BAYLE
Political Writings

Pierre Bayle was among the most important sceptical thinkers of the late seventeenth century. His work was an influence on the ideas of Hume, Montesquieu, Rousseau, and Voltaire (who acclaimed it for its insight on toleration, and emulated its candour on such subjects as atheism, obscenity, and sexual conduct). Banned in France on first publication in 1697, Bayle's *Dictionnaire Historique et Critique* became a bestseller and ran into many editions and translations. Sally L. Jenkinson's masterly new edition presents the reader with a coherent path through Bayle's monumental work (which ran to seven million words). This is the first volume in English to select political writings from Bayle's work and to present its author as a specifically political thinker. Sally L. Jenkinson's authoritative translation, careful selection of texts, and lucid introduction will be welcomed by scholars and students of the history of ideas, political theory, cultural history and French studies.

SALLY L. JENKINSON is part-time Visiting Professor at the Department of Political Science, University of California, Los Angeles, and a former Senior Lecturer in Political Studies at the University of North London. She has published widely on politics and toleration.

CAMBRIDGE TEXTS IN THE HISTORY OF POLITICAL THOUGHT

Series editors

RAYMOND GEUSS
Lecturer in Philosophy, University of Cambridge

QUENTIN SKINNER
Regius Professor of Modern History in the University of Cambridge

Cambridge Texts in the History of Political Thought is now firmly established as the major student textbook series in political theory. It aims to make available to students all the most important texts in the history of western political thought, from ancient Greece to the early twentieth century. All the familiar classic texts will be included but the series seeks at the same time to enlarge the conventional canon by incorporating an extensive range of less well-known works, many of them never before available in a modern English edition. Wherever possible, texts are published in complete and unabridged form, and translations are specially commissioned for the series. Each volume contains a critical introduction together with chronologies, biographical sketches, a guide to further reading and any necessary glossaries and textual apparatus. When completed, the series will aim to offer an outline of the entire evolution of western political thought.

For a list of titles published in the series, please see end of book.

A N

Hiftorical *and* Critical

DICTIONARY.

B Y

MONSIEUR BAYLE.

Tranflated into Englifh, *with many* ADDITIONS *and* CORRECTIONS, *made by the Author him-felf, that are not in the* French *Editions.*

VOLUME *the* FIRST.

A——B.

LONDON:

Printed for *C. Harper, D. Brown, J. Tonson, A.* and *J. Churchill, T. Horne, T. Goodwin, R. Knaplock, J. Taylor, A. Bell, B. Tooke, D. Midwinter, B. Lintott* and *W. Lewis.* MDCCX.

Bayle, *Historical and Critical Dictionary.* Title page of the first translation into English, 1710. (The engraving of Minerva is by Michael van der Gucht (1660–1725) from Antwerp, who settled in London in 1682 where he became known for anatomical drawings and as illustrator of Clarendon's *History of the Rebellion in England*, 1702–4.)

BAYLE

Political Writings

EDITED BY

SALLY L. JENKINSON
University of California, Los Angeles

CAMBRIDGE
UNIVERSITY PRESS

PUBLISHED BY THE PRESS SYNDICATE OF THE UNIVERSITY OF CAMBRIDGE
The Pitt Building, Trumpington Street, Cambridge CB2 1RP, United Kingdom

CAMBRIDGE UNIVERSITY PRESS
The Edinburgh Building, Cambridge, CB2 2RU, UK   http://www.cup.cam.ac.uk
40 West 20th Street, New York, NY 10011–4211, USA   http://www.cup.org
10 Stamford Road, Oakleigh, Melbourne 3166, Australia

First published 2000

Printed in the United Kingdom at the University Press, Cambridge

Typeset in Ehrhardt 9.5/12 pt [WV]

A catalogue record for this book is available from the British Library

Library of Congress Cataloguing in Publication data
Bayle, Pierre, 1647–1706.
Bayle: – Political Writings/edited by Sally L. Jenkinson
p.   cm. – (Cambridge texts in the history of political thought)
Includes bibliographical references and index.
ISBN 0 521 47094 3 (hb.)
1. Political science. – Early works to 1800.   I. Jenkinson, Sally L.
II. Title.   III. Title: Political writings   IV. Series
JC155.B39   1999
320.1′.01 – dc21   98–43279 CIP

ISBN 0 521 47094 3 hardback
ISBN 0 521 47677 1 paperback

To the memory of Elisabeth Labrousse, 1914–2000

For her commitment to intellectual liberty, and for making
Bayle's ideas accessible to future generations.

Contents

Contents

Acknowledgements

This selection of texts in part originates with Quentin Skinner's insight that Bayle's Dictionary should be read for its political theory. It has roots too in the doctoral thesis on Bayle's early political writing which I submitted to the University of Sheffield in 1975. That project was supported by the Morrell Studies in Toleration whose advisors included the late Sir Isaiah Berlin, and whose Director was Professor Bernard Crick. Earlier still, at the London School of Economics, I had been dazzled by the seminars on Logic and Scientific Method of Karl Popper and Imre Lakatos. So when I came to read Bayle's *Pensées diverses*, his *Critique générale*, and his *Commentaire philosophique*, I was able, thanks to such distinguished teaching, to perceive not just Bayle the reputed 'sceptic' but also the theorist of pluralism, equipped to support his convictions with an epistemology of conjecture and refutation.

No study of Bayle from a political perspective can ignore the debt that is owed to the recent work of Professors John Pocock, Quentin Skinner, and Richard Tuck. For their respective analyses of Renaissance humanism and Atlantic republicanism have recovered a framework which reveals many of the nuances to which Bayle responded. There are debts to be acknowledged too, both to Professor Patrick Riley and to Professor Jerome Schneewind: their interpretations of normative theory after Descartes and before Kant have elucidated a context in which Bayle as a moral thinker can find a place.

Throughout the continent of Europe and beyond, students of Bayle's ideas continue to build upon the historical and biographical erudition of Mme Elisabeth Labrousse. Many have been recipients too of her personal generosity of spirit. In 1996 colleagues paid their tribute in essays published by the Voltaire Foundation which they presented at the Sorbonne. Following that ceremony, Mme Labrousse sent me some comments on a draft introduction to these texts for which I thank her immensely. It goes without saying that I am responsible for the interpretation and for any errors of fact.

To Professor Patrick O'Brien, until recently Director of London University's Institute of Historical Research, I am doubly indebted. Firstly, because his Institute and its staff provided a base for completing this study, and secondly because it hosts beguiling seminars, including that in the History of Ideas led by Professors James Burns, Gregory Claeys, Janet Coleman, and Fred Rosen. At the University of California in 1997 and 1998, and as visitor to UCLA's Department of Political Science, this project has benefited from conversations, formal and informal, with Emeritus Professors Richard Popkin and David C. Rapoport, and Professor John Christian Laursen. Other friends and colleagues whose ideas have enriched this project include: Judith Evans, Mark Goldie, Sarah Hutton, John Hope Mason, Effa Okupa, and Professors Bernard Crick, Robert Goodin, Iain Hampsher Monk, Preston King, Marianne Horowitz, Cary Nederman, Melvin Richter, Amie and Donald Tannenbaum, Lyman Tower Sargent, Harry Bracken, and Giovanni Mori.

To the Nuffield Foundation I express my appreciation for providing, in 1996–8, a grant at the moment it was needed, and to Rudolf Richter who contributed word processing and other skills. Dr Lucy McGuinness, now of the Warburg Institute, is to be especially acknowledged for her learning in the classics and for her sensitive translations of Bayle's Latin citations. Responsibility for any errors, or over-free renderings, is, of course, mine. Finally, I thank the two editors of the Cambridge Texts for their constructive criticism, and the Cambridge University Press for their scholarly editing.

A note on the translation

The text

The excerpts selected for the present anthology have been newly translated. The text is based on the last complete French edition (ed. Beuchot) (Paris, 1820–4), 16 vols. in octavo, of which there is an easily accessible facsimile reproduction by Slatkine (Geneva, 1969). The earliest French editions, however, those of 1697 and 1702 in particular, carry non-textual messages which no translator can ignore. Likewise, the English translation of 1710, set in the same format, was a major event in English publishing. Its title page read: *An Historical and Critical Dictionary by Monsieur Bayle, with Many Additions and Corrections Made by the Author Himself that are not in the French Editions*. Subsequent English translations were published in 1734–8 in five volumes, in 1734–41 in ten volumes, and were read on both sides of the Atlantic.

Layout and referencing

The huge in-folio volumes of the eighteenth-century editions, whether of Rotterdam or London, carried visual information that is lost in modern format. By taking advantage of their length, width, and spacious margins, the printers could reinforce, with three font sizes, Bayle's three-fold distinction between fact, comment, and evidence. Accordingly, the framework of each article (referred to by convention as 'the body of the text', abbreviated here in cross-references to '*txt*') was outlined in the largest print. Footnotes (referred to by convention as 'remarks') contained the editor's critical comments and appeared on the same page, set in a medium-sized print. These 'remarks', frequently essays in their own right, imparted extra impact through their two-column format as in a gazette. We follow Bayle in sometimes altering slightly the wording of the body of the text to which the remarks are referenced. Thirdly, the sources relied on by Bayle were set in fine print and were located in the side margins.

Beuchot's edition of 1820–4 abandoned the in-folio page and the three sizes of font, as well as the use of the side margins for bibliographic references. It retained the format in two columns, and the system of notation. These excerpts follow Beuchot apart from the two-column format. That is, the 'remarks' are indicated by uppercase letters in round brackets: (A), (B), (Z) etc. and follow the 'body of the text', and the sources by superscript lower-case characters. Letters a, b, . . . z etc. denote the sources relating to the 'body of the text', while numerals 1, 2 . . . 9 etc. denote the sources relating to the 'remarks'. So that the reader can easily consult Beuchot's edition, we retain Bayle's system of notation for sources, but before Bayle's letter or number we place the appropriate character and an 'equals' sign if necessary to generate an unbroken sequential order. To take 'Elizabeth' as an example, Bayle's last lettered footnote in the body of the text of that article, note h, appears here as 'g=h', while Bayle's first numbered footnote to the remarks appears as '1= 8'. This means that our footnotes 'g' and '1' are footnotes 'h' and '8' in Bayle's original text, omissions in text and remarks having led to the loss of the footnotes attached thereto. Our sequence for notes and remarks omits 'j', following Bayle's preference. Omission of complete remarks is shown thus: '[Remarks (A)–(H) omitted.]'. Starred footnotes appear among the footnote sequences from time to time. Sometimes they represent Bayle's own afterthoughts, sometimes they indicate the comments of the editors of other editions, and when this is so, we point this out by an observation within square brackets. We have not attempted to verify all Bayle's references, nor identify all his sources. Comments added to this anthology are contained within square brackets, mainly in the headnotes that introduce each article; elsewhere (occasionally) to explain references. All footnotes to the texts, therefore, are Bayle's, unless expressly indicated otherwise.

Cuts within the text

Given that the Dictionary consists of some seven million words, and that even many 'remarks' run to several thousand, making cuts within an article could not be avoided. A strategy was to omit a whole 'remark' in order to leave as intact as possible the 'remarks' retained. Omitted 'remarks' and footnotes remain referenced in the 'body of the text' in square brackets, and can be consulted in the complete editions. Cuts are indicated by '. . .', whether within the 'body of the text' or within a 'remark'.

Translation from French

Many concepts in political thought pose pitfalls in translation. '*La politique*', for example, is more accurately translated as 'policy' than as 'politics', and this was as true in Bayle's day as in the present though, as the articles 'David' and 'Elizabeth' show, the word 'state-craft' can, on occasions, be even better. Additionally, it was requisite to consider context and Bayle's thought as a whole when deciding whether to render '*le mal*' as 'harm', or 'pain', or 'evil', or in some other way. Faced with such hazards, who would dare to omit Bayle's own caveat when he says in his 'Project' that he is certain that he will make 'only too many . . . mistakes', and that his critics will 'gratify him' if 'they correct and enlighten' him?

Translation from Latin

Bayle supposed that he had no need to translate into the vernacular many of his Latin quotations. No such assumption can be made today. Where a long passage is involved we have supplied the first few words of the Latin to indicate the language of the original, followed by the English rendering in brackets. All Latin quotations, excepting one, have been especially translated for this compilation. The exception, a passage from Augustine, occurs in the article 'Juno', Remark (AA), n. 12=168. In this case the translation, by R. W. Dyson, is reproduced from Augustine, *The City of God against the Pagans* (Cambridge University Press, 1998, pp. 258–9).

Abbreviations

For further details, see the Note on the Translation, the Bibliography and the headnotes to the selections in this compilation.

Dic I–XVI	Bayle, *Dictionnaire historique et critique* (Paris, 1820–4, based on original edns of 1697 and 1702), 16 vols.
Proj	Bayle, *Project for a Critical Dictionary dedicated to M. du Rondel, professor of* belles lettres *at Maestricht* (1692)

Articles from Bayle's Dictionary in this compilation:

Ald	'Sainte-Aldegonde'
Bod	'Bodin'
Brut	'Brutus'
Clar	'Clarifications'
Clar I	'First Clarification: On Atheists'
Clar IV	'Fourth Clarification: On Obscenities'
David	'David'
Eliz	'Elizabeth'
Greg	'Gregory I'
Hob	'Hobbes'
Hôp	'de l'Hôpital'
Hot	'Hotman'
Jap	'Japan'
Juno	'Juno'
Loy	'Loyola'
Mach	'Machiavelli'
Mâcon	'Mâcon'

Mar	'Mariana'
Nav	'Navarre, Marguerite, reine de'
Nic	'Nicole'
Ovid	'Ovid'
Sainc	'Sainctes'
Soc	'Socinus' (*F*, 'Faustus'; *M*, 'Marianus')
Syn	'Synergistes'
Xen	'Xenophanes'

Other works by Bayle:

OD I–V	Bayle, *Œuvres diverses*, ed. Labrousse (1964–82) [1727–31], 5 vols.
APD	*Additions aux Pensées diverses sur les comètes* (*OD* III, pp. 161–86)
Avis	*Avis important aux réfugiez* (1690) (*OD* II, pp. 578–633)
Com Phil	*Commentaire philosophique* (1686) (*OD* II, pp. 357–496)
CPD	*Continuation des Pensées diverses sur la comète* (1704) (*OD* III, pp. 187–417)
Cr Gén	*Critique générale de l'Histoire du Calvinisme de M. Maimbourg* (1682) (*OD* II, pp. 1–160)
FTC	*Ce que c'est que la France Toute Catholique sous le règne de Louis le Grand* (1686) (*OD* II, pp. 336–54)
NLHC	*Nouvelles lettres de l'auteur de la Critique générale de l'histoire du Calvinisme* (1685) (*OD* II, pp. 161–335)
NRL	*Nouvelles de la République des Lettres* (1684–7) (*OD* I, pp. 1–760)
PD	*Pensées diverses sur la comète* (1681) (*OD* III, pp. 1–160)
RNC	*Réponse d'un nouveau converti* (1688) (*OD* II, pp. 561–75)
Sys Abr	*Système abrégé de philosophie* (c. 1679) (*OD* IV, pp. 200–520)

Introduction: a defence of justice and freedom

> Diversity in religion has its inconveniences ... but, on the
> other hand, it prevents the development of corruption and
> obliges religions to treat one another with respect.
>
> 'Juno', Remark (AA)

What is the reputation of Pierre Bayle, and why should his ideas be
restored to the canon of political thought? For his *Dictionnaire historique et critique*, first published in 1697, was for nearly two centuries
rarely out of print. As one man's encyclopaedia of error the Dictionary, even at first glance, seemed remarkable. Its most celebrated
feature, however, was the extended footnote where the author elab-
orated his criticisms of current scholarship. Bayle's admirers in the
age of the Enlightenment were apt to distil the essence of these
comments into just two words: tolerance and scepticism. They were
notions with which Bayle's name became synonymous, even though
his concerns went deeper than his posthumous admirers supposed.
For in addition to tolerance and scepticism Bayle's Dictionary promoted justice as the end of government, and critical freedom as its
prerequisite.

The texts in this collection have been selected to highlight the
Dictionary's political ideas. Recent scholarship has in any case
begun to redraw the links between Bayle's historical criticism and
his convictions as a Huguenot who opposed persecution. Bayle's
biographer, Elisabeth Labrousse, uncovers in his *œuvre* as a whole
an engagement with a range of specifically political themes: for

example, *raison d'état*, absolutism, the philosophy of history, tolerance both ecclesiastical and civil, and liberty of conscience (Labrousse (1963–4), vol. II, pp. 449–591). Bayle sought also, through natural psychology, to explain political behaviour and especially the causes of intolerance. Reasoned argument, he believed, was among humanity's achievements, but it is noteworthy that, on the eve of the Enlightenment, Bayle warned persistently of reason's limitations. For though humanity has the capacity to make improvements, it has equally the capacity to abuse them.[1] The way is open, then, to re-interpret Bayle as analyst of both political thought and conduct – who responded to the great thinkers of early modernity such as Machiavelli, Bodin, and Hobbes – and as protagonist, before his time, of a political theory of diversity.

Bayle's Dictionary was far from eclipsed by the rivals it inspired. During the next two centuries it saw many re-impressions in French as well as translations into English and German and new editions.[2] It was read throughout Europe by successive generations alongside both the great *Encyclopédie* (1751–72) of Diderot and D'Alembert, and Voltaire's *Dictionnaire philosophique* (1764), and Bayle became, posthumously, an honorary figure of the Enlightenment. If great thinkers – for example Hume, Voltaire, or John Stuart Mill – reveal evident debts to Bayle's ideas, there were many others, for example Rousseau, Jefferson, Paine, Kant, Bentham, Hegel, Feuerbach or Marx, who absorbed his ideas selectively, or who turned to the Dictionary's sources.[3]

So what in fact did posterity value in Bayle's Dictionary? Scepticism and toleration undoubtedly, but also rigour in criticism, sources of new and recovered learning, and careful bibliographic notation. Educators could recommend the Dictionary because it exemplified these skills, and because it introduced useful ways of distinguishing between what was true, false or speculative. In addition, the Dictionary extended to the middle classes the idea of openness about questions which occur naturally to the young: about God, creation, Satan, atheism, generation, sex, violence, tyranny or insurrection. Bayle himself was convinced that free discussion

---

[1] See *Loy* (T); *Soc F* (A), (I), (L); *Xen* (E); *Brut.*
[2] For the Dictionary's reception see Rétat (1971); Labrousse (1983), p. 90; Popkin (ed.) (1991), pp. viii–x.
[3] *Ibid.*

provided a better antidote than censorship to every sort of problem whether factual or moral. In short, the *Dictionnaire* reassured an age eager for self-improvement that no topic need be thought too sacred, or too embarrassing, for serious discussion.

Today's historians of scepticism recognise that Bayle's Dictionary includes important articles on Pyrrhonism, and the philosophy of antiquity called 'sceptical'.[4] However, the present collection adds to that picture by showing that Bayle's approach to history, politics, and human conduct relies on a method of factual refutation. His critique of intolerance, these pieces show, was based not only upon 'sceptical' objections to dogmatic teaching, but also upon a public rhetoric in which empirical evidence plays a part. For Bayle maintains (*Proj*:§IX) that if some types of conjecture are too obscure for certainty, others are quite precise enough to be tested for their truth. A student of scientific method can see resemblances between this approach and that of Karl Popper.[5] From these texts we can ascertain that Bayle indeed held, as do today's theorists of conjecture and refutation, that a scientist of the natural world can get nearer to the truth by testing received ideas, and by discarding as fallacies those that are negated by sound evidence. Using this approach, Bayle rejected the *politique's* limits upon toleration, showing that freedom might safely be extended. His alternative was the plural society, committed to a diversity of schools and sects and, as in modern democracy, to imposing no religious tests upon citizens (*Greg* (G); *Com Phil*, p. 364). Bayle of course supported the existing practice of limited toleration for that was always better than the cruelty of persecution (see *Sainc* (F); *Soc* (A), (F)), but his long-term preference was for complete freedom. For Bayle questioned whether a case could ever be made, in logic, or in justice, or from Christ's example, for rewarding or penalising a citizen for refusing to believe in one metaphysical tenet rather than another (*Greg* (E); *Soc F* (L)).

Education, life and times

Bayle was born in 1647, the second son of Jean Bayle, a Calvinist minister who, in the era of Toleration, served the rural community of Le

---

[4] Pyrrho (*c*. 365–270 BC). The Pyrrhonian was one associated with the philosophic position that no indubitably true knowledge was possible. See 'Pyrrho' in Popkin (ed.) (1991), pp. 149–209. Cf. *Xen* (L).

[5] See Karl R. Popper, *Conjectures and Refutations* (1963).

Carla in southern France. Though poor, Jean Bayle was able to marry and to raise his three children in secure, even idyllic, surroundings. Jacob, his eldest son, was destined for the Calvinist ministry, and Pierre was expected to follow the same path (Labrousse (1963–4), vol. I, p. 30). Yet Bayle, like his contemporary John Locke (Cranston (1957), p. 97), side-stepped such a career. At home, he read, along with the Bible, the classics of humanism and scepticism he found in his father's small library (Labrousse (1963–4), vol. I, pp. 19, 43). Since the family could afford to send away only one son at a time, his adolescent education was probably neglected. At last, in 1666, Bayle attended the Huguenot college at Puylaurens, and then, in 1669, the Catholic Academy at Toulouse as an external student (*ibid.*, pp. 50–74). For a brief period between 1669 and 1670 he was a convert to Catholicism, but he returned to Calvinism and was dispatched by his family to the Protestant Academy of Geneva. Had he remained in France he would have incurred penalties as a Huguenot convert who had rescinded his conversion. In Geneva, Bayle continued to study philosophy and theology, and after various engagements as a tutor in Protestant households he completed his thesis and obtained a post in 1675 as Professor of Philosophy at the Huguenot Academy of Sedan where he remained until 1681 (*ibid.*, pp. 131–67).

Anticipating the suppression of the Sedan Academy, Bayle, like his colleagues, looked for employment outside France. He accepted an invitation from the city fathers of Rotterdam to assume the Chair of History and Philosophy at their new Ecole Illustre. Then, poised to take advantage of Dutch literary freedom, he quickly made a reputation in the 1680s as a critic of ideas, who had a rare additional gift for prolific journalism (*ibid.*, pp. 168–200). The trauma of the Revocation of the Edict of Nantes in 1685 was compounded for Bayle by the death of his brother. For Jacob Bayle, who by then had taken over his father's role as pastor at Le Carla, stayed with his flock as long as he might legally do so. He was, however, arbitrarily imprisoned by the authorities in consequence of Pierre's writings and died soon after in the foul prison conditions (*ibid.*, pp. 198–200). In the context of this tragedy and family involvement with the troubles of the nation Bayle used his talent to become, in addition to the teacher of science, a pamphleteer in exile, and distinguished author of works of criticism.

Whether Bayle intended his Dictionary from the beginning to be a vehicle for his political ideas, or whether it merely became so as he worked on it, is uncertain (see *Proj*). The themes of his writing career before the Dictionary, however, in both natural philosophy and in critical history, indicate the depth of his commitment to intellectual freedom.[6] Why, otherwise, after an intense decade between 1680 and 1690 of writing essays, reviews and pamphlets against Louis XIV's suppression of toleration for the Huguenots, would he have taken on so demanding a project? His first major publication, *Pensées diverses sur la comète* (1681), was followed in 1682 by a critique of Louis Maimbourg's hostile history of Calvinism. Next, Bayle founded and edited the review of books, the *Nouvelles de la République des Lettres* (1684–7). His third major work was the *Commentaire philosophique* (1686), which was translated into English in 1708, and reissued posthumously in French with the subtitle: *Traité de la tolérance universelle* (1713). In 1693, a prolonged quarrel with the Protestant theologian Pierre Jurieu, who had formerly been his patron, led to the loss of his post (but not his right to teach) at Rotterdam's Ecole Illustre. But by then, in 1692, Bayle had completed his proposal to undertake the *Dictionnaire Historique et Critique* for the publisher Leers. By devoting all his time to it he was able to complete two volumes by November 1696 (Labrousse (1963–4), vol. I, p. 183), which became the first edition of 1697 leading to a substantially augmented second edition in four volumes in 1702.

Bayle confessed to many hesitations before embarking on the Dictionary, for when he defended the project, he insisted that it was not 'out of inclination' but 'from choice' that he dealt 'in quibbles', and that he 'ought to be thanked for it, since it is a way of sacrificing oneself to the good of one's neighbour' (*Proj*:§ VII). And was not his departure from 'the path to glory' in order to bring others 'to a factual exactitude' to be thought of as 'a great sacrifice' (*ibid.*)? It turned out that by restating in a more popular medium certain themes presented in earlier essays and reviews, he attracted a wider audience and ensured a more prolonged influence, especially for his advocacy of intellectual freedom, and rigour in historical criticism.[7]

---

[6] An early work by Bayle (*c.* 1679) was *Dissertation . . . sur l'essence du corps*, a defence of Cartesian philosophy on the nature of substance, against the traditionalists who accused the Cartesians of heresy (*OD* IV, pp. 109–32).

[7] See Rétat (1971), pp. 475–7; there were ten posthumous editions in French, including those of Rotterdam (1740), Leipzig (1801–4) and Paris (1820–4). English translations were published in 1710, 1734–8, 1734–40, and 1826.

The Renaissance and Reformation do not, on their own, account for Bayle's defence of a politics of 'conciliation and decency' (*Syn* (C)). As a Huguenot and a layman, he was a direct heir to the *politiques* and moderate minds of the sixteenth century who worked for peace and supported the Edict of Nantes. For, as Bayle notes in his article 'Mâcon', the reign of 'tolerance' under 'the Edicts' had proved that it was possible for 'the people of France of different religions' to live in 'fraternity' (Remark (C)). Though Calvinism is often associated with puritan rigidity, or with the rise of the commercial spirit, it was not at all the case in France. (See Labrousse (1996c), p. 71.) Official toleration reflected and reinforced the common culture existing among France's professional classes of both religions: among for example the moderate jurists, the *literati*, and the members of the Third Estate. The education of a Calvinist in such a climate could be cultivated and egalitarian without falling into puritanism (Labrousse (1963–4), vol. I, pp. 14–17). Renaissance and Reformation had blended the study of the Scriptures with the study of the classics: the culture reflected the works of Cicero, Tacitus, and their modern disciple, Montaigne (*ibid.*, p. 55). Calvinists in France, therefore, not unlike certain Jansenist Catholics, could empathise readily with the Christians of the first three centuries and with the Stoics of the same era. The Christianity of those times had been a 'benign, gentle and patient religion', Bayle observed, and this contrasted sharply with the aberrant doctrine 'which was preached . . . in the sixteenth century' and which had been a 'bloody and murderous religion' (*Jap* (E)). It was likely that 'some men without religion' were more motivated 'to lead a decent, moral life by their constitution, in conjunction with the love of praise and the fear of disgrace' than were 'some others by the instinct of conscience' (*Clar* I:§III). In his Fourth Clarification, 'On Obscenities', Bayle remarked that 'whatever one's sex', one would need to have lived 'only four or five years' to know by hearsay 'countless rude things'; for 'in countries where jealousy is not tyrannical' there is an innocent freedom, and for children 'games, conversations, amusing parties, festivals and country outings are almost daily fare' (*Clar* IV, p. 338 below).

It seems that the regime of official toleration, though limited, permitted Bayle to draw insight from a scientific education through the two religious cultures of his community (Labrousse (1963–4), vol. I, p. 62). For it was through a Jesuit at Toulouse (*ibid.*, pp. 74, 95–6) that Bayle first encountered a critical account of the heliocentric cosmology of Copernicus and Galileo. The approach was to regard the new teaching less as new certainty that must replace a fallacious dogma, and more as a better tested replacement for the now refuted theory of the Scholastics. When in 1675 Bayle himself came to lecture on natural philosophy,[8] he indicated in his courses that new discoveries in science, like the ideas they replaced, were not necessarily indubitably true but must always remain theories that better explained 'the apparent facts' (*Syn* (C), n. 10=23).

If intellectuals in France disagreed passionately with their colleagues on matters of science, psychology and theology, through criticism and through sceptical epistemology they found an important way of discussing their disagreements.[9] Descartes's method in particular attracted critical minds from both confessions and in all disciplines, and Bayle thought he could use Descartes's well-known account of the interplay between feelings, body and brain to explain the prejudices of certain historians.[10] Why, for example, do scholars sometimes feel convinced of the truth of false propositions without further evidence, when at other times they dismiss true propositions without a second thought? Education, he surmised, might be a factor. For how far did intellectuals in fields other than physics deliberately foster critical learning by entertaining a proposition as a conjecture, or withhold judgement as to its truth, falsity or indeterminacy, until the evidence has been assessed (*Nic* (C))? Forbearance from judgement, though appropriate in the sphere of philosophic investigation, was unsuitable for everyday decision-making which is, quite properly, 'inclined to yield to the evidence of inward feeling' (*Soc F* (I)). It was appropriate 'in matters of morals', Bayle believed, whatever one's confession, to 'be satisfied with good sense' (*Loy* (T)).

In social life, Bayle observed, individuals are disposed to praise virtue and condemn vice even though few are able to live wholly by their own standards (*Juno* (Z), (BB); *Xen* (H), (K)). By analogy,

---

[8] See *Sys Abr.*

[9] On Cartesian thought, see Popkin (1979), pp. 110, 129; in the context of political theory see Keohane (1980); Tuck (1993).

[10] As e.g. in Descartes's *Discours de la méthode* (1637); and *Les Passions de l'âme* (1649).

a mature civil society would realise that the courts of conscience (*tribunaux de la conscience*) might condemn matters which, for reasons of prudent government (*sage gouvernement*),[11] should not, in courts of law, be punished with the same rigour.[12] Excessive zeal for making others virtuous contributed to public harm, whereas a civil regime which created the conditions of orderly diversity could further the general good (*Hôp txt*, (D), (E), (S)). Man seemed in nature to be a paradox, for though he was well intentioned, he seemed unwittingly to be 'so injurious and so destructive that if all other animals did as much in proportion, the earth would not be able to furnish them with sufficient sustenance' (*Ovid* (G)). Yet a remedy of a sort was available. For human kind, disposed to be troubled by its own conduct, seeks to ameliorate its passions and so mitigate their worst consequences.

Since human beings pursue both perfection and destructiveness to escape their disquiet, they can hardly avoid, Bayle supposes, inflicting their pathologies upon the world and upon one another (*Juno txt*, (Z), (BB); *Xen* (H)). Erudition provides little protection against objectionable behaviour, and biography teaches that scholars and theologians prove no more immune to dangerous passions than certain princes.[13] Even learned miscreants may well incite violence to alleviate their interior discomfort: hence their sermons of hatred, their vindictive essays, their biassed histories, their justifications of religiously motivated assassination, and support for cruel revenge in word and deed.[14]

It is possible, Bayle concedes, to conclude that the world is in the grip of Lucifer and irredeemable without supernatural assistance (*Xen* (E)). Yet a metaphysics of conjecture permits scholars to be aware that there are many other beliefs and theories about creation, and about the nature of mind, morals and society, which are equally consonant with the same facts (*Syn* (C)). One pre-Christian theory of creation, which Bayle brings before a general public through the

[11] These expressions are from *Dic*, article 'Ermite', Remark (I), para. 1 (not in this compilation). On the natural passions in general, see *David, Jap, Juno, Ovid, Xen, Ath*.

[12] On political prudence and *raison d'état* in general, see *Bod* (Q); *Brut* (C); *Eliz* (F), (H), (I); *Hôp txt*, (D); *Mach*.

[13] See *David txt*, (E), (G), (H), (I), (M); *Greg txt*, (E).

[14] See *David txt*, (D), (E), (H), (I); *Greg txt*, (E):§2; *Sainc txt*, (D), (E), (F); *Syn* (B), (C); *Xen* (E), (F).

Dictionary, is the notion of Chaos (*Ovid* (G):§III). For Ovid's
famous poem had mythologised the a-theism of the Epicureans.
Their school had taught that the cosmos was a self-created wilder-
ness, but perhaps susceptible to being shaped by humanity. Bayle's
method is to describe these theories without endorsing them. It
seemed evident, as he asserts in the article 'Xenophanes', that man
'by his nature' (*Xen* (E)), is 'prone to do harm (*au mal*)'. Yet when
he encounters the theologian's picture of a humankind motivated
by sin (which the age attributed to Augustine), or the cynical historian's picture of self-interest (which the age attributed to Guicciardini and Hobbes), Bayle counters with Montaigne's more amiable
view that 'the greatest number of men' were on balance only 'moderately reprehensible' (*Hob* (E)), and therefore able and willing to
limit the worst abuses.

The political ideas which Bayle opposed

To understand any political writer, it is important to place their
thought in its context. In Bayle's case this is to show how he criticised the ideas and institutions of early modernity which had
replaced those of the Middle Ages. Though a supporter of a Europe
of sovereign states, Bayle went further in his support of tolerance
and diversity within these states than did contemporaries, such as
Locke, whose political thought is better known to posterity. Despite
supporting the post-Reformation alternative to former Catholic
Christendom, Bayle objected to that part of the doctrine which
required each sovereign authority to uphold an official religion. For
the age which followed the era of the Wars of Religion did not
renounce this institution. Even the century's most enlightened
laymen – Bodin, Grotius, Justus Lipsius, Hobbes or Leibniz for
example – thought the issue to be not whether there should be an
official church to which all citizens should belong, but which articles
of faith to adopt, which sects to tolerate, and what methods to use
to enforce conformity. On these subjects, intellectual debate in
Louis XIV's France differed little from that which smouldered
throughout Europe as a whole. After the devastation of civil war it
was reluctantly agreed that there could be a majority and a minority
church. In direct consequence four distinct political tendencies had
emerged, which we call here Ultramontanism, Gallicanism, Hu-

guenotism, and *politique* realism. The following paragraphs will say something about the ideas of each tendency in order to show where Bayle stood, and why he sought to transcend them all.

Apologists in the 1680s, despite a changing social reality, based their respective positions on their perceptions of the purpose of the toleration forged in the previous century (see Skinner (1978), vol. II, pp. 239–84). The facts were that after some forty years of turbulence lasting from 1559 to 1598, Henry IV had come to preside over a regime supported by certain moderate Catholics on the one hand and the Huguenot party on the other (see *Hot txt*). Together these politicians – or *politiques* – sustained the Edict of Nantes of 1598: the constitutional settlement intended to consolidate 'justice and reason' (*Hôp txt*), and provide protection for the Calvinist minority (Labrousse (1990), p.138). In the 1680s, therefore, in the face of the Revocation of that Edict, supporters and opponents of this policy turned to the past to guide them through the new uncertainties. In favour of the reactionary policy was a zealous Catholic party led by the regime's administrators and its Catholic ecclesiastics. Opposing it were the Huguenots, now isolated and led mainly by their pastors (*ibid.*, pp. 77–80). For since 1629 these Huguenot communities had been deprived of their armed nobility, and after 1660 they had been depleted, through emigration or conversion, of their adherents in the civil professions. Despite toleration, none of the four tendencies asked whether religious unity or religious diversity was the more desirable end. Seemingly, the lesson of the Wars of Religion was that a nation divided in religion was a prey to disorder. Fearing a return of bloodshed, *politiques* everywhere, therefore, lent their support to the doctrine of *cuius regio eius religio* which said that prince and people should adopt an official religion and conform to it. Yet the doctrine recognised too that there could be exemption from conformity to official worship, and in particular for Christians who belonged to the confessions of Catholicism, Lutheranism, or Calvinism. Accordingly as early as the Peace of Augsburg of 1555 and the Treaty of Westphalia of 1648, Europe recognised limited toleration for approved minorities if their devotions were conducted in private. Compassionate minds recognised too that sectarians from whom toleration was withdrawn should always be permitted to emigrate peacefully with their possessions. A facet of political life, therefore, which Bayle alone seems to have regarded as a paradox, was that the diplomats, *politiques*, and *esprits forts* of the age could approve of toleration for a minority, while imposing civil disqualification, accompanied by financial inducements, to encourage the intransigent to unite with the majority.

We can return now to the four great tendencies in France in order to show why Bayle contested them all, and where, in these texts, to find the detail of his argument.

Ultramontanism: Ultramontane theologians continued to teach their seminarians the traditional theory of a former Catholic Christendom although the elites of the post-Reformation state were strongly opposed to it. Before the Reformation, Christian divines had asserted that there were two balanced authorities in Christendom, that of the *regnum*, which kept order, and that of the *sacerdotium* or priesthood, whose final authority was the Pope, which made supposedly inspired decisions for all Christendom, civil rulers included, concerning faith and morals (*Loy* (R); *Mar* (G)). During the Wars of Religion in France, the Catholic League, led by the ambitious House of Guise and its armed aristocratic supporters, rose to support the Ultramontane ecclesiastics. They pledged themselves to extirpate, in the name of the Pope, all Reformed opinion, and in particular that of Calvin, which the centrist monarchy was inclined to tolerate but which the church declared to be heresy. However, the House of Guise was finally subjugated militarily, and after the Edict of Nantes of 1598 the Catholic League pursued its policies more covertly. That is, ecclesiastics of the traditional religion solicited legislation that would bring all religious worship within the single official church (*Hôp* (D), (E), (F)).

Bayle seems to have judged that Ultramontane Catholicism by the turn of the century was no longer the main threat to his community. For an equally sinister force, namely Catholic sovereign extremism – allegedly popular, and a reverse image of Protestant popular sovereignty – posed the real danger to the tradition of the Edict of Nantes (see *Loy*, *Mar*). Power-seekers, he believed, were likely in every age to abuse religion to suppress their rivals and to further their ambitions. Yet, just as Catholic propaganda incited fear of unconverted Huguenots, so Protestant propaganda, in particular in the gazettes of Amsterdam (*Loy* (R)), incited public fear of Popery and Catholic tyranny (*Mar* (H)). History affords examples everywhere, Bayle noted, 'of kings deposed at the instigation, or

with the approbation, of the clergy' (*Loy* (S)). Injustice to the innocent was the likely result, he concluded, both from religious fanaticism and whenever a Christian community with 'power over others'
(*ibid.*) sought to use that power to further their ambitions.

Gallicanism: France had not broken with Rome at the Reformation but the civil authority had more or less brought the Gallican
church under its control. Its success depended, in part, on allowing
Catholic ecclesiastics to hope that in time it would re-integrate the
Calvinists into the one official religion. Laymen, on the other hand,
remained wary of ecclesiastical power. The Third Estate argued,
like Hobbes, that though unity in religion was best politically for
the nation, the unified church must be firmly in the hands of the
civil sovereign (*Hôp* (H)). Bayle, as a layman, adroitly uses his article on the founder of the Jesuits, Loyola, to make the significant
point that when the French Third Estate had proposed in 1615 that
the sovereign's authority was derived from neither aristocracy, nor
clergy, nor people, but from God (*Loy* (R)), they postulated no
theory of the king's divine right – although Ultramontane apologists
interpreted it in that way to discredit them (cf. *Sainc* (E)). Rather,
they implied defiantly that no allegiance to Pope or priest was owed
by any citizen of the French sovereign nation (*Loy* (R)).

The **Huguenots**, continuing to suppose that their liberty of
worship would always be protected, supported the crown. Furthermore, Huguenots no less than Catholics supposed that forced conversion, in the manner of the Spanish Inquisition, was alien to the
French idea of a civilised nation. Nevertheless, from 1660, the year
in which Louis XIV began his period of personal rule, they were
increasingly made to choose between service to their country and
loyalty to their religion. By the 1680s there existed many former
Calvinists – known as *nouveaux convertis* – who had joined the
official religion to avoid losing a livelihood, but who hoped that the
new compulsory conformity would, under Louis XIV's successor,
be reversed.

Politiques: Onto this web of religious and civil argument was
grafted the pragmatic realism of the *politiques*. The word had originally described the movement of the moderates, both Catholic and
Huguenot, loyal to the intentions of Michel de l'Hôpital, Chancellor
of France from 1560 to 1568. Their school promoted the new idea
of government that endorsed civil tolerance, and thereby prepared

the ground for Henry IV's Edict of Nantes and its reign of eighty-seven years. In Bayle's judgement, the better aspects of this movement, which had once united sovereign impartiality with religious toleration, deserved to be reinstated, since de l'Hôpital, Henry IV and their supporters among moderates and *politiques* had not only brought peace with justice, but had created a *corps* of civil jurists to implement the new arrangements (*Hôp* (L), (P), (S)). Legitimate authority for de l'Hôpital's *politiques* resided therefore neither in Pope, nor church, nor nobility nor even people. It lay rather in the will of a nation's public spirited leaders and in their commitment to a polity, secured against civil war, that could deliver a system of justice. For these statesmen, God, the sovereign, or the public good, were equally apt metaphors for a just society pioneering an experiment in governing a divided society. Yet after Henry IV's assassination in 1610, the word *politique* increasingly came to evoke the statecraft of Richelieu and Mazarin, for whom all instruments were valid – civil religion, toleration, or ecumenical negotiation – if they ensured the safety of the state as they perceived it (*Eliz* (H), (I); *Mach* (E)).

When he tried to explain the Revocation of the Edict of Nantes, Bayle concluded that it was motivated as much by a recovery of the supposed prudential case for religious unity, as by absolutism or religious zeal (see *FTC*). Many intellectuals, as their writings showed, were religiously indifferent, but believed – like the humanist Justus Lipsius – that diversity in religion was always prejudicial to security (see *CPD*, pp. 189–90). In consequence, with the end of the Dutch War in 1679, and convinced that there was a political case for eliminating the Huguenot communities, they debated only about methods and timing. It followed – so Bayle judged – that when his co-religionists protested only about what they called the theocracy and the absolutism of Louis XIV, they did so without having grasped the true cause of their persecution. The suppression of Calvinism in France was celebrated by the Gallican regime as a commendable consolidation of the nation's political unity, even though it was seen as a catastrophe in the eyes of Protestant Europe.

Was Bayle correct to suspect that the persecution of the Huguenots was driven by the *politique* conception of the general good supported by a Gallican majority church? The facts suggest that for the lay administrator, at least, the policy was intended not to extir-

pate a heresy, but to integrate a minority. Long before the Revocation, the regime had passed legislation to reward those who con-
formed (Labrousse (1990), pp. 153–63). Later, it suppressed
Huguenot academies and schools including the academy where
Bayle gained a livelihood. After the Revocation it was able legally
to demolish temples, harass householders with dragoons, invalidate
marriages, expel pastors, and remove children from parents.
Undoubtedly the Huguenots had been betrayed, for, by the terms
of the Peace of Alès in 1629, they had given up their right to bear
arms in return for the civil authority's protection of their liberty of
worship (Labrousse (1983), p. 9). Yet most Protestants opposed the
proliferation of sects (*Sainc* (F)), feeling at heart that unity of
religion was the ideal to be sought. They supposed that the best
arrangement would be to live in a Calvinist France which upheld
the true religion (as they understood it) even if a second-best
arrangement was to live under a Gallican regime which accorded
them toleration. Calvinists valued in particular the simplicity and
egalitarianism of their reformed religion. They prized its absence of
hierarchy, its voluntarism, and its commitment to private judgement, as well as its network of self-governing congregations and
synods; and they resisted those who attempted to lead or lure them
into union with the Gallican church. Moreover, given that they no
longer bore arms, Huguenots supposed that no opponent would
dishonestly portray them as a fifth column. Memories of resistance
and heroic self-defence against massacre during the sixteenth century were indeed a part of Huguenot mythology[15] but they had no
reality at the end of the seventeenth century. Huguenots lived in
dispersed communities loyal to the crown supposing, but wrongly,
that their protection was assured (Labrousse (1990), p. 96).

Despite Huguenot commitment to non-violence, Gallican apologists always emphasised that their sect, historically, had a tradition
of armed resistance (*Hôp* (F)). Maimbourg in particular, drawing
selectively on documents from the French Civil Wars, sought to
show that the mere presence in France of self-governing, self-
supporting, communities was a threat to civil order. Accordingly
Bayle, in his *Critique générale* (1682) of Maimbourg's *Histoire du*

---

[15] For resistance theory, Catholic and Protestant, see *Loy*; *Mar*; *Bod* (Q); *Hôp* (F);
Hot txt, (E); *Mâcon txt*, (C). Cf. Salmon (1991); Skinner (1978), vol. II, ch.7, ch.8.

Calvinisme, explored the historiography of this polemic to show the falsity of the accusation (see *Cr Gén* and *NLHC*). He even praised King James II of England, seeing a Catholic prince on the throne of a Protestant country as a mirror image of Henry IV's earlier role as a Huguenot prince in a Catholic country (*NRL*, pp. 293–4). As events turned out, the English Protestants did reject their Catholic king (*Eliz* (I)). Moreover, after the replacement of James II by William and Mary in 1688, certain Huguenots in exile – including Bayle's colleague Pierre Jurieu – began to 'prophesy' that Huguenots in France would rise in revolt and that William's Protestant army would march to Paris in their support.[16] Bayle, appalled by such imprudence (given the possibility of reprisals), wrote harsh declamations against such incitements to violence, especially those that posed as religious prophecy. To end the hostilities of the 1690s between William III and Louis XIV Bayle and his circle of moderates supported a negotiated peace between their adopted and their native countries (see *RNC* and *Avis*) and showed, in their private correspondence, that they were encouraged by England's revolution and Protestantism's triumph, hoping that a 'prompt restoration of the Edict of Nantes' (*OD* IV, p. 633) would be a consequence. Bayle's admiration for republican heroism in more auspicious circumstances may be inferred from his historical writings.[17] The Huguenot Francis Hotman had written his *Franco-Gallia*, Bayle noted, 'to show that the French monarchy' was not what it was thought to be, and that 'of right, the people are its true sovereigns' (*Hot* (H)). In the same vein he praised the Dutch nobleman and patriot who, in 1581, had dedicated both pen and diplomacy to 'the cause of liberty' to be free from 'the Spanish tyranny' and 'the yoke of the Inquisition' (*Ald txt*).

Bayle's modern reputation, as an astute interpreter of Machiavellian realism (*Mach* (E)) who was fascinated with the moral paradox of *raison d'état* (Labrousse (1963–4), vol. II, pp. 497–519), should be enhanced by today's revival of interest in the connection between *politique* ideas and Atlantic republicanism. For the movement which so engaged Bayle has been reassessed in recent years also, and for

[16] See Jurieu (*c.* 1689); cf. Labrousse (1983), pp. 36–9.
[17] See *Brut txt*; *Mach txt*, (E); *Hot txt*.

somewhat similar reasons.[18] When today's scholars reconsider the republican literature which flourished in Spain, France, England and the Netherlands during the years between 1572 and 1651, they tend to echo Bayle's interest. They associate the movement, as he did, with natural law in jurisprudence, republicanism in government, and neo-Stoicism in philosophy (cf. Tuck (1993), p. xiv). Bayle, considering the experience in France, made a finer distinction. He judged that neo-Stoicism in political theory was at its most admirable when it was allied with intellectual freedom for all people and not just for the elite. He sees it in the 'heroic magnanimity' of Marguerite of Navarre (*Nav* (P)), and in the honourable statecraft of de l'Hôpital and Henry IV, who had not only instituted the Edicts of Toleration, but had educated civilians to implement the arrangements (*Hôp* (S)).

To distinguish between the *politique* of the school of de l'Hôpital, and the hypocritical *politique* who a century later brought about the Revocation of the Edict of Nantes, Bayle devised an ingenious metaphor which is reiterated in the Dictionary (*Clar* I:§VIII). In his *Pensées diverses sur la comète* (1681), he had invited his readers to compare a 'government of atheists', or religiously impartial officials, to a 'government of idolaters', that is a government of corrupt persecutors. His purpose was to prove the proposition that, of the two types of rule, the former should be seen as the lesser evil. His argument had three stages. It sought first to establish as common ground the principle that, of two harms, it was always a duty to opt for the lesser. Then a 'thought experiment' was posed which asked whether – from behind a veil of ignorance[19] – a Christian of Roman times would have preferred to live under a regime of 'atheists', or impartial Stoics, or under a regime of 'idolaters' or persecuting pagans. Thirdly, his argument proceeded to the conclusion that, faced with the two options, the individual, both as citizen of the republic and as ethical agent, would be bound to choose the regime of 'atheists' (*Clar* I:§§III–VIII).

Decoding Bayle's paradox required familiarity with the debate among erudite sceptics, Cartesians, Jesuits, Jansenists, Calvinists,

---

[18] See Pocock (1975); Skinner (1978); and Tuck (1993).
[19] See Rawls (1972), pp. 136–42, who uses a similar argument in support of a not dissimilar project of moral persuasion.

nouveaux convertis and others, about faith, reason, prudence and the obligations of conscience.[20] He assumed that readers of the Dictionary would possess such familiarity, but he found that he had to explain himself before the Consistory of his own Calvinist church in Rotterdam before he could publish the Dictionary's second edition of 1702 (see *Clar*, editorial headnote, p. 311). His hypothetical demonstration in favour of civic impartiality as always a lesser harm than an obligatory civil religion had probably fallen on many receptive ears, but it also aroused incomprehension and anger. In the Dictionary, he repeated the assertion that there had been atheists and Epicureans whose virtue had surpassed that of most idolaters (*Clar* I:§§III–XV). Bayle's 'paradox' may be said to remain permanently relevant to the case for impartial rule in every religiously divided society seeking to avoid strife among its communities.

The political ideas which Bayle supported

It will now be clear that of the four tendencies, Bayle identifies most closely with the now isolated Huguenots and the *politique* realists, although he calls on all groups to reform their perceptions of their reciprocal involvement. He addresses his ideas to those raised in the spirit of the original Edict of Nantes, and it is with building blocks from that once powerful movement that he attempts to re-construct a religiously impartial opposition to the 'baroque' and Erastian state. In many articles, and in 'Mâcon' in particular,[21] Bayle reflects on the historian's responsibility to face the truth of past abominations. The moral is that the ruler's impartiality, and commitment to free utterance for all peaceful schools of thought, far from being an instance of supposed tyranny for which the prince must be deposed, should henceforward be re-asserted as a positive duty which he is required to discharge.

There are 'three sorts of person', Bayle counsels, who must learn from past atrocities to reform utterly their political ideas. They are: 1. those who 'govern states'; 2. those who 'govern ecclesiastical affairs'; and 3. those 'turbulent theologians' who 'take so much plea-

---

[20] See *Nic* (C); *Ovid* (G); *Soc F* (H), (I); *Syn txt*, (A), (B), (C); *Xen* (E), (F), (H), (K).

[21] See *Mâcon* (C); *David* (H):§VII; *Greg* (E).

sure in innovation'. Three conclusions follow: firstly, those who preside over states should respect at all times the maxim 'persecute no one for his opinions in religion and do not use the right of the sword against conscience'. Secondly, leaders of traditional parties should renounce their delusion that the concept of 'tolerance' is 'the most frightful and the most monstrous of all dogmas'. They mistakenly suppose that the right and the duty to extirpate heresy is 'the finest flower of the crown'. Nor, by the same token, should they argue that justice requires that rulers 'at least' be allowed 'to imprison and banish heretics'. For on grounds not only of natural justice but also of political prudence, rulers should recognise that 'sectarians' are likely to 'respond with raised swords' against the injustice of their oppressors instead of 'merely speaking or writing against [their] doctrines'. Thirdly, leaders of a party of reform, sincerely and properly seeking to correct error or superstition, are no less obliged than the party of tradition to be wise and judicious in respect of the methods they use to promote their opinions. For, 'if such people had rather disturb the public peace than contain their personal ideas, then their conduct cannot be too much deplored'. They should rather 'consider both the consequences of their innovations and the means they use to bring them about' (*Mâcon* (C), *passim*).

Bayle's historical recovery of his country's former diversity – of parties and communities interacting peacefully within a just civil order – had yet to be converted into constitutional precept. For though there were rare instances of 'reason and genius' (*Nav* (P)) in the Europe of his time which promoted limited tolerance, 'diversity' as a value had still to find its supporters even among reformers and republicans (*Ald* (L); *Sainct* (F)). He warned that certain parties 'too much addicted to disputes' needed reminding in some cases that 'the most fearsome intolerance does not come from sovereigns who use the right of the sword against sectarians, but that it comes from those individual divines who, without a very urgent necessity, rise up against errors protected by custom and the habits of peoples' (*Mâcon* (C)). Bayle assumes that decent minds already regarded as unjust the imposition of a religious dogma in the face of conscientious refusal (*Nic* (C); *Syn* (B), (C)). However, as an apologist for impartiality, he thought that opponents of religious persecution would have to be more theoretically coherent if their aspirations were to be transformed into codes of practice, accepted by leaders of sects and parties as well as by thinkers and jurists (*Sainct* (F)).

Because he distanced himself from all violent resistance, especially Jurieu's new defence of Protestant popular rebellion, some historians have supposed that Bayle must have opposed the English Revolution of 1688, or sympathised with ideas that were monarchist or 'absolutist'.[22] The accusations, first made by Jurieu to discredit Bayle, are not supported by the evidence. For Bayle clearly shows in his articles on the *politiques* and republicans that, above all, he supports intellectual liberty.[23] He insists that if government's first duty is to provide safety for citizens, its purpose is to create the orderly community in which all honest ideas can be freely taught. Bodin, Bayle pointed out, had been accused of asserting that princes might behave arbitrarily or do as they pleased. On the contrary, Bodin had maintained rather that it is not for 'one subject in particular, nor for all in general, to conspire against the honour or the life of such monarchs either by violence or in a juridical way'. Judged in the context of the turbulent times, Bayle concluded, it was clear that Bodin had intended to support 'the public good and . . . the peace and tranquillity of the state' (*Bod txt*). That is, he had shown that if liberty and order conflicted, one could still value liberty more than order while insisting that, chronologically speaking, order constituted a condition of liberty.

Those who write to inform the public, Bayle cautioned, will – like Bodin – advance sometimes ideas that are proved wrong by events. History was laden with such lessons, but what did this prove? Only that to err was no crime. The crime was to use violence to oppose error when the more effective weapon of the pen was available. In his 'Project for a Dictionary' Bayle points out that 'although one cannot reject historical Pyrrhonism in respect of a large number of propositions', a historian 'may show indubitably that many propositions are false, that many lack certainty, and that many others are true'. And he concluded with some passion: 'Now is it nothing to correct the unfortunate tendency we have to make rash judgements? Is it nothing to learn not to assent lightly to what we see in print?' (*Proj*:§IX). In short, to protect the freedom to err,

---

[22] See Touchard (1975), p. 369; cf. Jurieu (*c.* 1690/1).
[23] See *Ald*; *Bod*; *Hob*; *Hôp*; *Hot*; *Loy*; *Mach*; *Mâcon*; *Mar.* Cf. Jenkinson (1999b).

and to make corrections without having to resort to violence, was to protect the basis of the just and self-reforming society.

Values

If we were to systematise the theory of justice and freedom that emerges from Bayle's historical criticism, we should need to cast it as a series of connected propositions. Bayle supposed, above all, that the ruler must further the public good, a duty which entails protecting the conditions in which intellectual freedom, and its corollary of institutional diversity, may flourish. Bayle thought, too, that the good society must always be ruled according to laws justified by natural morality and natural reason. That is, he supposed that the quality of society, whether it is just, humane, efficient and consistent, has little to do with the supposed origins of authority or with the religion of its ruler or with the detail of its instruments of government. More important is the extent to which a society embraces agreed principles of justice and measures its laws and its policies against them. Since the proper end of government is not to fight a holy war, but to keep the peace and serve the well-being of the people, the ruler should institute good laws, implement them firmly, and safeguard the right of utterance and the right of reply.

There is, Bayle suggests, an implied contract of peaceful deliberation which is an essential preliminary to making a just public decision. The *avant garde* which teaches new ideas, and the majority which is disposed to defend the old, are equally obliged to renounce violence. Governments, for their part, must enforce this agreement, or presumed contract, by enabling all parties to speak peacefully in defence of what they believe to be right. Bayle rejects the doctrine that a diversity of sects is a threat to public peace. If it is argued that orthodoxy must be imposed because diversity threatens civil order, then this can be refuted. History shows, he pointed out, that many minority sects have a record of being reasonable and law abiding; and that many majority religions have a record of inciting violence without just cause (*Greg*; *Mâcon*; *Soc*; *Sainc*).

If it is argued that virtuous conduct in a citizen requires indoctrination in the fear and love of God, or in God's supposed retribution, this cannot, Bayle insists, be convincingly demonstrated. For though it was commonly held that sects that rejected this view must be outlawed as heretical, the evidence of fact (which the Dictionary cites) proved that there was no necessary connection between believing in or denying God's existence or providence, and the conduct of the believer. On the one hand, it was on record that some sects in antiquity, such as the followers of Epicurus, who had no belief in the deity or in the soul's immortality, had lived lives devoted to the pursuit of virtue. On the other, it was chronicled that some persons who asserted that they believed strongly in divine providence had, nevertheless, engaged in lawless conduct and vice. Therefore, the civil religion was not to be the sole determinant of human virtue.

From these demonstrations it seemed that received notions of a government's duty required revision. For if objective knowledge arose out of freedom for speculative thought, society must positively protect the conditions which made such trial and error possible. The matter at issue therefore was about government, not religion. If the society in which scholars offered free criticism of one another's conjectures was as orderly as the society which forbade it, then free communities had a better chance of acquiring knowledge and making improvements than communities which feared criticism and suppressed dissent.

Given his many references to those who had no religion, it is often asked if Bayle himself was an atheist. Was his Calvinism sincere? Or did he, perhaps, support the theory of Epicurus or some similar notion of creation *ex nihilo*?[24] The texts show that Bayle condemned only dogmatism, proposing, with enough orthodoxy for a Cartesian age, that 'the best position that our reason can adopt is to say that everything, apart from God, has a beginning' (*Xen* (L); cf. *Hob* (M)). Yet Bayle was indeed of the *avant garde*, as some modern critics recognise (see Popkin (ed.) (1993), pp. xix–xxix), and he was set further apart from orthodoxy because of his epistemology. For it was almost always the case that a philosopher of the Protestant confession defended a supposed Protestant reasonableness against a supposed Popish superstition. Bayle, however, held a different view of the philosopher's role. As a teacher of science in

---

[24] See the Christian interpretation of Bayle's faith proposed by Sandberg (1964), and Popkin's speculative approach which asks if Bayle might have been a 'secret Jew' (Popkin (ed.) (1991), pp. xxiv–xxix).

the Calvinist Academy in Gallican France, he acknowledged no duty to support either the majority or the minority religion's perspective on science. When he moved to the Netherlands, he maintained the same neutrality, asserting, as before, a commitment only to criticise error (cf. *Proj*:§ix).

The subtleties of Bayle's thinking are equally apparent when he assesses the political theory of post-Reformation Europe. He praises *politique* and sceptical thinkers for their scholarly opposition to superstition in public life, but he criticises those among them who fail to question the doctrine of *cuius regio eius religio*. Their position was permeated, he thought, by irrational fear, whether of ideas supposed pagan, or of diversity itself. To allay these fears Bayle had shown that faith in the deity was unconnected to a citizen's conduct. So his model of the society where even the atheist was protected from persecution need not be read as a defence of atheism. It can be read – and I think it should be read – as the defining principle of a new pluralism that favoured protection under the civil constitution for any unorthodox minority – including a Calvinist minority, or a Catholic minority, or a Jewish minority, or even an atheist minority.

It is perhaps because he played the three roles of academic, of spokesman for a persecuted political community, and of lay member of a dissenting church, that Bayle is so careful to separate types of judgement. He took for granted that there were appropriate occasions, apparent to every mature individual, for withholding a judgement (i.e. 'scepticism'); and appropriate occasions for according a judgement (i.e. 'faith'). Since Bayle perceived that the Huguenot intellectual of his day had three roles to play, something further should be said about his idea of each.

Firstly, there was the academic sphere with which the notion of scepticism was most closely connected. The goal of the scholar was always the pursuit of truth, and its quest involved identifying problems, formulating theories, and assessing them, in the light of available evidence, for their falsity, their truth or their uncertainty. The judging agent was the collectivity of the republic of letters, and the sanction was that of ridicule if agreed rules of reason and logic were broken. Secondly, there was the political sphere, or the domain of public policy. The purpose of government was the public well-being, including keeping the peace and defending the realm, and for that reason its ultimate sanction was 'the sword'. Governments must often take decisions in the face of immediate threats to civil order, so that suspension of judgement, notwithstanding uncertainty, was impossible. Accordingly, rulers should take decisions appropriate to agreed public ends, and their judgements should be informed by the best criticism, and the most rational evidence, available at the time. Thirdly, there was the ethical sphere where each person tried to pursue virtue. Doing the right thing rarely allows the suspension of judgement; yet an ethical choice differed from a political choice because, being of concern only to the individual who made it, it could be arrived at in more than one way: through faith, or reason, or ordinary common sense.

Given these distinctions, some conclusions can be drawn about Bayle's view of the proper place in each sphere for scepticism and conviction. To be competent as a philosopher of the natural and social world, an individual needed sound proof before pronouncing publicly on the truth or falsity of a proposition, including propositions about God's existence or providence. In this domain Bayle followed the Ancients by insisting that the philosophic art of suspending judgement – which required a particular training and effort – was a necessary part of the pursuit of truth.[25] For, in the quest for explanation, a diversity of hypotheses – whether arising from written texts, or scholarly observation, or even, initially, from visionary religion (*Soc F* (H)) – could co-exist. By contrast, to be competent as a ruler, or a politician, the decision-maker must choose and implement the best alternative (see *Mach* (E)). History tended to absolve princes from censure, Bayle noted, if they made their judgements in the general interest, and if they gave plausible reasons for what they did (*Eliz* (F), (I); *David* (I)). Yet to act rightly in everyday life, Bayle judged, one needed to be honest to one's conscience. Accordingly, he himself professed Calvinism as his guide to ethics, but not, he insisted, because it was more 'reasonable' than Catholicism, but because he chose to be loyal to the religion of his fathers and because it seemed right to him. He conceded, by the same token, that a Catholic, such as the Jansenist philosopher Nicole, was entitled – since it seemed right to him – to

---

[25] Cf. Bertrand Russell (1948): 'belief is something subtracted from an idea, by an effort, when the idea is being considered without being accepted' (p.116).

advance a similar case in defence of his choice of Catholicism (*Nic* (C)). This was his way of concluding that many factors – faith, reason and loyalty included – had their place in ethical commitment, but because an agent acted in an individual capacity, integrity of motive defined the psychology of the ethical act.

The axiom of public justice that seems to summarise Bayle's thinking was that the ruler was obliged to 'persecute no one for his opinions in religion' (cited above). Respect for private conscience had been sanctioned by the diplomatic community as early as the Religious Peace of Augsburg of 1555. Yet Europe's regimes, Catholic and Protestant, still treated their minorities as less than full citizens, even when they 'tolerated' them. For Bayle and his small circle, who sought to reverse Gallican public policy, a restoration of the former Edicts of Toleration on the same terms as before would have been lamentable. Citizenship in future, they thought, should be based on the same freedom for all parties, whether they proposed alternatives to received belief or whether they propagated orthodoxy. The outcome would be a new society that made no law concerning religion and in which a plurality of ideas could flourish.

Perhaps the Dictionary should be seen as a forum for a rising generation of dissenters, in Europe and in the New World, to whom Bayle could give new heart by showing that 'good sense' had a way of prevailing. Many of the Dictionary's ideas – especially concerning liberty and pluralism – have never subsequently left the public agenda. In particular, Bayle teaches reformers of the future, Voltaire among them, that to silence any marginal voice along the road to innovation could well be an error as well as an injustice. The Dictionary is always permeated with its author's ethical principles and, despite some intentionally frivolous asides, it is overwhelmingly preoccupied with grave themes at the heart of the human condition. For Bayle teaches that when dogmatic parties attempt to censor speech, their claims to be motivated by notions of truth, goodness, or even public order, have always to be tested. It is all too often the case, he warns, that they seek merely to silence humanity's collective anxieties.

Chronology

A: From religious war to limited toleration, 1515–1643: the age of Francis I to the age of Richelieu

Date	Events in France	Other events
1515	Reign of Francis I (1515–47).	Calvin: *Institutes of the Christian Religion* (1533).
1547	Reign of Henry II (1547–59). Reformers are persecuted as heretics.	Copernicus: *Revolutions of Heavenly Bodies* (1543).
1555		1555: Peace of Augsburg – establishment within the Holy Roman Empire of the constitutional principle of *cuius regio eius religio*. 1558: accession of Elizabeth I of England. She opts for the Protestant religion.
1559	Henry II dies. 25 May: first synod in France of Reformed Church meets in Paris. Reign of Francis II (1559–60). Catherine de	

	Médicis, Henry II's widow, becomes Regent on behalf of three sons successively.	
1560	Francis II dies. Reign of Charles IX (1560–74).	
1561	Colloque de Poissy.	Catherine and Chancellor de l'Hôpital make appeal for national unity.
1562	Massacre de Vassy. Beginning of Wars of Religion.	
1563	Temporary Peace of Amboise.	Rights of conscience and separate organisation for Calvinism acknowledged
1568	Catherine dismisses de l'Hôpital.	
1570	Peace of Saint-Germain.	Freedom of conscience formally re-affirmed.
1572	23–4 August: Massacre of Saint Bartholomew's Eve.	
1574	Henry III (1574–89) succeeds Charles IX.	Hotman: *Franco-Gallia*.
1576	Formation of the Catholic League. Henry III calls Estates General at Blois.	Bodin: *Six livres de la république*.
1573–84	Military alliance of Huguenots and Catholic 'Malcontents' under Henry of Navarre. Death of François d'Anjou, Catholic heir to Henry III. Protestant Henry of Navarre becomes legal heir.	Montmorency-Damville, and the Catholic heir, the Duc d'Anjou, support the alliance. Montaigne: *Essais* (1580). 1581: Dutch Declaration of Independence from Spain. William 'the Silent' leads the Protestant United Provinces.

1585	Renewal of repression of 'heretics', as under Henry II.	1584: Catholic resistance writing, supported by Pope and Spain, gains momentum.
1588	January: Catherine de Médicis dies.	Catholic Duc de Guise declared 'king of Paris', but is assassinated at the Estates General at Blois. Life of Hobbes (1588–1679).
1589	August: Assassination of Henry III. Protestant Henry IV (1589–1601) accedes to the throne. Brother of de Guise declared 'king'. Catholic Faculty of Theology releases subjects from loyalty to Henry III, or to Henry IV as his Protestant heir and successor.	Henry IV is refused recognition by Pope unless he converts to Catholicism (which he does in 1595).
1595	Pope recognises Henry IV as legitimate French sovereign.	
1598	Edict of Nantes guaranteeing limited toleration for the Reformed communities. Sully under Henry IV reorganises French finances.	
		Mariana: *De rege et regis institutione* (1599).
1610	Assassination of Henry IV; Catholic Louis XIII (1610–1643) accedes to the throne.	
1616–17	Richelieu's first ministry.	Grotius: *De jure belli ac pacis* (1625). Galileo: *Dialogue on the*

		Two Principal Systems of the World (1632).
1643	Death of Louis XIII. Louis XIV, a minor, becomes king.	1624–43: The age of Richelieu, limited toleration, and *politique* rule.
	The Regency of Anne of Austria. The age of Mazarin begins.	Hobbes: *Leviathan* (1651).
1660	Louis XIV (1643–1715) begins period of personal rule and policy of gradual restoration of a single official religion.	Restoration of monarchy and Anglicanism as official religion in Great Britain.

B: Events in Bayle's life

Date	Bayle's life	Other events
1637	Jean Bayle becomes pastor of the Reformed church at Le Carla, in southern France, in the Comté de Foix.	Descartes: *Discours de la méthode* (1637).
1647	Bayle born on 17 November. He is second son of Jeanne de Brugière and Jean Bayle.	1648: Treaties of Westphalia. *Cuius regio eius religio* re-asserted, entailing limited freedom of conscience.
1666	1666–7: begins studies at the Reformed Academy at Puylaurens.	
1669	Attends the Catholic Academy at Toulouse as external student. Converts to Catholicism.	

1670	Renounces Catholicism. Arrives in Geneva to attend Protestant Academy.	
1672	Becomes tutor in the household of Comte de Dohna.	
1674	Becomes tutor in Rouen.	
1675	Becomes Professor of Philosophy at the Reformed Academy of Sedan.	
1681	July: Closure of the Reformed Academy of Sedan on orders of Louis XIV's regime. October: Arrives in Rotterdam to take post as Professor of Philosophy and History at the Ecole Illustre. His patron is Adriaan Van Paets.	Bossuet: *Discours sur l'histoire universelle.*
1682	March: *Lettre sur la comète.* July: *Critique générale de l'Histoire du Calvinisme de M. Maimbourg..*	Maimbourg: *Histoire du Calvinisme.*
1684	November: *Critique générale,* 2nd edn. September: *Pensées diverses sur la comète,* 2nd edn.	
1685	Becomes editor of *Nouvelles de la république des lettres* (from 1684 to 1687). Death of younger brother, Joseph. Death in France of father, Jean Bayle. *Nouvelles lettres de l'auteur*	Revocation of Edict of Nantes in France. Accession of Catholic James II of England on death of Charles II.

de la critique générale.
Translates from Latin into
French Adriaan Van
Paets's *Lettre de Monsieur
H.V.P. à monsieur B****,
sur les derniers troubles en
Angleterre: où il est parlé
de la tolérance de ceux qui
ne suivent point la religion
dominante.*
October: death of Van
Paets.
November: death in
French prison of elder
brother, Jacob Bayle.

1686	*Ce que c'est que la France Toute Catholique.* October: *Commentaire philosophique*, Parts 1 and 2. *Commentaire philosophique*, Part 3.	European League of Augsburg to combat French territorial ambitions.
1688	Bayle ceases to edit *Nouvelles de la république des lettres* for reasons of ill health. Henri Basnage de Beauval relaces him.	England's Glorious Revolution.
1689	*Réponse d'un nouveau converti à une lettre d'un réfugié.*	Locke: *Letter on Toleration.*
1690	*Avis aux réfugiez.*	
1691	Bayle's quarrels with Jurieu continue.	
1692	*Projet* for the *Dictionnaire critique.*	
1693	Bayle is relieved of his post at the Ecole Illustre (but not of the right to teach).	

1694	*Addition aux Pensées diverses.*	*Dictionnaire de l'Académie française.*
1697	*Dictionnaire historique et critique*, 1st edn. November: Enquiry begins by the Reformed Church of Rotterdam into alleged impiety and obscenity in the *Dictionnaire*. Bayle agrees to make token changes.	Peace of Ryswyck. Louis XIV and William III make peace. Louis XIV obliged to recognise William and Mary as joint sovereigns.
1698	Publishers plan 2nd edn of *Dictionnaire*.	
1699	*Pensées diverses sur la comète*, 3rd edn. *Addition aux Pensées diverses*, 2nd edn.	
1700	Accepts invitation to the Hague to meet Princess Sophie-Charlotte of Hanover, Electress of Brandenburg and future queen of Prussia.	
1701	Licence granted in London to begin an English translation of the *Dictionnaire*.	
1702	*Dictionnaire historique et critique*, 2nd Amsterdam edn in French.	
1703	1703/4: *Réponse aux questions d'un provincial, part 1.*	
1704	*Pensées diverses*, 4th edn. August: *Continuation des Pensées diverses* *Réponse aux questions d'un provincial*, part 2.	

1705	November: *Réponse aux questions d'un provincial*, part 3.	1705–7: Jean Leclerc debates with Bayle in *La Bibliothèque choisie* (beginning 1705, vol. v).
1706	Bayle dies at his desk on 28 December 1706.	
1707	*Réponse aux questions d'un provincial*, part 4. Published posthumously.	
1710	*An Historical and Critical Dictionary by Monsieur Bayle*, London. Published posthumously.	Leibniz responds to Bayle's philosophic critique of theology, in *Theodicy*.

Bibliography

Further reading

The following guide to further reading refers as far as possible to works in English even though many invaluable items are published in French, Italian, and other languages. Key studies are Labrousse, *Pierre Bayle* (2 vols., 1963–4; vol. II, rev. edn 1996), and Solé, *Le Débat entre protestants et catholiques français de 1598 à 1685* (1986). The selected bibliography below gives their details in full.

On Bayle as a political and moral philosopher

Studies of synthesis, in the English language, have yet to appear, and Locke's biographer John Dunn thinks that 'there is no commanding analysis of Bayle's thought as a whole' ((1996), p. 114, n. 14). The work in English, *Bayle*, by Elisabeth Labrousse (1983), provides however a concise general introduction to her interpretive work in French. The view advanced here is that on pluralism in politics, and on the appropriate epistemology for supporting it, Bayle has in recent decades begun to receive the reappraisal that he merits. On this perspective, see Jenkinson, 'Rationality, Pluralism and Reciprocal Tolerance: A Reappraisal of Pierre Bayle's Political Thought' (1993). A common assumption until recently was that Bayle shared the ordinary view that the Christian commonwealth set necessary limits to institutional diversity. Harry H. Bracken is among a new group of scholars who disagree with this assumption. See, *inter alia*, Bracken's 'Toleration Theories: Bayle vs. Locke' (1991) and 'Bayle and the Origins of the Doctrine' (1994). Two articles, Mori's 'Pierre Bayle, the Rights of the Conscience, the "Remedy" of Toleration' (1997), and Jenkinson's 'Two Concepts of Tolerance: Why Bayle is not Locke' (1996), advance other objections. Perceptive critics, including the mathematician Leibniz, find some of Bayle's ideas enigmatic: see Leibniz, *Theodicy* (1710). On Bayle and Leibniz, see Jenkinson (1999a). See also John Dunn in 'The Claim to Freedom of Conscience; Freedom of Speech, Freedom of Thought, Freedom of Worship' (1996), as well as David Wootton, 'Bayle, Libestine?' (1997), and J. C. Laursen in 'Baylean Liberalism: Tolerance Requires Non-tolerance' (1998). On Bayle as passionate opponent of intolerance and political violence see, *inter alia*, Amie and Donald Tannenbaum, 'John Locke and Pierre Bayle on Religious Toleration: an Enquiry' (1992) or Jenkinson, 'Nourishing Men's Anger' (1998). Bayle's influence on Shaftesbury is referred to briefly in J. B. Schneewind's 'The Earl of Shaftesbury' (1990). Finally, John Kilcullen's monograph *Sincerity and Truth: Essays on Arnauld, Bayle and Toleration* (1988) opens an avenue for exploring Bayle as a normative thinker before Kant, echoing thereby a subtle thesis advanced by Delvolvé in *Religion, critique et philosophie positive chez Pierre Bayle* (1906).

On the general background of the sixteenth and seventeenth centuries

For an overview of the age of Reformation, civil war, and toleration in whose history Bayle was immersed, see the Chronology above. See also Mark Greengrass, *France in the Age of Henry IV* (1995) and its bibliography of recent social and economic research. Voltaire's *Le Siècle de Louis XIV* (1751; translated as *The Age of Louis XIV*) remains distinctive for reminding us that until 1685 Catholic France had set Europe's standards for civility and toleration. The chapters 'Calvinism in the Age of Louis XIV' and 'Chinese Ceremonies' show the influence of Bayle on Voltaire's perspective. Skinner's *Foundations of Political Thought* (1978), especially vol. II, provides theoretical depth, as does the work of J. H. M. Salmon, and in particular his *Renaissance and Revolt: Essays in the Intellectual and Social History of Early Modern France* (1987). For the political thought of a broad era see Nannerl Keohane's *Philosophy and the State in France. The Renaissance to the Enlightenment*

(1980). For two volumes that provide analyses of the public themes to which Bayle responded, see firstly A. Pagden (ed.), *The Languages of Political Theory in Early Modern Europe* (1987), and secondly Phillipson and Skinner (eds.), *Political Discourse in Early Modern Europe* (1993). For the humanist tradition and its emanations, see J. Pocock, *The Machiavellian Moment: Florentine Political Thought and the Atlantic Republican Tradition* (1975), and Richard Tuck's *Philosophy and Government 1578–1651* (1993). On Bayle's circle in the Netherlands, there are various articles, many in English, collected in M. Magdelaine *et al.* (eds.), *De l'humanisme aux lumières, Bayle et le protestantisme: mélanges en l'honneur d'Elisabeth Labrousse* (1996). An article which enlarges the vignette of the *philosophe de Rotterdam* presented by Hazard in *The European Mind* (1963) is that of Gerald Cerny, 'Jacques Basnage and Pierre Bayle: an Intimate Collaboration in Refugee Literary Circles and in the Affairs of the Republic of Letters, 1685–1706' (1996). On Protestant controversy, see Luisa Simonutti's bibliographic article 'Between Political Loyalty and Religious Liberty: Political Theory and Toleration in Huguenot Thought in the Epoch of Bayle' (1996). Toleration in the Netherlands is explored in depth in Berkevens-Stevelinck *et al.* (eds.), *The Emergence of Tolerance in the Dutch Republic* (1997). On the rise of toleration in France in the sixteenth century, see Yardeni (1971), *La Conscience nationale de France pendant les guerres de religion (1559–1598)*. On its erosion in seventeenth-century France, see the 'Baylean' analysis by Elisabeth Labrousse in *La Révocation de L'Edit de Nantes* (1990).

Scientific background to the sixteenth and seventeenth centuries

No interpretation of Bayle's political thought can overlook the impact of Galileo's critical science upon those who taught natural philosophy in the European university. For an overview see Roy Porter and Mikulas Teich (eds.), *Scientific Revolution in National Context* (1992), and for case studies there is John Henry and Sarah Hutton (eds.), *New Perspectives on Renaissance Thought: Essays in the History of Science, Education and Philosophy* (1990). On 'scepticism', including its impact on theology, see the many publications of Richard H. Popkin, in particular *The History of Scepticism from Erasmus to Spinoza* (1979). On the classical origins of Galileo's cosmology, I believe that Karl Popper's essay 'Back to the Pre-Socratics' in his *Conjectures and Refutations. The Growth of Scientific Knowledge* (1963) is crucial and cf. Thomas Lennon, 'Bayle's Anticipation of Popper' (1997). On science in the syllabus, see L. W. B. Brockliss, 'Copernicus in the University: the French Experience' (1990). The volume of essays entitled *Scepticism and Irreligion in the Seventeenth and Eighteenth Centuries*, edited by Popkin and Vanderjagt (1993), newly illuminates Bayle's engagement with natural philosophy as Christian theologians interpreted it. Of insight for Bayle's perspective are the respective pieces of Murr, 'Gassendi's Scepticism as a Religious Attitude', and of Bracken, 'Bayle's Attack on Natural Theology: the Case of Christian Pyrrhonism'.

Selected bibliography

For references to Bayle's own writings see, additionally, the key to abbreviations, pp. xvi–xvii. Of the many editions in French of the *Dictionnaire* an annotated list of twelve is appended to Rétat's study (1971) pp. 475–7. A comprehensive bibliography of secondary literature on Bayle in a range of disciplines can be found in Labrousse, *Pierre Bayle*, vol. II: *Hétérodoxie et rigorisme* (1996a) [1964]. This second edition of vol. II has a revised bibliography.

Works published before 1760

Augustine (1998) [AD 426], *The City of God against the Pagans*, ed. and tr. R. W. Dyson. Cambridge: Cambridge University Press.
Bayle, Pierre (*c.* 1679), *Système abrégé de philosophie*. In *OD* IV, pp. 201–520.
    (1682), *Critique générale de l'Histoire du Calvinisme de M. Maimbourg*. In *OD* II, pp. 1–160.
    (1684–7), *Nouvelles de la République des Lettres*. In *OD* I, pp. 1–760.
    (1685), *Nouvelles lettres de l'auteur de la Critique Générale de l'Histoire du Calvinisme*. In *OD* II, pp. 161–335.
    (1686), *Ce que c'est que la France Toute Catholique sous le règne de Louis le Grand*. In *OD* II, pp. 336–54.
    (1686), *Commentaire philosophique sur ces paroles de Jésus Christ 'Contrains-les d'entrer'; Où l'on prouve par plusieurs raisons*

demonstratives, qu'il n'y a rien de plus abominable que de faire des conversions par la contrainte: et où l'on réfute tous les sophismes des convertisseurs à contrainte, et l'Apologie que Saint Augustine a faite des persécutions. In *OD* II, pp. 355–60.

(1987) [1686], *Philosophical Commentary*, ed. and trans. Amie Godman Tannenbaum. Bern: Peter Lang.

(1689), *Réponse d'un nouveau converti.* In *OD* II, pp. 561–75.

(1690), *Avis important aux réfugiez sur leur prochain retour en France.* In *OD* II, pp. 578–633.

(1697), *Dictionnaire historique et critique: par M. Bayle.* Avec Privilège, 4 parts, 2 vols. Rotterdam: Rainier Leers.

(1702), *Dictionnaire historique et critique: par M. Bayle.* Seconde édition, revue, corrigée et augmentée par l'auteur. Avec Privilège. 3 vols. Rotterdam: Rainier Leers.

(1704), *Continuation des Pensées diverses.* In *OD* III, pp. 187–417.

(1710), *An Historical and Critical Dictionary by Monsieur Bayle. Translated into English with many Additions and Corrections, made by the Author himself that are not in the French Editions.* London: Printed for C. Harper, D. Brown, J. Tonson, A. and J. Churchill, T. Horne, T. Goodwin, R. Knaplock, J. Taylor, A. Bell, B. Tooke, D. Midwinter, B. Lintott and W. Lewis.

(1727–31), *Œuvres diverses.* 4 vols., The Hague.

(1730), *Dictionnaire historique et critique, par M. Bayle.* Quatrième édition, revue, corrigée et augmentée, avec la vie de l'auteur par M. Des Maizeaux. 4 vols. Amsterdam: P. Brunel; R. and J. Wetstein, G. Smith, H. Waesberge; P. Humbert; F. Honoré.

(1734–8), *Dictionary Historical and Critical*, 5 vols. London: J. J. and P. Knapton [facsimile edition, London: Routledge/Toennies Press, 1997].

(1734–41), *A General Dictionary, Historical and Critical*, 10 vols. By the Revd John Peter Bernard *et al.* London: printed by James Bettenham *et al.*

(1740) *Dictionnaire historique et critique*, 4 vols., Amsterdam, Leiden, The Hague, Utrecht [revised version of the edition of 1730].

(1820–4) [1696/7] [1702], *Dictionnaire historique et critique. Nouvelle édition augmentée de notes extraites de Chaufepié, Joly, La Monnoie, Leduchat, L.-J. Leclerc, Prosper Marchand*, etc. 16 vols., Paris: Beuchot. [Abbreviated to *Dic.*]

(1970–82) [1727–31], *Œuvres diverses. Avec une Introduction par Elisabeth Labrousse.* [Second reprographic reimpression of the edition of The Hague, 1727–31.] 5 vols. Hildesheim and New York: Georg Olms Verlag. [Abbreviated to *OD*]

(1987) [1686], *Philosophical Commentary* [trans. of *Commentaire philosophique*, 1686], ed. and trans. Amie Godman Tannenbaum. Bern: Peter Lang.

(1991) [1965], *Pierre Bayle: Historical and Critical Dictionary. Selections*, ed. R. H. Popkin; trans. R. H. Popkin and C. Brush. 2nd edn. Indianapolis and Cambridge: Hackett Publishing Company, Inc.

(1999–), *Correspondance de Pierre Bayle*, ed. Elisabeth Labrousse, Edward James, Antony McKenna, Maria-Christina Pitassi, Ruth Whelan. Vol. I, 1662–1674, Lettres 1–65. 10 vols. (Vols. II–X forthcoming.) Oxford: Voltaire Foundation.

Benoist, Elie (1693–5), *L'Histoire de l'Edit de Nantes*. Delft.

Bossuet, J. (1990) [1709], *Politics Drawn from the very Words of Holy Scripture*, ed. and trans. P. Riley. Cambridge: Cambridge University Press.

Des Maizeaux, Pierre (1820) [1740], *La Vie de M. Bayle*. In *Dic*, vol. XVI, pp. 44–275.

Descartes, R. (1963–1973) [1637–], *Oeuvres philosophiques*, ed. F. Alquie. 3 vols., Paris: Garnier.

(1964–76) [1637–], *Œuvres*. 12 vols., Paris: Vrin/CNRS.

Hobbes, Thomas (1991) [1651], *Leviathan*, ed. Richard Tuck. Cambridge: Cambridge University Press.

Jurieu, Pierre (1686), *L'Accomplissement de prophéties ou la délivrance prochaine de l'église*. Rotterdam.

(1687), *Des droits de deux souverains en matière de religion, la conscience et le Prince pour détruire le dogma de l'indifférence et de la tolérance universelle contre un livre intitulé Commentaire philosophique sur ces paroles de la parabole 'Contrains-les d'entrer'*. Rotterdam.

(*c.* 1690/1), *Examen d'un libelle contre la Religion, contre l'Etat, et contre la révolution en Angleterre entitulé l'Avis aux réfugiez sur le prochain retour en France*. The Hague.

Leibniz, G. (1985) [1710], *Theodicy. Essays on the Goodness of God, the Freedom of Man and the Origin of Evil*, ed. A. Farrer, trans. E. M. Huggard. La Salle, Ill.: Open Court.

Locke, J. (1966) [1689], *A Letter Concerning Toleration*. In *The Second Treatise of Government (An Essay Concerning the True Original Extent and End of Civil Government) and A Letter Concerning Toleration*, 3rd edn, ed. J. Gough. Oxford: Basil Blackwell, pp. 123–67.

Maimbourg, Louis (1682), *L'Histoire du Calvinisme*. 2 vols., Paris: Sébastien Marbre.

Mézerai, François Eudes de (1688) [1674], *Abrégé chronologique de l'histoire de France par le sieur de M . . ., historiographe de France.* 6 vols. Amsterdam.

Moréri, Louis (1674), *Le Grand Dictionnaire historique ou le mélange curieux de l'histoire sainte et profane.* Lyon: Jean Girin et Bartélémy Rivière.

Paets, Adriaan Van (1685), *H. V. P. ad B**** de nuperis Angliae motibus epistola in qua de diversorum a publica religione circa divina sententium disseritur tolerantia* [in Latin, French and Dutch]. Rotterdam: Leers, 1685. (For Bayle's translation, see *Lettre sur les derniers troubles en Angleterre, où il est parlé de la tolérance de ceux qui ne suivent pas la religion dominante, OD* v, 2, pp. 11–77.)

Thou, Jacques Auguste de (1734), *Histoire Universelle depuis 1554– 1607.* 16 vols., Paris.

Voltaire, Jean François Arouet de (1751), *Le Siècle de Louis XIV.* Berlin. [English trans. by Martyn P. Pollack, *The Age of Louis XIV* (1961). London and New York: Everyman's Library.]

Works published since 1906

Abel, O. and P. F. Moreau (eds.) (1995), *Pierre Bayle: la foi dans le doute.* Geneva: Labor et Fides.

Berkevens-Stevelinck, C., J. Israel and G. H. M. Posthumus Meyjes (eds.) (1997), *The Emergence of Tolerance in the Dutch Republic.* Leiden: E. J. Brill.

Bost, Hubert (*c.* 1989/90), 'Pierre Bayle et la Glorieuse Revolution d'Angleterre', in Michel Peronnet (ed.), *Protestantisme et Révolution. Actes du VIè Colloque Jean Boisset, XIe Colloque du Centre d'Histoire des Reformées et du Protestantisme.* Montpelier: Sauramps, pp. 75–88.

(1994), *Pierre Bayle et la religion.* Paris: Presses Universitaires de France.

Bracken, H. (1990), 'Pierre Bayle and Freedom of Speech', in E. J. Furcha (ed.), *Truth and Tolerance.* Montreal: McGill University Faculty of Religious Studies, pp. 28–42.

(1991), 'Toleration Theories: Bayle vs. Locke', in E. Greffier and M. Paradis (eds.), *The Notion of Tolerance and Human Rights. Essays in Honour of R. Klibanski.* [Ottawa, Ontario:] Carleton University Press, pp. 1–11.

(1993), 'Bayle's Attack on Natural Theology: the Case of Christian Pyrrhonism', in Popkin and Vanderjagt (eds.) (1993), pp. 254–66.

(1994), 'Bayle and the Origins of the Doctrine', in *Freedom of Speech: Words are not Deeds*. Westport, Conn.: Praeger, pp. 1–19.

Brockliss, L. W. B. (1990), 'Copernicus in the University: the French Experience', in Henry and Hutton (eds.) (1990), pp. 190–213.

Cerny, Gerald (1996), 'Jacques Basnage and Pierre Bayle: an Intimate Collaboration in Refugee Literary Circles and in the Affairs of the Republic of Letters, 1685–1706', in Magdelaine *et al.* (1996), pp. 495–508.

Cohen, R. S., K. Feyerabend and M. W. Wartovsky (eds.) (1976), *Essays in Honour of Imre Lakatos*. Dordrecht: Reidel.

Courtines, Leo (1938), *Bayle's Relations with England and the English*. New York: Columbia University Press.

Cranston, Maurice (1957), *John Locke, a Biography*. London: Longman.

Delvolvé, Jean (1906), *Religion, critique et philosophie positive chez Pierre Bayle*. Paris: F. Alcan.

Dunn, J. (1984), *Locke*. Oxford and New York: Oxford University Press.

(1996), 'The Claim to Freedom of Conscience; Freedom of Speech, Freedom of Thought, Freedom of Worship', in *The History of Political Theory and Other Essays*. Cambridge: Cambridge University Press, pp. 100–20.

Golden, R. (ed.) (1982), *Church, State and Society under the Bourbon Kings*. Kansas: Lawrence.

Goldie, Mark (1987), 'The Civil Religion of James Harrington', in Anthony Pagden (ed.), *The Languages of Political Theory in Early Modern Europe*. Cambridge: Cambridge University Press, pp. 197–222.

Goubert, Pierre (1997) [1973], *The Ancien Regime: French Society 1600–1750*. London: Phoenix Giant.

Greengrass, Mark (1995), *France in the Age of Henry IV*, 2nd edn. London and New York: Longman.

Gros, J. M. (1995), 'Sens et limites de la théorie de la tolérance chez Bayle', in Abel and Moreau (eds.) (1995), pp. 65–86.

Gross, Paul R. (1997), *The Flight from Science and Reason*. Baltimore: Johns Hopkins University Press.

Habermas, J. (1987), *The Philosophical Discourse of Modernity*, trans. F. Lawrence. Oxford: Polity Press.

Hazard, Paul (1964), 'Pierre Bayle', in *The European Mind*. Harmondsworth: Penguin, pp. 124–44.

Henry, John and Hutton, Sarah (eds.) (1990), *New Perspectives on Renaissance Thought: Essays in the History of Science, Education and Philosophy: in Honour of Charles B. Schmitt*. London: Duckworth.

Horton, J. M. and Susan Mendus (1991), *Locke, J., 'A Letter Concerning Toleration' in Focus*. London and New York: Routledge.

Hunter, Michael and David Wootton (eds.) (1992), *Atheism from the Reformation to the Enlightenment*. Oxford: Clarendon Press.

Jenkinson, S. L. (1987), 'Bayle', in D. Miller *et al.* (eds.), *The Blackwell Encyclopaedia of Political Thought*. Oxford: Blackwell, pp. 35–6.

(1993), 'Rationality, Pluralism and Reciprocal Tolerance: A Reappraisal of Pierre Bayle's Political Thought', in Iain Hampsher-Monk (ed.), *Defending Politics: Bernard Crick and Pluralism*. London and New York: British Academic Press, pp. 22–45.

(1996), 'Two Concepts of Tolerance: Why Bayle is not Locke', *The Journal of Political Philosophy*, 4 (4), pp. 302–22.

(1998), 'Nourishing Men's Anger and Inflaming the Fires of Hatred: Bayle on Religious Violence and the "Novus Ordo Saeculorum"', *Terrorism and Political Violence*, 10, 4 (Winter 1998), pp. 64–79.

(1999a), 'Bayle and Leibniz: Two Paradigms of Tolerance and some Reflections on Goodness without God', in J. C. Laursen (ed.), *The Variety of Rites: Religious Toleration from Cyrus to Defoe*. London and New York: St Martin's Press, pp. 173–89.

(1999b), 'Bayle's Dictionary and the Rhetoric of Tyrannicide.' Dublin: Tenth International Congress on the Enlightenment, 25–31 July. Typescript, 34 pp.

Kamen, Henry (1997), 'Toleration and the Law in the West', *Ratio Juris*, 10 (1) (March), pp. 36–44.

Kenshur, O. (1993), 'Bayle's Theory of Toleration: The Politics of Certainty and Doubt', in *Dilemma of Enlightenment: Studies in the Rhetoric and Logic of Ideology*. Berkeley: University of California Press.

Keohane, N. O. (1980), *Philosophy and the State in France. The Renaissance to the Enlightenment*. Princeton, New Jersey: Princeton University Press.

Kilcullen, J. (1988), *Sincerity and Truth: Essays on Arnauld, Bayle and Toleration*. Oxford: Oxford University Press.

King, Preston 1998 [1976], *Toleration*. London: Cass.

Labrousse, Elisabeth (1961), *Inventaire critique de la correspondance de Pierre Bayle*. Paris: J. Vrin.

(1963–4), *Pierre Bayle*, vol. I: *Du pays de Foix a la cité d'Erasme*; vol. II: *Hétérodoxie et rigorisme*. The Hague: Martinus Nijhoff.

(1964–82), 'Introduction historique' [Historical Introduction], in Bayle, *Œuvres Diverses* (1964–1982), 5 vols. Hildesheim; New York: Georg Olms Verlag, Vol. I, pp. ix–xx; vol. II, pp. vii–xvi; vol. III, pp. vii–xiv; vol. IV, pp. vii–xvi; vol. V, pp. ix–lviii.

(1983), *Bayle*, trans. Denys Potts. Oxford and New York: Oxford University Press.

(1990) [1985], *La Révocation de l'Edit de Nantes. Une foi, une loi, un roi?* Saint-Amand (Cher): Payot.

(1996a) [1964], *Pierre Bayle*, vol. II: *Hétérodoxie et rigorisme*, 2nd edn with annexes and a revised bibliography. Paris: Albin Michel.

(1996b), *Conscience et Conviction. Etudes sur le XVIIè siècle*. Paris and Oxford: The Voltaire Foundation. [Vol. II of M. Magdelaine *et al.* (eds.) (1996).]

(1996c), 'Mythes Huguenots au XVIIè siècle', in Labrousse (1996b), pp. 71–80.

(1996d), 'Les Idées politiques du Réfuge: Bayle et Jurieu', in Labrousse (1996b), pp. 160–91.

Laursen, John Christian (1998), 'Baylean Liberalism: Tolerance Requires Non-tolerance', in Laursen and Nederman (eds.) (1998), pp. 197–215.

Laursen, John Christian (ed.) (1995), *New Essays on the Political Thought of the Huguenots of the Refuge*. Leiden: E. J. Brill.

(1999), *The Variety of Rites: Religious Toleration from Cyrus to Defoe*. London and New York: St Martin's Press.

Laursen, John Christian and Cary Nederman (eds.) (1998), *Beyond the Persecuting Society: Religious Toleration before the Enlightenment*. Philadelphia: University of Pennsylvania Press.

Lennon, Thomas M. (1995), 'Taste and Sentiment: Hume, Bayle, Jurieu and Nicole', in Abel and Moreau (eds.) (1995), pp. 49–64.

(1997), 'Bayle's Anticipation of Popper', *The Journal of the History of Ideas*, 58 (4), pp. 695–705.

Magdelaine, M., M. Pitassi, R. Whelan and A. McKenna (eds.) (1996), *De l'humanisme aux lumières, Bayle et le Protestantisme: Mélanges en l'honneur d'Elisabeth Labrousse*. Paris and Oxford: Voltaire Foundation.

McKenna, A. (1996), 'Bayle moraliste augustinien', in *De la morale à l'économie politique*. Pau, France: Presses Universitaires de France, pp. 175–86.

Mill, J. Stuart (1910) [1859, 1861, 1863], *Utilitarianism. Liberty. Representative Government*. London: J. M. Dent and Sons Ltd.

Mori, G. (1997), 'Pierre Bayle, the Rights of the Conscience, the "Remedy" of Toleration', *Ratio Juris*, 10 (1) (March), pp. 45–60.

(1999), *Bayle – philosophe*. Paris and Geneva: Champion-Slatkine.

Murr, Sylvia (1993), 'Gassendi's Scepticism as a Religious Attitude', in Popkin and Vanderjagt (eds.) (1993), pp. 12–30.

Nederman, Cary J. and Laursen, John Christian (eds.) (1996), *Difference and Dissent: Theories of Tolerance in Mediaeval and Early Modern Europe*. New York and London: Rowman and Littlefield Publishers, Inc.

O'Cathasaigh, Sean (1996), 'Bayle and Locke on Toleration', in Magdelaine *et al.* (eds.) (1996), pp. 679–92.

Pagden, Anthony (ed.) (1987), *Languages of Political Theory in Early Modern Europe*. Cambridge: Cambridge University Press.

Paganini, Gianni (1980), *Analise de la fede e critica della ragione nella filosofia de Pierre Bayle*. Florence: La Nuova Italia.

(1999), 'Le Dernier Bayle et le problème théologico-politique.' Dublin: Tenth International Congress on the Enlightenment. 25–31 July. Typescript, 20 pp.

Peronnet, Michel (ed.) (*c.* 1989/90), *Protestantisme et Revolution. Actes du VIe Colloque Jean Boisset, XIe Colloque du Centre d'Histoire des Réformées et du Protestantisme*. Montpelier: Sauramps.

Phillipson, Nicholas and Quentin Skinner (eds.) (1993), *Political Discourse in Early Modern Europe*. Cambridge: Cambridge University Press.

Pocock, J. (1975), *The Machiavellian Moment: Florentine Political Thought and the Atlantic Republican Tradition*. Princeton: Princeton University Press.

Popkin, R. H. (1979), *The History of Scepticism from Erasmus to Spinoza*. Berkeley and London: University of California Press.

(1996), 'Pierre Bayle and the Conversion of the Jews', in Magdelaine *et al.* (eds.) (1996), pp. 635–43.

Popkin, R. H. (ed.) (1991) [1965], 'Introduction', *Pierre Bayle: Historical and Critical Dictionary. Selections.* Indianapolis and Cambridge: Hackett Publishing Company, Inc., pp. viii–xxix.

Popkin, Richard H. and Arjo Vanderjagt (eds.) (1993), *Scepticism and Irreligion in the Seventeenth and Eighteenth Centuries.* Leiden and New York: E. J. Brill.

Popper, K. R. (1963), 'Back to the Pre-Socratics', *Conjectures and Refutations. The Growth of Scientific Knowledge.* London: Routledge and Kegan Paul, pp. 139–65.

Porter, Roy and Mikulas Teich (eds.) (1992), *Scientific Revolution in National Context.* Cambridge: Cambridge University Press.

Rawls, J. (1972), *A Theory of Justice.* Oxford: Clarendon Press.

Rétat, Pierre (1971), *Le Dictionnaire de Bayle et la lutte philosophique au XVIIIè siècle.* Paris: Vrin.

Riley, P. (1982), *Will and Political Legitimacy: A Critical Exposition of Social Contract Theory in Hobbes, Locke, Rousseau, Kant, and Hegel.* Cambridge, Mass., and London: Harvard University Press.

(1990), 'Introduction', in *Bossuet: Politics Drawn from Holy Scripture*, ed. P. Riley. Cambridge: Cambridge University Press, pp. xiii–lxxv.

(1996), *Leibniz: Universal Jurisprudence. Justice as the Charity of the Wise.* Cambridge: Harvard University Press.

Russell, Bertrand (1948), *Human Knowledge. Its Scope and Limitations.* London: George Allen and Unwin.

Salmon, J. H. M. (1987), *Renaissance and Revolt: Essays in the Intellectual and Social History of Early Modern France.* Cambridge: Cambridge University Press.

(1991), 'Catholic Resistance Theory, Ultramontanism and the Royalist Response, 1580–1620', in J. Burns and M. Goldie (eds.), *The Cambridge History of Political Thought: 1540–1700.* Cambridge: Cambridge University Press, pp. 219–53.

Sandberg, K. C. (1964), 'Pierre Bayle's Sincerity in his Views on Faith and Reason', *Studies in Philology*, 61, pp. 74–84.

Schneewind, J. B. (1990), 'The Earl of Shaftesbury', in Schneewind (ed.) (1990), part 4: *Autonomy and Responsibility*, pp. 483–502.

(1993), 'Kant and Natural Law Ethics', *Ethics*, 104 (October), pp. 53–74.

Schneewind, J. B. (ed.) (1990), *Moral Philosophy from Montaigne to Kant: An Anthology*. 4 vols., Cambridge: Cambridge University Press.

Simonutti, Luisa (1996), 'Between Political Loyalty and Religious Liberty: Political Theory and Toleration in Huguenot Thought in the Epoch of Bayle', *History of Political Thought*, 17 (4), pp. 522–54.

Skinner, Q. (1978), *The Foundations of Political Thought*, vol. I: *The Renaissance*; vol. II: *The Age of Reformation*. Cambridge: Cambridge University Press.

(1996), *Reason and Rhetoric in the Philosophy of Hobbes*. Cambridge: Cambridge University Press.

(1998), *Liberty before Liberalism*. Cambridge: Cambridge University Press.

Solé, Jacques (1986), *Le Débat entre protestants et catholiques français de 1598 à 1685*. Lille: ANRT.

(1996), 'Les Débuts de la collaboration entre Adriaan van Paets, protecteur de Pierre Bayle à Rotterdam, et le gouvernement de Louis XIV', in Magdelaine *et al.* (eds.) (1996), pp. 477–94.

Stewart, M. A. (ed.) (1997), *Studies in Eighteenth Century European Philosophy*. Oxford: Clarendon Press.

Tannenbaum, Amie and Donald Tannenbaum (1992), 'John Locke and Pierre Bayle on Religious Toleration: an Enquiry', *Studies on Voltaire and the Eighteenth Century*, 303, pp. 418–21.

(1999), 'Bayle and Machiavelli: Dictionary, Texts and Interpretations'. Dublin: Tenth International Congress on the Enlightenment. 25–31 July. Typescript, 30 pp.

Tinsley, B. S. (1996), 'Sozzini's Ghost: Pierre Bayle and Socinian Toleration', *Journal of the History of Ideas*, 57 (7), pp. 609–24.

Touchard, J. (1975), *Histoire des idées politiques*. Paris: Presses Universitaires de France.

Tuck, Richard (1988), 'Scepticism and Toleration in the Seventeenth Century', in Susan Mendus (ed.), *Justifying Toler-*

ation: *Conceptual and Historical Perspectives*. Cambridge: Cambridge University Press, pp. 21–36.

(1992), 'The Christian Atheism of Thomas Hobbes', in Hunter and Wootton (eds.) (1992), pp. 111–30.

(1993), *Philosophy and Government 1578–1651*. Cambridge: Cambridge University Press.

Van Lieshout, H. H. M. (1997), 'Les Querelles lexicales sur la lice de la tolérance: Pierre Jurieu attaqué dans le *Dictionnaire historique et critique de Pierre Bayle*', in Berkevens-Stevelinck *et al.* (eds.), pp. 199–212.

Whelan, Ruth (1989), *The Anatomy of Superstition: a Study of the Historical Theory and Practice of Pierre Bayle*. Oxford: Oxford University Press.

(1993), 'The Wisdom of Simonides: Bayle and La Mothe le Vayer', in Richard H. Popkin and Arjo Vanderjagt (eds.), *Scepticism and Irreligion in the Seventeenth and Eighteenth Centuries*. Leiden, New York: E. J. Brill, pp. 230–53.

Wootton, David (1997), 'Pierre Bayle, Libertine?', in M. A. Stewart (ed.), *Studies in Eighteenth Century European Philosophy*. Oxford: Clarendon Press, pp. 197–226.

Yardeni, Myriam (1971), *La Conscience nationale de France pendant les guerres de religion (1559–1598)*. Louvain, Paris: Editions Nauwelaerts.

(1996), 'Pierre Bayle et l'histoire de France', in Magdelaine *et al.* (eds.) (1996), pp. 564–70.

Project for a Critical Dictionary

[In 1692 Bayle composed an essay to support his project for a critical encyclopaedia. It would aim, he said, to rectify the mistakes he had found in Moréri's dictionary. He addressed his proposal to Jacques du Rondel, a former colleague at Sedan, who had become professor of belles lettres at the university of Maestricht. The 'Project' shows that the idea of a dictionary of errors arises from Bayle's approach to scientific discovery; and from his perception that an accurate historical fact could serve to negate a false conjecture. For the scholar – whether historian or natural scientist – by being alert to evidence of mistakes in received thinking could often get nearer to the truth. Perhaps the essay inspired Mill's thoughts on poetry and pushpin: Bayle – citing the poet Malherbe's ironic rebuke – asks if the good poet should be thought less useful to the state than the good player at ninepins (p. 8).]

Dissertation

Which was printed as a foreword to some essays or fragments of this work in the year MDCXCII, under the title: Project for a Critical Dictionary to M. du Rondel, professor of *belles lettres* at Maestricht.

Sir,

You will doubtless be surprised at the resolution I have recently made. I have had the notion of compiling the largest collection that I can of the errors that are met with in Dictionaries and, so as not to limit myself to this project alone, vast as it is, I shall make digressions upon authors of every sort whenever the opportunity arises . . .

But there are some objections to dispose of which may take some time. . . .

[Sections I–V expand on this theme with reference to a wide range of the printed literature of Catholic and Reformed scholarship of the age of Renaissance and Reformation.]

VI Reply to certain difficulties
The first difficulty: that the work might make enemies

Firstly, Sir, the liberty I have taken to collect together the mistakes I have found dispersed throughout many books may be thought of as a sign of imprudence. Is it not to create without good cause a vast number of enemies? For, when we attack the Ancients we bring to the fray their numerous partisans among the Moderns; and when we censure the Moderns we expose ourselves to their personal resentment if they are living, and to that of their family if they are dead. Now the rancour of these authors is no small matter. They are, reputedly, exceedingly sensitive, short-tempered and vindictive; and it is said that after their death, their heirs think themselves bound to perpetuate their love for their kinsman's creations. As for the interest taken by many Moderns in the reputation of the Ancients, I cannot better represent it than in the passage I cite, in which La Mothe le Vayer fulminates against Balzac because he had criticised an argument from Pompey.[a=t]

In answer to this difficulty, Sir, I say that I do not envisage my enterprise as being at all hazardous in that respect. It may happen then that I am described in the following way,

---

[a=t] 'In truth I confess that such unjust treatment of antiquity as a whole elicits in my soul such indignation that I prefer you, or someone other than myself skilled at this sort of candour, to give it the name it deserves.' 'Exclamet Melicerta periisse / frontem de rebus': Macrobius, *Saturnalia*, 1.5. ['Melicerta would exclaim that shame had vanished from the earth.'] . . . [La Mothe le Vayer,] *Hexaméron rustique*, pp. 142, 143.

> Periculosae plenum opus aleae
> Tractas, et incedis per ignes
> Suppositos cineri doloso.[b=u]

without rightly speaking being called reckless. I do not see authors
in quite the way they are characterised by malignant pens. I imagine
they are too reasonable to take it amiss if, in the interest of the
public good, I show that they have not always got things right. I
declare that in doing this I have no intention of lessening the glory
they have acquired, and that I shall carefully abstain, above all
wherever honesty requires it, from any uncivil expressions concerning their personal character or the *corpus* of their work. Certain
small errors scattered here and there in a book do not determine its
destiny; nor do they diminish its just price or rob the author of due
praise. The injustice and malice of the human species, great as they
are, have not yet grown to such a point that they hinder most readers from praising a good book, notwithstanding the faults that may
be in it. This fine maxim of a poet from the court of Augustus will
always be relevant:

> Ubi plura nitent in carmine, non ego paucis
> Offendar maculis, quas aut incuria fudit
> Aut humana parum cavit natura.[c=w]

Above all, they will pardon the faults, though numerous, of those
who compile large dictionaries; and this maxim is particularly to be
urged on their behalf,

> Opere in longo fas est obrepere somnum,[d=x]

and it is because of this confidence that I shall have so few scruples
about criticising them, for I should be profoundly grieved to lessen
any of the respect that they are owed. The public is infinitely
obliged for all the instruction that is produced by the sweat of their

---

[b=u] ['You conduct a task fraught with hazardous risks and walk across flames concealed under deceptive ashes.'] Horace, *Odes*, 2.1.6–8.
[c=w] ['When the qualities which radiate from a poem are many, I am not bothered
by the few blots which either carelessness has spilt, or human nature has been
unable to avoid.'] Horace, *Ars poetica* [The Art of Poetry], 351–3.
[d=x] ['Drowsiness may prevail when a work is long and dreary.'] *Ibid.*, 360.

brow . . . You see, sir, where my excuses are leading: it is not my intention to undermine the worth of authors, nor to depart from the rules of civility towards them: and I have so good an opinion of their modesty and of their zeal for the instruction of the public that I do not believe that they will resent the liberty I shall take to show the places where they have made mistakes.

Generally speaking I shall not myself reveal their faults: I shall merely report what others have said. I make it a religion never to appropriate to myself what I borrow from others. So the reader may be completely assured that where I indicate a fault without citing a source I am unaware that it has ever before been made public. That is, I do not think I am required to show a greater indulgence to my neighbour than to myself, and it will be seen that I do not spare myself. Finally, one must suppose that the interest of the public must take precedence over that of private persons, so that an author who improperly prefers to have his own faults concealed than to see the public disabused[☞y] deserves no indulgence. . . . If these replies are inadequate, I add, on the one hand, that the public's instruction is worth self-sacrifice to the ill-humour of a few individuals; and on the other, that I am only too willing to yield the floor to the retaliation of authors whom I criticise. I consent willingly to have them point out my errors whether on their own account or as descendants of others. They will gratify me if they correct and enlighten me, and I urge any reader to do so. I shall try to make no mistakes though I am very certain that I shall commit only too many. No one will be able to charge me with the complaint made against those censors who print nothing for fear of reprisals (C).

VII The second difficulty: that it will censure very trivial faults.

In the second place it will be found very odd if I spend my time quibbling over nits or censuring trivialities . . . I have decided nevertheless

---

[☞y] 'Nimis perverse se ipsum amat . . .' ['A man has an excessively unhealthy self-love if he is willing to lead others into error in order to conceal his own. For it is far better and more beneficial, when he has himself made a mistake, that others do not make the same mistake, since upon their advice he might be disabused. But if he does not wish this, at least let him avoid having companions in error.'] Augustine, *Letters*, 7.

that I should ignore such mockery, and comment on even small errors. For the more one uses reason to criticise things, the more one can show how hard it is to be perfectly exact. Moreover, by taking the idea of perfect exactitude to the utmost degree, we oblige authors to be more guarded and to examine everything with maximum care. Man is only too accustomed to being on the wrong side of the rules set before him.[cc] So if he is to get as close as possible to the point of perfection we must require him to deviate from it as little as he can. Moreover, as this work can be of service to those who want a historical dictionary of utmost accuracy, towards which it is exceedingly important to aim, I have had to go into detail with a particular sort of precision, and even make digressions. It is not out of inclination that I deal in quibbles, but from choice and I ought to be thanked for it, since it is a way of sacrificing oneself to the good of one's neighbour.[dd] This is not a path to glory; it is done to bring others to a factual exactitude and that is a great sacrifice, is it not? There are not many who are willing to do likewise: I can cite Quintilian.[f=ee] I shall say something below which elaborates my discussion of this second difficulty.

VIII The third difficulty: that it will contain useless discussions

In the third place, I may be reproached for having given myself useless trouble. For some will say, why do we need to know if this Cassius Longinus has been confused with another, or whether he was capitally punished or merely banished? Does the public lose sleep over such things? What does it matter if Scaliger was or was not incensed against Erasmus when he considered him as a mere soldier; and so on? . . .

I say, however, that this objection which would perhaps be very sound, absolutely speaking and without reference to time and place, is worth nothing when one relates it to the present century and to this part of the world in which we live. For were man perfectly rational he would concern himself only with his eternal salvation,

---

[f=ee] 'Sive contemnentes tanquam . . .' ['Either they despise as trivial what we learn early, or, what is nearest to the truth, they expect no reward for ability in those subjects which, although necessary, are, however, far removed from showy display.'] Quintilian, *Institutio oratoria* [The Education of an Orator], I, proemium.

as the Lord told Martha: 'But one thing is needful.'[g=ff] Who does not also know the maxim: *de peu de biens nature se contente* [nature is content with very little]? Who will doubt that were we to contain ourselves within the limits of basic need we would have to abolish as superfluous nearly all the arts? But man can no longer be treated upon that basis. Since time immemorial it has been natural for him to seek the agreeable things of life and all sorts of comforts and pleasures. Among other non-necessary things which it has pleased Europeans to acquire are the Greek and Latin languages, or rather we seek to understand what is in the books that have been handed down to us in these two languages. Nor are our scholars content to know vaguely, but they have sought to examine if everything they found was indubitably true, and if new light emerged when one author contradicted another. Then, when it proved possible to resolve these difficulties and those in many other sorts of history, they felt a very intense pleasure. They have greatly entertained their readers and they have been bathed in glory notwithstanding that this enlightenment was of no use at all for diminishing the cost of living, nor for providing protection against the heat and the cold, or the rain and the hail. One should not, then, impute to me the impertinent audacity of wanting to reveal as a merchandise of great price a thing universally rejected as supposedly useless. For in this I am merely following a taste long established. Whether men are justified in feeling satisfied that they are not mistaken upon a point of geography, or chronology, or history, is not the issue; I am no way answerable for that. It is enough for me that the public[h=gg] wants to know in detail about all the errors in circulation, and to take account of these discoveries.[i=hh]

Let it not be said that our century, disabused and cured of the critical spirit of the preceding age, now looks upon the writings of those who correct factual error – whether concerning the specific

---

[g=ff] Luke, 10:42.
[h=gg] In using this word [the public] I do not mean to say that everyone . . . is interested in the same refutations; but only that some are interested in one sort, and others interested in another.
[i=hh] If it matters little for one not to know these things, it matters little also for one to know them . . . Lipsius wanted to know the truth of every small detail: 'Admirabilis Lipsius . . .' ['The admirable Lipsius says somewhere that he likes to know the truth even in the most minute matters.'] *Epistola Hoffmanni ad Reinesium* [Letter from Hoffmann to Reinesius], p. 100.

lives of great men, or the names of cities, or of anything else whatsoever – as mere pedantry. For it is certain, all things considered, that
men were never more devoted than they are today to this sort of
illumination. For every experimental physicist and for every mathematician, you will find five who study history and its related fields.
And never was the science of antiquities – by which I mean the
study of medallions, inscriptions, *bas relief* etc. – as cultivated as it
is today. Now where does this lead? To pin-pointing ever more
accurately the time at which certain events took place, or to pre-
venting a particular town or a particular individual from being confused with another; or to testing conjectures upon certain rites of
the ancients; and to establishing a hundred other matters of curiosity, in which the public is allegedly uninterested, according to the
disdainful maxims which make up the topic of this third difficulty.
Such maxims have not however discouraged one eminent man,[k=ii]
as consummate in the study of humane learning as he is in affairs
of state, from publishing a distinguished book upon the excellence
and usefulness of medallions.

You, Sir, are better persuaded than anyone that such maxims are
irrelevant. For if they lead anywhere it is to the destruction of all
the *beaux-arts* and nearly all the sciences which civilise and exalt
the mind.[l=ij] For should these fine precepts be followed there would
remain only the use of the mechanical arts and as little geometry
as is necessary for accurate navigation, carriages, agriculture and
fortifications. Amongst all our professors we should have scarcely
anyone but engineers bent on inventing new ways of destroying
mankind. It must, of course, be allowed that the public has a clear
interest in having such things [mechanical arts] since through them
we may make abundance reign in our towns, and pursue offensive
or defensive wars. But it must on the other hand be agreed, despite
Cicero,[m=kk] that all the beauties of painting, sculpture and architec-
ture serve to please only particular eyes and can elicit admiration

[k=ii] M. de Spanheim.
[l=ij] See *Nouvelles de la république des lettres*, September 1684, article 4 [*OD* I, pp.
123–5, p. 125].
[m=kk] In the Third Book of the Orator he tries to prove this thesis: 'In plerisque
rebus ...' ['In most matters, nature has designed things in a marvellous way,
so that what possesses the greatest utility has the most worth and often beauty
too.']

only from *connoisseurs*. The coarse productions of all these arts can supply man's needs: we can be housed safely and comfortably without the help of Corinthian or composite order, without friezes, cornices and architraves. Much less for life's amenities is it necessary to know everything that is taught about the [mathematical] incommensurability of the asymptotes, or about magical squares, or about the duplication of the cube etc. . . .

So that if one were disposed to despise a work as soon as it ceased to address *de pane lucrando* [bread winning] or to have any practical use . . . or, in short, when popular taste can do without it, there would be few books whatsoever that would not be paltry. They would deserve the rebuke which you have doubtless seen in the *Life* of the poet Malherbe. When M. de Méziriac presented the poet with his commentary on Diophantus, in the company of several parties who had 'praised this book exorbitantly' as being 'exceedingly useful to the public, Malherbe's comment was to ask if it would bring down the price of bread?' On another occasion he defended the award of stipends to those who served the King in his armies and his affairs; but said that 'a good poet was no more useful to the state than a good player at ninepins [*quilles*]'.

You must therefore grant me, despite what is said, that there are countless creations of the human mind which are esteemed not because we need them, but because they please us. And is it not right to contest the statements of authors who say the contrary, given that there are so many people who delight in knowing the truth, even in things where their fortune is not in the least concerned?

Certainly a shoemaker, a miller, or a gardener are infinitely more necessary to a state than the ablest painters or sculptors: than a Michelangelo or a Bernini. Certainly the most humble mason is more indispensable to a town than the most gifted chronologist or astronomer: than a Joseph Scaliger, or a Copernicus. It is possible, nevertheless, to make an infinitely stronger case for these great minds, whose work one could well do without, than for the absolutely essential work of these artisans.[n=mm]

[n=mm] 'Plus interfuit reipublicae . . .' ['The Republic attained more benefit from the capture of a Ligurian stronghold than from the defence of a law-suit by Manius Curius. Quite so, but the Athenians benefited more from having strong roofs on their homes than a beautiful ivory statue of Minerva. I would, however,

For there are some things whose price can be determined only with reference to an honest pleasure or to a simple adornment of the soul.

IX The same arguments which demonstrate the usefulness of other sciences demonstrate the usefulness of critical research

In this section, Sir, you will not fail to foresee that the enemies of *belles lettres* will concoct a hundred exceptions. Not being able to deny that their maxims tend to revive barbarism in all its aspects, they will draw our attention to the basic necessities which result from particular sciences. But the argument will get them nowhere, for as soon as they place in the class of basic necessities the learning from which useful things arise, whether by *résultance* [invented effect] or whether by *émanation* [inevitable effect] (permit me to use this old Scholastic vocabulary since it encompasses so well the two kinds of accessory utilities[o=nn] which are relevant here), they will realise that they are obliged to include in this utilitarian category both the humanities and critical learning. I can thus use all their own observations to oppose them. And herewith is a small example of what I mean.

If they tell me that the most abstract theorems of algebra are highly useful in life because they make the human mind more capable of perfecting certain skills, I will reply that scrupulous enquiry into historical fact is likewise capable of producing very great benefits. I am confident enough to assert that the perverse obstinacy of the first critics who dwelt upon trifles – for example upon the question of whether one ought to say *Virgil* or *Vergil* – has accidentally been quite useful. For such critics thereby inspired a strong veneration for antiquity; they disposed minds towards careful enquiry into behaviour in ancient Greece and ancient Rome. They thus created the condition that could benefit from these great examples. What effect do you suppose, Sir, that a grave and majestic passage

rather be Pheidias than the best of carpenters. Therefore, we must estimate the extent not of each man's usefulness, but of his value, especially since few can paint or sculpt outstandingly, but workmen or labourers are hardly in short supply.'] Cicero, in *Brutus*, 73.256–7.

[o=nn] More comprehension is given to this distinction here, than in Scholasticism.

taken from Livy or Tacitus and uttered as having formerly inclined the Roman senate to a certain resolution might have upon an audience so pre-disposed?

I could say that it is capable of saving a state, and perhaps has saved more than one. The president of an assembly pronounces these Latin words with a certain emphasis. He makes an impression on minds by virtue of the respect they have for the name of Roman. Each one goes home converted, and inspires in his locality a sense of loyalty, and thus you see a civil war stifled in its cradle. Malherbe grasped nothing of this when he said that a poet is no more useful to a state than a good player at ninepins. For without displaying here all the good that a poet can do,[p=pp] do you think, sir, that none of those men who are called parish worthy [*coq de paroisse*] has ever quelled the mischief of a factious troublemaker with a stanza of Pibrac, gravely uttered? And in the home, do you think that those golden phrases, whose reading[q=qq] Molière recommended, are always without effect? I would suppose that though very often they are, it is not always so; and that Horace, in the lines that I cite in the note, spoke of nothing other than the edification that comes from an idea.[r=rr]

It will be said, perhaps, that what seems most dry and abstract in mathematics brings us at least this advantage: that it leads us to indubitably true propositions; whereas historical discussion and investigation into human facts always leave us in some doubt, and always generate the seeds of new disputes. But there is little prudence in harping upon this string! Historical facts, I maintain, may be carried to a degree of certainty more indubitable than the degree of certainty which can be arrived at in the case of geometrical propositions; provided of course that we consider these two sorts of proposition according to the degree of certainty that is appropriate to each. Allow me to explain myself. In factual disputes that arise among historians, on knowing whether one prince has reigned

[p=pp] Horace, *Epistles*, 2.1.

[q=qq] 'Lisez-moi comme il faut, au lieu de ses sornettes, / Les quatrains de Pibrac, et les doctes tablettes / Du conseiller Matthieu, ouvrage de valeur, / Et plein de beaux dictons à réciter par cœur.' Molière, *Comédie du cocu imaginaire*.

[r=rr] 'Os tenerum pueri . . .' ['In representing the young, innocent speech of a boy, the poet diverts the ear from ugly utterances. Presently, he shapes the heart with his benevolent tutelage, preaching against harshness, jealousy and anger.'] Horace, *Epistles*, 2.1.126–9.

before or after another, it is supposed, on each side, that a fact has all the reality and all the existence outside of our understanding of which it is capable; provided of course that it is not of the sort related by Ariosto or by similar inventors of fictions, and that one pays no attention to the difficulties which Pyrrhonians raise to throw doubt on whether the things which appear to exist, really do outside of our minds. Thus a historical fact, once we have been able to establish its apparent existence, is in the category of the highest degree of certainty that can be accorded, since one requires that alone for this sort of proposition; and it would be to deny the common principle of the parties, and to move from one sort of argument to another, were we required to prove not only that it was apparent to the whole of Europe that a bloody battle was fought at Senef in 1674, but also the extent to which it appears to us that these events exist outside of our own minds.

In this way we are delivered from the tiresome quibbles which the Pyrrhonians call expedients of the age [*moyens de l'époque*], and although one cannot reject historical Pyrrhonism in respect of a large number of propositions, one can be sure that there are many which can be proved with a full certainty: so that historical research is not fruitless in that respect. For we may show indubitably that many propositions are false, that many lack certainty, and that many others are true, and thus you have demonstrations which can be used by a far greater number of people than those of the geometricians. For, if few people have a taste for the latter or find any occasion for applying them to the reform of manners, it will be granted me, Sir, that an abundance of people will benefit, morally speaking, by the reading of a great collection of historical refutations well documented, even if it were only to make them more circumspect in judging their neighbour, or better able to avoid the snares that calumny and flattery lay on all sides to catch the unsuspecting reader. Now is it nothing to correct the unfortunate tendency we have to make rash judgements? Is it nothing to learn not to assent lightly to what we see in print? Is it not the very essence of prudence not to accord belief too readily?[s=ss]

[s=ss] 'Sobrius esto atque . . .' ['Be sensible and bear this precept in mind: that to avoid believing anything too hastily is the power and the strength of wisdom.'] Epicharmus, in *Cicero, Polybius, Lucian* etc.

In vain should we seek these practical uses [*utilités*] in a collection of axioms of algebra. Besides, by leave of our mathematicians, it is not as easy for them to arrive at the sort of certainty which they need as it is for historians to reach the sort of certainty appropriate to them. No serious objection will ever be made against the factual truth that Caesar vanquished Pompey; and from whatever sort of principles one wants to dispute, one will find nothing more irrefutable than this proposition: 'that Caesar and Pompey existed and were not a mere modification of the mind of those who wrote their lives'. But in respect of the object of mathematics it is not only very hard to prove that it exists outside of our intellect, it is very easy to prove that it can only be an idea of the mind.[t=tt]

Indeed, the existence of a square circle outside of ourselves seems hardly more impossible than the existence outside of ourselves of the perfect circle of which geometry gives us so many fine demonstrations; I mean a circle from whose circumference one can draw to the centre as many straight lines as there are points in the circumference. One feels intuitively that the centre, which is only a point, cannot be the common meeting place of as many different lines as there are points in the circumference. In a word, given that mathematics concerns points absolutely indivisible, lines without breadth or depth, and surfaces without profundity, it is evident enough that its object cannot exist outside of our imagination. Thus it is metaphysically more certain that Cicero existed outside the understanding of all other men, than it is certain that the object of mathematics exists outside our understanding. I omit what the learned M. Huet[u=vv] has represented to these gentlemen to teach them not to be so disdainful of historical facts [*les vérités historiques*].

The abstract profundity of mathematics, it will be said, gives us great notions of the infinity of God. Amen to that: but do you not think that a great practical good can result from a critical dictionary? The oracle that cannot lie maintains that science is arrogant; and therefore there is no place more important to humble the pride of man. Whosoever speaks of pride speaks of the fault which is both furthest from true virtue, and most diametrically opposed to the

[t=tt] See [*Dic,*] article 'Zenon', the Epicurean philosopher, Remark (D), towards the end.

[u=vv] Huet, Pierre Daniel, Praefat. *Demonstrat. evangel.* [Demonstration from the Gospels].

spirit of the Evangelist. What could be imagined more suitable for giving man a true notion of the weakness of the mind, and of the nothingness and vanity of the sciences, than showing him, in abundance, the factual untruths contained in books? Innumerable men of letters, of the most penetrating and sublime minds, have, for many years, taken it upon themselves to throw light upon antiquity. That task of the critics, having as its object the actions of a few men, should be easier than the task of the philosophers, which has as its object the actions of God. And yet the critics have given so many proofs of human inadequacy as to leave room to compile vast volumes of their mistakes. These volumes may therefore mortify man with respect to his greatest vanity, I mean with respect to his science. Let them be considered, then, as trophies or triumphal arches erected to the ignorance and the inadequacy of man.

That being so, Sir, you will see that the very smallest faults will have their use here, since in that way one can collect a great number of untruths upon each topic; we can teach man better to know his weaknesses, and we can show him the diversity of ways in which he is susceptible to error. This will make him more aware that he is but the plaything of malice and ignorance: that the one takes hold of him where the other leaves off, and that if he is enlightened enough to recognise a lie, he is wicked enough deliberately to tell one. Or should he not be sufficiently wicked to tell a lie, he is insufficiently enlightened to see the truth. As for myself, when I think that perhaps I shall make it my serious employment for the rest of my life to gather materials for this kind of triumphal arch, I find myself thoroughly overcome by the conviction of my nothingness. It will be a continual lesson in humility. No sermon, not even from the author of the Book of Solomon, can hold me more firmly to the following great maxim:[v=ww] *I have seen all the works that are done under the sun AND BEHOLD ALL IS VANITY AND VEXATION OF SPIRIT*[w=xx] . . .

I would have ended with this fine moral precept when I realised that I had omitted to say that I intend to make use of the same freedom and the same civility towards my authors whatever their

[v=ww] Ecclesiastes, 1:14.
[w=xx] Compare this with what is said by M. Vigneul-Marville, *Mélanges d'histoire et de littérature*, vol. III, Rouen, 1701, p. 206.

nation or religion. Therefore I declare it here. Nothing is more absurd than a dictionary in which the author turns polemicist. It is one of the greatest faults in the dictionary of M. Moréri, where we find a hundred passages which seem to be extracted from a blatantly crusading sermon. For my part I shall not say with Hannibal, 'Whoever shall strike the enemy will be a Carthaginian in my eyes, from whatever city he may come' ['Hostem qui feriet mihi erit Carthaginiensis quisquis erit,[x=yy] civis'];[y=zz] but rather that all who depart from the truth shall be equal strangers to me. You will know people who will complain about this and who, deep in their hearts, will also rejoice since it will provide them with a pretext both for slander and for playing the zealot, two things which, with them, are always connected. But although I am not exceptionally complacent, I shall pursue my chosen path whatever they may say, and without begrudging them the bones that they will find to pick. Here is the justification for the method I propose to follow.

This dictionary will avoid being concerned with errors of judgement [*de droit*], given that partiality in that area would be incomparably more inexcusable than in historical dictionaries. For in such works one is obliged to report a thousand things that are true in the judgement of some, but false in the judgement of others: and one must presume a great difference of opinion among readers, and imagine that, in the hands of some, one will be in enemy territory, and in the hands of others, one will be in friendly country; and that it is appropriate to adjust to the situation one's style and one's manner of judging. But when one proposes to gather only errors of fact, one presumes with reason the same criterion among all one's readers. That is that there would be no individual who would not accept as false what one would demonstrate as such. For the proofs of a statement's factual falsity are neither the prejudices of a nation, nor of a particular religion. They are maxims that are common to all men. You will see from this, Sir, that erroneous theories in [moral] philosophy or theology do not enter into the plan of my work: notwithstanding that it is the case that the books in which they are

---

[x=yy] Thus Cicero cites the words of Ennius; but to rhyme he has to use *ferit* and not *feriet*. Cicero, *Pro Cornelio Balbo*, 22.51.

[y=zz] There are some critics who wish one might read *cujati' siet* ['from whatever country he may come'].

discussed represent factually false statements of a sort, and perhaps they will prove not the least useful to the reader.

It nearly always happens that written disputes on a given dogma degenerate into personal disagreement, and rarely continue to turn only upon the question of whether a passage of the adversary has been correctly or incorrectly cited, or whether it has been well or badly interpreted. The public abandons the disputants at that point and, as a fine wit has said recently, it is then that the parties are obliged to forsake the field for want of readers and booksellers. Whosoever has the patience to make an analysis of these personal differences will find a rich harvest of faults, a resource which will be collected in this dictionary: many false citations, many mistaken interpretations, and many errors of fact included. You will agree with me, Sir, that there is no logic to compare with that for teaching exactness in reasoning. In addition to this great practical use, the work will reveal also those countless vanities or at least inadequacies of the human mind. For what is not caused by bad faith arises from an extravagance or paucity of spirit. It is disturbing that self-deception of this sort enjoys its impunity largely because readers fail to make comparisons between reply and rejoinder. For were anyone to take the trouble to outline, in a few words, the progression of a dispute, it would be a way of learning all the tricks of the charlatan, and that one should abhor them.

Forgive me, Sir, for writing a dedicatory epistle of such length, and do not wait too long before enriching the Republic of Letters with those learned works it is expecting from you. Your modesty, and our friendship, forbid me from pronouncing an *encomium*, but when they appear, I hope that the public will immediately bestow upon you the praise they deserve. I am in every respect,

Sir,
Your most humble and most obedient servant,
5 May 1692

[Remarks (A)–(B) omitted.]

(C) Who print nothing for fear of reprisals.] Régnier in his ninth Satire calls upon his censor to publish something . . . to which he applies an Italian tale.

> Once upon a time a peasant
> A knowing man, and shrewd enough
> To judge from his request,
> Took himself off to the Pope in order to beg
> That the priests of those times might marry
> So that, said he, we others
> May caress their wives as they do ours.

Martial already had thoughts along these lines in the ninety-second epigram of his first book.

> Cum tua non edas, carpis mea carmina, Laeli.
> Carpere vel noli nostra, vel ede tua.

['Since you do not publish your own poetry, you tear mine to pieces, Laelius. Stop taking mine apart or publish your own.'] . . .

I have observed elsewhere that readers who have never written are very often more rigid and more unfair in their criticism than those who know from experience the pains of composition. I think I may say that there are two things that may hinder wholly unmerciful critics from revealing themselves. One is the fear that others will attack their work and make them suffer the penalty of ruthless retaliation. The other is that they themselves have not measured up to the idea of perfection which was the basis of their own criticism. 'It is easier to imagine the highest perfection than to attain it; and thus it is the fate of most critics to be able to find fault, but not to be able to do better. For, being so dry and so sterile, it seems that they have no talent for either speaking or writing.'[1=5] The author who judges thus observes that M. Conrart, 'who had an excellent judgement, a refined taste, and a confident and enlightened discernment, which penetrated every nook and cranny of a work, had the prudence to publish nothing of his own', and that 'the little [criticism] that has appeared is not very remarkable'.

[1=5] Vigneul-Marville, *Mélanges d'histoire et de littérature.*

Bodin

['Bodin' is one of several articles in which Bayle reflects on contemporary politics through the historiography of the French Wars of Religion, 1559–98. Historians, Protestant as well as Catholic, continued to misrepresent Bodin's impartiality in religious matters as support for 'absolutism'. Read in context, Bayle replies, Bodin was no absolutist but a politique, *whose brilliance in dark times had served the public good, and who, through his theory of sovereignty, had tried to put limits on Papal influence. As a deputy for the Third Estate he had opposed selling off royal lands to pay for religious persecution, and he had advocated, initially, legal tolerance for the Reformed religion. It would be more just, Bayle suggests, were posterity to recognise Bodin as a man of action as well as intellect whose compromises had been made to protect the innocent and forestall bloodshed and war.]*

BODIN (Jean), born in Angers and one of the most intelligent Frenchmen of the sixteenth century, studied the law at Toulouse[a] and having taken his degrees he then gave lectures there to the great acclaim of those who heard him.[b] His early ambition was to become a professor of law at Toulouse. Therefore to gain favour with the Toulousians he entitled his oration *De instituenda in republica juventuti* [On the Education of Youth in the Republic] which he dedicated to the People and the Senate of Toulouse, and which he delivered publicly in the University Faculty. It was said too that he composed, with the same end in mind, an epitaph to Clémence

[a] Ménage, *Rémarques sur la Vie de P. Ayrault*, p. 141.
[b] See his letter to Pibrac at the beginning of his *Republic*.

Isaure[c] . . . I shall include a list of his other works in a note [(D)], not forgetting his *Heptaplomères* which has never been published, and in which he discussed, it is alleged, many impious matters.

His reputation [according to Ménage] as a learned man with a fine mind brought him to the attention of Henry III [(E)], who loved men of letters and enjoyed associating with them.[d] Accordingly, Henry III sent for Bodin and since his conversation was delightful, for he had read much and remembered all that he had read, Henry III took pleasure in his company . . . But he was not in favour long. For those who envied him undermined him in the estimation of the king, and ensured that the king's regard ceased. It was at this time – finding himself courted by the brother of kings Francis II, Charles IX, and Henry III – that he became associated with François de France, Duc d'Alençon and Anjou. The Duc d'Alençon made him his executive secretary[e=*] . . . While they were in England he had the satisfaction and the honour of witnessing at the university of Cambridge a public reading of his books on the *Republic* [(F)]. They were by now translated into Latin by the English, for he had written them in French. This obliged him to translate them into Latin himself . . . On the death of the Duc d'Alençon . . . Bodin, seeing his prospects dashed, thought of going abroad. [Ménage, p. 145]

He took refuge in Laon where he married a woman who was a magistrate's sister [(G)]. He obtained an office in the administration of that town and it was apparently because of this post that he became, in 1576, deputy for the Third Estate of Vermondois at the Estates of Blois, though in the account which he gave of those Estates, he was merely deputy for the Third Estate of Vermondois.[f] In that capacity he proved himself very well disposed towards the rights of the people (I), and he believed it was for this reason that he failed to obtain the post of Master of Requests which had been promised him. He had the courage to stand up to those who wanted all the king's subjects to be compelled to profess the Catholic religion.[g] He argued very persuasively that this resolution would be

---

[c] Said, but erroneously, to have founded the floral games of Toulouse.

[d] Ménage, *Rémarques sur La Vie de P. Ayrault*, p. 145.

[e=*] See l'Abbé le Laboureur, *De Castelnau*, vol. II, p. 385.

[f] Ménage, *Rémarques sur La Vie de P. Ayrault*, p. 146.

[g] De Thou, bk 63, for the year 1576; see Remark (I).

an infraction of the Edicts, and that such a violation would be an inevitable provocation to war which could not fail to inflame the whole kingdom. The forthrightness with which he put this opinion made him many enemies. This was why – though having perceived that there was a conspiracy to have the resolution passed, and that because of the myopia of the king and his counsellors, those who could have thrown out this wicked resolution dared say nothing – he therefore refrained from speaking for the motion. For it would have been prejudicial to him as an individual and served no public good.[h] There were certain towns which complained that he had over-reached his mandate merely by objecting to the resolution. But the king's Council, which examined these complaints, acquitted him.[i] It is well known that in Boccalini's *Ragguagli di Parnasso* he was condemned to be burnt as an atheist, *notorio atheista*, for having said, in his books on the *Republic*, that religious sects should be granted liberty of conscience.[k]

He had once belonged to the Reformed religion. However in 1589 he persuaded the inhabitants of Laon to support the Duc de Maine [(L)], arguing that the uprising of so many towns and so many *parlements* in favour of the [Catholic] House of Guise should not be called rebellion but revolution:[l=m] and to support his position on the subject he published a *Letter*.[m=n] . . . He died of the plague . . . in Laon in 1596 in his sixty-seventh year [(M)] . . . It seems to me that there is as much exaggeration in the praise bestowed upon Bodin by Gabriel Naudé, as there is injustice in the contempt expressed by Cujas, Scaliger and certain others [(N)]. Nor is Possevin the only person to have accused him of having written many things that are contrary to religion [(O)], and there have been some who have suspected him of sorcery,[q] or who were convinced that he died a Jew.[n=r] Note that he spoke out very forthrightly against those who maintained that the authority of monarchs was unlimited

---

[h] M. de Thou is inconsistent on the subject and contradicts himself. See end of Remark (I).
[i] From de Thou, bk 63. See Remark (I), citation 7=31.
[k] [Boccalini], *Ragguagli di Parnasso* [Reports from Parnassus, 1614], in cent. 1, ch. 64, p. 195.
[l=m] Ménage, *Rémarques sur la Vie de P. Ayrault*, p. 147.
[m=n] Dated 29 January 1590, at Laon.
[n=r] Loscher, *De latrocinio in scriptis publicatis*, p. 41, in Diecmannus, *De naturalismo* [On Naturalism], p. 4.

(P) while failing to satisfy those of republican sentiments. I believe that was because – among other reasons – he maintained firstly that there were some absolute monarchs in Europe; and secondly that it is not appropriate for one subject in particular, nor for all in general, to conspire against the honour or the life of such monarchs either by violence or in a juridical way – and notwithstanding that they might have committed all the villainy, impiety or cruelty that can be named.[o=s] But that opinion does not seem to be very consistent with the doctrine that he also maintained: namely that the power of those monarchs had certain limits and that they were obliged to govern according to the law, though one may finally recognise that in [subscribing to] both these doctrines he had at heart the public good and the peace and tranquillity of the state (Q). The Germans condemn him strongly, and they malign him. You may see many such passages in the collections of Magirus,[p=t] and in those of Pope Blount . . .[q=v] Nevertheless, there are certain Germans who attribute to him a massive erudition and a sublime mind and judgement . . .

He had so sound a bodily constitution that in all his travels he was never seasick [(S)]. His opinion about comets was somewhat strange. . . .

[Remarks (A)–(H) omitted.]

(I) At the Estates of Blois he proved himself very well disposed towards the rights of the people.] To use the expression of M. de Mézerai,

> he maintained there with a 'Gallic liberty' that the income from the royal domains belonged to the provinces, and that the king's right was over only the use of them. Henry III did not take this unkindly saying that Bodin was an honest man. See Bodin's account. He also argued that the deputies

---

[o=s] Bodin, *De la République*, bk 2, ch. 5, p. 302.
[p=t] Tobias Magirus, *Eponymologium*, pp. 137 *et seq.*
[q=v] Pope Blount, Thomas, *Censura celebriorum auctorum* [Criticism of Famous Authors], pp. 524 *et seq.*

of two Chambers could decide nothing to the prejudice of the third and, in consequence of his demonstration, the deputies for the Ecclesiastical Order and the deputies for the Nobility, who had previously held a contrary opinion, changed their minds: which made king Henry III say that, on that day, Bodin was master of the Estates. See chapter 7 of book 3 of Bodin's *Republic*.[1=25]

See also the *Letter* in Latin that he wrote to Pibrac, which can be found prefaced to the French editions of his *Republic* . . .

What M. de Thou recounts on the same subject is to Bodin's lasting credit. He says that when the petitions of the Estates were laid before the king, it was proposed to the Third Estate that they should nominate twelve commissioners to attend the king's Council when those petitions were scrutinised.[2=26] This was approved initially, but on further consideration Bodin gave the opinion that it ought not to be done, and he advised his colleagues to nominate no deputy, and to oppose what the ecclesiastics and the nobility had wanted prior to the deputation. He was sent to the other two Chambers and by means of several arguments he demonstrated how dangerous it would be to delegate a decision made by the Three Estates of the realm to so small a number of persons. For even if the nominated commissioners were immune to bribery, the king's presence might intimidate them, or they might be won round by the prevarication and persuasiveness of the royal officials. A reply was made, Bodin responded, and finally he won his case because of the energy with which he persuaded them that the Third Estate should oppose deputations. Henry III was highly angered and he sought to penalise Bodin for it . . .[3=27]

This same Prince had the Estates notified of his pressing need to sell [*aliéner*] a part of his royal land [*domain*]. 'Necessitate, quae potentissimum . . .' ['He argued for the sale to be allowed, claiming that he was driven by necessity – that most powerful of weapons – since all agreed that the security of the people should be the highest law'];[4=28] but they rejected the proposal and it was Bodin mainly

[1=25] Ménage, *Rémarques sur la Vie de P. Ayrault*, pp. 147, 248.
[2=26] De Thou, bk 63, p. 187.
[3=27] *Ibid.*
[4=28] *Ibid.*

who brought it about, since the leading deputies, corrupted by graft, were already wavering.

> Pessimum de domanio ... ['Since the leading deputies, already corrupted by promises, were wavering, it was Bodin chiefly who demolished the weakest ploy about selling *domain* under the false pretext of necessity. For he argued that the land would have been pitiably squandered under an extravagant prince, had he then held possession of it.'][5=29]

The same Bodin resisted the cabals of the followers of Messieurs de Guise who had resolved to finish off the war against the Huguen-ots.[6=30] So we may infer from this that M. de Mézerai must be mistaken when he asserts that the king praised Bodin for opposing the selling of his *domain*. He confuses two issues which he should have kept distinct. Bodin's conduct was vindicated in the king's Council after certain towns made the complaint that he had opposed the resolution which proposed that two religions should not be allowed in the kingdom. 'Homines a factiosis ...' ['Representatives sent by the opposing parties came to report that Bodin's intervention had contravened his mandate. They were heard in the king's Council, but here it was still proclaimed that Bodin had most definitely acted as he should.'][7=31]

That event was prior to the two matters referred to by M. de Thou, above, and which caused Bodin subsequently to lose the favour of Henry III. Let us observe also a contradiction of M. de Thou. He says, p. 183, that Bodin, having perceived that his remonstrations – against the conspiracies of those who sought to undermine the Edicts of Peace – would be in vain, abstained from making a speech on the matter.

> Cum videret homo ... ['Anticipating the outcome, Bodin could tell what opinion favoured since a conspiracy had been formed. He could see that the fatal blindness of the king and his counsellors led to the affectation of a perverse caution in this matter by those very men empowered to put a stop to it. He therefore abstained from giving his advice to such an

[5=29] *Ibid.*
[6=30] *Ibid.*, p. 188.
[7=31] *Ibid.*, p. 183.

audience which would be ill-disposed towards him, and which would benefit in no way from his suggestions.']⁸⁼³²

But on p. 188, he [de Thou] informs us that our jurist vigorously opposed the faction of Messieurs de Guise on the occasion when it seemed, once the petitions of the Estates had been laid before the king, that the term of the deputies had expired. His opposition, in fact, was to the conspiracy to renew the war against the Protestants. The partisans of the Duc de Guise had won over the ecclesiastics and the nobility, since those two Chambers frequently held private cabals to subvert the overtures for peace. Bodin who, because the deputies from Paris were absent, found himself at the head of the Third Estate, courageously opposed those cabals;[9=33] and when they informed him that the matter had now been concluded in the Estates and that the Assembly had no further authority, he answered them firmly:

> You are, then, rebels, since you acknowledge that your term [of office] is over and that you have no right to assemble, and yet that does not stop you from meeting. But I am of another opinion: we may still present a solemn petition to the king, since the assemblies in which one seeks a truce can always be less formal than those in which one declares a war
> . . . [10=34]

It was necessary for me to draw attention to the inconsistency of M. de Thou, for he had considerably diminished Bodin's reputation and for no good cause.

[Remarks (K)–(O) omitted.]

(P) He spoke out very forthrightly against those who maintained that the authority of monarchs was unlimited.] He maintained that monarchs cannot impose taxes without the consent of the people, and that they are more obliged than their subjects to observe the laws of God and those of nature; and that the covenants

---

8=32 *Ibid.*
9=33 'Summa fiducia intercessu' ['intervening with great courage'], *ibid.*, p. 188.
10=34 *Ibid.*, p. 188.

which they make impose the same obligations on themselves as on their subjects. He says that most civil lawyers taught the contrary, and that he was the first who dared to contest the view of those who wrote on ways of extending the rights of the king. Here are his words:

> Miror tamen esse qui . . . ['I am however amazed that there are some who think that I attach considerably more weight to the power of one man than befits a steadfast citizen in the Republic, given that frequently in other places – in particular in chapter 8 of the first book of my *Republic* – I have not hesitated to refute those who have written on the law of taxation and on extending the powers of the king. I was the first to do so, notwithstanding the most perilous times. For these writers, drawing on divine law and natural law, attributed to kings infinite power. Yet, what could be more relevant to the people than the opinions I dared to advance, arguing that it is not permissible for kings even to raise taxes without the majority consent of the citizens? Or, of what importance is this principle which I have likewise propounded, namely: that in matters of divine law and natural law, princes should be held on a tighter chain than those who are subject to their rule? [For] should not kings also be committed to fixed agreements just as the other citizens are? But almost all teachers of jurisprudence advocate the opposite view.']11=82

Had he said no more than this, he would have offended no republican thinker, but because he maintained simultaneously that subjects should not depose a lawful monarch who governed tyrannically, many people were outraged by the doctrine. He informs us that the reason which persuaded him to adopt that opinion was that everywhere around him he saw peoples at war against their princes – that they were propagating everywhere a vast number of writings maintaining that peoples might overthrow kings and re-arrange the succession to crowns in whatever way they pleased – and that this was likely to shake the foundations of every society. He thought,

---

11=82 *Epistula ad Vidum Fabrum [Letter to Guy du Faur* (Seigneur de Pibrac)] at the beginning of the French edition of the *Republic.*

therefore, that his duty required him to oppose the maxims which he judged so pernicious.

> Sed cum viderem . . . ['But I was mindful of subjects everywhere taking up arms against their sovereigns, and noticed that books too were being publicly circulated which ignited fervent passions within republics. For they teach us that we must dethrone sovereigns whom God has assigned to humankind, so long as we can cite their tyranny as the pretext. These books teach also that it should not be birthright that appoints a king, but rather the decision of the people. Such teaching shakes the foundation not only of the sovereign's authority, but also of the whole republic. I denied that it was in the character of a good man or a good citizen to do violence to his sovereign, however great a tyrant he might be. I asserted that we should leave that punishment to other sovereigns and to the everlasting God; and I confirmed this with reference to divine law, to human law and to citations, and backed them with suitably persuasive argument.']¹²⁼⁸³

Note that having wanted to say that the Protestants played a considerable part in this sort of writing, he did it in a very restrained manner, and by exonerating Luther and Calvin. These are his words.

> To reply to the frivolous objections and arguments of those who say the contrary would be time wasted, but just as he who doubts that there is a God should be made to have a taste of the law's punishments without further ado, so also should those who question a matter as clear and as available in printed books as the following: whether subjects may justly take up arms against their tyrannical prince and put him to death in any manner whatsoever; notwithstanding that their most eminent and their most learned¹³⁼*¹ theologians hold that it is never lawful either to kill or to rebel against one's sovereign prince, unless there is a particular and incontrovertible command from God to do so; as we

¹²⁼⁸³ *Ibid.*
¹³⁼*¹ Martin Luther, and Calvin on St John's Gospel, and on the *Institutes*, final chapter.

read of Jehu[14=*2] who was elected by God and anointed king
by the Prophet with the express mandate of destroying the
race of Ahab.[15=84]

He believes also that he shows considerable moderation in respect of
the gentlemen of Geneva, notwithstanding that he thought he had
cause for complaint against them for the edition of his book that was
undertaken in their city. He does not get involved in detail. He does
not say like Possevin that the Genevans made many changes to his
work.[16=85] You will be convinced if you read the Latin.

> Alterum reprehensionis . . . ['Another kind of criticism was
> made by those Genevans who published a second edition of
> my *Republic*. Either they should not have printed this for
> their citizens to read, or they should have defended its
> author from defamation. They should have recalled the law
> introduced into the Senate of Geneva on 5 June 1559,
> which, in its second article, strictly forbade attacks upon the
> writers whom they translated. But what had I written that
> was inconsistent with either the dignity of a private citizen,
> or with the authority of the state? For I also commended
> what was praiseworthy in the teachings of these Genevans;
> having refuted what they judged deserving of criticism, and
> having thoroughly examined each of their remarks in turn
> in the light of my ideas as I see them, I embraced a due
> spirit of moderation of the sort that most people seek vainly
> among the writers of that city.'][17=86]

Take the care to note that he makes a major distinction between
a local tyrant on the one hand, and a foreign prince on the other.
For though he does not approve of subjects taking up arms to
deliver themselves from tyranny, he does approve of their neighbours coming to liberate them.

> There is a very great difference between saying that, on the
> one hand, a tyrant may be legitimately killed by a foreign

[14=*2] 2 Kings, 6–10.
[15=84] Bodin, *De la république*, bk 2, ch. 5, p. 305.
[16=85] 'Genevates Bodinum . . .' ['The Genevans censured Bodin and changed much
in his books on the Republic.'] Possevin [A. Possevino, the elder], *Bibliotheca
selecta*, vol. II.
[17=86] Bodin, *Epistula ad Vidum Fabrum.*

prince and, on the other, that he may be legitimately killed by a subject. For just as it is right and proper for anyone to defend, in practice, the goods, the honour and the life of those who are unjustly oppressed when the door to justice is barred to them – with Moses, for example, after seeing his brother abused and beaten, and without being given a reason – so it is a fine and splendid thing for a prince to take up arms to avenge a whole people unjustly subjugated by the cruelty of an oppressor. Such a person would be like the mighty Hercules who wandered the world to exterminate such tyrannical monsters, and who was deified for his great exploits. He would be like Dion, Timoleon, Aratus and other generous princes who earned the name of scourge and subjugator of tyrants.[18=87]

Richeome makes many reflections on this passage of Bodin in chapter 13 of his categorical analysis of the *Anti-Coton*.[19=88]

(Q) One may recognise that in both these doctrines on the power of monarchs he had at heart the public good and the peace and tranquillity of the state.] He came out with the first opinion when he saw that Henry III's sycophants and flatterers were making proposals from which great abuse would follow, costly and damaging to the people. He maintained the second opinion when he saw France inundated with faction – torn apart by civil wars that elicited a host of manifestoes and other writings which undermined the most essential and basic laws of government. For they wrote, and they spoke, of the power of peoples as freely as if they were already living under a democratic state, and as if they were seeking to reduce that power in practice, through plotting to reassign the crown. They even sanctioned those assassins who, under pretext of tyranny, conspired against the lives of kings. This could be followed only by the most dreadful devastation; and this was why Bodin, by opposing such licence, showed himself to be exceedingly concerned for the public good.

Qui regias opes et honores ... ['I have considered royal wealth and honour to be less important than the public

---

[18=87] Bodin, *De la république*, bk 2, ch. 5, p. 300.
[19=88] *Ibid.*, pp. 113 *et seq.*

good. At the same time, I have condemned in writing and in conversation those who attempt to overthrow their prince under the pretext of tyranny, or who endeavour to promulgate constitutional bills to establish kings by popular vote, or who seek to use violence to wrest sovereignty from the hands of a legitimate prince.']20=89

He had, however, the misfortune to retract his principles after the death of Henry III, for he joined the party of the League. A sinner's fall, however, does not prevent his worthy deeds from being good.

20=89 Bodin, *Epistula ad Vidum Fabrum.*

Brutus

[Idealism in public life, and the use and abuse of reason, are recurring themes in Bayle's work, but they are clarified in his interpretation of the tragedy of Brutus. Whether theist or agnostic, Christian or pagan, some politicians who pursue honourable goals are apt to pin their hopes on a word such as 'justice' which they mistake for a moral being. Accordingly, the idealist, confronting defeat by the party of opportunism, is apt to give way, like Brutus, to disillusion and despair. Bayle's response is to observe that the outcome of all public action is determined by general laws and the competence of the actor. He assures us that honourable policies are best – both for their own sake and because a just cause in no way 'averts or retards the victory'.]

BRUTUS (Marcus Junius), son of Marcus Junius Brutus, and of Servilia the sister of Cato, was one of the assassins of Julius Caesar. He was the greatest republican that ever lived. He believed that no one was obliged to keep their word or sacred oath with those who wielded a tyranny over Rome (A). He was imbued with those noble ideas of liberty and love of country which the Greek and Roman authors describe so gloriously. He was so beguiled, I say, that neither his obligation to Julius Caesar nor his certain prospect of rising as far as he could desire under the new master of Rome could outweigh the passion he felt to restore affairs to their former state through the assassination of the tyrant. He conspired against him with several others; and their plot was so well organised and executed, that on 15 March 709 [i.e. after the foundation of Rome in 753 BC], Julius Caesar was stabbed to death in the Senate. At first, the people approved that deed; but unexpectedly, like a sea moved by a sudden squall, they turned against the murderers. The latter were forced to seek safety in flight. Brutus and Cassius were not discouraged and they attempted to sustain their party in the provinces. Though they held out in Macedonia with a strong army, fortune declared for liberty's oppressors. These two great republicans, called the last of the Romans [(B)], were defeated by Octavian and Mark Anthony and they were obliged to kill themselves in the year 711. Brutus has been condemned for having used his dying words to decry virtue (C); but he was not quite as wrong as some imagine (D).[a] It is a tragedy that by the murder of his benefactor he should have ruined a combination of the greatest qualities that ever a person could possess [(E)]. His deed was condemned by many Romans of the era;[b] and, to say the least, one can hardly deny that it was disproportionate to the circumstances. I mean that it was inappropriate. You will find support for this in Dio Cassius (F). He followed the sect of the Stoics, he loved books and he wrote some [(G)]. He was a fine orator; and as he had, for his part, chosen a concise and serious style,[c] it is not surprising that he found the eloquence of Cicero destitute of character. Yet in that orator he found a matchless panegyrist by whom he had been infinitely esteemed from his youth.[d] ... I cannot pass over in silence the proof which Brutus gave of his love of justice at the beginning of the war between Caesar and Pompey ...

(A) He believed that no one was obliged to keep their word ... with those who wielded a tyranny over Rome.] In one of his speeches to the Roman people at the Capitol he told them: 'Cum tyranno Romanis nulla fides, nulla jurisjurandi religio.' ['Towards a tyrant, the Romans have neither loyalty nor sworn obligation.'][1] This maxim seemed unreasonable to Grotius. You may see the way

[a] See Plutarch's *Life of Brutus.*
[b] See citation from Tacitus, note 8=18.
[c] *Gravitatem Bruti* ['the *gravitas* of Brutus']: Quintilian, *Institutio oratoria* [The Education of an Orator], 12.10.
[d] See Cicero in the works *Brutus, Philippics* and elsewhere.

[1] From Appian, *De bello civili* [The Civil Wars], 2.

in which he has refuted it in § 15, chapter 7 of the second book of *De jure belli et pacis*. Boclerus supported this refutation in his notes on chapter 54, book 2 of Velleius Paterculus. However, the maxim of pagan Rome would be less unpardonable than that which Christian Rome is said to have established at the Council of Constance: namely, that faith is not to be kept with heretics.

[Remark (B) omitted.]

(C) He used his dying words to decry virtue.] 'Oh wretched virtue', he lamented, 'how I have been deceived in your service! I believed you were a real being, and I dedicated myself to you in that belief; but you were only a vain name, a chimera, the victim and slave of fortune.' He was not the first to have made use of these words. A Greek poet put them in the mouth of Hercules.[2=5] ... According to Plutarch, he who uttered the lament of having vainly followed virtue as a real thing adds that he abandoned injustice as an abundant source of wealth, and intemperance as the copious provider of every sort of pleasure ...

(D) ... but he was not quite as wrong as some imagine.] Far from deserving to be condemned in all respects, it should be said of him that, on the contrary, perhaps no pagan ever said a truer or more reasonable thing. However, to perceive this we must put ourselves in the position of this Roman. He had once considered virtue, justice, and right, as very real objects; that is to say as beings whose strength was superior to that of injustice, and which sooner or later would establish their followers above the accidents and hazards of fortune. But he experienced quite the contrary. He saw for a second time the party of justice, and the destiny of his country, on their knees before the party of rebellion. He had recently seen Mark Anthony, the most profligate of men, whose hands were steeped in the blood of the most illustrious citizens of Rome, subjugate those

---

[2=5] 'Aliaque voce recitato Herculis isto dicto: "O infelix virtus, itane, cum nihil quam nomen esses, ego te tanquam rem aliquam exercui, quam tu fortunae servieris!" ' ['In a different voice he recited this saying of Hercules: "Oh wretched virtue, although you were nothing but a name, I practised you as something real. How you are the slave to fortune!" ']: Dio Cassius, [Roman History], 47. See Plutarch, *De Superstit.* [*Moralia*, 1.14].

who upheld the liberty of the Roman people. Thus he found himself wretchedly disillusioned with the idea he had formed of virtue. He had gained nothing in her service other than a choice between killing himself or becoming the pawn of a usurper, while Mark Anthony, in the service of injustice, had been favoured with the opportunity of satisfying all his ambitions. Thus you see why Brutus said that virtue had no reality and that, if one did not want to be taken for a dupe, one should regard her as an empty name, and not as a real thing.

But was he not wrong to say this? Let us make a distinction. In the general proposition and absolutely speaking, he advanced a great absurdity and an impious fallacy. Yet, according to his own hypothesis and in the context of his own doctrines, his lament was well founded. It may also be said that the pagans, given the obscurity in which they lived concerning an afterlife, reasoned very inconsequentially on the reality of virtue. It belongs to Christians to argue correctly. For if to the exercise of virtue one does not add those blessings to come, which the Scriptures promise to the faithful, one might place virtue and integrity among the number of things on which Solomon has pronounced the definitive precept: *Vanity, vanity, all is vanity!* To trust in one's integrity would be to rely on a broken reed which pierces the hand of the one who leans upon it. God, as earthly disposer of events and the provider of good and bad fortune, has submitted virtue and integrity to general laws no less than health and wealth. One of the most considerable states of Europe alternately lost and won when it waged only unjust wars; or gained more than it lost. Since then it has engaged only in just wars and done nothing but lose. So how has this happened? It was powerful once, but is no longer! Our conclusion is that whoever attaches himself to the system of Brutus, and who regards virtue as the fountain of temporal success, runs the risk of having to complain one day of having taken for a reality what was only an empty name.

But let us beware, on the other hand, of the rash observation of that extravagant perspective which claims that to have an ill cause is the readiest way to succeed. We say, on the contrary, that, all other things being equal, to have reason and justice on one's side is a fair step along the path to victory. However grave the disorders of humankind, it cannot yet be said with truth that to be in the right averts or retards the victory. Not so long ago,[3=9] I found myself in company where the conversation turned to two princes who had been nominated for an important job. There was no division of opinion: everyone acquiesced in predicting which would succeed.[4=10] The reasons given were as follows: the endorsement throughout Europe for one of the two candidates, the situation of the country from which each could expect support, the excessive power of the patron of the one whose ill success was foretold, as well as a plethora of other considerations.[5=11] 'You may think you have considered everything' interjected a Frenchman who had not previously spoken,

> But that would be a mistake. I shall give you a stronger case. One party has right on his side, his candidature is honest and therefore he must sink. The candidature of the other party has all possible defects: it contravenes the basic formalities, including the fundamental laws of the nation; and that, on its own, is enough to secure him the victory and the triumph.

This argument was derided. Yet some were willing to take it further, but they concluded that injustice on its own was more likely to prejudice a cause than to further it; and that it is only coincidental if justice, in some circumstances, turns out to be an impediment to success. It happens very often that those who work for a good cause are less active than their adversaries. For they flatter themselves, as Brutus did, that Heaven will declare for them. They imagine that the true cause needs less support than the unjust cause, whereupon they slacken their vigilance, and sometimes they are such honest people that they refuse to resort to sordid means to further a good end. Those who are engaged in unwholesome causes, on the other hand, have no scruples about adding iniquity to iniquity and, given their doubts about their success, they have recourse to prodigious activity and make use of all imaginable

---

[3=9] I wrote this in 1698.
[4=10] In fact that was what happened.
[5=11] See [*Dic,*] article 'Bellarmine', note 81.

expedients. They omit nothing that could either advance their own candidature or impede the progress of the opponent.[6=12]

One may also imagine, by analogy with the hypothesis of good and bad angels, that the latter are far more energetic. Be that as it may, there is no correlation to be drawn between success and the justice or injustice of a cause. Moreover, except in cases where God works through a miracle – which happens but seldom – the outcome of an enterprise depends on the circumstances and the effectiveness of the means that are used to promote it. This is why injustice sometimes prevails, but why one may also proclaim: 'tandem bona causa triumphat' ['the right cause is eventually victorious'].

[Remark (E) omitted.]

(F) The act . . . was inappropriate in the circumstances. You will find support for this in Dio Cassius.] This historian makes two observations: 1. that a corrupt anger overcame some of those who vented their rancour against Julius Caesar, leading them to assassinate him unjustly; 2. that though they submitted the fine pretext of re-establishing liberty, their deed, in fact, was iniquitous and it plunged into sedition a state that was beginning to taste the advantages of a sound administration. He then declares that monarchy is preferable to democratic government, and that Greek history, and even Roman, proves that cities and individuals experience more moderation and far fewer adversities under the authority of one person than under a popular government; furthermore, that if there had been states that flourished under such conditions, then they lasted only until they had reached a certain degree of size and power, beyond which they experienced only a discord caused by envy and ambition. Thus – it was argued – since the city of Rome saw itself in that era as mistress of an infinity of nations, and was burdened with riches and glory, it was impossible for the inhabitants in the midst of such republican liberty to loosen the bonds of their passions; just as it was more impossible still to restrain their greed. On this they could all agree . . . Thus if Brutus and Cassius

---

[6=12] Note that in some encounters they fail because they lack the courage to be sufficiently base.

had considered matters carefully, they would never have assassinated the leader of the republic, and nor, in consequence, would they
have plunged themselves and the whole Roman Empire into an
unending train of misfortune. Note that Xiphilinus contested Dio
Cassius on that point.[7=17]

But I do not believe that anyone could reasonably deny – given
the level of greatness to which the Roman Empire had come, and
which had accustomed it to licence and ambition – that they could
have enjoyed peace or tranquillity under democratic government
either in the provinces or in the capital. For a long time Rome had
been a republic in name only. Changes of government will always
be inevitable in popular states which engage in conquest. Had they
wished to preserve themselves, they should have avoided like the
plague all offensive war, and been content with a smaller territory.
To use a Scholastic distinction, they should have sought to consolidate and strengthen themselves *intensively*, and not *extensively*.

I remarked in the body of this article that several Romans disagreed with the deed of Brutus. It is necessary therefore to cite a
witness.

> Die funeris [Augusti] milites . . . ['On the day of the funeral
> [of Augustus], soldiers were lined up like a guard. This was
> much ridiculed by those who had themselves witnessed (or
> whose fathers had described to them) that day on which
> servitude was still a new experience and freedom was
> reclaimed with adverse consequences, namely, the day of
> Caesar's murder, considered by some the worst of crimes,
> but by others the noblest of deeds.'][8=18]

[7=17] [Johannes] Xiphilinus, *Epit. Dion* [Epitome of Dio Cassius], 44.
[8=18] Tacitus, *Annals*, 1.8.

David

[Following an indictment before the Huguenot church in Rotterdam, Bayle removed from the 1702 edition of the Dictionary certain passages from the article 'David'. Seemingly he had flouted convention by condemning David more for his cruelties and his betrayals than for his lapses in sexual morals. Furthermore he had implied that there were political parallels between the opportunism of the House of David and that of the House of Orange. For David, having married Saul's daughter, had taken over Saul's crown and lands, while William, having married the daughter of James II, had not only acquired his crown and the government of the British Isles but had resorted to warfare to retain them. In Remark (I), Bayle suggests that his accusers had merely emphasised his observation that a ruler's opportunism was often venerated by the very clerics who had a duty to condemn it.

For the second edition of 1702 Bayle supplied an amended text removing Remarks (D), (H), (I) and (M). The Paris edition of 1820–4, from which these texts are translated, restored them, showing how the text of 1697 compared with the amended version. In the body of the text, we print the restored lines in italics.]

DAVID, king of the Jews, was one of the greatest men ever known, even though one should not consider him as a royal prophet who was after God's own heart. The first time the Scriptures represent him on the stage of history[a] is where they inform us that Samuel

---

[a] 1 Samuel, 16:13.

36

named him king and performed the ceremony of consecration. David was then a mere shepherd. He was the youngest of the eight sons of Jesse the Bethlehemite [(A)]. Afterwards, Scripture tells us, he was sent to cure king Saul[b] of his fits of madness with the sound of his instrument of music [(B)]. A service of such importance made him so much loved by Saul that he kept him in his household and made him his armour bearer.[c] The Scriptures say[d] that David sometimes returned home to care for his father's flocks and that his father sent him one day to Saul's camp with provisions for three of his sons who were in his service. David performing that mission heard of the challenge that a Philistine called Goliath, proud of his strength and tall in stature, made daily to the Israelites, none of them daring to accept it. He devised a plan to fight the giant whereupon he was brought to the king and assured him that he would triumph over the Philistine. Saul gave him his armour but David, finding it troublesome, removed it and resolved to make use only of his sling which he did with such ease that he felled the braggart[e] with a stone and then killed him with his own sword and cut off his head which he presented to Saul [(C)]. When he saw David confront Goliath the prince asked his General: 'whose son is that youth?'[f] The general answered that he did not know, and received orders from Saul to enquire about it. But Saul heard it himself from that young man, for when they presented him after the victory he asked him: 'whose son art thou?' and David answered him that he was the son of Jesse.[g] Then Saul kept him in his service without allowing him to return to his father.[h] But because the songs that were sung in every city on the defeat of the Philistines were more glorious to David than to Saul[i] the king conceived a violent jealousy which increased daily because the tasks that he gave to David to keep him from the court served only to make him more illustrious and to take from him the affection and the admiration of the Jews. With a devious intent he sought to make him his son-in-law, for he

[b] *Ibid.*, 16:20.
[c] *Ibid.*
[d] *Ibid.*, 17:15.
[e] *Ibid.*, 17:49, 50.
[f] *Ibid.*, 17:55.
[g] *Ibid.*, 17:58.
[h] *Ibid.*, 18:2.
[i] ... *Ibid.*, 18:7.

hoped that the conditions on which he was to give him his second daughter would deliver him from the object of his aversion, but his cunning confounded him. As his daughter's dowry he asked for a hundred Philistine foreskins, but David brought him two hundred;[k] so that instead of being destroyed by the undertaking he returned with a new glory. He married Saul's daughter, whereupon he became even more formidable to the king.[l] All his expeditions against the Philistines were highly successful. His name caused a great stir; he was held in such a remarkable esteem[m] that Saul, who knew his son-in-law's virtue much less than the humour of the people, imagined that the death of David would be the sole act that could prevent him from being dethroned. He resolved then to be rid of him for good and entrusted his eldest son with the plan, but he, far from sharing his father's jealousy, warned David of the dark conspiracy.[n] David fled and was pursued from place to place until he had given undeniable proof of his probity and his fidelity to his father-in-law, to whom he did no harm despite two occasions[o] on which he might easily have killed him. This made Saul resolve to leave him alone. But David, fearing the return of that prince's harmful intentions, did not grow less cautious. On the contrary, he provided himself with a better place of refuge than before in the country of the Philistines.[p] From the king of Geth he requested a town from which he made many expeditions into neighbouring territories *(D)*.[q] He returned into Judaea[r] after the death of Saul where he was declared king by the tribe of Judah. In the meantime the other tribes submitted themselves to Ish-bosheth, son of Saul, because of the loyalty of Abner.[s] This man, who had been army general under king Saul, set Ish-bosheth on the throne and kept him there despite David's efforts. But being displeased with Ish-bosheth, who censured him for having taken one of Saul's concu-

---

[k] *Ibid.*, 18:27.
[l] *Ibid.*, 18:29.
[m] *Ibid.*, 18:30.
[n] *Ibid.*, 19:1, 2.
[o] *Ibid.*, 24, 26.
[p] *Ibid.*, 27.
[q] *Ibid.*
[r] 2 Samuel, 2:4.
[s] *Ibid.*, 2:8.

bines,[t] he negotiated with David to give him possession of Ish-bosheth's kingdom. The treaty would soon have been completed to David's satisfaction, had Joab[u] not killed Abner to avenge a private quarrel. But this man's death did not merely hasten the downfall of the wretched Ish-bosheth. Two of his captains killed him and brought his head to David who did not reward them for it, as they had expected, but ordered their execution.[v=x] Ish-bosheth's subjects did not wait long before voluntarily submitting themselves to David's dominion. This prince had reigned seven and a half years over the tribe of Judah, and afterwards he reigned for some thirty-three years over all Israel.[w=y] The long reign was distinguished by great successes and glorious conquests; and it was little troubled except by conspiracies of the prince's own children (E). They are commonly the enemies from whom sovereigns have most to fear. David very nearly had to return to that mean condition in which Samuel found him. Humanly speaking, that reverse (F) would have been unavoidable had he not found some persons to perform the role of traitor in respect of his son Absalom.[x=z]

David's piety is so radiant in his psalms and in many of his actions that it cannot be sufficiently revered. He is a sun of holiness in the church where, by his works, he spreads a wonderful light of consolation and piety; but he had his faults (G). [Original text, 1697, cut from edition of 1702: *There is another thing no less admirable in his conduct; it is to see that he was able to make such a happy accord between this piety and the unscrupulous maxims of the art of reigning. It is generally held that his adultery with Bathsheba, the murder of Uriah, the counting of the populace, are the only faults with which he can be reproached. But that would be a great mistake; for throughout his life there were many other matters (H). One could not sufficiently admire him, but the deviousness of his politics may be discerned right up to his dying words (I). Holy Scripture reports these matters as history, which is why each individual is allowed to judge them for himself. Let us conclude*

---

[t] *Ibid.*, 3.
[u] He was the general of David's army.
[v=x] *Ibid.*, 4.
[w=y] *Ibid.*, 5:5.
[x=z] *Ibid.*, 15:34 *et seq.*

by saying that the history of king David may be reassuring to many crowned heads, given the warning of certain strict moralists who contend that for a king it is almost impossible to attain salvation.]

Though the life of this great prince published by the Abbé de Choisi is a fine book, it would have been better had he taken the trouble to put in the margin the year of each event, and the places in the Bible, or Josephus, that supplied him with his facts. A reader is irked if he does not know whether what he reads comes from a sacred source or a profane source. I shall comment on some of Moréri's mistakes. The article on David which I have recently read in the *Dictionnaire du Bible* (by M. Simon . . . Lyon, 1690) gives me an opportunity to make a comment. [Original text, 1697, cut from edition of 1702: *I should have mentioned that it would have been wrong to condemn David for having excluded his eldest son from the succession (M).*]

[Remarks (A)–(C) omitted.]

(D) From the king of Geth he requested a town from which he made many expeditions into neighbouring territories.]

[From text of 1697. The whole of Remark (D) was withdrawn from edition of 1702.]

Having lived for a period of time in the capital city of king Akis, David, with his small band of six hundred brave warriors, feared being a burden on this prince and begged for another dwelling place. Akis directed him to the town of Siceleg. David moved there with his army and he did not allow their swords to rust. He often led them on expeditions when they killed men and women without mercy, allowing only animals to live. This was the only booty which he took, for he feared that prisoners would reveal the secret to king Akis. This was his reason for taking none, and why he had both sexes exterminated. The secret that he did not want to be revealed was that these ravages took place not only in the lands of the Israelites, as it had been agreed with the king of Geth, but also in the lands of the former peoples of Palestine.[1=10] Frankly, this conduct

[1=10] 1 Samuel, 27.

was exceedingly wicked; for to hide one fault he committed another that was even greater. He deceived a king to whom he had an obligation, and he perpetrated prodigious cruelties in order to hide that deception. Had David been asked: 'by whose authority do you do these things?' what could he have replied? Does a fugitive like himself, who has found exile in the lands of a neighbouring prince, have the right to engage in hostilities on his own account without a specific commission from the sovereign of his country? Did David have such a commission? Did he not, on the contrary, work against the intentions and the interests of the king of Geth? It is certain that if an individual, whatever his birth, were to behave today as David behaved in this incident, he would be unable to avoid castigation with epithets far from honourable. I know very well that the most illustrious heroes, and the most famous prophets of the Old Testament, have sometimes agreed that one could put to the sword every living thing, and thus I would be very cautious about calling David's action inhuman had he been authorised by some prophet, or if God, though his own inspired command, had ordered him to use the sword in that manner. But it seems manifest, given the silence of Scripture, that he did it entirely on his own initiative.

I shall say something of what he resolved to do to Nabal. When this man, who was very rich, was nurturing his flocks, David had him asked, with courtesy, for certain services: that is, his messengers insisted that Nabal's shepherds had suffered no harm from David's men. As Nabal was somewhat direct, he asked in a very brusque manner who David was, and reproached him for having disregarded the orders of his master. In a word he declared that he was not so imprudent as to give to strangers and to people without status what he had set aside for his own servants. David, outraged by this reply, had four hundred of his soldiers take up arms and, putting himself at their head, resolved to leave no living soul unslain. He even committed himself to it by oath, and if he did not carry out this bloody resolution, it was because Abigail came to appease him with her fine words and her gifts.[2=11] Abigail was the wife of Nabal, a person of great worth, beautiful and intelligent, and so pleasing to David that he married her as soon as she was a widow.[3=12] Speaking seriously and in good faith, is it not undeniable

[2=11] *Ibid.*, 25.
[3=12] *Ibid.*, 25:42.

that David was planning to commit a highly criminal act? He had no right to the goods of Nabal, nor any authority to punish his incivility. He wandered over the earth with a band of companions, and though he could ask rich persons for favours, should they refuse he was obliged to respond with patience; and he could not coerce them with military force without plunging the world into that fearfully confused state called nature, in which one recognises only the law of the strongest. What should we say today if a prince of the blood in France, being disgraced at court, lived as he could with friends who wanted to be his companions of fortune? What judgement would we make, I ask, if he sought to live by contributions from the territories where he encamped, and put to the sword everyone in the parishes which refused to pay his taxes? What would we say if that prince, having equipped some ships, then trawled the seas to take what he could from all the merchant shipping? Frankly speaking, was David any better authorised to exact contributions from Nabal, or to massacre all the men and women of the country of the Amalekites etc., and to carry off all the livestock they could find? I agree that you could reply that today we are better acquainted with the rights of peoples, the *jus belli et pacis* [the law of war and peace], from which such remarkable systems have been constructed; and that such behaviour in those times was accordingly more excusable than it would be today. But the deep respect that we have for this great king and prophet should not prevent us from condemning the flaws that are to be found in his life. Otherwise we should give cause to secular people to reproach us by saying that for an action to be just, it is enough for it to be performed by people whom we venerate. Nothing could be more damaging for Christian morals than that. It is important for the true religion that the lives of the orthodox are judged by general ideas of rectitude [*la droiture*] and order [*l'ordre*].

(E) **The reign was little troubled except by conspiracies of David's own children.**] The most heinous of their conspiracies was the revolt of Absalom which compelled this great prince to flee from Jerusalem in mournful procession, with his head covered, bare-footed, dissolved in tears, and his ears resounding with the lamentations of his faithful subjects.[4=14] Absalom entered Jerusalem,

[4=14] 2 Samuel, 15.

as it were, in a triumphant manner: and, lest his supporters should complacently suppose that this discord between father and son would end eventually, he did a thing likely to cause the belief that he would never be reconciled with David. He lay with the ten concubines of that prince in the full view of the public.[5=15] It is probable that even this crime would have been pardoned: and David's extraordinary affliction over his death is proof of it. He was the greatest father that ever was: but his indulgence was excessive and he was the first to suffer for it. For had he punished the infamous action of his son Ammon[6=16] as the thing deserved, he would not have had the shame and vexation of seeing another take revenge for Tamar's injury. And if he had punished the one who avenged that affront as he ought to have done, he would not have risked dethronement. David suffered the fate of most great princes: he had wretched family relationships. His eldest son ravished his own sister, and for that incest he was killed by one of his brothers; and the author of the fratricide was he who lay with David's concubines.

(F) . . . the reverse would have been unavoidable . . . for little was needed for him to have returned to the condition . . . in which Samuel had found him.] This shows that no trust can be placed in the allegiance of peoples, for in general David was both a good and a great king. He made himself loved and esteemed and he had all the zeal imaginable for the religion of his country. Thus his subjects had reason to be satisfied and if they had been required to choose a prince, could they have wished for one better qualified? And yet so fickle were they in their duty to David, that his son .Absalom, in order to have himself declared king, needed only to court popularity from time to time and to give support to a few emissaries in each tribe. This maxim *casta est quam nemo rogavit* ['chaste is she whom no one has propositioned'] may be applied to the people. If we do not see kings dethroned more often than they are, it is because the people have not been incited to revolt by carefully managed intrigues. For that alone is required. Whether or not a prince is wicked, it is well known how to depict him as such or in thrall to wicked advisers. Pretexts are never lacking and, pro-

---

[5=15] *Ibid.*, 16.
[6=16] He raped Tamar and was killed for that crime, on the order of Absalom, who was Tamar's brother by the same father and the same mother. *Ibid.*, 13.

vided that they are cleverly presented, they pass for legitimate argument, however weak their foundation.

(G) He had his faults.] The numbering of the people was a matter which God considered to be a grave sin.[7=17] His love for Uriah's wife and the orders which he gave to have Uriah destroyed[8=18] were two enormous crimes. Yet he felt so much remorse and he atoned with such commendable sorrow that it is an aspect of his life which contributes not least to the instruction and the edification of faithful souls. It teaches one about the frailty of the saints, and it provides a fine example of the precept of vigilance, which is to be aware that one must pay for one's sins. As for the remarks of certain critics who wish to demonstrate that he deserves strong censure in certain other actions of his life, I suppress them in this edition, the more willingly since some persons, more enlightened than I in this sort of thing, have assured me that these fine objections are easily allayed as soon as one recalls the following:

1. that David was king by right during the life of Saul; 2. that he had at his side the High Priest who consulted God to determine what should be done; 3. that the orders given to Joshua to exterminate the infidels of Palestine had long existed; 4. that many other circumstances drawn from Scripture can prove David's innocence concerning conduct which, if considered in general, would appear wrong; and which certainly would be wrong today.

(H) It is commonly believed that his adultery etc. are the only things for which David can be reproached ... yet there were many other matters.]

[From text of 1697. Remark (H) was withdrawn from edition of 1702.]

We have already remarked on matters which belong to the period in which he was a private individual; but here are some which concern the period of his reign.

1. One cannot easily excuse his polygamy, for if God still tolerated it in those times one should not suppose that one can carry it that far without succumbing to lust. Mical, second daughter of Saul,

[7=17] 2 Samuel, 24.
[8=18] *Ibid.*, 11.

44

was David's first wife, but she was taken from him during his disgrace.[9=17] He married in succession several other wives[10=18] and yet he did not cease to consort with the first. To recover her he had to abduct her from a husband who loved her and who followed her as far as he could crying like a child.[11=19] David did not scruple to consort with the daughter of a gentile,[12=20] and though he had children by several women, in Jerusalem he procured still more concubines. Doubtless he chose the most beautiful he met; thus with regard to the sensualities of love one cannot say that he took much care to tame nature.

II. As soon as he had learnt of Saul's death, he sought immediately to reclaim the succession. He set off for Hebron; 'and as soon as he had arrived the whole tribe of Judah, whose leaders HE HAD WON OVER BY GRAFT, recognised him as king.'[13=21] If Abner had conserved for the son of Saul the remainder of the succession, it is certain that David, by the same method – I mean the method of winning over the leaders through favours – would have become king of all Israel. What happened after Abner's devotion had retained eleven tribes for Ish-bosheth? The same thing that would occur between any two highly ambitious infidel kings. David and Ish-bosheth made unceasing war[14=22] to establish which of the two would acquire the portion of the other, so that he might enjoy the whole kingdom undivided. What I am about to relate is far worse. Abner, dissatisfied with the king his master, aspired to remove his lands from him and transfer them to David. He confided his intentions to David. He sought him out in order to conspire with him over that deed. David lent his ear to this perfidy and resolved to gain a kingdom by the intrigue.[15=23] Could anyone say that these exploits were those of a saint? I agree that there is nothing here that does not conform to the precepts of statecraft or to the resourcefulness of prudence, but no one will ever convince me that the strict laws of justice, and the decent morality of a conscientious servant of

---

[9=17] I Samuel, 25:24.
[10=18] 2 Samuel, 3:5.
[11=19] *Ibid.*, 3:16.
[12=20] *Ibid.*, 3:3.
[13=21] Abbé de Choisi, *Histoire de la vie de David*, p. 47.
[14=22] 2 Samuel, 3:1.
[15=23] *Ibid.*, 3.

God, could approve of such conduct. Note that David did not claim that Saul's son reigned through usurpation; it was necessary for him to be an honest man[16=24] and he was therefore a legitimate king.

III. I make the same judgement about the subterfuge which David employed during the revolt of Absalom. He did not want Hushai, one of his most loyal friends, to support him. He instructed him to insinuate himself into the party of Absalom in order to give imprudent advice to his rebellious son and so be in a position to inform David of all the affairs of the new king.[17=25] Such deception in matters of state is doubtless highly praiseworthy if one judges these things from the perspective of public prudence or the statecraft of sovereigns. It saved David, and from that century on, our own included, statecraft has produced an infinity of political escapades – useful to some and pernicious to others. Yet a strict moral theorist would never take such cunning to be an action worthy of a prophet, or a saint, or a good man. A good man would, in that capacity, prefer to lose a crown than be the cause of the damnation of his friend. Thus, it is to damn our friend – if he is one – if we incite him to commit a crime. And it is as much a crime – in my view – to pretend to espouse a man's cause as to destroy him by giving him bad advice, or by disclosing the secrets of his council. Can one imagine a treachery more perfidious than that of Hushai? As soon as he saw Absalom he exclaimed: Long live the king! Long live the king! And when he was asked why he did not support his intimate friend, he feigned a devout expression and claimed a reason of conscience, saying: I shall be for him whom the Eternal One has chosen.[18=26]

IV. When David because of his old age could get no warmth from the blankets which covered him, he was advised to find a young woman to look after him and lie with him. For this purpose he allowed them to bring him the most beautiful girl that could be found.[19=27] Could anyone say that this was the act of a chaste man? Would a man replete with ideas of purity, and wholly resolved to do what dignity and propriety required, have consented to such a remedy? Would anyone agree to it who did not prefer the instincts

[16=24] *Ibid.*, 4:11.
[17=25] *Ibid.*, 15.
[18=26] *Ibid.*, 16:28.
[19=27] 1 Kings, 1.

of nature and the claims of the flesh to those of the spirit of God?

v. It is a long time since anyone has condemned David for having committed a blatant injustice against Mephiboseth, the son of his bosom friend, Jonathan. The fact is that David, no longer fearing the faction of king Saul, was content to seem generous towards all those of this family who had survived. He learnt that there remained an indigent called Mephiboseth, son of Jonathan. He sent for him and gave him all the estate which had belonged to king Saul and instructed Siba, former servant of this house, to look after these lands on his behalf and to support the son of Mephiboseth. As for Mephiboseth, for the rest of his days he would enjoy a place at the table of king David.[20=28] While this prince was escaping from Jerusalem to avoid falling into the hands of Absalom, he met Siba who brought him some supplies and who told him in three words that Mephiboseth was in Jerusalem in the hope that in the course of these revolutions he might recover the kingdom. On this David gave to this man all the possessions of Mephiboseth.[21=29] After the death of Absalom he learnt that Siba had been a false informer and nevertheless he removed from him only half of what he had awarded him; and he gave back to Mephiboseth only half of his possessions.

There are some authors who claim that this injustice – which was the greater since David's ultimate obligations were to Jonathan – was the reason why God permitted Jeroboam to divide the kingdom of Israel.[22=30] But it is incontrovertible that the sins of Solomon were God's reason for permitting this division.[23=31] Not every interpreter has repudiated the case for David. There are those who claim that Siba's accusation was not false, or at least that it was founded on so many probabilities that one could believe it without making a rash judgement.[24=32] But there are few people who are of this opinion. The greater part of the Fathers and the Moderns believe that Siba was a false witness, and that David allowed himself to be misled. Observe carefully the opinion of Pope Gregory: he concedes that Mephiboseth was calumniated and nevertheless he

[20=28] 2 Samuel, 9.
[21=29] *Ibid.*, 16.
[22=30] . . . Théophile Raynaud, *Hoploth.*, sect. 2, series 2, ch. 10, p. 231.
[23=31] 1 Kings, 11:2.
[24=32] See Petrus Joannes Olivii, in Théophile Raynaud, sect. 4, p. 523, and *ibid.*, p. 232.

asserts that the sentence whereby he was deprived of all his possessions was just. He asserts this for two reasons: 1. because David pronounced it; 2. because a secret judgement of God intervened.

> Non me latet . . . ['It has not escaped my notice that, contrary to those interpreters who were convinced of the opposite opinion above, Saint Gregory takes a stand against David in line 1 of his fourth dialogue. He concedes that David believed he was just in pronouncing sentence against the innocent son of Jonathan, since it was David who pronounced it, and the sentence was in accordance with the hidden judgement of God. Nevertheless, Gregory clearly admits that Mephiboseth was innocent. It plainly follows from this that David's action was unjust . . .][25=33]

The author that I cite takes another tack. Since David's saintliness, he tells us, is very well established, and since he never ordered the restitution of the wrong done to Mephiboseth, it must be concluded that the sentence was just. Now that is to establish a highly dangerous precedent: namely, that we can no longer examine the conduct of the prophets for the purpose of condemning actions that do not seem to conform to morality. It would follow that libertines could accuse our moral theorists of favouring actions which are visibly unjust: of judging, I say, in favour of certain people because of who they are. Let us suggest something better: let us apply to the saints what has been said of great intellects, 'nullum sine venia placuit ingenium' ['A genius is always disliked if he never has to be forgiven']. The greatest of saints need to beg forgiveness in some matters.

VI. I shall say nothing of the reproach that was made to David by Mical, one of his wives, about the company he kept when he danced in public. Had he flaunted his nakedness his action might have passed for improper, morally speaking; but if he had merely made himself ridiculous through his postures, or failed to sustain the majesty of his position, that would have been an imprudence and not a crime. For one would need to consider the occasion on which he danced, since it was when the Ark of the Covenant was carried into Jerusalem;[26=34] and consequently the joyful exuberance in his

---

[25=33] Théophile Raynaud, p. 232.
[26=34] 2 Samuel, 2:6.

movements reflected his emotion and his attachment to holy matters. . . .

VII. David's conquests will be the subject of my final observation. There are exacting moralists who do not believe that a Christian prince may legitimately engage in war for the purpose of self-aggrandisement. These moralists approve only of defensive wars, or, in general, of those which aim merely to make restitution to each party of his rightful possessions. According to this maxim, David must have undertaken unjust wars, because Holy Scripture, as well as frequently representing him to us as the aggressor, reveals also that he envisaged 'Egypt to the Euphrates' as the 'limits of his Empire'.[27=37] It might be better to say, in order not to condemn David outright, that conquests can sometimes be permitted, and thus one must be very careful if, in inveighing against modern princes, one does not inadvertently undermine this great prophet. But if, speaking in general terms, the conquests of that holy monarch were indeed glorious, one has difficulty, when one gets down to the detail, in agreeing with the proposition without prejudicing his justice. Let us not become engulfed in conjecture about secrets which history has not revealed, but let us assume – since David wished to profit from the treachery of Abner and Hushai – that there were few machinations which he did not use against the rebellious kings whom he brought to heel. Let us dwell then only on what history tells us of the manner in which he treated the vanquished. 'He seized all the people who were in Rabba[38] and he attached them to ratchets, to iron harrows and to metal choppers and he dragged them through the ovens where the bricks were fired. He acted likewise in every town where there were children of Hammon.'[28=39] The Geneva Bible observes in the margin of this verse that 'these were methods of torturing people to death that were used in former times'. Now let us see how he treats the Moabites.[29=40]

'He measured them with a tape, making them lie on the ground, and he calculated two measurements for those who should die, and one measurement for those who should live.' That is to say, he sought to annihilate precisely two thirds of the people, neither more

---

[27=37] Abbé de Choisi, *Histoire de la vie de David*, p. 64.
[28=39] 2 Samuel, 12:31.
[29=40] *Ibid.*, 8:2.

nor less.[41] Edom received an even ruder treatment since he had every male inhabitant put to death; 'Joab remained there with the whole of Israel until he had exterminated every male in Edom.'[30=42] Can anyone deny that this method of prosecuting war deserves to be execrated? Do not the Turks and the Tartars have a little more humanity? And if an infinity of contemporary pamphlets make daily protest against military executions as truly cruel and highly reprehensible but sweet in comparison with those of David, what would the authors of these pamphlets say today if they had to condemn the ratchets, the harrows, and the ovens of David, and the mass murder [*la tuerie générale*] of every male in the population, great and small?

(I) The deviousness of his politics may be discerned right up to his dying words.]

[From text of 1697. Remark (I) as a whole was withdrawn from edition of 1702.]

Consider the sense of my words: I do not mean that in that state David did not always say what he really thought: but rather that the frank and direct manner in which he revealed his heart witnesses that he had previously, in two noteworthy episodes, sacrificed justice to utility. He knew clearly that Joab deserved death and that not to punish the assassination with which Joab's hands were stained was a blatant injury in the eyes of the law and of reason. Joab, nevertheless, retained his responsibilities, his reputation, and his authority. He was brave, he served his master, the king, faithfully and usefully; and there was a fear of violent discontent should any attempt be made to punish him. Such are the reasons of state which make the law defer to expediency. But when David no longer needed this general he gave the order for him to be put to death; it was one of the clauses in his will.[31=43] His successor Solomon was charged with a similar execution against Semei. This man, knowing that David had escaped from Jerusalem in great disarray because of the revolt of Absalom, came to insult him in public and to make reproaches against him that were sharper even than the stones

---

[30=42] I Kings, 9:15.
[31=43] I Kings, 2:6.

which he slung.[32=44] David suffered this injury very patiently. With
a singular piety he recognised and revered the hand of God in the
incident; and when matters were restored he pardoned Semei who
was among the first to capitulate to him and beg for clemency.[33=45]
David solemnly promised that he would not put him to death, and
he kept his word until he was on his deathbed. Then, seeing himself
in this condition, he ordered his son to put this man to death.[34=46]
This is clear evidence that he had let him live only in order to
acquire firstly the glory of a compassionate prince, and secondly to
avoid being reproached for having failed to keep his word. I should
like to ask if, strictly speaking, a man who promises an enemy his
life keeps his promise if, in his will, he orders that he shall be
executed. From everything I have said in the preceding remarks
and in the present one it can easily be inferred that if the people of
Syria had been as adept at fabricating lies as today's Europeans,
they could have strangely distorted the glory of David. With what
names, and with what infamous expressions, might they not have
sabotaged that band of marauders who joined him after he left the
court of Saul? The Scriptures suggest that everyone who was persecuted by creditors, every malcontent, and everyone whose affairs
were going badly, came over to his side, and that he made himself
their chief.[35=47] Nothing is more susceptible to a malign interpretation than such a circumstance. In that respect the historians of
Catiline and Caesar supply many of the colours for a rancorous
artist. History has in fact preserved a small treasure house of the
malicious libels to which David was subjected by the accomplices
of Saul. The collection testifies that they accused David of being a
bloody murderer, and that they regarded the revolt of Absalom as
just punishment for the evils which he had perpetrated against Saul
and his family[36=48] . . . [37=49] He committed abominations, for it is a
fact, that according to the testimony of God himself, David was a
murderer. This is why God did not wish to permit him to build

---

[32=44] 2 Samuel, 16:5.
[33=45] *Ibid.*, 11:19.
[34=46] 1 Kings, 11:9.
[35=47] 'Convenerunt ad eum omnes . . .' ['About him there congregated all who had
    troubles, who were plagued by debt, or who were dissatisfied, and he became
    their leader.']: 1 Samuel, 22:2.
[36=48] . . . 2 Samuel, 16.
[37=49] [Josephus,] *Antiquitates judaicae* [Jewish Antiquities], 7, 8.

the Temple.[38=50] It is also a fact that to appease the Gabaonites he handed over to them the two sons and the five grandsons of Saul, whom they crucified – all seven of them.[39=51] But it is false that he ever conspired against either the life or the crown of Saul.

Those who find it strange that I should state my opinion about certain actions of David in relation to natural morality are requested to consider the three following points.

1. That they are themselves obliged to admit that the conduct of this prince towards Uriah constituted one of the greatest crimes that could be committed. There is thus between them and me, more or less, only one point of difference. For I recognise that the faults of this prophet did not prevent him from overflowing with piety and with a mighty zeal for the glory of the Eternal Being. He was subject by turns to passion and to grace. This is an inevitable consequence of our nature since the sin of Adam. For though he was very often directed by the grace of God, in certain encounters he was overtaken by cupidity: and in those cases statecraft [*la politique*] imposed silence on religion.

2. That it is perfectly permissible for insignificant individuals such as myself to judge the facts contained in Scripture when they are not expressly qualified by the Holy Spirit. Where Scripture, in recounting an action, praises it or condemns it, it is no longer permissible to question that judgement; each must regulate his approval or his condemnation according to the example of Scripture.[40=52] I have not acted contrary to this obligation: the facts upon which I advance my own small opinion are reported in Sacred History without the caveat of the Holy Spirit, and without any character of approbation.

3. It would do a very great wrong to eternal laws and, in consequence, to true religion, if one were to give to profane persons grounds to object that as soon as a man has been a party to God's inspiration one must consider his behaviour as a model for good morals; or that we dare not condemn public deeds completely opposed to ideas of justice [*l'équité*] if it is he who has committed

---

[38=50] 1 Chronicles, 22:8; 28:3.

[39=51] 2 Samuel, 21.

[40=52] I note that Scripture reveals that David consulted and followed God's orders when it was a question of repelling aggressors, 1 Samuel, 23 and 30; but he did not consult God when he sought to ruin Nabal, etc.

them. Yet there is no middle ground: either these actions are unworthy, or actions similar to them are not wicked. Accordingly, since one must choose one or the other of these two alternatives, is it not better for us to favour the interests of morality [*la morale*] than the glory of an individual? Otherwise, would it not be to proclaim that it is better to compromise the honour of God than the honour of a mortal man?

[Remarks (K)–(L) omitted.]

(M) One would be wrong to condemn him for having excluded his eldest son from the succession.]

[From text of 1697. Remark (M) was withdrawn from the edition of 1702.]

David left his kingdom to Solomon to the prejudice of the right of the eldest, a prerogative which in hereditary kingdoms should be inviolably maintained – at least if one does not wish to open the floodgates to a thousand civil wars. Nevertheless David had very good reasons for overriding this right since Adonija, his eldest son, was so eager to reign that he ascended the throne before David had ceased to live.[41=63] This good father had not dared to express his resentment against a rapacity which, in fact, did not differ from usurpation. He had always shown tenderness towards his children, but his near decrepitude was not very conducive to remedying the weakness which accompanies tender hearts. Yet Solomon's mother, alerted by a prophet[42=64] that Adonija had failed to pay homage at a royal ceremony,[43=65] averted the *coup*. She and the prophet obliged David to declare himself in favour of Solomon, and to give all the necessary orders for the investiture of this young prince. Adonija, believing himself lost, took refuge at the foot of the altar, but Solomon assured him that he would do him no harm, provided that he was seen to maintain a good and wise conduct.[44=66] He had him executed, however, for a reason that appears rather trivial – I mean

---

[41=63] I Kings, I.
[42=64] The prophet Nathan.
[43=65] I Kings, 1:10, 26.
[44=66] *Ibid.*, vss. 51, 52.

because Adonija had asked in marriage the Sunamite woman who had been employed to keep David warm.[45=67] This confirms what I said above, that this king-prophet was unfortunate in his children. They had no natural feeling either towards him or towards one another. See how the wisest of them all spills blood for a trifle. For one should not imagine that Solomon put Adonija to death because of a matter relating to his love life ... It was rather because his request awakened Solomon's suspicions, and made him fear that if he grew accustomed to asking favours he would soon seek to revive the prerogative of the eldest son.[46=68] Thus a politics in some respects like that of the Ottomans brought about his demise.

[45=67] *Ibid.*, 1:2.
[46=68] *Ibid.*, vs. 22.

Elizabeth

[Statecraft, combined with the ideas of salus populi suprema lex esto, *was taken for granted in Bayle's day as well as in the sixteenth century. In 'Elizabeth', as in his articles 'Machiavelli' and 'David', Bayle defends the notion of* raison d'état, *but he warns against supposing that it may support any act whatsoever. For subjects are rightly shocked if they learn that rulers have acted from motives of self-interest. In Remarks (F) and (I), Bayle asks if Elizabeth was wise in 1558 to choose Protestantism as the official religion in England. He concludes that she acted to avoid civil war, and that therefore she took the correct decision for the times. Yet he does not overlook the effect, in 1688, of the memory of this policy. For Elizabeth's action could have precipitated the consequence that James II's promise to uphold the Protestant religion inspired no confidence at all among Protestants, thereby causing them to decide that he must be replaced.]*

ELIZABETH, queen of England, daughter of king Henry VIII by Anne Boleyn, is one of the most illustrious figures recorded in history. To say that no woman did more gloriously wield the sceptre would not do her sufficient justice, unless we add that few great monarchs have been her equal [(A)]. Her reign provides the choicest part in the finest era of English history, for it was a school in which many great statesmen [(B)] were raised, so much so that England could never boast of more. We may say the same thing of her military men.[a] I shall relate nothing of the chief events of her glorious life. They may be found in an abundance of books which each individual may read, and which in some cases have come out very recently.[a=b] My interest is rather to collect certain particulars which, though of less moment, are not less curious, and which few other authors have observed. When Holland and Zealand offered to recognise her as sovereign of their country, she told their ambassadors that it would be neither honest nor decent for her to take over the possessions of another; and that the Dutch were in the wrong to incite so many troubles on account of the Mass [(C)]. Then she continued her conversation in a bantering strain. It was perhaps at this audience that a young man in the entourage of the ambassadors expressed rather bluntly what he felt within himself at the sight of so beautiful a queen [(D)]. It did him no harm but on the contrary it made her take notice of him. The resentment which this queen harboured against Buzneval who found fault with her way of speaking French is highly remarkable, and should serve as a caution to others [(E)]. At her accession to the throne she fluctuated between the two religions, and chose eventually the Protestant (F). That, by general agreement, was to take the side of prudence. She would never have been queen had the king of Spain not felt more hatred towards France than zeal for the Catholic religion [(G)]. It was that which saved Elizabeth's life, a circumstance that would be enough to weaken the accusation laid against her of ingratitude (H). It is rather hard upon her memory to reproach her for having broken the promises she made when she succeeded her sister.[b=c] She committed herself to maintaining Popery which was then the dominant religion, and yet she abolished it soon after. This policy perhaps rendered a very great service to the Protestant religion in the celebrated Revolution of 1688 (I). To what extent this queen has been spitefully calumniated is hard to tell [(K)]. It was unavoidable given the severe laws which, for reasons of state, she was obliged to enact against the Papists. If some lost their lives, a great many others suffered either the penalty of prison or the inconveniences of exile (L), and it was principally the latter who wrote a variety of pamphlets damaging to Elizabeth's reputation. They made her

---

[a=b] See, especially, de Larrey, *L'Histoire d'Angleterre*, Rotterdam, Reinier Leers, 1698.
[b=c] See Elizabeth's history [*L'Histoire*] by M. Leti, vol. I, p. 331, etc.

a monster of barbarity, greed, and immodesty. There are few Protestant authors that do not extol to the heavens her chastity, and there are memoirs which assert that she could not, without hazarding her life, have borne a child [(M)]. Her chastity is made an issue in the writings of a modern author who is a Protestant [(N)]. It is far easier to save her reputation both in this regard and in her proclamations against the Papists than in the affair of the unfortunate queen of Scots [(O)]; and moreover one cannot justly bestow upon her the praise which a Roman historian accords to Agrippina, of having overcome the weakness of her sex through her application to manly affairs [(P)]. Pope Sixtus had a particular esteem for Elizabeth [(Q)], and it is even reported that he exchanged diplomatic correspondence with her to the prejudice of the king of Spain. What M. Leti reports on that score does not lack probability [(R)]. I have said nothing about the erudition of this queen which is, however, an attribute for which she deserves admiration.[c=d] Her reign, so long suffused with the blessings of providence, ended in the darkest melancholy [(S)]. Some will have it that the death of the earl of Essex caused that grievous sorrow [(T)]. Certain polemical writers published a malicious jest which is highly unlikely.[d=e] It was said that the Maréchal de Biron boasted of having seen the head of the Protestant church dancing. They should have attributed this story to another ambassador. For Elizabeth was no longer of dancing age[e=f] when Henry IV sent her the Maréchal de Biron. Had Balzac considered the maturity of this queen,[f=g] he would certainly have avoided saying that she was so charming that the earl of Essex chose rather to die than to beg his life of her for fear of being still importuned by her love and her caresses.[g=h] There is more than one ambiguity in that comment. M. Moréri's faults will be indicated in the last remark . . .

[c=d] See Bohun, *Le Caractère de la reine Elizabeth*, The Hague, 1694, p. 5; see also the words of Balzac, Remark [(Q)].

[d=e] See Osiander, in Grotius, *De jure belli et pacis*, p. 465.

[e=f] Several historians say that she danced, but others are content to say she played the spinet . . .

[f=g] The earl of Essex was executed in 1601, and the queen was born in 1533.

[g=h] Balzac in his *Prince*, no. 62. Note that he says this satirically and to mock the poets who had placed this queen's beauty above that of Helen. A pitiable refutation!

Pope Clement VIII made exceedingly disparaging remarks about this queen which proved that he was not well informed about the state of England [(X)].

[Remarks (A)–(E) omitted.]

(F) She fluctuated between the two religions and chose eventually the Protestant.] Had all other things been equal, she would, without question, have preferred the Protestant religion to the Roman, for she had been raised in it. But I believe, also, that, to avoid the dangers she feared from the overthrow of the religion she found established, she would have followed Catholicism had she had seen any advantage in it. The hard usage she met with from the Pope,[1=8] however, obliged her to turn to the party of the Protestants. It was clear that by remaining Catholic she would have been unable to undo the disadvantage of owing her crown to a usurpation, and to a condescension from the court of Rome which would constantly have exposed her throne to innumerable disputes. As a Catholic she would have been obliged to admit that the divorce of her father from Catherine of Aragon was void, and that Anne Boleyn had been merely a concubine of Henry VIII. Now, in hereditary monarchies an illegitimate offspring cannot take precedence over the legitimate successor without overturning a constitutional law and without, in consequence, becoming a usurper. It was necessary then for Elizabeth to leave the Roman church so that she might maintain that the court of Rome was in the wrong to disallow the marriage of Anne Boleyn. But in addition to this, her penetrating mind was too well acquainted with the situation of affairs in general to leave her one moment in doubt that, by declaring against the Pope, she would be combining her interests with those of all Protestant Europe, and that through this means she could foment civil wars among her neighbours as much as she wished. Mézerai remarks that the court of France intentionally put the Pope in a very

---

[1=8] He had it declared that she was a bastard, and that he would not revoke the bulls of his predecessors; that she had been very impertinent to accede to the throne; that she could expect no grace from God if she did not renounce her claim and submit herself entirely to the Holy See. Leti, *Histoire d'Elizabeth*, 1558, vol. I, p. 315.

unfavourable humour concerning Elizabeth[2=9] since the exclusion of this princess might well have secured the kingdom of England for Mary Stuart, queen of Scots and wife to the Dauphin. The idea was a shrewd one, but France happened to play an unlucky card. . . .

[Remark (G) omitted.]

(H) . . . this circumstance would be enough to weaken the accusation laid against her of ingratitude.] The Jesuit who concealed his identity under the name of Andreas Philopatrus,[3=13] and to oppose the law of 1591 which this princess proclaimed against the Papists, made certain criticisms concerning her complaints about the behaviour of the king of Spain. She showed little recognition, he said, of the gratitude she had to that monarch who, on three occasions, had opposed those who threatened her life. Having come over to England in July 1554, he married queen Mary and found her ready to put Elizabeth to death as an accomplice in Thomas Wyat's conspiracy;[4=14] but he dissuaded her and even prevailed upon her to recall Elizabeth to court. Another plot in which Elizabeth was suspected of complicity was discovered in 1555, and it was formally debated as to whether to proceed against her with the severity of the law. The queen's counsellors were for it, but king Philip and the Spaniards who advised him supported a milder course. And therefore it was resolved that two Catholic gentlemen should be placed close to Elizabeth to watch her actions.[5=15] She was so adept at deceiving them without attracting their attention that she contrived that Thomas Strafford, exiled in France, should return to England to assume the title of king and to marry her. Accordingly he came over in April, 1557, and took possession of a maritime town. Yet he was soon captured and along with some of

---

[2=9] The king, who had an interest in . . . not letting Elizabeth take a crown that he believed belonged to the wife of his son, the dauphin, ensured that the Pope gave a cool reception to the envoy of this princess, treating her as illegitimate. Mézerai, *Abrégé chronologique*, vol. IV, p. 714, for the year 1558.

[3=13] He was Robert Parsons. See Alegambe, p. 415.

[4=14] Andreas Philopatrus, *Responsum ad edictum reginae angliae* [Response to the Edict of the Queen of England], pp. 88, 89.

[5=15] *Ibid.*, pp. 90, 91.

his faction punished with death. Elizabeth then perceived that she was in great peril and would not have escaped capital punishment had the protection of the king of Spain not played a part.[6=16]

I shall not enquire into the truth or falsity of the facts relating to these three plots, for they are discussed in detail by the British historians. I am saying only that the reproach of ingratitude, based on those three good turns of king Philip II, is not legitimate. For, from the time when Elizabeth acceded to the throne to the date of the Edict of 1591, his conduct towards her justified the complaints she made for which the so-called Philopatrus condemned her; and thus he deserved no gratitude for having saved the life of that princess. For he did not do it out of affection for her but only out of motives of utility [*l'utilité*]; and he had found his reward amply and sufficiently in Elizabeth's preservation. It was not out of a principle of clemency that he acted thus, but out of malignity towards France, or at least out of a political prudence necessary to his ambition. When a good deed proceeds from such a source we must remind those who complain of ingratitude of one of the fables of Phaedrus.[7=17] Here is another consideration: gratitude between sovereigns is not governed by the same rules as gratitude between one private individual and another. Louis XII has been greatly praised for having said that the king of France ought not to avenge the injuries done to the Duc d'Orléans. It could have equally been said and no less correctly that the king of France is not obliged to be grateful for the services rendered by the Duc d'Orléans. Do you suppose that a Duc d'Orléans, who ascends the throne by a civil war whereby success is owed to the powerful assistance provided by a neighbouring prince, should be obliged either to enter into an alliance with that prince, or to refrain from making a league with the enemies of that prince? Yet, if he does not espouse the interests of his benefactor, will he not be ungrateful? Or, will he not be even more ungrateful if he supports the interests of princes who attack his benefactor? To resolve these questions there is only one fact to establish. Namely, is it in the interest of the state, of which our

[6=16] *Ibid..*
[7=17] '... Faceres si causa mea ...' ['If you were acting on my behalf, I would be grateful ... But now you are toiling away for leftovers which the mice would have eaten, and are devouring the mice as well. So don't burden me with a favour which isn't one at all.'] Phaedrus, *Fabulae* [Fables], 1.22.

Duc d'Orléans has become master, for the neighbouring prince, who has so strongly assisted him, to increase his power or even lose part of those conquests which make him so formidable to all his neighbours? In such a case he may forget past benefits and say: it is not for the king of France to show gratitude to the Duc d'Orléans; or that he should out of gratitude ally with a prince whether victorious or vanquished. Such is the law of politics [*la loi de la politique*], and such is the jurisprudence of the state; and it was by virtue of this jurisprudence that Elizabeth was fully justified in opposing Philip II. The United Provinces had the greatest obligations both to that queen and to Henry IV of France, the two staunchest supporters of their newborn liberty. Nevertheless, if the state's interest had required the power of either the English or the French to be weakened, they would have had to concur in it with the enemies of those two nations; and there is every appearance that they would have done so. To know how this policy [*cette politique*] can be reconciled with the eternal laws of morality, and how such a contrast between the duties of private individuals and the duties of sovereigns does not destroy the immutable certainty of notions of individual decency and virtue, is another question. It is enough to say that, as human societies are now constituted, the public interest [*l'intérêt publique*] is a sun with respect to a considerable number of virtues. These virtues are stars which disappear and which evaporate, in the presence of this interest. '*Salus populi suprema lex esto.*' ['Let the safety of the people be the highest law.'] Naudé has touched on something of this in his *Coups d'état.*

(I) This policy perhaps rendered a very great service to the Protestant religion in the revolution of 1688.] A solemn promise made to a whole people and confirmed by an oath is a restraint that one can hardly violate without compromising one's reputation. Therefore there are grounds for believing that a prince bound by such a promise will keep it, even if it is only to avoid damaging his reputation. But if we see in some cases, for example a special prerogative in matters of religion, that a great queen has broken a promise of that nature, without ceasing to appear as a heroine and as the wonder of her century, we dare no longer depend upon the effects which the fear of being condemned for breaking an oath can produce. Thus the English have been able to persuade themselves that James II would not fear the consequences that might proceed from breaking his word in the matter of religion; and that since he would only be following Elizabeth's example, he could expect that his memory would receive no more condemnation than hers. Having therefore no reason whatsoever to feel confidence in his oath, they have moved smartly to prevent him from imitating their heroine. Thus you see how there are matters which serve more than one cause, both in the present and for the time to come. In general one may be confident that in statecraft there is nothing that does not have its uses.[8=18]

[Remark (K) omitted.]

(L) ... Many others suffered either the penalty of prison, or the inconveniences of exile etc.] The Protestants of England acknowledged the debt; that is, they did not deny the fact[9=25] but maintained at the same time that the conspiracies of the Papists against the government and the queen deserved those punishments. But have no fear that you will find this observation in the pamphlets of the English Catholics! You will find many condemnations along with the rhetoric appropriate for enlarging them, but they do not acknowledge the seditious activities which preceded and occasioned them. There are few accounts in which the order of these events is not obscured. It is not always bad faith which produces this confusion; a too turbulent zeal is sometimes its cause; and nature does the rest without any premeditated malice. The constitution of man is such that he fancies the afflictions that he suffers to be great, and those that he makes others suffer to be small. He feels the former but not the latter, and thus even when he remembers having been the aggressor, he insists that he had cause for complaint. He does not record in the balance sheet the harm he has inflicted; he mentions only what he has endured. Zeal, if it is not properly guided, brings memory to bear only on the injuries of truth persecuted, and it forgets the provocation given to the persecutors. If these two causes are not sufficient, bad faith, which can cause disorder on its

---

[8=18] See [*Dic,*] article 'Dolabella', vol. v; in the text, citation e from Publius Cornelius, p. 547.

[9=25] See Bohun, *Caractère d'Elizabeth*, p. 411.

own, completes the confusion. Whatever the cause, I have observed that the principal difference between the histories of the Papists and those of the Protestants consists in the ordering of the facts. Each party endeavours to dwell upon the harm which they have suffered, which they elaborate, while passing carelessly over what they have inflicted by way of reprisal or as just punishment. That is what both parties claim. Nothing is more likely to trouble the judgement of the non-partisan reader: for in order to know precisely what is to be condemned and what is to be excused in each party, it is absolutely necessary to consider the facts in their true order. If the Catholics had laid no hand upon the Protestants until after they had seen the latter pull down their churches, altars, images and crosses etc., then their violence would not have been so criminal. That is why it seems important to represent an adversary as the aggressor. A modern author has declared that he does not wish to read those whose histories transpose the order of events.[10=26] The enquiry in some cases presents no great difficulty, but in others one finds oneself so confused that without the help of some revelation to reverse the order of the Apocalypse[11=27] one could not legitimately attain any certainty.

[10=26] See letter 1 of *La Critique générale de l'Histoire du Calvinisme de M. Maimbourg* [i.e. Bayle, *OD* II, pp. 7–12].

[11=27] In saying that, one is merely supposing, as M. Jurieu has done, that the Holy Spirit had confused the facts, which he, M. Jurieu, had disentangled. Here is a part of the title of ch. 12 of his *Accomplissement de l'Apocalypse*: part 2: 'Arrangement en abrégé des événements que le Saint-Esprit avait dérangés dans les visions' ['An Abridged Ordering of Events which the Holy Spirit had Confused in Visions'].

Gregory

[Bayle takes for granted that Pope Gregory I had wielded massive civil power and that the historian should ask if he had used it well. He accuses Gregory of lacking principle in making conversions. For when his missionaries preached to the English pagans, he had taught that in Christ's kingdom there were only voluntary subjects. Yet within the Empire itself, the mission of 'conversion' had degenerated into debating the relative effectiveness of inducements vs. punishments. In Remark (E), Bayle shows that Gregory's ambiguity remained Christendom's received wisdom. He concludes, augmenting the thesis of his Commentaire philosophique *(1686), that the society that was not tyrannical would propose to the unorthodox neither punishments nor rewards. In Remark (R), he shows how a critical scholar should approach a text that apparently gave credence to miracles.]*

GREGORY I, known as the Great, was born in Rome of a patrician family. He revealed so much ability in the exercise of the office of senator that the Emperor Justinian the Younger made him prefect of Rome.[a,b=*1] He gave up this dignity when he found it was too worldly, and retired[c=*2] to a monastery [(A)] under the discipline of

[a] M. Maimbourg, *L'Histoire du pontificat de saint Grégoire-le-Grand* [Paris, 1686]. [Bayle had reviewed it in *NRL*, February 1686, pp. 493–8.]
[b=*1] This was about the year 537, according to Abbé L.-J. Leclerc. [The foregoing note was inserted by the editor of the edition of 1820–4. Abbé Leclerc was editor of the *Dictionnaire*'s edition of Trevoux, 1734.]
[c=*2] This was about the year 575, according to Leclerc.

the Abbot Valentius.[d=b] He was recalled a short time later by Pope Pelagius II, who made him his seventh deacon[e=*3] and sent him as *nuncio* to Constantinople to solicit assistance against the Lombards. He returned to Rome[f=*4] after the death of the emperor [(B)], serving for some time as secretary to Pope Pelagius after which he obtained leave to return to his monastery.[g=c] When he thought he was at last to enjoy peace and tranquillity he was elected Pope: by the clergy, by the Senate, and by the people of Rome. Eventually, after seeking all imaginable ways of avoiding this burden [(C)], he was finally obliged to accept it.[h=d] It appeared from his conduct that they could not have elected to this great responsibility a more deserving person. For besides being learned and instructing the church through his personal example of writing and preaching, he proved very able at directing the minds of princes in the interests of religion whether spiritual or temporal. I could get carried away by the intricacies of this activity so I shall refrain from enlarging upon it since anyone may inform themselves of it in the work of a modern writer.[i=e] I shall observe only that our Pope undertook the conversion of the English (D), and that he brought it to a fruitful conclusion through the assistance of a woman,[k=f] according to the familiar pattern of revolutions in religion. His maxims concerning the constraint of conscience were far from consistent and he sometimes fell into gross negligence (E). And indeed it is very difficult to have rules for a thing so contrary to reason. As if to make up for it, his requirements concerning the chastity of ecclesiastics were extremely strict [(F)]. For he claimed that a man who had lost his virginity should not be admitted to the priesthood, and he ordered that postulants should be interrogated upon this point. He exempted widowers from that condition provided they had been constant in their marriage, and that they had lived for a long period in a state of continence. He was also very severe with respect to

---

[d=b] Others called him Valentine.
[e=*3]   That is to say one of the seven archdeacons of Rome, according to Leclerc who adds that, according to Fleuri, it was [Pope] Benedict I who conferred that dignity upon him.
[f=*4] In 583 according to Leclerc.
[g=c] Maimbourg, *Histoire du pontificat de saint Grégoire*, pp. 7, 8.
[h=d] His investiture was on 3 September 590.
[i=e] Maimbourg, in *L'Histoire du pontificat de saint Grégoire*.
[k=f] See Remark (D).

calumny [(G)]. All things duly considered he deserves the epithet 'great', but one cannot excuse the way he perverted praise in order to ingratiate himself into the friendship of a usurper [(H)] who was appallingly involved in one of the most execrable assassinations that history has known. It is a glaring instance of the enslavement into which a man may fall when he seeks to sustain himself in high office. If we compare his manner of flattering the Emperor Phocas with the way in which he exploited an exceedingly corrupt queen of France [(I)], we must acknowledge that they who obliged him to be Pope knew him better than he knew himself. They perceived that he had all the cunning and all the subterfuge that were needed to procure powerful protectors and provide the church with worldly blessings. It is highly probable that the zeal which he displayed in thwarting the ambition of the Patriarch of Constantinople was insincere [(K)].

It is unlikely that he ordered the destruction of the fine monuments to the former magnificence of the Romans [(L)] lest those who came to Rome should give more attention to the triumphal arches than to holy things. Let us make the same judgement about the accusation that he was responsible for burning a vast number of pagan works [(M)], and in particular those of Titus Livy [(N)]. He died on 10 March 604. I shall make no observation concerning his works, referring my reader instead to M. du Pin whose work is more readily available than this Dictionary will ever be. I almost forgot to mention this Pope's great fondness for the psalmody of the church [(O)].

The work which Father Denys de Sainte-Marthe[l=g] has had published[m=h] under the title *L'Histoire de Saint Grégoire-le-grand* had not appeared when I wrote this article. I have recently seen this history and it seems to me that were it not for the fact that the author regularly intersperses his praise with various observations explaining the context or illuminating the facts or offering a refutation of some writer, it would have been an uninterrupted panegyric to the great man. In his preface he gives a catalogue of other authors who have written the life of Saint Gregory, and it is there that he censures certain shortcomings of the minister

---

[l=g] Benedictine of the Congregation of Saint-Maur.
[m=h] Rouen, 1697, in quarto.

Pierre du Moulin in addition to those which I myself mention in Remark [(C)]. He seems little enraptured with Maimbourg [(P)]; he refutes Cardinal Baronius on the noviciate of Saint Gregory and he objects to several opinions of M. de Goussinville.[n=i] . . .

I do not find that he censures Pope Gregory for anything. Indeed he [de Sainte-Marthe] acts the part of his apologist in everything: on the praise he bestowed on Phocas and Queen Brunehaud, on the many amazing miracles related by this pope in his *Dialogues* (R), and on the inconsistency of his principles concerning religious persecution etc. He is one of those who deny that Saint Gregory delivered the soul of the Emperor Trajan[o=k] from hell. If it were true that some of this Pope's writings were burnt after his death – and that other papers were saved only after an incident [(S)] similar to the one that had formerly led the Roman people to kill their senators as murderers of Romulus[p=l] – some people might conclude that the glory of this Pope, like that of several other ancient fathers, resembles certain rivers which though minute at their source become exceedingly large when they are a long way from it. Something might be said against this comparison but, generally speaking, the objects of memory are of a nature different from the objects of sight. For the latter tend to lessen proportionately to our distance from them, whereas the former commonly increase in proportion to our remoteness from their time and place.[q=m] . . .

[Remarks (A)–(C) omitted.]

(D) He undertook the conversion of the English.] He sent some monks from his monastery[1=16] to England under the leadership of Augustine their abbot[2=17] whom the bishops of France consecrated

---

[n=i] Editor of the *Œuvres de saint Grégoire* [Works of Saint Gregory], 1675.
[o=k] See [*Dic*,] article 'Trajan', Remark (A), vol. xiv.
[p=l] See Plutarch, in the *Life of Romulus*.
[q=m] 'Omnia post obitum . . .' ['The passing of time makes all things greater long after their disappearance.']

[1=16] That is from the monastery which he had founded at his own house in Rome.
[2=17] Maimbourg, *Histoire du pontificat de saint Grégoire*, p. 201.

first bishop of the English nation by virtue of the authority they had received from Saint Gregory.[3=18] Ethelred reigned in England at that time, and he had married Aldeberge or Berthe, daughter of Charibert, king of France, a young princess of much learning, well instructed in letters and exceedingly zealous for the Catholic faith.[4=19] She encouraged him to listen to the Pope's emissaries. He bade them to come into his presence but, in conformity with one of the ancient superstitions of the people, he would hear them only in an open field, so that had they planned to use any charm or secret spell to deceive him, it might dissipate in the open air and lose its potency ... After listening to them in silence, he told them that everything he had heard pleased him immensely. But, given that their inspiring words did not appear to him indubitably true, especially the magnificent promises they had made concerning an eternal life, he thought it inexpedient to forsake what he had learned from his ancestors to chase after what was uncertain.[5=20] He permitted them to preach in his kingdom just as he permitted all who found their doctrine pleasing to embrace it. He himself was converted.[6=21] And because the example of kings is commonly very persuasive, either for good or for ill, the greater part of the English embraced the Christian faith as he did, though what finally brought about their conversion was that their method was as gentle as it was moderate. For he used no violence and he forced no one to renounce their ancient superstitions against their will, having learnt from his divines that the homage rendered to Jesus Christ must be voluntary.[7=22] The queen contributed greatly to these conversions. For she encouraged the king, her husband, not only to deal favourably with the missionaries, but additionally to become a convert himself. There has hardly ever been a revolution in religion, either for good or for ill, in which women have not been a party to the commotion. M. Maimbourg has given us certain examples.[8=23] One may say that,

---

[3=18] *Ibid.*, p. 206.
[4=19] *Ibid.*, p. 207.
[5=20] *Ibid.*, p. 208, in the year 597.
[6=21] *Ibid.*, p. 212, year 600.
[7=22] See the *Nouvelles de la république des lettres*, February 1686, for objections to Maimbourg's comparison of the methods used for making conversions by Ethelred and Louis XIV [*OD* I, pp. 493–8].
[8=23] *Histoire du pontificat de saint Grégoire*, p. 69.

as the devil made use in former times of three empresses,[9=*] one from Licinius, one from Constantius, and the third from Valens, to establish the Arian heresy in the East, so God, in order to use the same weapons as the enemy, sought the help of three illustrious queens: Clotilde wife of Clovis, Ingonde wife of saint Ermineigilde, and Theodelinde wife of Agilulphe. Thus he sanctified the West by converting the French from paganism, and he exterminated Arianism from Spain and Italy through the conversion of the Visigoths and the Lombards. In another work, however, Maimbourg speaks only of the service rendered by women to evil causes . . .'[10=24]

(E) He sometimes fell into gross negligence.] The lack of consistency in Gregory's maxims is manifest; for though he disapproved of forcing the Jews to be baptised, he did support the use of force to bring heretics back to the church. 'Saint Avit, bishop of Clermont in the Auvergne, was one day accompanying his clergy in a procession through the town . . . suddenly, all the people who were following him fell upon the Jewish synagogue and ransacked it so that nothing of it remained but the land completely flattened and without so much as one stone upon another.'[11=25] The prelate, hoping to take advantage of so favourable an opportunity, ordered that the Jews should be told that they must convert or depart from the diocese. Three hundred were converted and the rest were obliged to depart. This example was followed soon afterwards in Spain, in Italy, and above all in Provence where what was done was worse. For without even taking the trouble to attempt to convert them to the Christian faith by sacred instructions and by good example, they forced them to receive holy baptism whether or not they were willing, which caused as many profanations of a sacred ritual and as many sacrileges as there were baptised Jews.

Saint Gregory, to prevent [the return of] such a great evil, wrote[12=*1] to Virgilius, archbishop of Arles, and to Theodore, bishop of Marseille – two extraordinarily good men – commanding them

---

[9=*] Constantia, Eusebia, Dominica.
[10=24] *Histoire du grand schisme d'Occident*, bk. 2, p. 183, bk. 4, p. 69 . . .
[11=25] Maimbourg, *Histoire du pontificat de saint Grégoire*, p. 239.
[12=*1] 'Dum quispiam ad baptismatis fontem . . .' ['When anyone comes to the baptismal font led there not by preaching but by force, if he returns to his former superstition, his "rebirth" causes him to die a worse death.']

to see that the Jews should not be forced to receive baptism lest the sacred fonts, whereby men are reborn to a divine life through baptism, should be an occasion for a second death through an apostasy more fatal than the first. Some time earlier he had written the same thing to the bishop of Terracina.[13=26] He ordered him to 'permit the Jews complete liberty to assemble in the place that was granted them for the celebration of their feasts'.[14=27] This is what he added some time after to the bishop of Cagliari in Sardinia. The laws, he told him,

> certainly do forbid the Jews to build new synagogues, but they permit them, nevertheless, to possess the old ones without any molestation on that account.[15=*2] And he adds what he said some time later in respect of the Jews of Marseille: that it was through preaching and not violence that they were to be won to the faith; that God requires sacrifices that are made by the mind and the heart to be voluntary; and he adds that those who are converted only by force and by necessity return to their vomit as soon as they can.[16=28]

How very true that is! But here follows a strange distinction which makes a monstrous illogicality of his system. [For in Maimbourg's words]

> There was not, in his opinion, a very great difference between infidels and heretics, especially at the beginning of heresies, because the latter had to be treated as rebels, traitors, and perjurers, who had violated their faith to God and to the Catholic church from which they had departed by reason of rebelling against her and by attempting, as far as they could, to destroy her. One can thus require them to return to their duty and to the obedience which they owe; and if they do not, one may properly punish them – according to Imperial Laws, according to the fathers of the church, and according even to Calvin who, to justify his conduct

---

[13=26] Maimbourg, *Histoire du pontificat de saint Grégoire*, p. 240.
[14=27] *Ibid.*, p. 241.
[15=*2] 'Quia sicut legalis definitio Judaeos . . .' ['For although the prescriptions of the law do not allow Jews to build new synagogues they permit them to retain the existing ones undisturbed.']
[16=28] Maimbourg, *Histoire du pontificat de saint Grégoire*, p. 242.

towards Servetus whom he caused to be condemned to the flames at Geneva, wrote a treatise upon this subject. The same treatment is not appropriate for pagans, Jews, or Mahometans, nor even for those heretics who, being born in a heresy which they have acquired from their ancestors, have no more been raised in the church than have infidels. One should not use direct force to convert them, particularly if they have been tolerated for some time. But Saint Gregory teaches us, as much by his doctrine as by his example, that it is right to compel them indirectly, by virtue of the Gospel which says, *Compelle intrare* ['Compel them to come in'].[17=29]

The task could be undertaken in two ways: the first was through treating the obdurate with severity, the second was through giving rewards to those who converted. [In Maimbourg's words:]

This was why Saint Gregory required the Manicheans, obstinate in their heresy, to be persecuted; and why he gave orders to the bishop of Cagliari to tax excessively the peasants and those pagans who were under the church and worked its lands, and who refused persistently and stubbornly to embrace Christianity; but why, at the same time, he enjoined that those Jews who converted should be exempted from one third of what they were obliged to pay to the Roman church in respect of the inherited lands which they cultivated in Sicily, so that other Jews, attracted by the expectation of a similar concession, would more readily turn Christian. Moreover, to those who might consider these opportunistic conversions to be suspect, he says[18=*] that if these people merely dissemble and are not truly converted much will still be gained, since their children, at least, will become good Catholics. [Maimbourg, pp. 243, 244]

The whole [of Maimbourg's text] could provide the subject for a long treatise [Bayle's reference is to his *Commentaire philosophique*] but here I shall have to be content with a few notes.

[17=29] *Ibid.*, pp. 243, 244.
[18=*] 'Etsi ipsi minus fideliter . . .' ['Although they themselves come with little faith, their children are baptised who will soon have greater faith. We convert, therefore, either these men or their sons.']

1. It is undeniable that the choice between conversion and exile is very harsh and highly likely to produce hypocrites. For what will people of an ordinary piety not do, in order not to be parted from the sweetness of their native land? And, in fact, all who put forward this alternative condemn it as the act of a tyrant wherever they themselves are subjected to it: a clear sign that they are judging the justice of an action merely by the rule of their own interest. 'Quod volumus sanctum est.' ['What we will is sacrosanct.']

2. If it is asserted that the church can treat all who leave her in the way that civil states [*états humains*] treat rebels, it is to confer upon her a power which she does not possess. The church can have none but voluntary subjects; she can never require an oath which derogates from the law of the directive which requires us, at all times and in all places, to follow the light of conscience. Consequently, those who break the oath which they have given to obey that light must be compared to those who prefer primitive and absolute oaths to posterior and conditional oaths. For it would be an act of impiety to commit oneself to a body of faith without pre-supposing it to be right and true. And thus each oath by which one links oneself to the church is conditional, while the commitment to the light of conscience is natural, essential, and absolute. The worst that can be said of those who, to obey their conscience, break the oath they have given to the church is that they were once enlightened but have become ignorant. But where are the well-governed states that enact penalties against those who forget their learning, or who acquire ideas which persuade them that what they once took for error is the truth? Let us say, therefore, that if the church could punish as rebels those who leave her, she would have more power than the most despotic prince.[19=30] For she could punish changing one's mind about certain things as a capital crime.

3. It is not difficult to discern the fallacy of the distinction; for a man who has been raised in a church could never renounce his right [*la faculté*] to leave it once his conscience prompted him to side with another communion; and thus he has as much right [*droit*] to follow that communion as those who have been raised in it. For the

---

[19=30] That is, considered only as a sovereign; for note that sovereigns who punish what they call heresy do it only in respect of their own religion and, properly speaking, therefore, it is their religion which punishes: QUOD NOTANDUM ['note this'].

full justification [*tout le droit*] of the latter consists in their being persuaded that their religion is right and true.

4. My maxims are so incontrovertible that every party agrees with them when it does not presuppose his own principle. A Jew, far from castigating as a traitor and a rebel a man who renounces Christianity to embrace Judaism, calls him faithful to God, to the truth, and to the true church. He calls none perfidious save those who renounce the Jewish religion. This is the way of every religion.

5. As to the two methods of *Compelle intrare* ['Compel them to enter'], I refer the reader to the *Philosophical Commentary*. I shall observe only that the expression 'traffickers in the word of God'[20=31] would apply *par excellence* to those who use either of these methods [inducements or punishments] in the profession of making converts;[21=32] and that it is impossible, morally, for the sovereigns who authorise them not to be dragged down by those who instigate these affairs into consequences where there is not only great injustice but also massive corruption.[22=33]

6. The reason given by Saint Gregory for not wishing to see the Jews converted by punishment is completely sound: it is, said he, because those who are converted in such a manner 'return to their vomit as soon as they can'. But, by the same token, he was very much in the wrong to order that conversions should be made by surtaxing the obdurate, and by exempting from a third of the tax those who turned Christian. For it is manifest that those who are converted in this manner likewise must 'return to their vomit as soon as they can'.

7. And if the reasons he gives for requiring the Jews to be converted by increasing the taxes upon the obdurate and by remitting those of the converted are sound, then he was mistaken to object to

---

[20=31] 2 Corinthians, 2:17.

[21=32] This evokes the following two verses of Ennius: ' Nec mi aurum posco, nec mi pretium dederitis, / Nec cauponantes bellum, sed belligerantes.' ['I ask not for gold, nor will you pay me any price: we are not trading but waging war.'] Cicero, *De officiis* [On Duties], 1.12.

[22=33] See *Nouvelles lettres sur l'Histoire du Calvinisme de M. Maimbourg*, vol. I, pp. 205 *et seq.*; and what is said concerning the ways of making converts by Queen Mary in England. *Nouvelles de la république des lettres*, November 1685. [See *OD* I, pp. 416–19. The book reviewed by Bayle was *Histoire de la réformation de l'église d'Angleterre* ... 'translated from the English of M. Burnet by M. Rosemond', London, 1685.]

the policy of forcing them to receive baptism; for consider his argument: 'if these converts dissemble, one will still gain much, in that their children, at least, will become good Catholics.' Could the very same not be said of those who are baptised under compulsion? One cannot rescue him therefore from lamentable inconsistency.

[Remarks (F)–(Q) omitted.]

(R) . . . the credulity with which this pope reported so many miracles in his *Dialogues*.] 'Some scholars who object to the recounting of so many miracles have questioned whether Saint Gregory is actually the author of those *Dialogues* since they consider them unworthy of so great a divine.'[23=86] Father Denys de Sainte-Marthe, who speaks thus, resolves the doubts of those learned persons with sound arguments and shows them that those *Dialogues* are genuinely the work of Saint Gregory. M. du Pin confirms this factual opinion.[24=87] But he admits, at the same time, that 'it seems to him' that they are unworthy of the 'gravity and discernment of this holy Pope', being full of 'extraordinary miracles, and tales that are almost incredible. It is true [du Pin says] that he relates them upon the faith of others; but he should not so lightly have accorded his own belief nor related them subsequently as reliable material . . .' The stories which are told in these dialogues are rarely based on anything other than the tales of unlettered old men or upon hearsay accounts. They perform such extraordinary and frequent miracles, and often concerning matters of so little consequence, that it is very difficult to believe anything at all. There are stories which, with a little trouble, could have been checked against the lives of those who tell them, as for example the voluntary imprisonment of Saint Paulin under the king of the Vandals. Visions, apparitions, and dreams are more frequently recorded there than in any other author. Also Saint Gregory admits that one had discovered more about other worlds in those times than in any preceding century. But I do not believe that anyone would wish to subscribe to all

---

[23=86] Sainte-Marthe, *Histoire de saint Grégoire*, p. 273.
[24=87] Du Pin, *Bibliothèque des auteurs ecclésiastiques* [Collection of Ecclesiastical Authors], vol. v, p. 138, Dutch edition.

those tales. Father Denys de Sainte-Marthe acknowledges, 'that he himself would not have vouched for the truth of every miracle or every vision that one reads about in those *Dialogues*'.[25=88] Nevertheless he does not condemn the practice of this Pope. 'Our saint', he [de Sainte-Marthe] writes, 'believed that he should not scorn these things given the edifying content of the matters he related. It is for the reader to examine prudently, as he reads, what degree of certainty Saint Gregory attributes to them, and who his authorities are.' Manifestly one observes here the language of the apologist who holds that Saint Gregory is in no way at fault. Harm is done because the arguments, which he puts forward to support his view, are unsound. For if a story could be accepted as true on the pretext that there were edifying matters in it, what fables and what pious histories purporting to be true might not be permissibly uttered? Simply to refrain from stating in specific terms 'I record this as certain and reliable' is not acceptable practice; nor is neglecting wholly reputable contemporary authors in favour of ancient tradition; nor is it permissible as a precaution whereby an author could absolve himself. For if he wishes to demonstrate that he does not place the facts in such a degree of certitude that he would seriously and energetically wish to persuade his readers of them, he is obliged to say, formally and specifically: 'I put this to you as a doubtful matter, you may believe it if you wish, but I have no good evidence for it.' Every author who relates a miraculous event without indicating – by whatever means are necessary to make it known – that he doubts it, or that others ought to doubt it, manifestly indicates thereby that he relates it as a matter of fact. Let it not be retorted to me that no historian is permitted to suppress whatever seems false to him; and that his duty requires him to give an account of all matters which are well attested, though he himself does not believe them to be true. Let no one – I say – make this objection to me since it does not address my point. My thesis concerns the historian who fails to indicate his own suspicions – by whatever means are necessary to make them known – and the liberty he imparts thereby to his reader to reject his narration. Every good historian who discusses a matter which he judges to be fanciful adds

---

[25=88] Sainte-Marthe, *Histoire de saint Grégoire*, pp. 275, 276.

'it is said' or some other phrase which shows even more precisely what he himself thinks of it;[26=89] and therefore when he adds nothing of that nature, it is a sign that he is convinced of the truth of what he has reported, and that he would like his reader to give credit to it. Now that is the usual aim of all who relate things of which they are themselves persuaded. They want to seem persuasive to those whom they address, and it would be to disoblige them, and to express contempt, were a reader to reply that he believed nothing of what had been said. Now if these maxims are true – with respect to a theologian who tells of miracles either in a work of morals, or in a treatise of devotion, or generally in a work such as that of Saint Gregory – one must suppose not only that this Pope recounted no miracles which he believed false, but also that he wanted all his readers to acknowledge as true all the prodigies which he related. He is thus guilty of too much credulity. Nor would he have had any discernment if it had not occurred to him that not all his readers would overlook his faults; for if one has the prudence to reject a part of what one relates, clearly it is not because of the assistance it provides. Observe then that a person would justify himself very inadequately were he so foolhardy as to reply that he did not believe all that he had uttered. In that case, I would ask: did he want his readers to give credit to everything he said? If he did, then he was an impostor; if he did not, then why did he take the trouble to write such material? The option which is the least disadvantageous to his memory is to say that he was both too credulous and too short on judgement.

This is how one could oppose the apology which de Sainte-Marthe seeks to make for those alleged miracles reported by this great Pope. The apologist does not insist that he believes that there were many miracles in this category in the *Dialogues* of Saint

---

[26=89] 'Equidem plura transcribo . . .' ['I for my part copy down more than I believe. For I cannot bear to present as fact those matters about which I have my doubts. Nor can I bear to overlook the tradition I have received.'] Q. Curtius [The History of Alexander the Great], bk. 9, ch. 1. See the Commentary of Freinshem where you will find many similar passages relating to other historians. See also Tacitus, *Annals*, 4.11; and Maimbourg, bk. 5, *De l'histoire des croisades* [History of the Crusades], cited in *Les Pensées diverses sur les comètes*, p. 293 [see *APD, CPD, PD*]; La Mothe le Vayer in *Discours sur l'histoire* recounts various passages where Titus Livy takes various precautions when reporting prodigies.

Gregory, but one may easily presume it. He goes to great lengths to explain why the prodigious things related in those *Dialogues* were very frequent in those days. One of his arguments relies on the fact that there were at that time many heretics to convert, and that there were many Catholics who did not believe in 'the immortality of the soul and the resurrection of the body'.[27=90]

> It is a reliable fact [*une vérité constante*] that in the time of Saint Gregory the age saw many people vacillate in respect of those two capital points of our doctrine and religion. He[28=*] had the humility to confess that he himself had entertained doubts about the resurrection. It is for this reason that, in many of his homilies, he was particularly concerned with persuading his readers of these facts. Since there have always been libertines within the Catholic church, both at its core and in its exterior communion, there have always been many people who, having an interest in there being no life beyond the present, no resurrection, and no last judgement, were accordingly easily persuaded of such matters. For it is a short step from a corrupt heart to an erroneous mind. Whatever the reason, it is certain that Italy in the age of Saint Gregory and Rome, in particular, abounded with such unbelievers. It would be pointless for me undertake to prove it after what the most recent translator of the *Dialogues* has said in an excellent preface. Gregory of Tours[29=*1] recounts a debate which he had with a priest of his church who asserted dogmatically that he did not expect a resurrection. He speaks similarly of a deacon of the church of Paris who, in order to seem clever, fell into the same error by appearing very eager to discuss this article of faith. We can judge from this that there were many others in France engaged in so dangerous a heresy. Those who read the *Dialogues* will learn there of Peter the Deacon who knew of

---

[27=90] Sainte-Marthe, *Histoire de saint Grégoire*, p. 274.
[28=*] *Homilia 26 in Evangeliis* [Homily 26 on the Gospels]: 'Multi enim de resurrectione . . .' ['For there were many who had doubts about the resurrection, just as I once did.']
[29=*1] Gregory of Tours, *Historia francorum* [History of the Franks], 1.10.13 and 14.

many among the Christians who doubted whether the soul continued to live after it was separated from the body.[30=*2]

Was it not therefore in conformity with the mercy of God that, to remedy the weakness of these unfortunate unbelievers, he brought forth miracles in abundance at that time? And can Saint Gregory be blamed for having collected them together?

In respect of the above quotation I shall make two short observations. One is that if those unbelieving Catholics questioned only whether the soul was immortal, or whether bodies might be raised from the grave, they were very poor logicians; for from the moment that one first concedes the truth of the Gospel, it is absurd and paltry to form any doubts about those two particular articles. The other is that there have never perhaps been so many unbelievers as in the sixteenth and seventeenth centuries – I mean unbelievers who were not content to wreck the building while retaining the foundations, but those who rejected everything whatsoever, foundations included. Furthermore in those two centuries there were a great many heretics[31=91] to convert. It follows therefore that miracles in these two recent centuries should have been at least as frequent as in the century of Saint Gregory. You may conclude from this that the reasoning of Father Denys de Sainte-Marthe proves nothing because it proves too much.

[30=*2] [*Ibid.*,] bk 3, ch. 38; and bk 4, ch. 4.
[31=91] That is, according to the definition of Father Denys de Sainte-Marthe, above, bk 4, ch. 7, p. 613.

Hobbes

[Hobbes, Bayle observes, had constructed an elegant theory of a society that was apparently secure against troubles. His mistake was to suppose that because order was an initial condition of justice it was a sufficient condition. For Hobbes's fear of sectarian diversity had led him to defend the very arguments advanced in Gallican France for revoking the toleration accorded to Huguenots. Bayle finds less to contest in Hobbes's treatment of monarchy and democracy in the ancient world. Polemicists who disputed the merits of these rival institutions would always be able to make a case for condemning their opponents' favoured system. In Remark (M), Bayle defends Hobbes against malicious pens which had alleged that the philosopher's materialist physics were incompatible with the piety of an ethical Christian.]

HOBBES (Thomas), one of the greatest minds of the sixteenth century, was born at Malmesbury in England in 1588 [(A)]. He had made great progress in languages [(B)] when at fourteen years of age he was sent to Oxford where for five years he studied Aristotle's philosophy. Afterwards he joined William Cavendish, who a little after was made earl of Devonshire, to become tutor to his eldest son. He travelled in France and in Italy with his pupil; and, becoming aware that he remembered little of his Greek or his Latin, and that the philosophy of Aristotle, in which he had made such great progress, was despised by the wisest heads, he devoted himself entirely to literature as soon as he returned to his country. Since among the Greek historians he preferred Thucydides, he translated him into English and published his translation in the year 1628 with a view to showing the English, through the history of the Athenians, the disorders and confusions of democratic government (C). In the year 1629 he undertook to travel into France with a young English lord[a] and during that tour applied himself to the study of mathematics [(D)]. In the year 1631 he joined the household of the countess of Devonshire,[b] who had a son of thirteen to whom he became tutor, and who travelled under his direction in France and Italy. During his stay in Paris he studied physics, making a special study of the causes of instinctive behaviour. He discussed the topic with Father Mersenne. He was called back to England in the year 1637, but foreseeing the Civil War after reflecting on the events which occurred at the first sessions of the Parliament of 1640, he sought a quiet refuge in Paris where he might philosophise in peace with Mersenne, Gassendi, and certain other men of distinction. He there wrote his treatise *De cive* (E), publishing just a few copies in the year 1642. He taught mathematics to the prince of Wales who had been forced to withdraw to France, and devoted the rest of his time to writing his *Leviathan* (F) which he had printed in England in 1651. He continued to stay in Paris. Though he testified that he believed in worship according to the rites of the Anglican church [(G)], it did not prevent him from being made odious to the Episcopalians, and so effectively that he was ordered to stay out of the king's circle.[c] This was the reason for his return to England where he lived with the earl of Devonshire [(H)] in an obscure manner, considering his great merit. He drew from his obscurity the advantage of having more leisure to work on his book *De corpore*, and some others[d=*] [(I)].

He received great marks of esteem from Charles II who was restored in 1660 [(K)] . . . He loved his country, he was loyal to his king, was a good friend, and was charitable and reliable. He was nevertheless thought to be an atheist, though those who wrote his

---

[a] He was called Gervais Clifton. The father of his first pupil died in 1626, and this pupil in 1628.

[b] Widow of the earl of Devonshire, father of his first pupil.

[c] See Remark (F).

[d=*] [Note by the editor of the edition of 1820–4:] Chaufepié gives a list of forty-two works written or translated by Hobbes. His small work on logic was, says M. Barbier, translated into French by M. Destutt-Tracy at the end of the third part of his *Eléments d'idéologie.*

Life$^{e=*}$ maintain that he held wholly orthodox opinions about the nature of God (M). It was said too that he was frightened of phantoms and demons (N). They replied that this was a fabrication. They frankly stated that in his youth he had loved women and a little wine;$^{f=d}$ and that nevertheless he lived a bachelor's life in order not to be distracted from his studies in philosophy. He reflected far more than he read [(O)] and was never concerned with acquiring a large library. He died on 4 December 1679 at the house of the earl of Devonshire after an illness of six weeks.$^{g=c}$

[Remarks (A)–(B) omitted.]

(C) The disorders and confusions of democratic government.] I have known men of intelligence who are astonished that in kingdoms where the authority of the prince is almost boundless the instructors of youth are permitted to use the works of the ancient Greeks and Romans in which anti-monarchical theories abound, and where there are many examples of the love of liberty. But this is no more surprising than to see that republican states permit professors of law to lecture on codes and digests which presuppose the supreme and inviolable authority of an emperor. We see here two things which might be thought equally surprising but which fundamentally ought to surprise no one. For, setting aside many explanations that might be offered, might we not say that works which contain the poison, whether concerning monarchies or republics, also contain the antidote? If you see, on the one hand,

---

$^{e=*}$ [Editorial note to the edition of 1820–4:] *Thomæ Hobbes Angli, Malmesburiensis philosophi, Vita.* Carolopoli, 1681, in octavo, containing three pieces: (1) *Thomæ Hobbes Malmesburiensis Vita,* formerly attributed to Hobbes, but which according to Wood is by Rymer. (2) *Vita Hobbianae auctarium,* by Richard Blackburn, doctor, d. in 1716 (and not Radulphe Bathurst as Bayle had said initially, an error which he acknowledged in his letter to [Pierre] Coste of 8 April 1704); (3) *Thomæ Hobbes Malmesburiensis Vita carmine expressa, auctore seipso.* The latter piece had been published in London in 1680 . . . These three pieces were reprinted in 1682, and it was on this edition that Bayle relied. For details consult the note by Desmaizeau to the letter from Bayle, 8 April 1704. [For the text of the letter to Coste, see *OD* IV, pp. 840–2, and for Desmaizeaux's comments on Bayle's initial error, see *ibid.*, p. 841, n. 4.]
$^{f=d}$ . . .*Vita Hobbesii* [*Life of Hobbes*], 1682.
$^{g=c}$ Taken from his *Life*, printed in 1682.

those great precepts of liberty and those fine examples of courage
with which republics have been sustained or restored, you see, on
the other, the tumultuous events and the factions and conspiracies
that afflicted, and finally ruined, an infinite number of small states
which in ancient Greece showed such opposition to tyranny. Does
this picture not offer a lesson to disabuse those who are scared by
monarchy's very idea? Hobbes supposed so,[1=3] since, with that end
in view, he published the viewpoint of an Athenian historian. But
reverse the coin, and you will find the picture to be capable of
teaching a completely different lesson, and one which is likely to
confirm one's horror of monarchy: for how did it happen, one will
ask, that the Greeks and the Romans preferred exposure to such
abominations to living under a monarchy? Did it not come about
because of the deplorable conditions to which their tyrants had
reduced them? And must monarchy not have seemed an evil very
severe, very unbearable, and highly disgraceful, if they were willing
to pay so high a price to deliver themselves from it? It is undeniable
that the description given in history of the conduct of some monarchs indeed arouses horror and makes our hair stand on end. Do
not reply to me that more disorder, generally speaking, has been
generated by the conspiracies that have put an end to tyranny than
there would have been by patiently enduring it. Do not point out
to me what I have already said in the article on Hiero.[2=4] The Syra-
cusans who had enjoyed a wonderful prosperity under the long
reign of that prince soon lost heart under his successor who governed tyrannically. They killed him in the second year of his reign,
and shortly after they put to death Hiero's two daughters and three
grand-daughters. Of these five women there were only three against
whom there was any complaint, and furthermore they were fugitives
at the foot of the altar. Was this not to overthrow one tyranny to
set up another that was worse?[3=5] Was Titus Livy[4=6] wrong to
observe upon this subject that people are unable to keep within the

---

[1=3] See [*Dic,*] article 'Pericles', Remark (Q), vol. XI.
[2=4] See [*Dic,*] article 'Hiero II', Remark (E).
[3=5] 'Ne tyrannos ulciscendo . . .' ['Lest those who punish tyrants end up themselves
by repeating the very atrocities which they themselves had abhorred.'] This was
the case that Heraclea, Hiero's daughter, put to her murderers. Livy, *Ab urbe
condita* [The History of Rome], 24.
[4=6] See his words, at citation 21 of [*Dic,*] article 'Hiero II'.

limits of moderation? They are humble to the point of servility when they obey; but insolent in the highest degree when they command. Nor was the massacre of these five women the impetuous action of a few private men; it was commanded by the Senate and the People of Syracuse while the memory of Hiero II was still fresh in their minds: a prince whom they had loved so tenderly and so rightly. The iniquity of their barbarous decree was so patent that they soon recognised it and revoked it; but it served no purpose for it had already been carried out.

> Tandem vulneribus confectae . . . ['Finally they were overcome by their wounds and collapsed dying, their blood spilt everywhere. Chance made the slaughter more pitiable than it already was. For a messenger arrived shortly afterwards to put a stop to the execution, since violent emotions had suddenly turned into pity. Pity was followed by anger, because there had been such haste in exacting the punishment and no room had been left for either changing their mind or stepping back from their anger. And so the people protested.']5=7

The in-fighting of the factions did not end with the elimination of the entire royal family. It increased day by day and in a very short time it overturned the liberty and the sovereignty of their country. The factions improperly exposed Syracuse to the hostility of the Romans who besieged and conquered her. Silius Italicus has given an adequate description of the chaos into which that city sank following the extermination of the tyrant and his family. The Romans knew precisely how to build a famous conquest upon that sort of disarray. The town's turmoil encouraged them to besiege it.

> Saevos namque pati fastus . . . ['Those men who were no longer willing to endure the young ruler's violent pride, passion for blood-feasts and combination of shamefulness and cruelty formed a conspiracy. Inflamed by anger and fear, they slew him. There was no end to their slaughter. They even massacred the women. His innocent sisters were seized and put to the sword. New-found freedom wielded arms and threw off subjugation. Some chose the Carthaginian

---

5=7 Livy, 24.26.

side, some the Italians, since they knew them. There was no shortage of men who were incensed but who preferred to join neither side.']⁶⁼⁸

This you may interpret as you wish, but you will never argue convincingly enough for those who are determined to oppose monarchy. They will reply that since the disorders of monarchy can be remedied only by such abominable disturbances, you must conclude that it is a mighty evil.

[Remark (D) omitted.]

(E) He wrote his treatise *De Cive* in Paris.] He revised it soon afterwards and enlarged it for the Amsterdam edition of 1647. It was Sorbière who was responsible for the second edition. He did more since he translated it into French and published it in that language.⁷⁼¹¹ The work made Hobbes many enemies but he obliged the more far-sighted to admit that the fundamentals of politics had never previously been analysed so well. I have no doubt that he took certain things too far; for that is common among those who write in opposition to a party which they strongly dislike. Hobbes was offended by the principles of the Parliamentarians;⁸⁼¹² their conduct caused him to live out of his country; and in his exile he had to hear daily that their rebellion was prevailing over the royal authority. He took matters to the other extreme since he taught that the authority of kings should have no limits, and in particular that the external aspects of religion, being the most virulent cause of civil war, ought to depend upon their will. There are people who believe that his system, if one considers it from the perspective of its theory only, is elegantly constructed and wholly consonant with the idea of a state well secured against troubles. But because the most reasonable ideas are subject to a thousand inconveniences when they come to be put into practice – that is to say, when attempts are made to implement them in the face of that fearsome train of emotions which reigns amongst mankind – it was hardly difficult to

⁶⁼⁸ Silius Italicus [*Punic Wars*], 14.101.
⁷⁼¹¹ Amsterdam, 1649.
⁸⁼¹² *Vita Hobbesii*, p. 45.

find many faults in this author's political system. He could have replied that the opposite system, even in its theory, contains a necessary principle of confusion and rebellion. Whatever the case, it is claimed that love of country inspired his work, and that his aim was to disabuse his countrymen of the false principles which had produced such a frightful contempt for royal authority.

> Grassante interim per Angliam ... ['The civil war was meanwhile raging throughout England. On account of his deep love for his country, as greatly befitted a good and loyal subject, Hobbes strove to instruct his own countrymen in sounder ideas than they had up to then acquired from their leaders. He endeavoured to dispel people's anger and to put them in mind of the reasons for peace and concord and to make them more devoted to obedience to the highest power. He therefore put aside his other pursuits and spent as much time as he needed on political science. He revised his book, *De cive* (of which he had published only few copies in Paris in 1642), adding useful notes. In this work, he utterly condemned subjects' plots and rebellions against the supreme ruler, as well as those monstrous opinions about stripping a prince of kingdom and life. He restored to the civil power the jurisdiction which had been appropriated by ecclesiastics in the exigencies of those dark ages, and with heroic audacity he dethroned the dreadful hydra of the sectarians: namely that unbridled freedom of conscience.']$^{9=13}$

I am persuaded that no one will be displeased to see here the judgement of M. Descartes upon this work of Hobbes. 'I believe', says he,$^{10=14}$

> that the author of the book *De cive* is the same as he who opposed the third objection to my *Meditations*.$^{11=15}$ I find him far more skilled in morals than in either physics or metaphysics, though I can by no means approve his maxims and principles, which are extremely pernicious and very dangerous, in as much as he supposes all men to be base or

---

$^{9=13}$ *Ibid.*
$^{10=14}$ Vol. III of his *Letters* cited by Baillet, *Vie de Descartes*.
$^{11=15}$ He was not wrong.

gives them reason to be so. His whole purpose is to write in favour of monarchy: which could be done so much more effectively than this by proceeding from maxims more virtuous and more substantial. He writes equally strongly against the church and the Roman religion, so that unless he is protected by some exceedingly powerful commendation I do not see how he can exempt his book from being censured.

M. Descartes is right to express disagreement if a person supposes 'all men to be base', which reminds me that Montaigne, though aware of the imperfections of the human race, did not approve of Guiccardini's attributing ill motives to every deed he relates in his history.[12=16] It is undeniable that there are some men who conduct themselves according to ideas of decency [*honnêteté*] and out of desire for a noble glory, and that the greater part of men are only moderately reprehensible. This ordinariness [*la médiocrité*] suffices, I admit, to ensure that the history of human affairs is saturated with iniquity, which leaves almost everywhere the imprint of the heart's corruption; but it would be far worse[13=17] were the greatest number of men not in many instances able to repress [*réprimer*] their unsavoury inclinations, either through fear of dishonour or from the hope of praise. And, moreover, it is proof that corruption has not taken hold to the ultimate degree. I am not here considering the good effects of true religion but rather mankind in general.

As for the inconveniences that might arise from Hobbes's suppositions once they are put into practice, I say, once more, that it is not here that he ought to be contested. For does not the opposing system, once put into practice, also have many great inconveniences? A man may aim for the best, he may build systems better than Plato's *Republic*, or More's *Utopia* or Campanella's *Republic of the Sun* etc., but all such ideas will turn out to have some inadequacies and deficiencies once you try to put them into practice. Men's passions, which feed upon one another in prodigious variety, will soon ruin the hopes which these fine systems inspire. Note what happens when mathematicians attempt to apply to the material world their speculations concerning points and lines. They can do

---

[12=16] See [*Dic*,] article 'Guicciardini', Remark (E), vol. VII, p. 331.
[13=17] Innocence is not suppressed in many encounters because of the ordinariness which I mention here.

everything they want with their lines and their areas, for they are pure ideas of the mind; and the mind allows us to strip away what we please of their dimensions, which is why we can demonstrate the most elegant things possible concerning the nature of the circle, or the infinite divisibility of the continuum. But it all founders when we apply it to matter which exists outside of our minds – hard and impenetrable matter. This may serve as a metaphor for real human passions when confronted by the speculative theories of a man who has formed an idea of perfect government. You will find a very perceptive critique of Hobbes's political system in the author whom I cite below.[14=18]

(F) He devoted the rest of his time to writing his *Leviathan*.] He denoted the body politic by the name of this beast. The theologians of the Anglican church who accompanied Charles II to France protested greatly about the work, saying that it contained many impieties and that its author was not of the Royalist party.[15=19] Their complaints were heard since Hobbes received the order to come to court no more. And since he had vexed the Papists exceedingly, he believed that it was no longer safe for him in France once he was without the protection of the king of England ... [16=20] He translated his *Leviathan* into Latin and had it printed, with an appendix, in the year 1668.[17=21] Ten years later it was translated into Flemish. The *précis* of this work is that without peace there is no safety in a state, and that peace cannot exist without command, nor command without arms; and that arms are worth nothing if they are not in the hands of one person; and that fear of arms cannot bring peace to those who are motivated to fight one another through an evil more terrible than death, that is to say: through dissension over matters that are necessary for salvation.

> Eius autem summa ... ['But this is a summary of his thought, that safety is impossible without peace, that peace

---

[14=18] Galeottus Galeatius Karlsbergius, in J. Dekherrus, *De scriptis adespostis, pseudepigraphis et suppositiis conjecturae* [Conjectures about Anonymous, Pseudonymous or Falsely Attributed Writings], p. 328.

[15=19] *Vita Hobbesii*, p. 61.

[16=20] *Ibid.*, p. 62.

[17=21] Amsterdam, chez Jean Blaeu, with his other *Œuvres philosophiques*, 2 vols. He was unable to obtain permission to print it in England. *Vita Hobbesii*, p. 70.

is impossible without rule, that rule is impossible without arms; arms have no power without troops collected under one command, and that anyone who is not motivated to fight because of an evil to be feared more than death can progress towards peace through fear of arms. Certainly, peace among citizens cannot endure while there is no consent about the factors thought necessary for eternal salvation.'][18=22]

There was fierce criticism of *Leviathan*, principally in England.[19=23]

[Remarks (G)–(L) omitted.]

(M) Those who wrote his *Life* maintain that he held wholly orthodox opinions about the nature of God.] Of all the moral virtues, there was hardly any except religion that could be thought problematic in the person of Hobbes. He was open,[20=40] civil, and communicative of what he knew,[21=41] a good friend, a good relation, charitable to the poor,[22=42] a great observer of equity,[23=43] and he cared nothing for possessions.[24=44] This latter quality is an indication of the goodness of his life; for there is not a more potent cause of harmful deeds than avarice. So if one knew Hobbes, one had no need to ask if he valued and loved virtue; but one might have been tempted to put to him the following question.

> Heus age, responde, minimum est quod scire laboro,
> De Jove quid sentis?

['Come on then, tell me; it is a very minor question which I am striving to have you answer: What do you think about Jupiter?'][25=45]
    The answer he could have sincerely made, if we believe those who wrote his life, would have been this: that there is a God who

---

[18=22] *Ibid.*, p. 45.
[19=23] The list of published writings against *Leviathan*, and the other *Œuvres* of Hobbes, are listed at the end of his *Life*.
[20=40] *Vita Hobbesii*, pp. 30, 111.
[21=41] *Ibid.*, p. 111.
[22=42] *Ibid.*, p. 108.
[23=43] 'Justitiae erat cum scientissimus tum tenacissimus' ['He was extremely knowledgeable about justice as well as highly committed to practising it'], *ibid.*, p. 30.
[24=44] 'Cum esset pecunia negligentissimus' ['Since he did not care at all about money'], *ibid.*
[25=45] Persius, *Satires*, 2.17.

is the origin of all things but who ought not to be circumscribed within the sphere of our narrow reason.[26=46] He would have added that he embraced Christianity as it was by law established in England;[27=47] but that he had an aversion to theological disputes; that he esteemed principally what tends to the practice of piety and sound morals [*bons mœurs*], and that he habitually condemned priests who corrupted the simplicity of religion by mixing with it superstitious worship and a plethora of vain and worldly speculation. 'Quicquid autem ...' ['But he thought whatever brought about the practice of piety or good morals of greatest importance. For him it seemed holier and more respectful to have belief in God rather than knowledge of him. But he would criticise priests who either spoiled the complete simplicity of Christianity with superstition, or who involved themselves in pointless, sometimes profane, speculations.'][28=48]

They conclude that those who accuse him of atheism are worthless slanderers who could perhaps maintain no other grounds than this: that he had rejected several Scholastic doctrines which had ascribed to God certain attributes modelled upon our own small intelligence. 'Quare fortiter ...' ['A great slander has therefore been committed by those who accused him of being guilty of atheism. This perhaps followed from the fact that he had rejected the custom of Scholastics and others of that breed, who, sitting at ease among their archives, shape the hidden attributes of the divine nature in accordance with the paltry capacity of their own intelligence.'][29=49]

It is undeniable that no accusation has been more seriously abused than that of atheism. Many small minds and people of malice bestow it upon all who – drawing on sound metaphysics and the general doctrines of the Scriptures – put limits upon claims about great and sublime truths. In addition, they want them to adopt every little article with which they continuously indoctrinate the people. If one believed certain divines, anyone with the courage

---

[26=46] 'Deum agnovit eumque rerum ...' ['He acknowledged that God existed and that he was the origin of all things, but that he should in no way be circumscribed within the narrow enclosure of human reason'], *Vita Hobbesii*, p. 105.
[27=47] 'Religionem christianam ...' ['He sincerely embraced Christianity, as it was established in the Anglican church by the laws of the kingdom, with the foolish superstitions cut out'], *ibid.*, p. 106.
[28=48] *Ibid.*, p. 107.
[29=49] *Ibid.*

to withdraw from this routine is impious and an *esprit fort*. This was
how Monconys was falsely accused. For he [Monconys] sometimes
debated very freely against those who debased the greatness of God
by the belief which they attributed to him, and by the paltry evidence which they provided. They did him the injustice of treating
him as a libertine: he, who was suffused with the most sublime idea
of God that can be conceived. Read what follows:

> That affable manner in which he was sometimes seen to
> contradict certain piteous minds – who demeaned with their
> proofs the facts which they wished to establish – permitted
> those who accused him to argue that his frankness and his
> candour should be taken as a depraved liberty. But the
> firmness of his virtue and the sincerity of his piety – of
> which he gave testimony in his *Voyages* – shone through. In
> his last illness he confessed to one of his friends that, in his
> heart, he had always held for the Divinity – of whom his
> idea was more noble than any man had conceived – a deep
> deference and an infinite respect. When he was in Alexan-
> dria – at a time when it seemed that nothing was inexplic-
> able – and finding himself, one night, alone on one of those
> terraces which serve as a roof for Levantine buildings, he
> was suddenly overwhelmed by a palpable knowledge of the
> Divinity. He then spent almost the whole night in continu-
> ous adoration of the principle of all beings, and filled with
> an inexplicable sense of consolation.[30=50]

**(N) It was said too that he was frightened of phantoms and
demons.]** His friends treated this as a fable . . . But it seems that
he admitted that he did not like to remain alone, and they allowed
it to be implied that he feared assassins. If his philosophy exempted
him from the latter but not the former, he still would not have been
prevented from feeling uneasy, and one could cite a thought of
Horace.[31=52] It can be noted in passing that his principles of natural
philosophy were not sufficient to remove his fear of apparitions for,

---

[30=50] Preface to *Voyages de Monconys*, p. 7.
[31=52] 'Somnia, terrores magicos, miracula . . .' ['Do you laugh at dreams, the terrors
of magic, strange marvels, soothsayers, night-time ghosts, and Thessalian por-
tents? What use is it for you to remove just one of many thorns?'] Horace,
Epistles, 2.208–12.

to reason logically, there are no philosophers who are less justified in rejecting magic and sorcery than those who deny the existence of God. But – you will say – Hobbes did not believe in the existence of spirits. Speak more circumspectly! For in fact he believed that there are no substances distinct from matter. Thus, since that would not have prevented him from believing that there exist many substances bent on doing harm and good to others, and which succeed, he could and should have believed that there are beings in the air and elsewhere just as capable of mischief as the corpuscles, which, he would have said, make up all the thoughts in our brain. Now why do these corpuscles have more knowledge of the means of doing mischief than other beings? And what proof is there that these other beings are unaware of the way in which they must act on our brain in order to make us see an apparition?

Let us consider the matter from another perspective. If one sought to claim that no one whatsoever ever believed he had seen a ghost, one would not only be very bold but also very extravagant. And I do not think that the most opinionated and the most extreme among unbelievers have ever maintained this. What they do can be reduced to saying that persons who have thought that they witnessed an apparition have had a damaged imagination. They admit, therefore, that there are certain places in the brain which, being affected in this or that manner, excite the image of an object which has no real existence outside of ourselves. They make the man, whose brain is thus affected, believe that he sees, at two paces from him, a fearsome spectre, or a fury, or a menacing phantom. Similar things take place inside the heads of even unbelieving people, either while they sleep, or when they are disturbed by a violent fever. Dare one maintain after this that it is impossible for a man awake, who is not delirious, to receive in certain parts of his brain an impression somewhat like that which, in accordance with the laws of nature, is connected with the appearance of a ghost? Once they are obliged to acknowledge this possibility, they cannot reply that a ghost will never appear before them, or that when they are awake and alone in their room they will never think that they are seeing either a man or a beast. Hobbes could have imagined, therefore, that a certain combination of atoms when excited in his brain would expose him to such a vision, though he would have been persuaded that no angel and no soul of a dead man had played a part in it. He was timorous to the last degree, and consequently he had good reason to mistrust his imagination when he was alone in his room at night. For in spite of himself, recollections of what he had read and heard concerning the apparition of spirits would reawaken, although he was not persuaded that these things were real. These images, in conjunction with his timidity of temperament, could play him a wretched trick. And it is certain that a man as unbelieving as he, but more courageous, would have been surprised had he seen someone whom he knew to be dead enter his room. Such apparitions are very common in dreams whether one believes in the immortality of the soul or whether one does not. Let us suppose it happened one day, that they appeared to an unbeliever who was awake, as they had appeared to him when he was asleep. Now even though he had great courage, we would understand his fear. All the more reason for us to suppose, then, that Hobbes would have been very scared.

De l'Hôpital

[Michel de l'Hôpital, chancellor from 1560 to 1568, was, in Bayle's judgement, a statesman comparable to Cicero. For he had sympathised with the ideas of reform and he had taught future generations that even in corrupt times an honourable law maker could pursue peace through persistent negotiation. Bayle draws on letters and memoirs from both sides to explain de l'Hôpital's reluctant severity towards the parlements *of his day. Zealots among the Catholic majority, contemptuous of the royal edicts of toleration, had voted for violence against the Reformers. In such conditions only heroic measures could have prevented the majority from fighting illegally, or the minority from arming in self-defence.]*

HÔPITAL (Michel de l'), chancellor of France in the sixteenth century, was one of the greatest men of his time. He was from the Auvergne of an ordinary family, and rose to prominence only gradually [(A)]. He was counsellor in the *parlement* of Paris when princess Marguerite, sister of king Henry II, having been assigned the duchy of Berri, chose him for her chancellor.[a] He continued with her in the same post in Italy after she had married the duke of Savoy and he was in Nice when he was raised to the office of chancellor of France in 1560 during the reign of Francis II.[b] It was believed that the House of Guise procured that office for him, and that it did so because they supposed that if he were under an obligation [(B)] to them he would do all that they wished. They were mistaken, for he

---

[a] Pasquier, *Lettres*, vol. II, bk 22, p. 758.
[b] La Planche, *Histoire de François II*, p. 228.

93

laid down for his maxim the good of the kingdom and the just interests of his master the king. It is true that he was obliged to operate circumspectly [(C)], for had he openly opposed the schemes of the Guises he would have been in no position to remedy the disarray of France. He was thus forced to swim between two streams; but through this manner of operating he deflected some of the storms which threatened the kingdom, and delayed others; and thereby he found the means of rendering good service to his country insofar as the wretched conditions of the times would allow. Among other things he prevented the introduction of the Inquisition by consenting to an edict[c] that was far more severe towards the Protestants than he would have wished (D). It was that of Romorantin [1560]. There is no doubt at all that had he possessed a completely free hand in those matters, he would have procured a full toleration for those of the Reformed religion. His responsible administration and his persuasiveness were very certainly among the factors that altered the disposition of men's minds towards them. So remarkable was the change in attitudes that by the second year of his ministry there were – in the council that examined the petition which they [those of the Reformed religion] presented to the king (E) to request the free exercise of their religion – almost as many votes for as against them. His influence was no less effective in respect of mitigating the Edicts of July 1561,[d] and in the freedom they acquired to be exempted from its observance.[e] The Edict of January [1562], which they obtained some time later, was his work undoubtedly; moreover this Edict permitted them public meetings and many other privileges. That was the only proper remedy for the afflictions of the state; furthermore all the dreadful troubles that were to beset it for the next thirty years arose from infringements of that Edict; and in the aftermath of those dismal calamities, it proved necessary, eventually, to impose the same remedy but in a stronger measure. It proved essential to negotiate the Edict of Nantes [1598] which was so much more favourable to the Reformed church than that which Chancellor de l'Hôpital had obtained for it. But I concede also that the Roman church took less risk when it accepted the Edict

---

[c] In May 1560.
[d] These restrictions angered zealous Catholics.
[e] See Remark (F), note 10=33.

of Nantes than when it agreed to the Edict of January (F). The
obstacles that he had to overcome did not cease once he had signed
it: they arose again over its ratification and he had to show all his
firmness of purpose and strength of mind to bring an end to the
mistrust and ill-humour of the *parlement* of Paris [(G)]. The
speeches he delivered to inspire a spirit of tolerance made him very
much suspected by the Catholics, and odious to the court of Rome
(H); and because he always argued against civil violence they
excluded him from the councils of war.[f] He was very distressed
when he saw preparations being made on both sides to take up arms
after the affair of Vassy; he declared his thoughts frankly upon it,
and made a most excellent answer to the Connétable who told him
that 'it did not belong to those of the robe [the judiciary] to give
opinions on matters of war. "Better there be such men", answered
he, "than those who, knowing how to bear arms, do not know when
they should be used".'[f=g] Cardinal Hippolyte d'Est, Legate *a latere*
in France, received orders to work on getting him dismissed from
office; but he told the Pope that he saw no likelihood of succeeding
in such an affair.[g=h] He proposed it nevertheless to the queen regent
who became exceedingly angry. If Varillas had known this he would
not have made the error which we shall see below.[h=i] This chancellor's counsels of peace contributed more to his downfall than any
other cause; and I have provided strong evidence for it.[i=k] He
resigned voluntarily as soon as he perceived that his enemies had
turned the king against him and he passed the rest of his life in the
country home[k=l] which he owned at Beauce. He made that withdrawal in June 1568. They sent for his seals of office some days
afterwards. He returned them very readily saying, in addition, that
he was no longer suited for the business of a world which was so
depraved.[l=m] We ought to think it more strange that he maintained
his ground for seven or eight years in so corrupt a court, than

---

[f=g] Pasquier, *Lettres*, vol. I, bk 4, p. 226. See also Baptiste le Grain, *L'Histoire de
Henri IV*, pp. 129, 130, where he praises as much as he condemns those who
excluded him from the war council.
[g=h] See [Remark (H), below,] the quotation at note 30=58.
[h=i] Citation [note] 32=60.
[i=k] In Remark (H), towards the end.
[k=l] Named Vignai and not Vignan as Mézerai calls it on p. 186 of vol. III of his major
history. He is [ordinarily] nothing less than exact in his proper names.
[l=m] Brantôme, in *Discours du Connétable de Montmorenci*, vol. II, p. 87.

that he was finally dismissed from office. There would have been something lacking in his virtue and his glory had he continued as chancellor until his death; for under such a reign it would have been a sort of stain or mark of ignominy to be thought suitable for that great employment. An honest man was not what was needed by those who were then in charge of public affairs. Let us observe that M. de l'Hôpital did not fail to establish some very good laws [(I)] and that he flattered neither subjects nor prince. He was very zealous in maintaining and supporting the royal majesty and authority, and through the gravity of his censures he was able to make the *parlements* appreciate the wrong that they did to undermine their monarch (K); but, on the other hand, he made it his business to see that the prince should obey justice and reason. He opposed unjust edicts as far as he could but if, nevertheless, he had to attach his seal to them he made it known that it was against his advice (L) . . . He wrote a noble testament which was published and which showed among other things his partiality for peace (P) and his indifference to funeral ceremonies. He died on 15 March 1573 at about sixty-eight years of age [(Q)] . . . I might have recounted many other things but I have omitted them because they may be found in Moréri . . .

Ronsard's Ode,[m=q] conceived as a eulogy to this great minister of justice, has been looked upon as superb but in certain respects I find nothing to surpass the portrayal by Brantôme. It represents M. de l'Hôpital as a man who could be compared with the greatest and most eminent men of the robe in ancient Greece and Rome. Since I shall cite so many other passages in the Remarks, I shall, for brevity's sake, omit what has been said by Brantôme. I beg my readers only to consider the two following matters. The first concerns what Brantôme remarks about the chancellor's firmness against the Cardinal de Lorraine, who wanted the Council of Trent ratified in France.[n=r] The second concerns the courage which he showed after the Massacre of Saint Bartholomew [1572] when he had reason to believe that the assassins had been sent to his home.[o=s] I shall say this as well. A famous

---

[m=q] See bk 1, 10 . . . Richelet who has commented on it says that it is a masterpiece of poetry. See also Pasquier, *Lettres*, bk 22, p. 758.

[n=r] Brantôme, *Mémoires*, vol. II, p. 85. See Varillas, *Charles IX*, bk 6, for the detail of this dispute.

[o=s] Brantôme, *Mémoires*, vol. II, pp. 87, 88.

author[p=t] – having described strength of mind as 'a certain temper and disposition of the intellect; always balanced within itself, firm, steady, courageous; able to see everything, hear everything and do everything, without being troubled, upset, distressed, or shocked' – adds that it is 'rather as Juvenal describes it' in the six 'fine verses of the tenth Satire'.[q=u] Chancellor de l'Hôpital, Naudé continues,[r=x] 'who was endowed with this strength of mind as well as any man who preceded or followed him, described the quality even more succinctly – if more robustly – whereby he derived his maxim: "Si fractus illabatur orbis / impavidum ferient ruinae." '[s=y] See note t=z. Should I not also mention the services that he rendered even after his death? And is it not proper to observe that the maxims of state by which he acted were highly beneficial for France – since he educated disciples who, at the right time and place, were able to oppose the League, thereby causing their pernicious schemes to miscarry (S)?

[Remarks (A)–(C) omitted.]

(D) He prevented . . . the introduction of the Inquisition by consenting to an edict that was far more severe towards the Protestants than he would have wished.] . . . M. Varillas[1=20] observes that such moderate action displeased the Calvinists and did not satisfy the Catholics.[2=21] . . . He was assumed to be a Huguenot although he went to mass; but at court they said: may God preserve

---

[p=t] Naudé, *Coups d'état*, ch. 5, p. 784.

[q=u] 'Fortem posce animum . . .' ['Pray for a brave heart free from fear of death, which ranks length of life as the least important of nature's gifts; the sort of a heart which can bear any suffering whatsoever, which does not know anger, which desires nothing; a heart which prefers the toils and hard labours of Hercules to the enchantments, feasts and feather cushions of Sardanapalus.'] Juvenal, *Satires*, 10.357–62.

[r=x] Naudé, *Coups d'état*, ch. 5, pp. 785, 786.

[s=y] These words are from Horace, *Odes*, 3.3.7–8, and as they are translated by Naudé's commentator they mean: 'should the earth be destroyed, its ruin would affect me but I should not be panic-stricken'.

[t=z] The vigour with which the French court testified, in 1563, against the Pope, in favour of the queen of Navarre etc. . . . was the work of M. de l'Hôpital and the Connétable de Montmorenci. See de Thou, bk 82, pp. 32, 33.

[1=20] Varillas, *Histoire de l'hérésie*, bk 22, p. 170.

[2=21] This edict allocated competence to judge the crime of heresy to bishops alone, and removed it from the royal judges.

us from the mass of M. de l'Hôpital. It is the common fate of those who seek to keep a temper between the claims of two opposing parties to please neither the one nor the other. But this inconvenience is sometimes a lesser evil than to comply with one side or the other, and there are many occasions when the greatest good that can be done is to divide the disadvantages so that everyone may have his share of them. Our chancellor would have ruined everything had he undertaken from the beginning to give complete satisfaction to the enemies of the House of Guise. For that would have been to pit himself against a rock. Prudence required that he confronted that faction only from a side angle. They had the wind in the stern and he could not steer into that sort of squall. I believe that many Calvinists, who had more zeal than understanding of the world, always condemned this chancellor's conduct. They would have had him declare himself loudly and vehemently as the protector of their cause. But could he have preserved his post for even three months had he not trimmed somewhat? He understood well that the way to survive a storm was the one to which Plutarch refers when speaking of the government of republics.

> For as the mathematicians say the sun neither completely follows the course of the firmament nor yet directly and diametrically opposes it; but, by having a small bias and following a roundabout path, it makes an oblique line which is not too violently straight, is able to turn gently and, by its very tilt, is thus able to conserve the whole of creation and ensure a world with a steady temperature. So, in the matter of governing a republic, too great a severity in opposing the will of the people [*la volonté du peuple*] on every occasion and in every matter is too extreme and too rigid. So is the facility of letting oneself be drawn into the errors of the people when they have a mistaken fondness or taste for certain things, which is a slippery and dangerous slope. But the middle way: at no time to cede to the appetite of the people so as to make them obey better; but, rather, to bestow upon them something agreeable in order to ask from them something useful, is a salutary means of administering and governing men. It permits one eventually to bring about, gently and usefully, many good things, provided that

one seeks to acquire them neither through an indulgence too great, nor through an arrogant and seigneurial authority.[3=23]

Our chancellor was not unaware that Cicero had observed that politicians should emulate helmsmen.

> An, cum videam navem . . . ['Imagine I am on a ship being carried along on a fair wind not making for that harbour which I have visited before, but heading for another which is no less safe or calm; would I rather take the risk of struggling against the conditions of the weather, or prefer to conform and comply with them, especially when it is a question of safety? I do not think him a fickle man who decides to adjust his course in the Republic just as he would steer his ship away from the storm.'][4=24]

Though he did not have the good fortune of that Lepidus who kept himself in favour with Tiberius by observing a fine balance between gross flattery and too much honesty, he deserves the following praise bestowed by Tacitus. 'Hunc ego Lepidum . . .' ['This Lepidus was, I am informed, a man of authority and good sense for his time. For he diverted most matters away from other men's dangerous flatteries and towards a better course. But he did not lack discretion, since he was held in high regard by Tiberius, possessing influence and favour in equal measure'].[5=25] . . .

(E) There were almost as many votes in favour of those of the Reformed religion . . . as there were against them.] This detail strikes me as curious, and I imagine that it would offend no one to hear more about the ins and outs of the matter. I shall make use here of what I find in a Catholic author.[6=26]

> The Huguenots petitioned the king for a right to set up a church separate from ours. The king sent this request to the *parlement* so that they might receive the advice of the nobles of his council. The case for each side was debated very vig-

---

[3=23] Plutarch, at the beginning of the *Life of Phocion*. I am using Amyot's version.
[4=24] Cicero, *Pro Plancio*, 39.94. See also *Epistulae ad familiares* [Letters to his Friends], 1.9.
[5=25] Tacitus, *Annals*, 4.20.
[6=26] Pasquier, *Lettres*, bk 4, p. 196.

orously. On the one side were those for the Catholic party, on the other were those for the Reformed religion. The Catholics carried the following resolution by three votes: that citizens must either follow the Roman religion like their fathers, or leave the kingdom with the right to sell their possessions. When it came to the vote, the murmurs were not few, because the other side argued that in a matter of such importance, three small votes were no reason for the whole of France to go up in flames. For banishment was impossible to implement ... M. de Guise, on the other hand, though time seemed to militate against his contention, declared vehemently that, since it had been so concluded, it was necessary to implement this decision and that his sword would never remain in its scabbard as long as it was a question of executing this law. Such matters were considered but to no conclusion.[7=27] ... After that, and to appease each side through a form of neutrality [giving the Reformers limited freedom of worship], the government promulgated the Edict of last July.[8=28] The French Catholics complained about this Edict, and said that those of the Reformed religion, or the supposed Reformed religion, were not to be found in their homes, which was effectively to render the first part of the Edict illusory, and was nevertheless to accord them the 'right of the magistrate': which would give them a reason, in due course, for seeking to shake off the burden of their allegiance completely.[9=29]

(F) The Roman religion did not run as great a risk later ... as it had when it agreed to the Edict of January.] It was little noticed that those of the Reformed religion had gained the advantage at the beginning of the reign of Charles IX; and that had they won, God alone knows what might have become of the religion which had persecuted them for so many preceding reigns ... I am now going to cite a passage which will show just how far they [the Protestants] were advantaged in the region of Orléans, and the extent of the liberty that they enjoyed there. They publicly

[7=27] *Ibid.*
[8=28] That is, in 1561.
[9=29] ... Pasquier, *Lettres*, vol. I, bk 4, p. 198.

assembled in the capital of the kingdom even before there were
edicts which permitted them to do so. But it must be noted that
the regent, Catherine de Médicis, had agreed this with king [An-
toine] of Navarre.[10=33]

The Huguenots[11=34] placed their confidence in this king[12=35]
completely; as one whom they had carried upon their shoul-
ders, and into whose hands they had consigned the government of France through their alliances and their stratagems
in the assembly of the Three Estates. And, by way of an
acknowledgement of this, he had permitted, by a very great
connivance, that their services might be held in public not
only in Paris, but also at the king's court in Saint-Germain-
en-Laye. Furthermore he was not very perturbed to maintain his grandeur only by the endorsement of those who
reciprocally undertook to maintain themselves by his support and favour. Nevertheless, on changing his mind, he
became the first tool through which the Catholics armed
themselves against the rest. But by means of confidential
letters by which these affairs are conducted – a way of
operating perhaps unknown to you – the Pope, seeing the
disagreements that existed among ourselves, sent the Cardinal de Ferrare, legate in France, the uncle of Madame de
Guise, very ample resources.[13=36] ... Or, such was the
common opinion.[14=37]

Anyway, I can inform you that in an instant his attitude and his
intentions towards the Huguenots were seen to change. For he forbade their ministers to preach henceforth in the château when they
had permission and liberty to do so five or six months previously.
Even in the Assembly of Saint German where there were two
churches, he still opposed the Huguenots as far as he could. But
the Prince de Condé, the Admiral de Coligny, and others who were
in the lower ranks of those near the king, opposed him, and carried
the day in respect of the promulgation of the Edict.[15=38] The same

[10=33] See Beza, *Histoire des églises*, bk 4, p. 670, and Beaucaire, bk 29, no. 34, p. 966.
[11=34] Pasquier, *Lettres*, vol. I, bk 4, p. 218.
[12=35] That is to say, the king of Navarre.
[13=36] Pasquier, *Lettres*, vol. I, p. 219.
[14=37] The common opinion was correct. More exact historians concur with it.
[15=38] That is, the Edict of January 1562.

author can show us also the great numbers which the Huguenots had attracted even before the Edict of January [1562] when they had enjoyed the favour of the king of Navarre 'this very day', that is 29 September 1561:

> the queen of Navarre, in the presence of all the people, had the marriage solemnised by Beza and according to the rites of Geneva, of the young Rohan and La Brabançon, niece of Madame d'Estampes in the town of Argenteuil . . . And in fact, in the following month of October, the Reformers preached outside the city walls of Paris by the monastery of Saint-Antoine-des-Champs, before eight or nine thousand people . . . [16=39]

You may see in other letters of Etienne Pasquier[17=40] the extent of these gatherings and the degree of the support that was accorded to them by the secular arm. One may consult also the letters of Hubert Languet,[18=41] where one finds, among other things, that the assemblies that were held near Paris were often of fifteen thousand people, women in the middle protected by men on foot, and the latter in their turn surrounded by men on horseback and that, during the sermons, the governor of Paris had the avenues guarded by soldiers who would beat back, or arrest, or restrain, in some other manner, all those who might trouble the devotions of the congregation.

Many people who judge these things only by their outcome might argue that those of the Reformed religion would have been more prudent had they displayed less presumption at that time. For the display of their numbers was looked upon as bravado which embittered their enemies, and drew down upon them violent retaliation. We see from a letter from the Cardinal Legate that he hoped to gain an advantage from such audacity. His letter from Saint-Germain is dated 27 February, 1562: here is a part of it.

> There happened lately a skirmish between those of the two religions which has left several dead; the danger however has proved greater than the damage. The Catholics instantly flocked here to complain of the insolence of the

[16=39] Pasquier, *Lettres*, vol. I, bk 4, pp. 200, 201.
[17=40] *Ibid.*, pp. 203, 205 etc.
[18=41] Bk 2, pp. 145, 150, 155, edition of Hall, 1698.

Huguenots; they have complained that they themselves, in accordance with the express order of His Majesty, have laid down their arms; while their enemies have done quite the opposite ... The reply given by the king and the queen of Navarre has been extremely favourable to those of our side; for they bade them take courage and also promised them that they would take care to provide collectively both for their particular safety, and for the general repose of their city ... To this I add the not unimportant particular that not only Their Majesties but everyone in general is extremely scandalised by Beza, who never walks in Paris unless he is escorted by M. Dandelot and followed by a great number of mounted horseguards. Notwithstanding all that ... given the present state of mind among the most powerful, it is likely that these disorders will quite soon be revisited upon the heads of those who are causing them.[19=44]

Nevertheless, let us say to these critics that it was very natural that those who had complained for nearly forty years about so hard and so cruel an oppression should take advantage of their liberty and spill over like water upon the opening of a sluice. Furthermore, there were even some motives of prudence that might have governed their conduct. For they could reasonably have supposed that there would be some motive to show respect for a party whose power was seen to be capable of making itself feared. Lastly, I say that neither minister nor layman could prevent Dandelot and the other gentlemen of quality from combining their zeal for religion with the demeanour of soldier and cavalier which they had acquired through custom and experience. Whatever the reason, the other church escaped narrowly: for since the Protestants withstood the first war so well – despite their desertion by [Antoine] the king of Navarre – what would they not have done under the protection of the Lieutenant-General of the kingdom who would doubtless have brought over the queen mother? Languet shows us what a generous estimate may be given of their strength. 'Re patefacta plerique ...'

[19=44] ['Negotiations, or Letters on Policy written to Pope Pius IV, and to Cardinal Borromeo, by Hippolyte d'Est, Cardinal de Ferrare, Legate in France'], pp. 93, 94.

['When the matter had become known very many of our men came armed to the meeting, as they do today, and of those who remain, a great number are filled with zeal . . . Indeed, our men assembled, filling the main streets of the city with some forty thousand soldiers . . .']20=45

[Remark (G) omitted.]

(H) His speeches . . . made him suspected by the Catholics, and very odious to the court of Rome.] We have seen above21=49 what was jokingly said in France, in a passage from Varillas, of the chancellor's mass. Beaucaire de Péguillon, speaking of the assembly of Saint-Germain22=50 and reporting the summary of the speech made there by Chancellor de l'Hôpital, observes that the first magistrate served as a model for the judges who sympathised with the sectarians, and who cared only for Calvinists . . .23=51 This historian had the effrontery to brand the great man as an atheist. The following is what he said when he observed that the Cardinal de Lorraine had procured him the office of chancellor.

> Interim Olivario cancellario . . . ['Meanwhile, following the death of Chancellor Olivaire, Cardinal de Lorraine, against the judgement of his whole household and all his friends, arranged for Michel de l'Hôpital to be chosen as the new chancellor, who was a man of some learning, but of no religion; in fact, I would call him atheist.']24=52

Something has been said elsewhere25=53 about this accusation. Oderic Raynaldus renewed that cruel castigation and used the same terms as Beaucaire. It is where he refers to a certain enterprise of President Ferrier, of whom I have spoken above.26=54 M. Cousin is

---

20=45 Hubert Languet, *Epistulae* [Letters], bk 2, letter 70. It is dated March 1562, at Paris. See also letter 67.
21=49 In Remark (D), n. 1=20.
22=50 Held in 1561.
23=51 Beaucaire, bk 29, no. 30, p. 964.
24=52 *Ibid.*, bk 28, no. 57, p. 937.
25=53 See *Pensées diverses sur la comète*, p. 350, and *Critique générale de l'Histoire du Calvinisme de Maimbourg*, letter 16, no. 2, of the 3rd edition.
26=54 See [*Dic*,] article 'Ferrier (Arnauld)', Remark (C).

angry about this injustice, as he ought to be, and with the excess of Raynaldus; and he has related a significant passage from the letter which de l'Hôpital wrote to Pius IV on 29 September 1562.[27=55] Fra Paolo[28=56] teaches us that Pius IV found the speech which this chancellor made to the Colloque de Poissy to be heretical in many places. He adds that the same Pope even threatened to bring him before the Inquisition, and that the court of Rome, where he distributed copies of this speech, spoke very ill of that person, and speculated that all the ministers of the kingdom held the same sentiments as he: so much so that the French ambassador was hard pressed to defend him. Note that Pius IV, having determined to give the king of France a hundred thousand écus as a pure gift, and to lend him as many again, stipulated, among other things, that the chancellor, the bishop of Valence, and certain others he would name, should be imprisoned.[29=57]

Let us relate here a passage of a letter which the Cardinal Legate Hippolyte d'Est wrote to the Pope on 14 June, 1562. It is headed 'Bois de Vincennes':

> Among other difficulties not one of the least is to dislodge from court, as your Holiness desires, the chancellor and several other relevant persons. For your Holiness puts in this number both heretics and those who are suspected of heresy. But if all the latter were to be banished from court it would undoubtedly be deserted, these new opinions having already made such an impression on the minds of courtiers that there are few to be found who have not some small tincture of them ... But as to the dislodgement you would have of the chancellor,[*] that is entirely another thing. For, as well as having an appointment that does not permit him to be away from the court except on urgent business, he cannot be deprived of his office except by the express order of the king, or for some great fault should he have committed one. Nor, legally, may one assert that he deserves death if one cannot back it up with indubitable proof ...[30=58]

[27=55] See *Journal des Savans*, Holland, 28 February 1689, p. 118.
[28=56] *Histoire du Concile de Trente*, bk 5, p. 438 of Amelot's version.
[29=57] *Ibid.*, bk 11, p. 487, year 1562.
[30=58] *Négotiations ou lettres d'affaires escrites par le Cardinal de Ferrare légat en France*, p. 224, 225.

The letter that he wrote the following day to Cardinal Borromeo is evidence that Catherine de Médicis did not appreciate the proposal to get rid of certain persons, and that she was far more angry than before when, following the express order she received from Pius IV,[31=59] the chancellor in particular was named. From which it would seem that M. Varillas was wholly mistaken when he said that the triumvirs required M. de l'Hôpital to withdraw, and that the queen sacrificed him.[32=60] He wanted this supposed dismissal to have taken place before the declaration of 7 April 1562 and for it to have lasted for the whole of the first War.[33=61] That is refuted as much by the silence of other historians as by the letters of the Legate dated 15 June and 8 July 1562.[34=62]

They were not wrong to believe that M. de l'Hôpital approved in his inner soul of the doctrine of the Reformed Church. In the speech reported by Mézerai, Catherine de Médicis did not dissemble on every detail.

> She applied all her skill to undermining the credit he had acquired in the mind of the young king; to whom she had it said, through her henchmen, that he [de l'Hôpital] undoubtedly supported the heretics; and that his wife, his daughter, his son-in-law, and all his family, were of that religion; that there was no doubt that he also was a Calvinist in his heart and that it was only fear of losing his office that prevented him from openly professing it. However, since secret enemies are more dangerous than open ones, it was more important to be apprehensive of him than of the Admiral de Coligny; and that His Majesty should no longer allow him to go on poisoning his advice with his fine maxims of peace beneath which – as beneath the skin of serpent adorned with colours most agreeable to the eye – there was secreted a poisonous venom, which, when caressed, would lead to death.[35=63]

[31=59] *Ibid.*, pp. 240, 241.
[32=60] Varillas, *Histoire de Charles IX*, vol. I, p. 151.
[33=61] *Ibid.*, p. 353.
[34=62] See *Négotiations du Cardinale de Ferrare*, p. 308.
[35=63] Mézerai, *Histoire de France*, vol. III, p. 185.

She was not right to say that M. de l'Hôpital was a dangerous enemy. For if he treated the Protestants favourably it was not for subversive motives, but on account of maxims completely instrumental to the good of the state and to the service of the king. The integrity of his behaviour, and his experience and wisdom in the conduct of affairs, were recognised everywhere; as also was his incorruptible attachment to the good of the state, to the preservation of its laws, and to the welfare of peoples. In addition, his generosity, always constant, in resisting injustice on the part of the powerful, was highly praised by people of good will.[36=64] However, Catherine de Médicis declared the truth indeed when she said that the family of the chancellor was of the [Protestant] religion.[37=65] So this is strong proof that he disapproved of the dogmas of the communion of Rome. In the portraits of him by Theodore Beza, there is a lighted candle painted behind him to represent – according to M. Sponde – that he carried that flame to bring enlightenment to others rather than to illuminate himself.[38=66] The words which accompany that portrait tell us that there were two reasons which caused him to abstain from making a public profession of the truth. He feared that he might deprive himself of the means to serve the cause, and he hoped that the time would come when he was no longer obliged to dissimulate. He waited in vain for the moment and then, having wanted to declare himself, he was unable to execute his resolution. He sacrificed himself for others. The Latin of Theodore Beza expresses this very well.

> Huic . . . ad justum laudis . . . ['He seems to be denied the full measure of the praise due to him. This praise he deserves: partly because, by not professing the true religion openly, he avoided closing his routes to assisting those pious believers, and partly because, being misled by a certain vain hope, he longed for everyone to be pulled from the quagmire. But since he had long neglected to extricate himself from that mire, he could not manage it later when he wished to. But will anyone fail to celebrate his memory because, in

[36=64] *Ibid.*, p. 296.
[37=65] See de Sponde, for the year 1573, no. 15, p. 745.
[38=66] For the year 1561, no. 19, p. 609.

his attempt to help others, he was inclined to neglect his own interests for so long'?][39=67]

His will and testament is proof that his heart was not Papist: for he makes no mention of it, nor of the mass, nor of purgatory, nor of priests, nor of anything similar; and he observes in it that 'Christians have no great esteem for funeral ceremonies and sepulchres.'[40=68] M. de Sponde asserts that this is the language of a profane mind,[41=69] and M. Maimbourg asserts that such sentiments are unworthy of a Christian.[42=70] . . . Father Garasse, carried away by a blind urge to censure the Protestants, accused them of calumny when they tried to persuade everyone in France that Chancellor de l'Hôpital was of their faith . . .[43=73] However, he merely exposed his ignorance.

I cannot resist setting down here two observations which I find in an anonymous work which is excellent. They reveal to us the causes of this chancellor's downfall.

I strongly oppose the view (says this unknown author),[44=74] that a great minister, employed by a prince on important affairs, should remain silent whatever the circumstances; otherwise he would be as much the cause of the ruin of his master and his affairs by his silence, as might another by his enterprise and his cunning. And this is why I cannot be of the opinion of those who judge that M. de l'Hôpital went too far in opposing so strongly the resolution that had been taken by ****, against the prudent advice of the late M. le Connétable: [that is], to have the king leave ***, at the beginning of the second troubles. This wise and prudent minister judged, however – and judged very wisely as events turned out – that such a sudden departure . . . would undoubtedly have prevented any reconciliation, and carried matters beyond

[39=67] Beza, *Icones*, fol. v, iii.
[40=68] See Colomiés, *Bibliothèque Choisie*, p. 70.
[41=69] Spondanus [de Sponde], for the year 1573, no. 15, p. 745.
[42=70] Maimbourg, *Histoire du Calvinisme*, p. 105. See what was replied to him in the *Critique générale* of his book, letter 16, no. 3.
[43=73] See Garasse, *Doctrine curieuse*, p. 28.
[44=74] Excerpt from *L'Examen du Prince de Machiavel* [Analysis of Machiavelli's Prince], edition of 1622, p. 95.

the point of no return. We can be in no doubt that had he hidden his feelings and had he not made the stand that he did, he would have committed a dereliction of duty unworthy of a man whom virtue alone had raised to such a position. For from that time on, he was no longer fighting with one hand tied behind his back, and from that moment his enemies – that is, the enemies of his virtue, integrity, and sincerity – had begun to plot his downfall . . . Since the goal of those who are honoured to be employed in such responsibilities is not to maintain themselves to the prejudice of their honour and their conscience but to serve well and faithfully, a great states-man – as able and well intentioned as was this worthy chancellor – should be very content to resign, especially when he sees affairs taking a course he has long since foreseen. . . .

A good and truly virtuous minister . . . will never offer advice contrary to his real beliefs, but being *ordered* to speak and to give his advice, he will offer it faithfully and boldly. This is what this chancellor did when the matter under discussion concerned the papal bulls giving permission to sell ecclesiastical property, for a hundred and fifty thousand livres of revenue, for the purpose of extirpating heretics. Since this clause was contrary to the Edicts of Peace – the implementation of which M. de l'Hôpital judged necessary for the good of the kingdom, apart from having been solemnly agreed – he judged that no one should contravene them, and that this was one of the disservices of the League which would fester from then on. Therefore at his instigation the advice was fol-lowed of obtaining, purely and simply, new bulls without this clause. But it proved the stumbling block which they used to have this fine person suspected of heresy, to remove his seals of office, and to put them in the hands of a man thought to be more appropriate for the times, and disposed, very shortly afterwards, to be completely in favour of the war.[45=75]

[45=75] *Ibid.*, pp. 97 *et seq.*

[Remark (I) omitted.]

(K) He knew how to make the *parlements* . . . appreciate the wrong they did to undermine their monarch.] No attorney better reprimanded a clerk who is guilty of a grievous impropriety than did our chancellor when he reprimanded the *parlement* of Bordeaux. The occasion was when Charles IX held his court of justice there before Easter, on 12 April 1564. 'The king', said he,[46=79] 'has found many faults with your *parlement* . . . We see here a house ill managed, and it is requisite for you to give us an account of yourselves . . . For though his ordinances are presented to you, you observe them if it suits you. If you have remonstrances to make, present them immediately and he will hear them. For you rob him of his royal power when you do not wish to obey his royal decrees.' . . .

Note the summary of what the king said to this *parlement*: 'that in future he wants to be better obeyed than he has been, that he would in no way permit any of his subjects to take up arms without his permission, and that he would also have his edicts respected'.[47=81] There is no doubt that M. de l'Hôpital had proposed this speech, as well as the vigorous declaration he had the same prince pronounce before the deputies of the *parlement* of Paris, some time earlier . . .[48=82] . . .[49=84] ,[50=85]

It is here that I must examine briefly an argument which is heard daily, and which considers any curtailment of the right, which *parlements* formerly had, of rejecting Edicts which appeared unjust to them to be a harmful principle. It was a dyke, they say, which prevented the people from being suffocated under the arbitrary power of the monarch. The rupture of this barrier ought to be compared to the blow which Aeolus dealt to the mountain which served to imprison the winds.

> Cavum conversa cuspide montem . . . ['He struck with the butt-end of his spear the side of the hollow mountain, and

[46=79] See the *Recueil* of various memoirs, Paris, Pierre Chevalier, 1623, p. 424.
[47=81] *Ibid.*, p. 426.
[48=82] Mézerai, *Abrégé chronologique*, vol. v, for the year 1563, p. 80.
[49=84] Brantôme, *Eloge de Charles IX*, volume of *Mémoires*, vol. IV, pp. 33, 34.
[50=85] Undoubtedly Brantôme referred to the same speech of Charles IX as that mentioned by Mézerai, *Histoire*, vol. III, under year 1571.

the winds, drawn up as if in a battleline, rushed through the point where an exit had been granted them, and blew across the earth in a whirlwind . . .']⁵¹⁼⁸⁶

They embellish this with many maxims which appear exceedingly sound, but they never look deeper; they never turn the coin; they never consult experience, nor do they examine whether a rejoinder might be made. But I appeal to practice. For here is its weakness: it is easy to prove that France was never so desolate or so wretched as when, under Charles IX and Henry III, its *parlements* enjoyed the full authority of rejecting the edicts and ordinances of the prince. It is easy to demonstrate also that the exercise of that authority was the main cause of the troubles in the kingdom between the year 1562 and the year 1594. Chancellor de l'Hôpital had laid down the foundations of the public peace by the Edict of the month of January. The Roman church had no further need to fear the danger to which I have referred above;⁵²⁼⁸⁷ king [Antoine] of Navarre had distanced himself from the Huguenots; Catherine de Médicis thought no more of coming out in their support. They were content to preach; and thus the kingdom could have remained at peace but only provided that the Edict of January had been respected. But the Catholics disregarded it, and from that point proceeded the first Wars of Religion, the root of all the afflictions which beset the state until the extinction of the League. For all those abuses were connected with one another or resulted from a directly linked sequence of cause and effect.⁵³⁼⁸⁸ So to what should this violation of that Edict of January principally be ascribed? Was it not to the *parlement* of Paris? Did it not encourage everyone to refrain from observing it? For they ratified it only by undermining it,⁵⁴⁼⁸⁹ that is to say, not until after three peremptory orders, and they hedged it with restrictions and clauses which caused it to be understood that they registered it unwillingly and as a transitory and unworkable command. Who, after this, would have feared to violate such an edict? Would one not feel assured that a *parlement* that judged in

---

⁵¹⁼⁸⁶ Virgil, *Aeneid*, 1.81–3.
⁵²⁼⁸⁷ See Remark [(G)].
⁵³⁼⁸⁸ Compare with this the remark made by d'Aubigné, *Histoire*, vol. III, bk 5, ch. 2, p. 628.
⁵⁴⁼⁸⁹ See Remark [(G)].

this manner would be unlikely to take the trouble to punish offenders? Now at that time to be a party to a breach of the peace and to sound the clarion for civil war was one and the same thing. Observe carefully the words used by Varillas at the beginning of his account of the measures that were taken against those of the Reformed religion immediately before the massacre of Vassy. 'The House of Guise', says he, 'judged, from the opposition that it had met in the *parlement*, that the Edict of January would not last, and doubted no longer that the civil wars would soon begin.'[55=90] Let us say in general then that the *parlements* of France, by refusing to ratify the edicts of peace, or by ratifying them with such an ill grace; and then, as a natural consequence, by not observing them, constituted one of the greatest chains of prolonged calamity that wasted the state and almost ruined the monarchy root and branch. Had Charles V been reigning at that time, France would unquestionably have become a province of his dominions, or rather she would have been divided into a thousand parts.

You demonstrate, someone will point out to me, only the abuse by the *parlements*, of the right they had then, to reject the edicts of the prince. But, I will reply to him: are tyranny and most other disorders anything other than an abuse of a good thing? To refute your reflections, it is sufficient to tell you that this dyke, or barrier, you speak of, and which, properly speaking, embraces the contradiction that a state is both monarchical and not monarchical, cannot be presented as a sound remedy given that it did far more harm than good. What comparison is there between the advantages that may accrue from the defeat of a few domestic edicts[56=91] and the deplorable devastation suffered by the whole kingdom for more than thirty years? It was much less to the court that one should attribute these calamitous events, than to the *parlements*. The court became wise through the enlightenment of a brilliant and virtuous chancellor. By the Edict of January, M. de l'Hôpital had forestalled the troubles, and he had excised the roots of the civil wars. But the *parlements*, instead of supporting him, undermined him, and rendered fruitless the remedy he had found – a remedy which could

---

[55=90] Varillas, *Histoire de Charles IX*, vol. I, p. 121, for year 1562.
[56=91] On 9 September 1578, the *parlement* registered only two out of twenty-two financial edicts presented to it. See *Fastes du Père du Londel*, p. 88.

not have failed to work since there was no other.[57=92] The court had taken the path which the chancellor had indicated, and left it only because of the chaos into which the kingdom had fallen through the fault of those who disobeyed that edict; and it was the *parlements* which opened the wide road to this disobedience. They, therefore, are responsible for so many profaned, plundered, and overturned churches of which catalogues are made to render the Huguenots odious. It is no credit to them that the wretchedness into which the state fell was not permanent even after the Catholic League was put down. They opposed the Edict of Nantes [1598], the unique remedy for the internecine disorders. For the *parlement* of Paris would never have ratified it had Henry IV had not implored them, though in a tone which suggested that he knew how to make himself obeyed.[58=93] Note that the speech by M. de l'Hôpital to the *parlement* of Bordeaux[59=94] shows that in those times when little weight was given to the king's ordinances, the administration of justice was full of corruption and shameful irregularities. I will conclude by saying that the government of peoples is so full of turmoil that the remedies which may seem the best are sometimes worse than the disease and the beginning of an even more terrible calamity. In the foregoing, I think, I have given an important example.

(L) If he had to attach his seal to unjust edicts he made it known that it was against his advice.] A minister of state, and a chancellor to a monarch above all, should do two things if he wishes to discharge his duties properly. The first is earnestly to recommend to all subjects compliance and obedience; he should assume nothing else. It is not for him to stand arguing with them about whether they have sometimes a right to take up arms or to refuse obedience to ordinances that they find unjust and burdensome. He must suppose as an incontestable point that they have not that right. The second thing he must do is to represent actively and incessantly to the prince that his royal authority never dispenses him from an absolute submission to justice, and that it confers no right and no privilege to depart from reason [*la raison*], or from equity [*l'équité*], and from his word etc. M. de l'Hôpital acquitted

---

[57=92] 'Optimum remedium quia unicum.' ['The best remedy because the only one.']
[58=93] See Matthieu, *Histoire de la paix*, bk 2, narrat. 1, no. 7, p. 210 *et seq.*
[59=94] I have cited this at note 46=79 above.

himself punctiliously in all these duties. He took the part of the king before his subjects and the part of the subjects before the king. He put down with great resolution those who sought to undermine the royal authority. You see[60=95] the censures he made to the *parlements* – or which he had the king make on his advice. You see likewise[61=96] what he answered to the deputy from the *parlement* of Dijon. But you will now see with what integrity, and with what strength of will, he resisted unjust propositions which were suggested to the prince. He withstood them by his arguments as far as he could; but if his remonstrances did not prevent the matter from being implemented, he would distance himself from them; and he would indicate that he had not consented ... De l'Hôpital would usually write the following words in his own hand, on the back of such letters: *me non consentiente* ['without my consent']. This meant: they have obliged me to append my seal against my advice. It was in this manner that he treated the letters of appointment relating to Cardinal de Ferrare who had been sent to France as Legate by Pope Pius IV.[62=*] In response to such an elaboration by the chancellor, the court of the *parlement*, reading the words on the back, joined with him and would not ratify that power.[63=97] Everyone knows about the absolute power possessed by M. de Guise under Francis II; nevertheless even that power was not capable of bending this chancellor; for it was he alone who refused to sign the warrant for the execution of the Prince de Condé.[64=100]

Languet has preserved for us a sharp rejoinder which the chancellor made to the papal legate. The latter had dared to accuse him of knowing nothing of the duties of his office. At least, replied the chancellor, I have endeavoured to learn them, but you, who have several bishoprics, have never dreamed of instructing yourself in the duties of the episcopacy.

> Solus cancellarius pertinacissime ... ['The chancellor alone tenaciously stood his ground, saying that in this affair the greatest affront was made to the young king, and that the

---

[60=95] In the preceding remark.
[61=96] See, [*Dic*,] article 'Bégat', vol. III, p. 252.
[62=*] La Popelinière, bk 7.
[63=97] Le Grain, *Décade de Henri-le-gran*, bk 8, p. 898.
[64=100] *Ibid.*, bk 1, p. 118.

laws and majesty of the French realm were brought into disrepute. He said that he would not allow them to abuse in this affair the royal seal entrusted to him. At these words Cardinal Legate de Ferrare was furious. He claimed that de l'Hôpital knew nothing of the duties of his office. The chancellor replied: "I, at least, have undoubtedly made the effort to find out what they are. But you have never even given a thought to what the episcopal office involves, although you hold several bishoprics." But he was eventually overcome by the insolence of others and handed back the royal seal, while wanting, nonetheless, to have access to that instrument of authority, and claiming a right to it.']^[65=101]

[Remarks (M)–(O) omitted.]

(P) He showed in his last testament his partiality for peace.] In that last act of his life he wished passionately to honour the very thing that Cicero had extolled before the whole senate.

'Quo quidem in bello' (said this great Roman orator), 'semper de pace ...' ['During that war I indeed always believed that we should have acted to achieve peace and taken any advice that furthered this end. I was always aggrieved that it was not peace alone that was rejected but also the speeches of those citizens who demanded peace. For I never supported that civil war nor any other. I always counselled peace and civilian life, not warfare and arms. Nor did I ever make a secret of my advice, for not only did I often plead for peace in this Senate while the matter was still open, but I also maintained the same stance during the actual war at a risk to my life.']^[66=118]

There is hardly anything here that M. de l'Hôpital might not have said. But see what he wrote in his will and testament.^[67=119] 'I can attest that though we took up arms on four occasions, and that

---

65=101 Languet, *Epistulae*, 62, 2, p. 157.
66=118 Cicero, *Pro Marcello*, 5.14.
67=119 *Testament de Michel de l'Hôpital*, reported by Colomiés, *Bibliothèque Choisie*, p. 61.

we went into battle on four or five, I have always advised and urged peace, judging that nothing is so damaging to a country as civil war, nor more advantageous than peace in any conditions whatsoever.'[68=120] Having then spoken of the enemies which that maxim drew down on him, and the miseries into which France was plunged etc., he adds:[69=121]

> I gave way before arms which were the strongest and retired into the country with my wife, family and grandchildren, entreating the king and the queen on my departure for just one thing: that since they had decided to break the truce and to pursue, through war, those with whom only a little before they had negotiated a peace; and since they had dismissed me from the court because they had heard that I was opposed and ill disposed to their campaign: I implored them, I say, since they did not acquiesce in my advice, that at least some time later, after they had glutted their hearts and slaked their thirst with the blood of their subjects, to embrace the first opportunity for peace that should come along, before things were reduced to complete ruin. For whatever the outcome of that war, it could only be exceedingly prejudicial to the king and the kingdom.

[Remarks (Q)–(R) omitted.]

(S) He educated disciples able to oppose the ... League ... thereby causing their pernicious schemes to miscarry.] An anonymous author, whom I have already cited, supplies me with the commentary that I need. He says,

> that if the 'religious devotion' of the minister or counsellor of the prince is not well grounded and his zeal well controlled, it is impossible to imagine the harm he may do. Firstly, he allows himself to be taken unawares, and then he himself does the same in turn to his chief. For in the matter of religious confession, advantage is taken of the cleverest

---

[68=120] See Pasquier, *Lettres*, vol. I, bk 10, p. 626, *et seq.*, where he describes the depravity of these wars.

[69=121] *Testament*, etc., *Bibliothèque choisie*, p. 62.

men. Many think themselves to be exceedingly pious and devout if they remain largely in ignorance of what goes on within religion, and of what is discussed privately among its leaders; some of whom, being experienced, engage them subsequently in a fine chicanery. We have spoken of the great disasters which have engulfed certain princes – though noble and well advised – through a lack of having understood this collusion.[70=133]

Let us say a word about some of the advisers . . . They were of two types, since those who had been schooled under the discipline of Chancellor de l'Hôpital held principles in conformity with Christian piety and moderation, and which were also useful for the conservation of peace and the maintenance of the king's authority. The rest, by contrast, whether because of conscience without much ability, or whether to consolidate an elite faction, were so attached to the externals of religion that they judged it better to let the kingdom be incinerated, than to put up with the least compromise in religious affairs. So the outcome of this divergence of attitude was that the second type [of adviser] has greatly aided to create, foster, and strengthen the League; just as the first type of adviser has helped to achieve the League's destruction: thereby rescuing the kingdom from the brink of the ruin to which the other type had brought it.

[70=133] *Fragment de L'Examen du Prince de Machiavel*, p. 83 *et seq.*

Hotman

[After the English Revolution of 1688, and the outbreak of war between William III and Louis XIV, Huguenots in the Netherlands were torn between loyalty to their native land and loyalty to their adopted republic. Some, such as Jurieu, wrote in favour of William, Protestantism, and popular sovereignty, while others stayed silent. In his account of the Huguenot author of the Franco-Gallia, *Bayle reveals another strategy. He reminds contemporaries that in the sixteenth century Protestants and Catholics had taught, in turn, that peoples were sovereign. For some doctrines were like 'birds of passage' – in 'one country in summer' and in another 'in winter'. In 1673, Hotman had proposed an elected ruler as an alternative to the Catholic regency; but the elective argument had 'migrated' to the Catholic House of Guise in 1584 when the Protestant Henry of Navarre acceded as legitimate heir.]*

HOTMANUS (François) . . . was one of the most learned lawyers of the sixteenth century. He was born in Paris on 23 August 1524 . . . [(A)] As soon as he was fifteen he was sent to Orléans to study law . . . His father, a counsellor in the *parlement* who had already planned his career, brought him back and entered him for the bar; but the young man was soon repelled by the wrangling of the courts, and immersed himself in the study of Roman law and the humanities. He encountered the new opinions for which so many in the kingdom were being put to death; but, finding that he could not profess them in Paris, he went in 1547 to Lyon where he published a book. It was the second he had sent to the press [(B)]. . . .

His ability was so widely recognised that the magistrates of Strasbourg offered him a chair in jurisprudence . . . and he found himself
courted by the duke of Prussia and the landgrave of Hesse. Though
he was not interested in those invitations he did not refuse to go to
the court of the king of Navarre at the beginning of the troubles.
He travelled twice to Germany to seek help from Ferdinand on
behalf of the Princes of the Blood and even on behalf of the queen
mother[a=c] . . . He allowed himself to be persuaded by Jean de
Monluc to teach law at Valence [(D)], which he did so effectively
that he raised that university's reputation . . . Three years later, at
the invitation of Marguerite of France, sister of Henry II, he went
to Bourges, but he left five months later for Orléans in order to be
in the circle of the leaders of the [Huguenot] party who put his
advice to great use. The peace which was made shortly afterwards
did not prevent him from fearing a return of the turbulence. This
was why he withdrew to Sancerre to wait for more favourable times.
It was there that he wrote an excellent book, *De consolatione*.[b=d] He
then returned to his chair at Bourges where he had feared for his
life during the massacre of the year 1572. Having had the good
fortune to escape . . . and vowing never to return, he fled to Geneva
where he published certain books against the persecutors of such
impact that he was offered great inducements to refrain from
further writing of that sort. He ignored them, however (E). . . .

He . . . composed a work in support of the rights of the king of
Navarre [(F)], after which he returned to Basle where he died on 15
February 1590. He declined to go to Leiden where he was offered a
professorial chair. He was able to arrange a new edition of his
works[c=e] which appeared only after his death . . .[d=f] Not everything
he had written was included [(G)]. Of all his writings, the *Franco-
Gallia*, which he himself greatly valued,[e=g] is the work which others
have approved the least, and it has persuaded some people that he
was author of the *Vindiciae contra tyrannos* (H), a book completely

---

[a=c] See below, note 6=23.
[b=d] His son had it published after his death.
[c=e] Taken from his *Life* by Petrus Neveletus Doschius. It is one of ten *Lives* in
Leickherus, *Vies des jurisconsultes*. I use the edition of Leipzig, 1686.
[d=f] . . . printed by Jacques Lectius, Geneva, 1599.
[e=g] See Remark (E).

devoted to republican ideas. Some time later his own maxims were turned against him (I). It is hard to avoid that inconvenience if one writes on certain subjects . . . I am surprised that in François Hotman's *Life* a matter has been forgotten that is particularly resplendent to his memory: namely, that at the age of twenty-three he delivered public lectures in the Faculty of Paris [(M)]. There is no mention either, and this does not surprise me, of certain things that Baudouin published against him, and which would have stained his memory horribly had they been true [(N)]. One could only believe them by supposing that it is easier to become superbly learned and a great enemy of religious persecution, than it is to become an indifferently honest man. . . .

[Remarks (A)–(D) omitted.]

(E) He published in Geneva certain books against the persecutors of such impact that he was offered great inducements to refrain from further writing of that sort, . . . but he ignored such propositions.] This is what is said of . . . [the *Franco-Gallia*] by the author who wrote his *Life*.[1=17]

> Ad Allobroges igitur . . . ['He returned to the people of Savoy . . . and in several of his learned works he steadfastly defended against the faith – or rather through faith – the innocence of those who had been persecuted. Indeed he accomplished this with such skill that certain persons, who thought his spirit would be weakened by such adversity, urged him with sweeping promises to refrain from writing again in that vein. He replied that he had never defended a cause that was unjust. Nor had he ever abandoned a legal case in the hope of profit or through fear of danger. He insisted that in a just action it was better to be defeated than weakly to concede; since though assassination must not go unpunished, the cause of the innocent must equally be defended.']

Immediately after this, the author discusses the book *De regni Galliae statu* [On the Constitution of the Kingdom of Gaul] which

[1=17] [Nevelet, *Vita,*] p. 221.

Hotman brought out at about that time under the title of *Franco-Gallia*. If we are to accept the opinion of certain Protestants, the work was commendable from the standpoint of learning but unworthy of a French constitutional lawyer. M. Teissier speaks of it thus: his book entitled *Franco-Gallia* drew upon him, WITH REASON, the censure of good Frenchmen. For in that work he endeavours to prove that this kingdom, the most flourishing in Christendom, is not hereditary as are the successions of private persons, but that crowns were formerly obtained only on election by the votes of the nobility and the people.[2=18] Therefore, since the power and authority to elect kings formerly belonged to the Estates of the Realm and to the whole nation assembled in a body, so the Estates could depose them. Hereupon he brings in the examples of Philippe de Valois, Jean, Charles V, Charles VI, and Louis XI. But what he principally insists on, is to show that since women have always been judged ineligible for royal office, they ought also to be excluded from all public posts and administration.[3=19]

Add to this the judicious words of Bongars taken from a letter to M. de Thou.[4=20]

> ...Grief gave some colour to the work when it was first printed, for we allow many words to escape us in extreme distress which we should blush to hear repeated when the trouble is over. I write to you of my thoughts about it, not knowing what judgement you make. . . . I am well aware that the good man was well pleased with that piece since he proved it by the frequent reimpressions. It is a malady with which too many of our people are afflicted: they would too willingly have our monarchy reduced to an anarchy. But even if something does have disadvantages, it does not follow that it must be destroyed.[5=22]

Bongars, you will say, has put his finger on it. Hotman was in a rage when he wrote that book, and, not content to avenge himself on the rulers of the time, he endeavoured to discharge

[2=18] From de Thou, Latin version, p. 49 for the year 1573.
[3=19] Teissier, *Additions aux éloges de M. de Thou*, 2, p. 139.
[4=20] The letter was written from Strasbourg in 1595 on the subject of the book by Nevélet, *La Vie de François Hotman*.
[5=22] *Lettres de Bongars*, La Haye, 1695, p. 651.

his resentment upon the monarchy itself and on the whole body of the nation; and with so little judgement that he provided the supporters of the League with powerful arguments for their exclusion of Henry IV. For according to his principles, the Catholics would have been completely in the right to elect the Ducs de Guise as kings of France to the prejudice of the Princes of the Blood. An impassioned writer, you will continue, is little able to think of the future, his thoughts are intent upon the present; it does not occur to him that times may change and that a doctrine which today was in the interest of our cause will, on another day, be as favourable to the cause of our enemies. That was what happened in France under Charles IX and Henry III. Each party was obliged to contradict themselves, as Montaigne has so exquisitely observed. See Remark (I). It is certain that if Catherine de Médicis had embraced the Reformation and established it throughout France, Hotman would have written a fine book to prove that the regency of women was a very fine thing in accordance with the spirit of our fundamental laws. With what vigour would he have refuted the Papists who would have written against this queen? The strongest argument advanced by the Protestants of France to justify their initial call to arms was because Catherine de Médicis wrote to the Prince de Condé. They therefore acknowledged the authority of this woman. Did not Hotman solicit help in Germany in the name of this queen? 'Ab his paullo . . .' ['A little later he was sent to Germany by these men, and in fact by the queen who was regent for the under-age king. His mission was to obtain some reinforcements from Emperor Ferdinand and other German dignitaries for their collapsing fortunes. The speech he delivered to the emperor's Frankfurt Committee survives.'][6=23] We shall see elsewhere[7=24] that he is accused of bad faith in his *Franco-Gallia*, and we shall try to say something in defence of this learned man.

[Remarks (F)–(G) omitted.]

(H) It was believed that he was the author of the *Vindiciae contra tyrannos*.] . . . When I spoke of this work in the 'Pro-

[6=23] Nevelet, in *Vita Hottomanni*.
[7=24] In Remark (H).

ject'[8=37] for this dictionary, I said that the error of those who attributed to François Hotman the book by Junius Brutus was trivial. Hotman, I continued, left France for his religion, and though he was not like those who flee from persecution breathing threats of murder as vengeful[9=38] as those of the persecutors themselves, he did not fail to criticise and protest in his exile. He wrote the *Franco-Gallia* to show that the French monarchy is not what it is thought to be, and that, of right, the people are its true sovereigns. This, in addition to the fact that it contains many maxims from the *Franco-Gallia*, is why it is believable that he was also the author of the work by Junius Brutus. Barclay refutes only this last argument which seems to him plausible enough, but claims to overturn it by something that is rather more plausible which is, he says,[10=39] that Junius Brutus made use of many arguments which Hotman mocked and refuted, and falls into elementary errors of the sort which Hotman could not have made concerning the civil law. This was more obliging to our learned lawyer than what was said by Boeclerus. 'I wish', says he,

> that Hotman had not so obstinately wished to appear among those authors who sound the clarion against kings, who, on their private authority, convert them into tyrants with a subterfuge which corrupts not only sound philosophy, but also Holy Scripture. I wish he had not in his *Franco-Gallia* given such a wretched example to others, and that he had not falsified history more than once to outrage others and to satisfy his prejudices with a too facile indulgence.

[8=37] [*Dic*,] vol. xv, p. 126. [*Vindiciae contra tyrannos* by 'Junius Brutus' was a pseudonymous sixteenth-century pamphlet justifying the overthrow of a tyrant. Bayle, ever concerned to prove that he raises no matter considered subversive, unless it had already been aired in print, indicates that his account, in Remark (H), of Hotman's republican theory is an excerpt from his own previously published *Projet d'un dictionnaire critique* (1692). He may have meant not the 'Project', but the 'Dissertation concernant le livre d'Etienne Junius Brutus imprimée l'an 1579', a long essay which had accompanied the 'Project', later reprinted in the Dictionary in 1697. In short, though a footnote in the 'Dissertation' refers back to the article 'Hotman' (see *Dic*, vol. xv, pp. 124–48, note g, p. 126), the passage had not appeared before in either of the earlier essays.]

[9=38] Acts of the Apostles, 9:1, concerning Saul.

[10=39] Barclay, *Contra monarchomachos*, p. 311.

The Greek phrase of Boeclerus has much more emphasis . . . 'To do a supposed service, he corrupted history more than once.'[11=40] . . . [12=41] I cannot refrain from saying that Boeclerus greatly maltreats Hotman, who was not among those men who, like certain English Catholics of the last century, left their country for religion in a menacing way, spewing out fire and flame, vomiting a thousand imprecations, thundering mantras, and seeking to return with sword in hand, or by the help of exterminating armies; in a word, seeking to return preceded, like the departure from Egypt, with all the plagues of Pharaoh, not excepting the passage of the exterminating angel. Hotman contented himself with some good strokes of the pen, and with a discussion of certain things which displeased him. It is true that unintentionally he worked for the League[13=42] and forged some weapons for [Cardinal] Bellarmine. It is true too that his arms were like those of the Parthians.[14=43] I mean that from a position of flight he hit harder than he would have done had he not retreated. But it needs to be said that his writings do not deserve the castigation merited by other outpourings that emerge from similar circumstances. For example, the Catholics from England in vain produced satires and bitter invectives against Queen Elizabeth,[15=44] for it was all wasted paper which the wise in any party neither make use of nor take seriously. Whatever the facts, appearances were somewhat against Hotman as to the work of Junius Brutus. For, as I have said, it was a very trivial error to have made him the author of the *Vindiciae contra tyrannos*.

(I) His own maxims were turned against him some time later.] It was by accident, and through a common enough eventuality whereby the interests of parties change, that Hotman's own work became subject to the inconvenience I speak of. The revolutions of France so changed the scene that the maxims of each party

---

[11=40] 'Etiam historiam non semel corrumpit.' Cited in Grotius, *De juri belli et pacis*, bk I, ch. 4, p. 275.

[12=41] [*Dic,*] *Projet*, vol. XV, p. 92.

[13=42] See following remark.

[14=43] 'Navita Bosphorum . . .' ['The Punic sailor is terrified of the Bosphorus . . . The soldier fears the Parthian's arrows fired during swift flight. The Parthian fears lying in chains in the Roman prison. But death as an unforeseen force has long carried people off and will go on doing so.'] Horace, *Odes*, 2.13.17–20.

[15=44] See 'Elizabeth', Remark [(K)].

were reciprocally metamorphosed into their contraries. Montaigne pleasantly ridicules the Catholics for it.[16=45]

> See (says he), with what horrible impudence we toss about divine arguments, and how irreligiously we throw them away and catch them again, as fortune alters our position in these public storms. That solemn proposition: that it is permitted for subjects to rebel and to take up arms against their prince for the defence of religion, was maintained last year by a certain party, and denied by the other party: but see now who maintains the affirmative and whether sabres rattle less for this cause than for that. We burn [at the stake] those people who say that it is necessary to harness truth to the yoke of necessity, but does not France do worse in what she does, than in what she says, etc.?

As long as the world lasts there will always be ambulatory doctrines, dependent on time and place: true migratory birds, which are in one country in summer and in another country in winter: wandering lights, which like the Cartesian comets illuminate successively several vortices. Whoever seeks to condemn that would be taken for an unrealistic critic, a citizen of Plato's *Republic*. And thus Hotman should not be held responsible for what, in the *Franco-Gallia*, was afterwards used to his own advantage by the prominent advocate for the Catholic League.

> They [the Protestants] cannot complain (it is Louis d'Orléans in the name of the English Catholics, who speaks thus) if they are treated in the way they have treated others. Follow their advice, tread in the path they have devised to gain ascendancy, and you will establish yourselves and involve them in shame and confusion. In their *Franco-Gallia*, one of the most detestable books that ever saw light of day and composed to ignite the whole of France, they say that it is lawful to choose a king at one's pleasure. Tell the heretics, then, that you do not like the king of Navarre, and therefore let him stay in Béarn until you desire to have him. Thus they should be whipped with their own rods so that

---

[16=45] Montaigne, *Essais*, bk 2, ch. 12, p. 193. Mézerai, *L'Histoire de France*, vol. III, p. 792.

they may know that the potent hand of God chastises them with their own pernicious writing and wicked advice.[17=46]

Fundamentally, Hotman's book is a fine work, well written and full of erudition, and all the more vexatious to the opposite party because the author, as he himself informs his critics, limits himself to the facts. 'Why was Matharele', he asks, 'so outraged by the author of the *Franco-Gallia* as narrator of plain historical fact? For, as he says in Bk 1.10, how could anyone be angry with a mere rapporteur? The *Franco-Gallia* is devoted only to exposition and straight reporting, so that were the words of others effaced the paper would be blank.'[18=47]

He was condemned on the grounds that his book seemed to have been the creation of a besotted, outraged madman, but he replied that this castigation was an actionable offence; since throughout the book he had maintained the stance of a calm and objective scholar.[19=48] That was a singular advantage in such a work. Furthermore, although the rejoinder was indeed written in a humorous style, it did not prevent him from including many things that were intended to be taken seriously. 'Ridentem dicere verum quid vetat?' ['What is to prevent the man who jokes from speaking the truth?'][20=49] That is, it warns the adversary that it is not sufficient for him to make his accusation, it refers to legal proceedings *de lite prosequenda*; and warns that he will be liable to pay compensation in the event of being convicted of calumny . . .[21=50] If we are to believe a historian who was a pastor, this work by Hotman did not please every Protestant, but neither did it displease every Catholic; and it was not written without some involvement with the Cabal of the Maréchal

[17=46] *Avertissements des catholiques anglais*, 1587, pp. 74, 75.

[18=47] It was a satire by Hotman himself. Matagonis de Matagonibus (pseud.), *Monitoriale adversus Italo-Galliam sive Anti-Franco-Galliam Antonii Matharelli* [A Warning against Antoine Matharel's *Italo-Gallia* or *Anti-Franco-Gallia*].

[19=48] 'Quod dicit Franco-Galliam . . .' ['He (Matharel) alleges that the *Franco-Gallia* was composed by an author who had imbibed too much in some wine-shop and vomited up a piece of scrawl overflowing with spleen and stupidity. But I can confirm as fact that many friends of the *Franco-Gallia*'s author call this accusation vulgar impudence deserving flogging and imprisonment. For where in the whole book is there one word which springs from a disturbed mind, rather than from a calm and balanced exposition?'] *Ibid.*

[20=49] Horace, *Satires*, 1.1.24–5.

[21=50] Matagonis de Matagonibus [Hotman], *Monitoriale adversus Italo-Galliam sive Anti-Franco-Galliam Antonii Matharelli.*

Damville. 'Shortly after', he tells us 'the Duc d'Alençon, his majesty's brother, withdrew from court with several gentlemen, who had been won over by the said Maréchal Damville; and, taking the name of Malcontents, they joined forces with the Huguenots of whom none renounced what they had said previously'.[22=51] And Hotman in his *Franco-Gallia* undertook to write that the French people had a sovereign authority not only to elect their kings but also to repudiate the sons of kings and to elect strangers. And upon that subject he says many things, praising those peoples who curb the licence of their kings and bring them to reason. He devotes his attention, after several other discussions, to attacking the regency of queen mothers. He did so because the queen mother [Catherine de Médicis] had been declared regent until the return of her son, the king of Poland. In short, he explored many ancient histories in his usual manner, first from one side, and then from the other. This book was agreeable to certain Reformers and certain Catholics who formed a group in favour of innovation, but not at all to everyone. D'Aubigné[23=52] also attributes that purpose to the book, but he says that it was published in 1573 while Charles IX was alive. De Thou[24=53] and Mézerai,[25=54] who suggest the same motive, place it during the reign of Charles IX, and the latter before the departure of the king of Poland. That overthrows Cayet's hypothesis: that the regency conferred on Queen Catherine at Charles IX's death was one of Hotman's grievances. It is certain that his work was printed before the queen, under the Edict of 30 May 1574, was declared regent. But perhaps he foresaw that it would be so, and it is very likely that he had her in mind in what he said against a female regency. He was thinking of the harm brought about by this princess during her first regency. This talented professor of jurisprudence – who had renounced the post of Counsellor in the *parlement* of Paris for the sake of religion – would have done better to rebut his adversaries seriously and directly instead of resorting to satire. . . .

[22=51] Pierre Victor Cayet, Foreword to *Chronologie novenaire*.
[23=52] De Thou, *Histoire universelle*, vol. II, p. 670. Simler in his *Epitome de la Bibliothèque de Gesner* places the printing of the *Franco-Gallia* in 1573, and he is right. This book was printed in Geneva by Jacobus Stoerius in the year 1573. The Epistle dedicatory to the Elector Palatine is dated 21 August 1573.
[24=53] De Thou, *Histoire universelle*, 57.
[25=54] Mézerai, *Histoire de France*, vol. III, p. 293.

Japan

[When he writes about Japan, Bayle intentionally makes comparisons with public life in Europe. Most Europeans were merely entertained by travellers' tales from the East, but scholars of human behaviour could see in these writings the evidence of similar dispositions and similar political and religious institutions. In Remark (E), Bayle condemns the recent bloody slaughter perpetrated by soldiers and missionaries upon indigenous peoples of the East and in the Americas, which he contrasts to the mildness of the Christianity of the first three centuries. When he assesses a work by a Jesuit missionary concerning the expulsion of Christianity from Japan, he remarks that he would like to see such a history written from the Japanese point of view.]

JAPAN. This is the name of a great country situated to the east of China and divided into many islands. It is treated so amply in Moréri's Dictionary[a] that few things remain for me to observe. Nor will I add anything that he has omitted, but I will confine myself instead to certain aspects of the theology of those islanders.

> The monarchy of Japan is divided into two estates, the ecclesiastical and the secular. The first is composed of the bonzes and the second of the nobility and the people. The name of bonze is given to all those ministers who are dedicated to the service of the Japanese Gods. They make a profession of a celibate life (A), and . . . they recognise a sovereign whom they call Iaco or

---

[a] Especially in the edition of 1699.

Xaco, who has authority over all others: who judges matters of religion, who determines what ought to be practised concerning the worship of the Gods, and what must be believed concerning their nature. He elects the Tundes who attend to matters less important, and who are analogous, in a way, to our bishops . . .[b] The Japanese have two sorts of God. The first are demons whom they venerate under various forms, not in the hope of receiving good from them but through fear of being hurt by them. The second sort are the kings, the conquerors, and the sages, whom they have designated as Gods. The main ones are Amida and Xaca [(B)] . . . It is estimated that there are as many as a dozen sects or religions in Japan, and each individual has the freedom to follow the one of his choice, which causes no division because it is said that ideas, unlike bodies, have no connections with one another. Among these religions, there are three principal creeds. The first does not hope for an afterlife and recognises no substance other than that which is discernible through the senses . . . The second, which believes in both the immortality of the soul and in an afterlife, is followed by the best people, and is called the sect of the men of the most high God. The third belief is that which gives veneration to Xaca.[c]

The bonzes may be compared to our monks.[d] Some authors maintain[e] that the basic division among the sects of Japan is between those who make their religious profession stop at appearances, and those who seek a reality which does not makes its impression on the physical senses, and which they call truth. Those who rely on appearances acknowledge a hereafter [(C)] in which there are eternal rewards for the good, and eternal punishments for the wicked. But those who seek interior and intangible reality reject heaven and hell and teach notions which are very similar to the ideas of Spinoza [(D)]. They are analogous to the Epicureans in that they do not attribute to God the government of the world, given that it would be contrary to his supreme tranquillity which, according to them, constitutes his felicity. Indeed, they go even further than Epicurus

---

[b] *Journal des savans*, 18 July 1689, p. 492, in the abstract of *L'Histoire de l'église du Japon* [History of the Church of Japan] by M. l'Abbé de T.
[c] *Ibid.*, p. 494.
[d] See Remark [(B)].
[e] See Possevin [A. Possevino, the elder], *Bibliotheca selecta*, vol. I, bk 10, ch. 2, p. 410.

for they attribute to him neither reason nor intelligence. They fear undoubtedly lest these qualities would disturb his repose, since they find that the activity of reasoning is attended with some fatigue.[f]

The Christian religion which Francis Xavier, and subsequently many other missionaries, preached to the Japanese found the greatest obstacles to be those which were caused by the bonzes; but not in consequence of their doctrines and their arguments, but because of the usual behaviour of ecclesiastics. I mean their recourse to the secular arm, and the care they took to arouse king and the people to give support to the traditional religion, and to persecute the followers of the new.[g] It must nevertheless be acknowledged that the Japanese priests engaged in discussions with the Christian priests and posed objections to them which proved that they were not lacking in intelligence.[h] They were unable to prevent the Christian religion from making great progress in a very short time. Yet finally they impelled the emperor to resort to the violence which extirpated it entirely from Japan, which has considerably enlarged the martyrology (E). Father Possevin strongly condemned those decrees (F) of the Japanese legislature.

(A) The bonzes make a profession of a celibate life.] But 'they do not always observe it very exactly. They abstain from meat and fish, they shave their beards and hair and they conceal their debaucheries under the appearance of an austere life.'[1] Their most profitable activity comes from burying the dead. For the people, being persuaded that the souls of their relatives may have needs in the next life, spare nothing to procure for them the comforts which the bonzes promise if they pay substantial alms. Another device which they use to enrich themselves is to borrow money by promising ordinary people that they will repay it with substantial interest in the world to come. And when they borrow in this way they say among themselves that the terms are worth the rate.[2]

[f] *Ibid.*, ch. 3, p. 415.
[g] See the *Journal des aavans*, above, p. 499.
[h] See *L'Histoire des ouvrages des savans*, September 1691, p. 8 *et seq.*, in the extract from *L'Histoire de l'église du Japon*.

[1] *Journal des savans*, 18 July 1689, p. 492, Dutch edition.
[2] *Ibid.*, p. 493.

Those who seek to draw parallels between the East and the West would be hard put to find an equivalent for debts payable in the world to come. Nevertheless, celibacy ill observed, deceit hidden under the appearances of a rigid morality, profit-making out of burials, and solace dispatched to souls separated from the body, would afford a great many comparisons. I am therefore persuaded that few people could read the extracts from the work of M. Cousin[3] without exclaiming inwardly: *thus it is with us*. It would be very entertaining to read an account of the West written by an inhabitant of Japan or China who had lived many years in the great cities of Europe. They would indeed pay us back in our own coin. Missionaries returning from the Indies publish accounts of the deceptions and frauds they have observed in the worship of these idolatrous nations. They laugh at them, but they should worry lest they are reminded of the saying 'quid rides? mutato nomine de te fabula narratur'[4] ['Why do you laugh? Just change the name and the same tale can be told about you'] and of the deserved reproaches and reprisals to which they are exposed when they ignore their own faults but reveal in the most minute detail the vices of others.

[Remarks (B)–(D) omitted.]

(E) The violence of the Japanese has considerably enlarged the martyrology.] Read *L'Histoire ecclésiastique du Japon* written by the Jesuit, François Solier, and *L'Histoire de l'église du Japon* by M. l'Abbé de T.[5=20] This abbé 'admires the profundities of God's judgement, and is amazed that he has permitted the blood of so many martyrs to be shed without making use of it, as in the first centuries of the Church, as fertile seed for producing new Christians'.[6=21] Without taking the liberty of delving into the reasons which God's wisdom may have for permitting at one time what it does not permit at another, one can maintain that the Christianity of the sixteenth century had no reason to hope for the protection and favour of God which could compare with that of the Christian-

---

[3] Author in *Journal des savans*, cited above and below.
[4] Horace, *Satires*, 1.6.
[5=20] Published in Paris, in 2 vols., in quarto, in 1689.
[6=21] *Journal des savans*, 25 July 1689, p. 507.

ity of the first three centuries. The latter was a benign, gentle and patient religion which recommended subjects to submit to their sovereigns; nor did it aspire to raise itself to thrones by way of rebellion. But the Christianity which was preached to the non-believers of the sixteenth century was no such thing: it was a bloody and murderous religion which had become accustomed to slaughtering for five or six hundred years. It had contracted a deeply entrenched habit of sustaining itself and expanding its dominions by putting to the sword all those who resisted it. The stake and the gibbet, the terrifying tribunal of the Inquisition, crusades, papal bulls to incite subjects to rebel, seditious preachers, conspiracies, and assassinations of princes, were the ordinary methods they employed against those who did not submit to their commands. Would that bring down the benediction that heaven granted to the primitive church, to the Gospel of peace, and patience and gentleness? The best choice the Japanese could have made would have been to convert to the true God: but not having sufficient illumination to renounce their false religion there remained a choice only between persecuting and being persecuted. They could preserve their traditional government and their traditional worship only by ridding themselves of the Christians. For the latter, sooner or later, would have ruined both these institutions as soon as they had been capable of making war. They would have armed all their proselytes and they would have introduced into the country the support and the cruel maxims of the Spaniards. And by means of killing and hanging, as in America, they would have brought all Japan under their yoke. Thus when one considers these matters only from the perspective of public policy one is obliged to acknowledge that the persecution suffered by Christians in that country was a consequence of the means which prudence uses to forestall the overthrow of the monarchy and the dishonour of the state. The ingenuous confession of a Spaniard justifies the precautions taken by those unbelievers. It gave a specious pretence to the bonzes to vent their hatred and to urge the extirpation of the Christians. For, asked by the king of Tossa how the king of Spain became master of such great tracts of lands in both hemispheres, he all too naïvely replied that he had sent monks to preach the Gospel to foreign nations, and once they had converted a good number of pagans, he then sent his troops who united with the new Christians and subdued the country. This indiscretion cost the Christians dearly.[7=22]

(F) Father Possevin has ... condemned the decrees of the Japanese legislature.] The first fault he finds with them is that they command idolatry, and in particular that of the cult and worship of *Camus* and *Fotoque*. He gives a good account of the enormity of that idolatry, and he places it in the highest degree of the injuries that can be committed against God. He demonstrates this with reference to the example of rebellion. For he says that the greatest crime that can be committed against a sovereign is to take away his power and confer it on another.

> Sicut nullum crimen in regem ... ['No worse crime can be perpetrated against a king and sovereign than to banish him from his kingdom, cast him down from the station of his kingly rank, and elevate another to the heights of royal grandeur. Likewise it is the greatest offence against God, and the worst wickedness is committed against him when religious honour and worship, which he alone is owed, are transferred to some other deity. They are stolen from him to be bestowed upon another.'][8=23]

The second fault of those laws is that though they strictly forbid the bonzes to have recourse to women, they permit pederasty. They forbid the former practice as something vile and abominable, yet they approve the latter practice as something decent and holy. 'In bonziis omnem ...' ['Among the bonzes, copulation with a woman is utterly condemned as vile, base, and abominable. But the enjoyment of boys is allowed. In fact, among these same men, sex with boys is considered honourable and sacred.'][9=24] Possevin shows with many arguments the nefariousness of sodomy. The third fault of these laws is that though they prohibit the slaughter of certain animals dedicated to *Camus* and *Fotoque*, they permit men to kill one another, and even to put an end to their own lives. They suppose

---

[7=22] *Histoire des ouvrages des savans*, September 1691, pp. 13, 14.
[8=23] Possevino [the elder], *Bibliotheca selecta*, vol. I, bk 10, ch. 6, p. 435. See *Pensées diverses sur les comètes*, pp. 340, 390.
[9=24] Possevino, *ibid.*

it to be not only an action acceptable to these divinities, but also
the true path to deification. And thus it comes about that great
numbers of Japanese kill themselves, either by throwing themselves
into water, or by burning themselves, or by burying themselves, or
by leaping from high cliffs. Many also slit their bellies on slight
pretext. Possevin shows the derangement of all such conduct.[10=25]
The final fault which he censures is that the laws of Japan declare
that by the invocation of 'NAMUAMIDABUT' or by shouting
'FORENGUELIO' men expiate all sorts of sin without the need for
repentance. The Japanese, he continues, make no mention either of
expiatory penalties or of good works. They claim that such acts
would be injurious to the merit of Xaca and Amida, who are themselves sufficiently wounded by the crimes of men, and have, through
their sufferings, fully expiated them. This doctrine opens the way
to sin since, given that nothing is easier than to utter an invocation
or a shout, one is easily assured of escaping all the penalties that
one would otherwise have to fear for indulging in the most heinous
crimes. Possevin clearly shows the effrontery of that doctrine,[11=26]
and the pernicious effects that follow from it. In condemning this
doctrine, no reader need fear being mistaken on the question of
right [*droit*]. But if he ventures to join the right [*droit*] to the fact
[*fait*]: to affirm that the doctrine of the bonzes is exactly as Possevin
represents it, then he may properly fear that he judges too hastily.
For one should never condemn people on the testimony of their
enemies. It is important to satisfy oneself first that they agree that
their doctrine has been faithfully represented. It would not be a
faithful representation if one stopped at the literal sense of some
laws, without having considered the interpretation of their doctors.
By that criterion, one could impute to the most reasonable religion
an abundance of absurdities. There are some harsh things in the
Scriptures which it would be wrong to consider as the laws of Christians. For they are not taken in the literal sense: they are explained
and softened by other passages and according to the analogy of faith.
We would need to know whether or not the bonzes do the same
thing in respect of some of the laws of their own legislators. I find
no difficulty in believing what is said of the frauds and hypocrisies

[10=25] *Ibid.*, p. 436.
[11=26] *Ibid.*, p. 437.

of those idolatrous priests, but I think it probable that they cloak their dogmas as well as they can, no less than their conduct, with some show of outward severity. So perhaps we should only impute to some of them what Possevin imputes to the whole body of their sects. It is taught by some monks that gross reprobates have been saved by the simple intercession of the Holy Virgin. The extravagance of those [Christians] who talk of the treasury of indulgences, or who say that the merits of the saints and their works of supplication make up for the lack of penitence in many mortal men, would afford substantial chapters in an account that a Japanese traveller might publish. Would it not be unfair if he related all that as articles of the Christian faith? On that score too, I should like to know what the bonzes would reply to the following question: do you in fact teach what Possevin imputes to you? Nor would I mind seeing a history which they may have written about the establishment and the extirpation of Christianity in their islands. And were they to write it after having read the accounts of François Solier and M. l'Abbé de T.,[12=*] it would be worth even more than a public debate.

[12=*] [Note to edition of 1820–4.] There is by Father Solier an *Histoire ecclésiastique des Isles et Royaume du Japon*, 1627. As for l'Abbé de T., he is none other than Father Crasset. This author is the true author of *L'Histoire de l'église du Japon* ... Paris, 1689, reprinted in 1715 under the author's name ...

Juno

[Juno is one of the Dictionary's several articles which allude to the power of the feminine. Neither paganism nor Christianity had been able to erase the emblem of a great queen from the heart of public life whether she is Juno or the Virgin Mary. Like the Virgin, Juno must bear children and yet remain pure. She is deceived by Jupiter, tormented by jealousy, and must perform impossible tasks. Erasmus had sought vainly to have the Virgin expunged from Christian worship. Bayle supposes that myth and its exegesis permit an interplay between imagination and reality, and that metaphor releases insights into human conduct that the age had yet to fathom. In Remark (EE), Bayle recounts one of his light tales, but it anticipates, nevertheless, a psychology of the libidinous unconscious.]

JUNO, sister and wife of Jupiter, was the daughter of Saturn and Rhea. Her father, being determined to devour his children for fear that one day they would dethrone him, gave her no more quarter than his two other daughters[a] whom he had already eaten. But he was obliged to disgorge them some years later. He was given a brew which made him regurgitate all the children he had the inhumanity to ingest.[b] Thus it came about that Juno was returned to the world.

Various accounts are given of her marriage to Jupiter. One tradition says that they were in love, and lay together without the knowledge of her father and mother [(A)] and without, it would

---

[a] Vesta and Ceres, older sisters of Juno. Apollodorus[, *On the Gods*], 1.
[b] *Ibid.*

seem, keeping her lover waiting too long.[c] Other traditions say that like a dutiful daughter raised to be honourable, she resisted Jupiter's advances [(B)] and that in order to be importuned by him no more sought refuge at a shrine. They add that there she met a man whose counsel so melted her heart in favour of Jupiter that she resolved there and then to please him. There are others who say that if this was the first time that she lay with Jupiter it was not her first amorous experience. For they claim that before her seduction by Jupiter she had been in the grip of Eurymedon, a lascivious giant, by whom she bore a son called Prometheus [(C)]. Jupiter knew nothing of this until after the marriage, and he then vented his resentment against this bastard under other pretexts. There were various occasions when the chastity of his wife appeared to him to be in doubt. [(D)] He would certainly have deserved it since his own adulteries were so exorbitant. There was hardly an animal whose shape he did not borrow in his pursuit of maidenheads. Everybody knows that he changed himself into a cuckoo in order to have his way with Juno [(E)]. This goddess presided over marriages,[d] but she ought not to have had that employment. It was an ill omen: for she and her husband had an unhappy household, and despite the good reasons that obliged her to put up with it, their quarrels, following the many legitimate occasions which he gave her for jealousy, led them to the extremity of divorce [(F)]; and I believe that before getting that far, he had attempted to bring her to reason by brutalising her. On one occasion he hung her up for some time between heaven and earth [(G)]. Since she held, on the one hand, responsibility for marriages and the supervision of weddings, she was responsible on the other for the regulation of their natural consequences. I mean by this that she presided over child-birth and over the many things that follow from it [(H)] ... Authors do not agree about the place where Juno was raised. Some say it was Samos;[d=e] others say it was in the ocean [(K)]. But there was no town where she was more honoured than at Argos [(L)]. She was also greatly venerated at Carthage (M) and at Olympia ... There were in the latter town sixteen matrons appointed to supervise the games which were celebrated in her honour every five years. Three

---

[c] See [*Dic*,] article 'Achille', vol. I.
[d=e] See Remark [(K)].

classes of young women competed there for prizes and entered the Olympic events . . . But to return to the subject, Jupiter's unfaithfulness to his wife was the more inexcusable because Juno had the secret of becoming a maid again every year [(N)] . . .

The cult of Juno in Rome was very ancient [(X)]. The honours she received in other towns in Italy were also very great [(Y)]. She was responsible for many miracles. She had a temple at Falerii before Rome was built. It resembled that of Argos and the ceremonies used were the same as those which the people of Argos had consecrated to her worship. We learn this from Dionysius of Halicarnassus in [*The Early History of Rome,*] book 1.21.

I should very much like to know if anyone, among the pagan sages, ever drew attention to a matter which seems patently obvious to me: namely that no one ever had less experience of a happy life than the greatest of the goddesses, though the condition of happiness is very necessary to the divine nature.[n] We can scarcely conceive of a condition more wretched than that of Juno. I do not base my judgement upon the nature of her employments, difficult and disagreeable though they may have been (Z), and however appropriate they may have been for turning to ridicule the theological system of the pagans (AA). No, I base it upon the need to which she found herself reduced, of persecuting the mistresses and bastards of her husband in order to seek some relief from the jealousy that overwhelmed her. She was vulnerable to this passion because of the proud and imperious disposition with which she had been imbued in consequence of her status as sister and wife of the greatest of the Gods. This sensitivity rendered her torment the more unbearable and obliged her to move earth and sea to procure the satisfaction of revenge. To obtain it she omitted nothing and gave herself no rest. But she never had the fulfilment of a complete and entire success (BB). She had always to begin anew. The misfortune she had to lose her case in a dispute about her beauty [(CC)] must be reckoned not least among the humiliations with which her life was beset. The resentment for that affront which she harboured against Paris, judge of the trial, was very violent and was followed by a thousand aggra-

---

[n] 'Quae nobis natura informationem Deorum ipsorum dedit, eadem insculsit in mentibus ut eos aeternos beatos haberemus.' Cicero, *De natura deorum* [On the Nature of the Gods], bk 1.17 . . .

vations and many afflictions. It was doubtless an agony more severe than the blow of the trident which she received from Hercules in her right breast.[f=o] It is said that after the consummation of her marriage she washed herself in a fountain between the Tigris and Euphrates and from that moment on, the waters of the fountain exuded a most marvellous fragrance which perfumed the air about it (DD). Juno was beautiful and for that reason it might be said that Jupiter's adulteries were all the more inexcusable (EE). But it would be small-minded of me to criticise Arnobius who has judged it in this manner. The superstition of the Romans was so great that some women honoured Juno by pretending to comb and dress her, and to hold up a looking glass before her [(FF)]. But others were little in awe of her and each seated herself in the Capitol before her husband, fancying herself as his mistress. . . .

[Remarks (A)–(L) omitted.]

(M) . . . She was also greatly venerated at Carthage.] I have long thought that Virgil used poetic licence without any regard for history when he depicted Carthage as the city most favoured by Juno;[1=78] and I am not persuaded to change my mind when I see in Ovid and in Silius Italicus a confirmation of what Virgil asserts, since one cannot reasonably doubt that it is he who is the source of Ovid speaking thus of Juno,

> Poeniteat quod non fovi Carthaginis arces,
> cum mea sint illo currus et arma loco.

['I would regret not having given my support to the Carthaginian stronghold, where my chariot and armour are to be found.']][2=79] . . .

I do not here take into account the theologies of those who reduce several pagan divinities to one, since I tend to support the popular view that Juno was venerated as the sister and the wife of Jupiter, and as an entity wholly distinct from Minerva, Diana, the moon,

---

[f=o] See Homer, *Iliad*, bk 5, vss. 392 *et seq.* which say that that wound was very painful. '. . . Tunc ipsam gravissimus occupavit dolor.'

[1=78] *Aeneid*, 1, near the beginning.
[2=79] Ovid, *Fasti*, 6.45–6.

Proserpine, etc. In general I can never see the many references to the widespread cult of this goddess[3=83] without supposing that there is mixed with it I know not how many instances of a custom which is everywhere observed concerning women. For when a woman plays a part in government she is far more assiduously served, honoured and respected than a man who holds a comparable authority. Consider the manner in which the wives of governors of provinces are courted when they are known to be held in high esteem. The honours that are paid to them exceed those which are given to their husbands. This is the practice on earth and it is carried into heaven. Jupiter was served as a king and Juno as an ambitious, proud and vengeful queen, who shared with him the government of the world and attended all his councils.[4=84] I dare to say that the extravagances into which Christians have fallen regarding the Virgin Mary, and which surpass anything that the pagans may have invented in honour of Juno, spring from the very same source; I mean from the habit which there is of honouring women and making one's court to them with much greater zeal and reverence than to the other sex. One cannot do without women in either civil or religious life. He who would remove from the Roman communion their devotion to saints, and especially to the one whom they call queen of heaven and queen of angels, would leave an irreparable gap in it; for the whole would fall apart: *arena sine calce, scopae dissolutae.* Erasmus, condemning the custom of honouring the Virgin Mary from the pulpit at the beginning of the sermon, says that 'it flew in the face of all the fathers of the church who should be imitated in preference to those who, probably to please women, thereafter trod in the steps of the heathens'.[5=85] . . .

[Remarks (N)–(Y) omitted.]

(Z) The nature of her employments, difficult and disagreeable as they may have been.] She had the oversight of marriages

---

[3=83] Additional matters relating to her cult in Italy are treated in Remark [(Y)].

[4=84] See Homer in the *Hymn to Apollo,* 344, when he notes that Juno, because of the birth of her daughter Minerva, was apart from her husband for a year.

[5=85] Erasmus, *In Ecclesiasten* [On Ecclesiastes], in Colomiés, *Rome protestante,* p. 25.

and their consequences. Consider the many commentaries on the following words of Virgil: ' . . . mactant lectas de more bidentes . . .' [' . . . according to custom, they sacrifice choice animals to law-giving Ceres, to Apollo, and to Father Bacchus, but especially to Juno, whose concern is marriage ties'].[6=157]

Commentators will draw to your attention a multitude of suchlike passages and they will refer you to the epithets of *Pronuba* [Matrimonial] and *Jugalis* [Nuptial], etc. which were appropriated by the spouse of Jupiter because she presided over commitments of marriage. This obligation required great attentiveness; for the cases were without number and it was exceedingly difficult to perform it with honour. Had it been only a matter of making matches, the difficulties would not have been so great, for the disposition of the participants and the inclination of nature would have saved the Intendant-General a great deal of trouble. But a Goddess of the highest rank would be committed by virtue of reputation and glory to ensure that people should marry well. I mean by this that the assortment of various qualities and dispositions brought together ought to create an indissoluble bond of affection and concord; and therefore all the marriages that were ill suited and all the correspondingly unhappy households could only give her a great deal of distress by being so many blemishes on her reputation, and so many just reproaches that all the efforts that had been made to invoke and worship her on the wedding day were labours lost. All who had a mind to abuse her thus had a fair opportunity. For in short, either she did all she could to procure happy marriages, or she did not. If she did, then there was reason to conclude she was very wretched since she had an employment which exhausted all her strength and all her industry; and yet ended in failure on countless occasions. The vast number of instances which showed the vainness of her enterprise was a proof that either she had to work with material impossible to shape, or that her powers were ineffective and limited. In the first case, her misfortune and the deplorable cruelty of her fate, or her lack of prudence, were patent. For if she was not free to resign an office, in which, though doing her best, she could only produce ill-success on a thousand occasions, the inevitability of her fate elicits compassion. But if she had been free to resign from her

<hr />

[6=157] Virgil, *Aeneid*, 4.57.

office, and had obstinately continued in it, she would have lacked judgement and prudence,[7=158] and would have maintained herself wrongly in a position which exceeded her strength and which she discharged only to her dishonour. It would have been a poor excuse for her to assert that her good intentions were thwarted by the caprice of another goddess. 'Sic visum Veneri cui placet impares . . .' ['Such is Venus's pleasure, for she enjoys the cruel joke of subjecting to the iron yoke (of matrimony) those of differing beauty and intellect].'[8=159]

This would have been to acknowledge the limitation and the dependence of her powers, a confession more mortifying than any that can be imagined for a goddess as glorious as Juno. This is what could be argued if it is assumed that she discharged her duties to the best of her capacity; but if it had been supposed that she could have done better, she should rightly have been looked upon either as guilty of extreme negligence, or of doing extreme harm; and consequently as highly unworthy both of the honour that was bestowed upon her, and of the responsibility invested in her.

Now these are reflections which the pagans ought to have made independently. For the outcome of these thoughts is to judge that her condition was wholly wretched, whether because of the great labour her employments required, or because of their ill success. The anguish appears to be inseparable from her state: that is she was of a status and of a sex which rendered her extraordinarily sensitive to contempt and humiliation; and one can well imagine that she had the intelligence not to be ignorant of the criticism that might be made against her administration, and to expect that the other Gods would criticise her because of it,[9=160] and that if they had the mendacity neither to utter it to her face, nor to report the attacks that were made behind her back, they would not fail to calumniate her in her absence, or at least harbour unkind thoughts about her. Nothing further is needed to bring anguish to a heart which is vulnerable, ambitious and superb: all that was needed was for her to have been aware that her inadequacies were known.

[7=158] Horace, *Epistles*, 7.1, last verse.
[8=159] Horace, *Odes*, 1.33.
[9=160] The pagans believed that jealousies, quarrels, divisions and similar disorders had their place among the gods.

All the reflections I have just related could be applied to Juno in her role of presiding over child-births. What an ordeal! It was to be without a moment of repose and to be compelled to work in a thousand places at once. The office is subject to innumerable distressing accidents. The art of the most adroit surgeons cannot prevent many infants from emerging in the breech position – some one way and some another – or from dying along with their mothers. These misfortunes provided good grounds for the reproaches of Juno's critics, uselessly invoked under particular and specific names according to the nature of the ailment.[10=161] I know well enough that it can be argued with some probability that one should not reduce to one deity, named differently, all the divinities of marriages, childbirth etc.; but on the other hand it is equally probable that all those other deities ought to be looked upon as the sub-delegates of the Intendant-General. From which it follows that every such malady could well be laid at the door of the Goddess Juno, just as maladministration by provincial governors is imputed to the sovereign authority if he does not produce a remedy for it. Besides, the proliferation of substitutes shows that Juno's employment was thought too arduous. . . .

(AA) . . . **however appropriate they may have been for turning to ridicule the theological system of the pagans.**] The suffixes 'Pronuba' [Matrimonial Goddess] and 'Jugalis' [Nuptial Goddess] which have been discussed above were not the only ones given to Juno in her capacity as patron of marriages. She had other special titles based on her various roles as patron of new brides, or of the matrimonial home, . . . or of assisting the groom to untie the virginal knot.[11=165] . . .

It can in no way be claimed that her duties stopped at the door of the nuptial chamber, for her assistance was also required in the nuptial bed, which she entered under the titles 'Dea Mater' [Mother-Goddess], 'Prema' [Goddess of Newly-weds], and 'Dea Pertunda' [Goddess of Loss of Virginity] accompanied by Deus Pater Subigus [Father-God of the Wedding Night]. It was on this account that Saint Augustine could turn paganism to ridicule; and

---

[10=161] See Remark [(H)].
[11=165] Du Boulay, *Trésors des antiquités romaines*, pp. 149, 150.

since it was very difficult to use only grave expressions on such a subject, he conveyed the impertinence of it in a free and playful language. It would be to expose oneself to the censure of every puritanical or prudish reader were one to translate the exact words of this father of the church. Let us, then, give them in Latin:

> Cum mas et femina conjunguntur ... ['When a man and a woman are united by the yoke [*iugum*] of marriage, the god Jugatinus is invoked. So far, so good. But the god Domiducus is then invoked to lead the bride home [*domum ducere*]. And the god Domitius is employed to install her in the house [*domum ire*]. The goddess Manturna is added, to ensure that she is to remain [*manere*] with her husband. What more is required? Let human modesty be spared: when a proper privacy has been secured, let the desires of flesh and blood run their course. Why fill the bedchamber with a swarm of deities when even the wedding attendants have departed? What is more, it is filled in this way not in order to secure a greater regard for modesty by the presence of the gods, but so that the woman, being of the weaker sex, and made bashful by novelty, may with their assistance surrender her virginity without any difficulty. For the goddess Virginensis is there, and the father-god Subigus, the mother-goddess Prema, the goddess Pertunda, and Venus, and Priapus. What is this? If, at any rate, the man, labouring at his task, needed to be helped by the gods, might not some one god or goddess have been sufficient? Would not Venus alone have been equal to the task? For her name is said to be derived from the fact that it is not without force [*vi non sine*] that a woman ceases to be a virgin. If there is any shame among men, even if there is none among the gods, why, when a newly married couple believe that so many gods of both sexes are present and viewing the proceedings, are they not so overcome with modesty that he is less aroused, and she made even more reluctant? And certainly, if the goddess Virginensis is present to unfasten the virgin's girdle; and if the god Subigus is present to ensure her husband will be able to subdue [*subigere*] her successfully; and if the goddess Prema is there to press her down [*premere*] once she has

submitted, so that she will not struggle – then what is the goddess Pertunda doing here? Let her blush and go forth; let the husband himself have something to do. It is surely dishonourable for any but him to do the act which is her name. But perhaps she is tolerated because she is a goddess and not a god. For if she were believed to be a male, and hence called Pertundus, the husband would require more assistance to defend his wife's chastity against him than the newly delivered woman does against the god Silvanus. But what am I saying? For Priapus is also there, and he is all too masculine. On his immense and most horrible phallus the newly married woman used to be required to sit, according to the most honourable and religious custom of the matrons!']^12=168

These objections [of Augustine] are devastating and I cannot conceive how the most able apologists of the pagan religion could easily have assailed them. The reproach which Saint Augustine proposes for the unnecessary multiplication of beings was, on its own, capable of demolishing it. What mistrust of human powers was shown in supposing that Venus needed to be assisted by three or four other divinities? One may suggest that an apologist would have been able to reply only that Saint Augustine was mistaken to reproach as useless the addition of the goddess Pertunda, and the goddess Mater Prema, and an intervention which left a husband nothing to do. For in this base theology, the one was neither more nor less necessary than the other, and neither, in fact, excluded the participation of husbands. There was, then, a small inexactitude in this aspect of the objections of Saint Augustine. The general argument of the pagans of that era was to reply that the multiplicity of gods objected to was only a multiplication of the names of the same deity. It was a weak answer, given that the works of the ancient pagans afforded its own refutation.

Note, by the way, that the philosophers who undertook to answer the Christian divines deserve our sympathy, for they carried the

---

12=168 Augustine, *De civitate dei* [The City of God], 6.9. [The French original supplies the citation in full in Latin with no translation. Cf. below, *On Obscenities*, p. 328. The translation from the Latin into English is by R. W. Dyson (Cambridge University Press, 1998), pp. 258–9.]

burden of the folly of others. The ancient priests had foolishly committed the fault of ridiculously transplanting the fictions of the poets into official worship; and the philosophers of later ages had to clear up the shame of those absurdities, and so torment themselves in parrying thrusts that hit the mark. Had those who framed so absurd a worship been subject to so dextrous and so powerful an adversary as Saint Augustine, they would have been more circumspect, and they would not have given so free a rein to their impostures. Thus in this you see the disadvantage of the unity of religion. Diversity in religion has its inconveniences which, it must be conceded – and even agreed – are much to be feared; but, on the other hand, it prevents the development of corruption and obliges religions to treat one another with respect.

(BB) Her jealousy obliged her to move earth and sea to produce the satisfaction of revenge ... But she never has the fulfilment of a complete and entire success.] ...

This is merely an outline of the history of this goddess but it is sufficient to show that the heathens must have looked upon her as one of the most unhappy persons who was ever in the universe. For she was no less suited to be considered as an image of extreme misery than Prometheus on Mount Caucasus, Sisyphus, Ixion, Tantalus and the Danaids, and the rest of the great sinners delivered over to eternal punishment. Nothing is more true than the remark of Horace when he said that the cruellest tyrants have been unable to invent a torture more intolerable than envy.[13=185] It arises principally from conjugal jealousy. For what can it be like to be subjected to a continual fatigue in the pursuit of an unsuccessful revenge? Natural immortality in no way sweetens the bitterness of this sad condition but instead increases it; since hope that death will bring an end to the pain and grief would be a consolation.

> Nec finire licet tantos mihi morte dolores,
> Sed nocet esse deum, praeclusa ianua lethi
> Aeternum nostros luctus extendit in aevum.

[13=185] 'Invidus alterius macrescit ...' ['An envious man grows thin over the abundance of another's possessions. Sicilian tyrants could have discovered no torture worse than envy.'] Horace, *Epistles*, 1.2.57–9.

['I may not put an end to such great suffering by dying. It is indeed painful to be a god, for the door to death is closed and my grief is thus prolonged for eternity.']¹⁴⁼¹⁸⁶

The proud title 'Queen of Heaven', a seat upon a fine throne, a sceptre in hand and a diadem on the head, are all useless in the face of an inward disquiet of the soul. One is even more vulnerable to these misfortunes when in the highest posts and offices. Or let us say, at least, that anxiety is like a fever which is not more easily cured in a good bed than upon straw . . . It is not wealth that can drive away a fever or uneasiness of the mind. It is to be noted that if the pagans did not make the observations which I have set down in the preceding remark they are wholly inexcusable. For it was not only through the poets that they were informed of Juno's distressing life. Official worship had adopted these stories: they were to be found on monuments in the temples, in the consecrated statues, the pictures of devotion, or all those objects which are called the books of the unlettered. All served to reveal to everyone in general the jealous distress of that goddess . . .

[Remark (CC) omitted.]

(DD) She washed herself in a fountain . . . and . . . its waters . . . exuded a most marvellous fragrance which perfumed the air about it.] Aelian has preserved this tale for us. He says¹⁵⁼²⁰⁴ that the fountain was wholly translucent and that the inhabitants of that country, as well as the Syrians, were familiar with the tradition which I have reported, and gave it as the cause of the agreeable odour in the surrounding air . . .¹⁶⁼²⁰⁵ One may detect here a characteristic which is both superstitious and imaginative at the same time. People are readily led into deriving from some celestial origin all the particular properties which they find in certain places of the world. And since the pagans allowed themselves to be seduced with a chimerical and vernacular tradition concerning the amours and marriages of the gods, they believed also that Juno, needing to bathe

---

¹⁴⁼¹⁸⁶ Ovid, *Metamorphoses*, 1.661–3.
¹⁵⁼²⁰⁴ Aelian, *De natura animalium* [On the Characteristics of Animals], 12.30.
¹⁶⁼²⁰⁵ *Ibid.*

on the morning after her wedding, chose a very clear fountain and left there some marks of her presence. Note that according to Turnebus they imagined that divine natures would make themselves known by their perfume.[17=206] . . .

The pagans would have easily believed that the saliva of the gods, and so on, was rose-water at the very least. Balzac[18=211] observes that the poet Furius 'makes Jupiter spit snow',[212] while 'another poet creates sufficient nectar to form the rivers of the golden age'. Balzac adds that 'he, whom the History of Matthew calls the Chrysostom of France, when preaching before the late king Henry the Great, did actually say: "Sire . . . Your Majesty sheds pearls for tears, Your Majesty spits emeralds, sneezes rubies, and blows diamonds from his nose", etc.' There would have been little difficulty in persuading the pagans that the gods really did these things. It is thus that we can persuade children that, once upon a time, Urgande the fairy asked of those who combed her hair: 'What are you making fall from my head?'; and heard with delight the following reply: 'Why, gold and silver, of course!' Most of those who believe such a thing in their childhood would believe it all their lives should they see that these things are the common opinion in matters of faith, and were they not disabused of it when they become older. In other matters too, there are many natural phenomena which the traditions of Christian people attribute to miraculous causes, just as the pagans attributed to Juno the fragrance of their fountain. Behold, it was once said to me, that little strip of land where the grass is so pale: it was that path that such and such a martyr trod when he was led from the prison to the place of execution. The way he went has borne the marks of it ever since. The wheat, the grass, whatever is sown there has a tincture of it, and never regains the greenness which you see to the right and the left. There is hardly a parish where you will not hear such stories. I wish some traveller would make a large collection of them. They like to gather material relating to great towns, but a collection of what concerns the country parishes would have its value too.

And in this connection I recall hearing a man of judgement say that his taste was not like that of an ancient father of the church

[17=206] Adrianus Turnebus, *Adversaria* [Journal], bk 30, ch. 39 . . .
[18=211] Balzac, *Entretien* 5, ch. 2, p. 88.

who wished he had been in Rome for a triumphal entrance. For my part, said he, I would rather I had been present for some months among the Roman townsfolk, and had been able to discover from their conversation how women practised their devotions, and how they spoke of Jupiter and Juno; or the content of their common talk on a wedding day, or a day of child-birth, or at a public procession, or on a day of *lectisternium* [parades] and so on, concerning the gods and goddesses, Subigus or Subiga [of weddings], Fabulinus [of early learning], Pertunda [of loss of virginity], and the others. Books do not teach us about those particulars; for it is only through conversation that we can gain an understanding of such minute details.

(EE) Whether, because of Juno's beauty, it could have been said that Jupiter's adulteries were all the more inexcusable.] This was how Arnobius reasoned. 'Et quid regi Saturnio . . .' ['What business did the Saturnian king have interfering with other people's marriages? Was Juno not enough for him, and could he not calm the impulse of his lusts with the queen of the gods, commended by her superior beauty, the grace of her face, the snow-white marble of her arms?']¹⁹⁼²¹³ [19=213] A sophist or a competent casuist could very easily attack Arnobius for that line of reasoning, and say that, after a certain period of time, women's beauty loses its allure with respect to their husbands; the nature of things being such that they are no longer affecting when one has become used to them: *ab assuetis non fit passio* [passion is not inspired by things one has become used to]. He would maintain that the axiom of the *politiques*, that the best means of preserving dominion are those that have been used to acquire them, is false in the empire of beauty.²⁰⁼²¹⁴ [20=214] For if beauty makes conquests, it is not how she retains them. A husband who falls in love merely because his mistress is beautiful will not remain in love because, as his wife, she continues to be so; habit hardens him against that sort of enchantment . . . A sophist might compile many observations of the same sort but at the end of the day he will be dismissed for quibbling. For it is evident that Arnobius bases his remark upon a commonly held notion. A neighbour-

---

¹⁹⁼²¹³ [19=213] Arnobius, *Disputationes adversus gentes* [Disputations against Pagans], 4.
²⁰⁼²¹⁴ [20=214] 'Imperium facile . . .' ['Dominion is retained easily by means of the arts by which it was first procured']. Sallust, in the proemium to the *Bellum Catilinae* [War against Catiline].

hood is more shocked by the amorous intrigues of a man whose
wife is handsome, than by those of one whose wife is plain. By the
same token, a nation, however great, agrees unanimously that the
philandering of its king is more excusable if its queen is ugly than
if she is a fine or rare beauty. Someone has included in the *Scalagérana* a story which has some relevance to this observation.

> Porthaise, a famous divine preaching at Poitiers, had heard
> tales of the infidelities of a local physician named Lumeau
> who, though he had a handsome wife, could not be happy
> without variety. One day, after having spoken against this
> vice in general, he came to particulars. Pointing at him con-
> genially from the pulpit, he then said: nay, we have heard
> with sadness that there are some men who are so profligate
> as to commit adultery even though they have a wife in their
> own house who, for our part, would satisfy us very well.[21=216]

[21=216] *Scalagérana*, p. 192.

Loyola

[In 'Loyola' Bayle pays a guarded tribute to the Spanish Counter-Reformation and to the founder of the Society of Jesus. He directs his main criticism at recent political casuistry, including the war of propaganda being waged in the Netherlands in the 1690s between Jesuits and Calvinists, and warns that posterity should treat such material with caution. Through referring, in Remark (S), to a historic resolution proposed in the French Estates General in 1615, Bayle exonerates the Third Estate from allegedly supporting the divine right of kings. The resolution, Bayle explains, far from supporting the doctrine of divine right, was a repudiation of Jesuitical casuistry posing as popular sovereignty, which claimed that princes who failed to extirpate heresy must be forced from office by popular insurrection.]

LOYOLA (Ignatius), founder of the Jesuits, was born in 1491 in the province of Guipuscoa in Spain. He was educated at the court of Ferdinand and Isabella and as soon as his age permitted him to bear arms, he sought opportunities to distinguish himself. He showed great courage at the siege of Pamplona[a] where he was wounded by a cannon shot which shattered his right leg. While he was recovering from his wound he made the resolution that he would renounce the vanities of the world, go to Jerusalem, and lead a very particular sort of life . . .

He began the rudiments of grammar in 1524 but finding that reading a book by Erasmus cooled his devotion [(D)], he could no

---

[a] This was the siege by the French which ended in the town's surrender.

longer hear that writer mentioned and took up Thomas à Kempis. After two years he was thought to have made sufficient progress to be admitted to courses in philosophy. Accordingly in the year 1526 he departed for Complutum . . .

He then decided to go to Paris, arriving there at the beginning of February 1528 with a firm resolution to study assiduously. But the poverty to which he was reduced obliged him to beg his bread in the streets and to seek help at the hospital of Saint-Jacques, which severely frustrated his plans. He tried several expedients to overcome these obstacles, but as soon as he had solved one difficulty he became caught up in others. It was observed that the intensity with which he exhorted young people to holiness led them to take up a very unusual manner of life. He was accused before an ecclesiastical inquisitor, and narrowly escaped a flogging in the college of Sainte-Barbe [(F)]. None of these difficulties prevented him from completing his courses in philosophy and theology, or from attracting a certain number of companions who committed themselves by oath to a new way of living. This they did in the church of Montmartre on 15 August 1534 and they renewed their dedication twice successively in the same place and on the same day and with the same ceremonies. At first there were seven including Loyola, but later there were ten. They decided that Ignatius should return to Spain to settle certain affairs and then go to Venice, and that they should leave Paris on 15 January 1537 to join him. He went to Spain in 1535 to preach repentance [(G)] and attracted prodigious audiences. Then, bearing in mind the plans of his companions, he travelled by sea to Genoa and thence to Venice where they were reunited on 8 January 1537.[b=f] In the meantime he did not remain idle. He won souls and he made the acquaintance of Jean-Pierre Carassa [(H)] who afterwards became Pope. Since they were sworn to the journey to Jerusalem they prepared themselves, but they wanted above all to honour the Pope and obtain his blessing and permission. They went therefore to Rome and obtained their objective. Returning to Venice with the intention of embarking they found no opportunity, since the war against the Porte [Ottoman Empire] had put a stop to the movement of pilgrims. There-

---

[b=f] They left Paris on 5 November 1536, and did not wait to the end of the period they had agreed.

upon, to avoid being idle, they resolved to travel around the towns under the Venetian jurisdiction. They preached in the streets and then moved into the academies to win over the scholars and finally they returned to Rome. It was there that Ignatius conceived the idea of a new society, which Pope Paul III confirmed in the year 1540 with certain conditions, but in 1543 without conditions. He was created General of this new order and in 1541 he set up his headquarters in Rome, while his companions spread themselves across the earth. He applied himself to various projects such as the conversion of the Jews (I), saving women of a dissolute life [(K)], or caring for orphans. He soon found himself exposed to the most outrageous calumnies [(L)] which did not, however, prevent him from pursuing whatever might contribute to the glory and establishment of his order. . . .

You will find in Moréri that Pope Paul V beatified Ignatius in the year 1609$^{c=h}$ and that Pope Gregory XV put him in the catalogue of saints in the year 1622. Innocent X and Clement IX increased the honours accorded to this new saint [(P)]. But regardless of what was done on his behalf, nothing in the story is more surprising than the prodigious growth of the order in so few years, both in the old world and in the new, despite strong opposition from its adversaries. I believe that no community ever had – and still has – more enemies than the Jesuits, both within and without. Yet their authority, which rose to so high a point so rapidly, has seen an increase rather than a decline. The books which have been published against them would, on their own, make a large library. It may be said that if many people condemn them through prejudice [(Q)], they do not fail to make the most of this, so that without taking the trouble to reply to the pens that malign them, they have a general way of weakening the accusations (R). But it is true also that there are those who, without any appearance of prejudice, maintain that many things have rendered this Society justly odious. They have not acquired so great a power, they say, nor preserved it for so long, without the assistance of a highly refined political strategy. Now is this not the height of immorality in the realm of spiritual sins? Moreover, it is the Jesuits who have extended furthest, and pursued

---

$^{c=h}$ and not in 1605, as Sotuel asserts, *Bibliotheca scriptorum societatis Jesu* [Library of the Writings of the Society of Jesus], p. 2.

with the most energy, the consequences of several doctrines which were conceived before their time, and which expose sovereigns to continual revolution (S), Protestants to slaughter, and Christian morality to the most deplorable laxity that one can imagine (T). Let us return to Loyola. . . .

His life has been written by some twenty authors of whom one is called Jean-Eusèbe de Nieremberg. His work was severely censured if we believe Baronius [(AA)]. I need not add, since this is common knowledge, that the Jesuit Bonhours is one of his patriarch's historians. What Grotius has written of Loyola and the Jesuits provides not the least fascinating section of his history.[d=i] His words are measured, serious, and honourable, and there is nothing in them to suggest invective rather than objectivity and balance. But the more he shows himself free from hatred and partiality, the more he can persuade us of a matter which, to say no less, remains open. He maintains that the profession of a Jesuit does not exclude marriage [(BB)], and that a man who is a member of the Society may live where he pleases and keep a separate home with a wife. Pasquier said the same thing, and was publicly rebutted. I have not found that he replied to the adversary who treated him as a common slanderer. Grotius would have been reprehensible had he possessed no better evidence than this.

[Remarks (A)–(H) omitted.]

(I) He applied himself . . . to various projects such as the conversion of the Jews.] In the residence of the Jesuits he gave a home to certain baptised Jews, and he secured through negotiation a house for the use of every Jew who converted to the true faith. At his request Pope Paul III ordered that they could keep all their goods, and that if they were members of a family and converted in opposition to their parents' wishes, then they would retain their inheritance.[1=43] And as for goods acquired through usury and whose

---

[d=i] Grotius, *Historia*, bk 3, pp. 273 *et seq.*

[1=43] 'Immo vero Judaeorum . . .' ['Indeed, whenever the children of Jews converted to Christianity against their parents' wishes, they were to be allowed to keep all their property completely intact.'] Ribadeneira, in *Vita Ignatii* [Life of Ignatius], bk 3, ch. 9, p. 213.

original owner was unknown, it was ruled that they would be given to converted Jews. Julian III and Paul IV added a new rule which was that every synagogue in Italy must pay an annual tax of a certain sum each year which would be used for these converts.[2=44] In our own times the agents of conversion in France have borrowed some of these ordinances.

[Remarks (K)–(Q) omitted.]

(R) They do not fail to make the most of this, so that ... they have a general way of weakening every accusation.] At one time they used to reply to all the books that were written against them, but now they are weary of it. The reason they give for their silence is that they are no more obliged to refute their enemies' pamphlets than the king of France is obliged to rebut the gazettes of Amsterdam. 'Why should it not be wished' (it is the Jesuit, Father Tellier, who speaks),

> that the Jesuits should neglect to reply to certain pamphlets which were, in their opinion, neither less fabulous nor less contemptible than the gazettes of Amsterdam or the historical and prophetical system of M. Jurieu? Ought they to be more sensitive in the matter of reputation than the God-given sovereign? Ought they not, or at least might they not, be permitted to despise what concerns only their individual honour?[3=99]

Here are further arguments: they concern the pointlessness of reply, and the disposition of a certain part of the public to presume to be true everything that is written against them.

> No sooner have we replied to one of their pamphlets than they have half a dozen more ready to be published. They keep stocks of them, and they distribute them to all parts of the world. Those which were refuted a hundred years ago, or which everyone scorned though they were not refuted,

---

[2=44] *Ibid.*, p. 213.
[3=99] *Défense des nouveaux Chrétiens* [In Defence of the New Christians], part 1, Paris, 1687, p. 27.

are dredged up again today with the same effrontery as if they were new; or as if they had remained unanswered; and those who follow them forty or fifty years hence, will do the same with those that are invented in our own day, despicable and scorned as they are. For instance, what use will it be to the Jesuits of China to have been the first, and almost the only men, to have submitted without the least resistance to the Apostolic Vicars as soon as they appeared in 1684, when this has not hindered their enemies from publishing, as recently as last summer, through the pen of their secretary the Gazetteer of Holland, that the Holy Father was extremely irritated with the Jesuits because they were unwilling to recognise the bishops he had sent to China? Can it be doubted that in a few years time this falsehood will reappear once again? . . .[4=100]

Then let us not have him [the editor of the Amsterdam Gazette] repent the publication of these absurdities, nor a hundred more besides. Let him make no changes to his style in the future. For if they are currently despised, he can be assured that one day, at least, they will provide good copy for the twentieth or thirtieth volume of *La Morale pratique*.[5=101]

Thus you see how artfully they [the Jesuits] take advantage of the prejudice of their enemies, and how they conform to the maxim: *misfortune is good for something*: they profit from the hatred that is felt for them. *Fruuntur diis iratis* ['they relish the gods' anger']. Undoubtedly they would be damaged more if their enemies were more circumspect in their attacks. For when a person indiscriminately mixes accusations that are well founded with those that are not, he helps the accused. He gives him the chance to render questionable those accusations which are, in fact, true. One would need to be very blind not to see that the many pamphlets that daily appear against the Society[6=102] put powerful weapons into their

---

[4=100] *Ibid.*, p. 28.
[5=101] *Ibid.*, p. 31. On this, see the responses of [the Jansenist] M. Arnauld, in vol. III of *La Morale pratique des Jésuites*, ch. 9, bk 12.
[6=102] For example, the one which is entitled *Les Jésuites de la maison professe de Paris, en belle humeur*, printed in 1695. Cf. [*Dic*,] article 'Annat', Remark (B).

hands. It could be said that if they had paid these authors to publish such stories, they would have spent their money well. See the comments I have made on the art of defamation.[7=103] Note that the Jansenists[8=104] pride themselves immensely on being less credulous in respect of the Jesuits, than those of the [Reformed] religion.

(S) ... the Jesuits have ... extended ... the consequences of several doctrines which were conceived before their time, and which expose sovereigns to continual revolution.] The opinion that the authority of kings is inferior to that of peoples, and that he [the king] may be punished by the people in certain cases, has been taught and practised in all countries in all ages, and in all Christian communities that have had any significance. History in every age shows kings deposed at the instigation, or with the approbation, of the clergy. The opinion that sovereigns have received the sword from God to punish heretics is more common still, and it has been carried out in practice by Christians from the days of Constantine to the present by every Christian community that has power over others. Indeed, one would hardly dare write against such an opinion in Holland. Doubtless the Jesuits have not invented these two doctrines, but it is they who have drawn from them the consequences that are the most pernicious and the most prejudicial to the public peace. For by combining these two principles they have concluded, and in their view by impeccable reasoning, that a heretical prince ought to be deposed and heresy extirpated, and by fire and sword if it cannot be done in any other way. For, if sovereigns have received the sword to punish heretics, it is evident that the people, the true sovereign of their monarchs according to the first principle, ought to punish them when they persist in heresy. But the lightest punishment that can be inflicted on a heretic is clearly imprisonment, banishment, or confiscation of goods; and consequently a heretical king ought at least to be removed from his throne by the people, his sovereign and executive [*commettant*] – if I may be allowed to use an appropriate Walloon expression – since, according to the first principle [i.e. that of popular sovereignty], monarchs are no more than officials to whom the people – not able

[7=103] *Ibid.*; [*Dic*,] article 'Bellarmini', Remark (E); see also [*Dic*,] article 'Gregory VII', Remark (P).
[8=104] Arnauld, *La Morale pratique*, vol. III, last page.

to exercise their sovereignty for themselves – delegate the duties and the exercise of sovereignty, but with reservations and with an inalienable right to remove these officials from office as soon as they perform badly. Now there is no case in which it is more fitting to remove them [monarchs] than when they deserve the penalty which sovereigns – understood according to the second principle – are charged by God with inflicting on heretics. But as in most cases it is impossible to remove from monarchs by judicial means the goods whose right to possess they have forfeited under the laws God wishes to be established against heresy, because – so I argue – they normally have sufficient power to maintain themselves when they exercise a royal authority – an exercise which can only be a usurpation as long as they are heretics – so it follows that, in order to impose the punishments which they have justly incurred, recourse must be had to intrigue. That is to say, one may engage in conspiracies against their person, since otherwise the sword to punish heretics, which God has given to the people as the true sovereign, would be unused. Furthermore, if sovereigns have received the sword to chastise those who violate the two tables of the Decalogue [the Ten Commandments], it follows that they must punish with more vigilance the heretics who violate the First Table [blasphemy and idolatry] than the murderers and the thieves who violate the Second. For infractions against the First Table are crimes against divine majesty and affront God directly; whereas infractions against the Second Table attack Him only indirectly. It is therefore the duty of the clergy to urge sovereigns to punish heretics as violators of the First Table of the Decalogue. And if princes are permissive in this respect, clergy should inveigh far more loudly against this neglect than against that which is shown in respect of murder and theft. They should even insist that if the present safety of the realm obliges them to grant edicts of tolerance to heretics, then they are not required to keep their word for longer than the danger lasts. And when this danger has passed, they should resume the sword to extirpate heresy, just as they would resume it against robbers and murderers when the danger, which forced them to make a truce with them, has passed. In a word, if God has placed the sword in the hand of sovereigns to punish heresy, the granting of an indulgence would render them as criminal before God, as would the granting of an indulgence for theft, for adultery or for murder.

Therefore, the only thing that could excuse it would be to argue that they had to promise to suspend the application of the penal laws to avoid a far greater harm: the certain ruin of state and church; from which it follows that they are obliged to resume their prior commitment as soon as the danger has passed; for every oath that binds a person to disobey God's law is essentially null and void. Such are the principles on which the Jesuits have built a system which has rightly rendered them odious, and has justly aroused horror of the maxims contrived by some of their members. They have built upon a foundation already in existence, just as they have elevated consequence upon consequence far beyond sight of the original, without being astonished at the ugliness of the outcome. They believed that, on the one hand, they served the good of the church and that, on the other, they did nothing against the art of reasoning. I shall not examine whether logic could in fact have guided them through all these consequences, for the matter would be too odious. I am content to say that France, having seen two of her kings [Henry III and Henry IV] successively murdered on the pernicious grounds that they protected heretics, asserted that there was no better way of attacking this wretched train of consequences than to demolish its basic premise. It was for this reason that the Chamber of the Third Estate of the Realm[9=105] sought to have condemned as a pernicious dogma the opinion that the authority of monarchs was founded on anything other than God.

I add to this an observation of M. Jurieu: for he cannot be suspected of partiality to the Jesuits, and yet undoubtedly he has praised the following line of reasoning: *princes can put heretics to death: therefore they should put them to death*, and he has ridiculed a man who would condemn neither those who wanted them executed, nor those who did not want them executed ...[10=106] ...[11=107]

M. Jurieu reasons as well in that passage as he reasons ill in another book[12=108] where he maintains that magistrates are obliged to punish idolaters – though he does not condemn the exemption from punishment which Holland has permitted idolaters [Catholics]

[9=105] In the year 1615.
[10=106] [Jurieu,] *Vrai Système de l'église*, p. 638.
[11=107] The words of this passage [from Jurieu's book] printed in italics are taken from a book by [the Jesuit] M. Ferrand, *Réponse à l'apologie pour la Réformation*.
[12=108] [Jurieu,] *Tableau du Socinianisme*, bk 3.

to enjoy for whole centuries. Note that when I say that he [Jurieu] reasons well, I have supplied in my imagination a clause which is highly essential for his discourse, and which he has omitted. The last sentence is absurd unless this, or something equivalent, is added: 'and nevertheless I am for those that do not put them to death, and it is my opinion that we should follow their example'.

(T) . . . and Christian morals to the most deplorable laxity that one can imagine.] The Jesuits did not invent mental reservations, nor the other opinions for which M. Pascal has reproached them,[13=109] nor even the philosophical sin.[14=110] They found all that in other authors; either specifically, or in the sense that a doctrine is contained in a principle of which it is a consequence. But since in their Society we have seen a greater number of supporters of these opinions than in any other community; and since in their hands these remiss maxims become daily more fertile by virtue of the energy which they give to discussing such things, they have been attributed to them – both in name and more substantially. Oh unhappy fruits of disputation, since their methods of study have been at least as much to blame as the corruption of the heart. For, before beginning moral theology, they teach one or several courses in philosophy; they have made a habit of quibbling about everything; they have wrangled a thousand times on the elements of reasoning; they are heard defending as often the *pros* as the *cons* of universal categories [*des universaux*], and of many other things of the same sort; their minds are so geared to matters of objection and distinction that when they come to handling morals they find themselves wholly inclined to confuse them. Distinctions proliferate; arguments *ad hominem* oblige you to retrench on everything; to give way on one thing today, and on another tomorrow. All this is highly dangerous: for dispute as long as you please about questions of logic, but in matters of morals be satisfied with good sense and with the light suffused through your mind by reading the Gospel.

[13=109] In *Les Lettres provinciales*.
[14=110] This dogma is an almost inevitable outcome of the definition of *liberté* [free will], by which it is established that in order for an act to be free, the agent must be able to position himself either to the right or to the left, but of necessity nowhere else. Moreover, this definition is the most common in the Roman church.

For once you start to dispute in the manner of the Scholastics you will soon be unable to escape from the labyrinth. He who said that the books of the casuists reflect the art of quibbling with God was right;[15=111] for these advocates at the bar of conscience find more distinctions and more subtleties than the advocates of the civil law. They make the tribunal of conscience a sort of moral laboratory in which the firmest truths evaporate into smoke, *sal volatile*, and hot air. What Cicero has said of the subtleties of logic[16=112] describes admirably those of the casuists; since you are caught in your own webs, you get lost in them without knowing which way to turn; and you can save yourself only by letting go of almost everything. They who have read Father Pirot's book[17=113] will tell me that it is easier to censure it and to feel that it contains a harmful doctrine than it is to explain one's objections.

In short, though the Jesuits are not the inventors of these remiss opinions, which are practised all the time by other parties, they ought not to regard it as unfair that they are attributed to them. For the principle is one which they themselves use in respect of the Mons version of the New Testament.[18=114]

[15=111] See *Journal des savans*, 30 March 1665, p. 249, for what M. Bernier [in] *Abrégé de Gassendi*, vol. VII, bk 2, ch. 8, p. 529, relates of the first president [of the *parlement* of Paris], de Lamoignon.

[16=112] 'Dialectici ad extremum . . .' ['Logicians prick themselves severely with their own shuttles; for by asking many questions they not only discover arguments which they cannot then refute, but unravel what they had begun and had almost finished weaving.'] Cicero, *De oratore* [On the Orator], 2.38.

[17=113] Entitled *L'Apologie des casuistes* [In Defence of Casuists].

[18=114] See the remarks of Father le Tellier on *La Défense de la version française du Nouveau Testament* [Defence of the French Version of the New Testament], Mons, p. 377 *et seq.*

Machiavelli

[Bayle's Dictionary shows how Machiavelli's writing at the turn of the eighteenth century was continuing to inspire new translations and editions. To express his own opinion Bayle reprints a book review of a recent translation of The Prince *from his journal* Nouvelles de la république des lettres. *Having reported the adverse criticism, Bayle defends, with reservations, the school which exonerated Machiavelli from the charge of advocating a statecraft without moral purpose. Machiavelli's aim according to scholarly opinion, Bayle shows, had never been other than to defend the republic against tyranny. He differed from other thinkers in his acknowledgement of the paradox that government must sometimes set itself above ordinary morality.]*

MACHIAVELLI (Niccolò), a native of Florence, was a man with much insight and an excellent pen. He had a sprinkling of Latin[a] but he started off in the service of a learned man who, having shown him many fine passages of the ancient authors, gave him the task of inserting them in his books [(A)]. He wrote a play in the style of the ancient Greeks [(B)], which proved so great a success that Leo X used it to entertain the city of Rome. He was secretary and afterwards historiographer to the republic of Florence. The Medicis procured this employment for him with a good salary to compensate him for having been tortured upon the rack.[b] He suffered in this way when he was suspected of complicity in a conspiracy on the

---

[a] 'In nulla vel ...' ['He had hardly any or just a moderate knowledge of Latin literature']. Paolo Giovio, *Elogium doctorum virorum* [Sayings of Learned Men], 87.
[b] *Ibid.*, p. 206.

part of the Soderini against the House of the Medicis. He had the fortitude to withstand the torture and to confess nothing.[c] The praise he gave Brutus and Cassius in his speeches and in his writings brought him under grave suspicion of having been the ringleader of a plot which was exposed [(C)].[d] Nevertheless no proceedings were ever taken against him. From then on he lived in poverty ridiculing everything and having no religion.[e] A tonic which he took for his health brought about his death in 1530 [(D)]. Some say that the public authority had to oblige him to receive the sacraments.[f] Others assert that he died vomiting blasphemies.[g] Of all his books, the one which has aroused the most controversy[h] is a work of politics which he called *The Prince* (E). Many authors have written against it. Nevertheless it was Possevin, who had not read it at all, who caused it to be condemned by the Inquisition [(F)]. Machiavelli published seven books on the art of war, which made him seem to the Duke of Urbino to be a man highly capable of drawing up an army in battle. He was however sufficiently prudent never to try out his theory on a single battalion [(G)]. A new edition of the greater part of his works has recently been published in French [(H)]. His novel *Belphégor*, an exceedingly clever piece, was published by M. le Fèvre of Saumur in 1664 . . .[i]

Those who say that he intended to portray Charles V [in *The Prince*] are very much mistaken [(M)]. It has been said that Catherine de Médicis made a particular study of this work and that she recommended it to her children [(N)]. Those who make this observation never fail to accompany it with many injurious epithets relating both to this queen and to Machiavelli. There are not many authors who write of him without attempting to denigrate his memory.[k=o] Yet some excuse him and attempt to defend him.[l=p] And

[c] Varillas, *Anecdotes de Florence*, p. 247.
[d] Paolo Giovio, *Elogium doctorum virorum*, 87, p. 206.
[e] See Remark [(D)].
[f] See Varillas, *Anecdotes de Florence*, p. 249.
[g] 'Blasphemans evomuit improbum spiritum.' ['He was blaspheming even as he spewed out the last breath of his shameless life.'] Théophile Raynaud, *De malis et bonis libris* [On Good and Bad Books], no. 46, p. 48.
[h] Théophile Raynaud, *ibid.*, gives us a list of authors who have refuted Machiavelli.
[i] See *Journal des Savans*, 12 January 1665.
[k=o] See Clasen, in ch. 9 of his treatise *De religione politica* [On the Political Religion], p. 162, edition of 1682.
[l=p] See Remarks [(D)] and (E).

there are even those who regard him as a writer who was motivated by a passion for the public good [(O)] and who think that he represented the art of politics for no other purpose than to inspire men with a horror of tyrants, and to encourage peoples everywhere to stand up for their liberty. If his true motives are a matter of controversy, one must at the very least acknowledge that in his conduct he showed himself to be formidably inspired by the spirit of republicanism [(P)]. One of his recent opponents is the Italian Jesuit, Father Lucchesini. See his *Saggio della sciocchezza di Nicolò Machiavelli*, printed in Rome in 1697.[m=q] The author of the appendix to the treatise *De litteratorum infelicitate* [On the Misfortunes of Men of Letters] has included Machiavelli in his catalogue,[n=r] and he was not mistaken; for this Florentine was besieged by ill fortune in more ways than one [(Q)] . . .

[Remarks (A)–(D) omitted.]

(E) A work of politics entitled *The Prince*.] The maxims of this author, it is said, are extremely pernicious; for public opinion is firmly persuaded of the proposition that Machiavellianism and the art of reigning tyrannically are expressions which carry the same meaning. This work of Machiavelli has been translated into French by M. Amelot de la Houssaye. The author of the *Nouvelles de la République des Lettres*,[1=26] referring to the third edition of this translation, makes the following comment.

> The Preface is full of salient reflections. We read there, among other things, this notion of M. de Wicquefort: 'that, almost always, Machiavelli tells us what Princes do, and not what they ought to do'.[2=27] It is surprising that there have been so few who contest that Machiavelli imparts to princes

---

[m=q] The *Journal de Leipsic*, 1698, p. 352, gives an excerpt.
[n=r] See Cornelius Tollius, appendix to *Pierrium Valerianum* [Giovanni Piero Valeriano], pp. 20, 21.

[1=26] [i.e. Bayle himself,] January 1687 [in *NLR, OD* I, pp. 740–1].
[2=27] Chancellor Bacon, *De dignitate et augmentis scientiarum*, 1.7.2 [The Advancement of Learning (revised version)]. 'Est quod gratias . . .' ['There is reason to thank Machiavelli and writers like him, for they openly and undisguisedly make public how men do act, not how they ought to act.']

a dangerous politics, given that, on the contrary, it is princes who have imparted to Machiavelli everything that he writes. His masters have been the study of the world and the observation of real involvements, not a fanciful closet meditation. So whether they burn his books, or refute them, or translate them, or comment upon them, it will not affect actual government one jot more or less. Politics, through a wretched and fatal necessity, must set itself above morality: this is not admitted, but it does as Achilles did: 'jura negat sibi nata' ['he breaks his own laws']. There is a distinguished philosopher of the present age who cannot bear it to be said that it is inevitable for man to sin. I believe, however, that he now acknowledges that sin in the case of sovereigns, without being excusable, is a necessary thing; yet not only are so few content with what is necessary, they would not need to be in this wretched condition of necessity if they were all decent men.

To this may be added the saying of an ancient poet: that the most innocent would learn to be reprehensible through the bare exercise of royalty and with no need for any tutor:

> Et nemo doceat fraudem et sceleris vias,
> regnum docebit.

['Kingship will teach us the ways of deceit and crime, if no one else does.']³⁼²⁸

Everyone has heard the maxim 'qui nescit dissimulare nescit regnare' ['the man who does not know how to dissemble, does not know how to rule'], and to deny it to be completely true one would need to be very ignorant of affairs of state. Boccalini with great subtlety conveys to us that Machiavelli learnt the politics in his *Prince* from the reign of certain popes.

> Io in tanto non intendo ... ['I shall not attempt to justify my writings, but I publicly indict and condemn them as wicked and execrable rules for the government of a state.

---

³⁼²⁸ Seneca, *Thyestes*, 312. He had said in vs. 217, 'Sanctitas, pietas, fides ...' ['Integrity, piety, loyalty, are qualities which belong to the private citizen, but kings may do as they please.'] *Ibid.*, 217.

Wherefore, if what I have printed is a doctrine of my own invention, or if it was originally devised by me, then let me suffer the sentence pronounced against me. But if I can show that I have written nothing except such remarks as I have collected from the actions of certain princes whom I can name whenever it pleases Your Majesty to command me to reveal them, what reason would there be for those who were the authors of what I have transcribed to be considered innocent, and for me to be condemned to die as a knave and an atheist? What reason is there for an original to be accounted holy, and the copy burnt as impious and execrable? And why should I be so violently persecuted when the reading of history (a liberty allowed and commended by all mankind) is able to turn anyone who peruses it with a politic eye into so many Macchiavellis?']⁴⁼²⁹

Note the last words. Boccalini claims that since the reading of history is both permitted and recommended, it is wrong to condemn the reading of Machiavelli. That is to say that one learns from history the same maxims as one learns from this author's *Prince*. In the former they are actually put into practice, while in the latter they are merely suppositions. Perhaps it is on this account that certain men of intelligence assert that it were to be wished that no histories were ever written.⁵⁼³⁰ This is not to absolve Machiavelli completely; for he advances maxims which he does not condemn while a good historian, who gives an account of the application of these maxims, does indeed condemn them. This puts a considerable distance between the book of this Florentine and a work of history. Yet it is incontestable that the reading of history tends incidentally to produce precisely the same effect as the reading of Machiavelli. There are able persons who have defended Machiavelli⁶⁼³¹ by saying

---

⁴⁼²⁹ Boccalini, *Ragguagli di Parnasso* [Reports from Parnassus, 1614], cent. 1, ch. 89.
⁵⁼³⁰ See Mascardi, *De arte historica* [On the Art of History].
⁶⁼³¹ 'Pro Machiavello inter alios . . .' ['Gaspius Scioppius among others has written a defence of Machiavelli in his *Political Education*, and in his *Dissertation against Paganino Gaudenzio*.'] [See] Bosius, Joannes Andreas, *De comparanda prudentia civili* [On Attaining Political Wisdom], no. 93, in Magirus, *Eponymologium*, p. 552.

that anyone who has attacked him reveals only their ignorance in matters of public affairs.[7=32]

> 'Quicunque sane hactenus Machiavellum ...' ['Those who have up to now taken it upon themselves to confute Machiavelli have, to tell the truth, very openly betrayed their own "lack of education" in political philosophy. This I call ignorance of the nature and quality of political science, as does that great master of definitions, Aristotle.[8=33] For you can see that practically all men in their political discussions talk as if there were no states except those which are concerned, before all else, with the safety of the people, or which actually strive for full and genuine happiness in our lives. They claim that, for them, and for any teacher of politics, these criteria alone should be considered. Therefore they condemn any thinking not concerned with those states which they judge to be the only ones anyone need know about. Indeed, they place outside the limits of political instruction any other thinking.']

You will find many remarks of this sort in the foreword which the learned Conringius has attached to Machiavelli's *Prince*. Note well that our Florentine is there accused of having enriched his work with ideas taken from Aristotle. It follows that Machiavelli's maxims must have been available in books for a long time.

> Nicolaus Machiavellus ... ['Niccolò Machiavelli, that hollow cymbal of the political arts, could give his *Prince* almost no original counsel about ruling: he gave him specifically Aristotle's previous observations in his *Politics*, book 5, about what to do to preserve tyranny and dominion.

[7=32] Conringius, preface to his edition of *De principe* [The Prince], in Magirus, *Eponymologium*, p. 554.

[8=33] Let us add to this these words of M. Naudé in ch. 1 of his *Coups d'état*: 'To attempt to speak of politics as it is practised and exercised today, without saying anything of its acts of statecraft [*coups d'état*], is to be unaware of the art, the teaching, and the means, used by Aristotle in his *Analytics*; that is, to speak of each thing correctly, and according to the principles and demonstrations that are appropriate and essential to it. "Est enim paediae ..." ["In education it is ignorance not to be aware of those matters for which one should seek a demonstration, and those matters for which, in fact, one should not"], as he [Aristotle] says in his *Metaphysics*.'

But this most insidious teacher of wickedness probably rep-
licated all those ideas as if they were his own, concealing his
plagiarism of Aristotle. But there was this difference: this
man wickedly and shamelessly recommended to every prince
what Aristotle had earlier prescribed, very rightly and sen-
sibly, only to chiefs and tyrants.']⁹⁼³⁴

Gentillet[10=35] accuses him of having plagiarised Bartolini. I am
astounded that no one has suggested that he lifted his maxims from
that angelic doctor, the saintly Thomas Aquinas. For see in Naudé's
Coups d'état[11=36] a long passage from the commentary by Aquinas
on the fifth book of Aristotle's *Politics*. M. Amelot[12=37] proves that
Machiavelli is only the disciple or interpreter of Tacitus, and on
this point he makes the same observation as Conringius. Among all
who censure Machiavelli, he says, you will find that some confess
that they have never understood him, as it certainly seems from the
literal sense that they give to certain passages, just as politicians 'are
fully able to interpret him otherwise'.[13=38] So that in reality he is
censured only because he is misinterpreted; and he is misinterpreted
by many who would understand him better were they to cease reading him from so prejudiced a perspective. For if, by contrast, they
were to judge him impartially – that is to say by putting an equal
distance between him and his adversaries – they would see that the
maxims which he discusses are absolutely necessary to princes who,
to use the words of the great Comte de Médicis, cannot govern
their states with the rosary in their hands.[14=*] He said also[15=39] that
it was not surprising that Machiavelli was censured by so many,
since so few people know what *raison d'état* means, and in consequence there are few persons sufficiently competent to judge the
quality of the precepts he advances or the maxims which he teaches.
And I say, in passing, that his maxims and his practical advice

---

⁹⁼³⁴ Conringius, Introduction to Aristotle's *Politics*, ch. 3, p. 583, in Thomasius, *De
plagio litterario* [On Literary Plagiarism].
¹⁰⁼³⁵ In the preface to bk 3 of *Commentariorum adversus Machiavellum* [Commentaries
against Machiavelli].
¹¹⁼³⁶ In ch. 1, p. 16.
¹²⁼³⁷ In his notes to *Le Prince de Machiavel*.
¹³⁼³⁸ Amelot de la Houssaye, Préface to *Le Prince de Machiavel*, 7.
¹⁴⁼* [Citation in edition of 1820–4:] 'Che gli stati non si tenevano con paternostri.'
['States are not governed by paternosters.'] Machiavelli, *Historiae*, VII.
¹⁵⁼³⁹ In *L'Epitre dédicatoire* [Dedicatory Epistle].

should be judged, and even examined step by step, from the perspective of a minister or the perspective of a prince; that is, by those persons who, before coming to the throne, might well have condemned them and detested them – so true is it that one needs to have become a prince, or at the very least a minister, to understand not the utility, I say, but the absolute necessity of these maxims. This is to apply to Machiavelli what another has said of Tacitus.

> Those who accuse him of supporting maxims which are impious and immoral will forgive me if I point out to them that no *politique* ever treated the rules of statecraft more reasonably than he; and that the more scrupulous sort of person, who condemned him when they were private individuals, studied him, and applied his precepts, once they were called to the government of public affairs.[16=40]

M. Amelot, who cites these words of M. de Chanvalon, then confirms them with an example. Germany, says he,[17=41] has recently seen a good example in the last bishop of Vienna who, when he was plain Father Emeric, inveighed in all his sermons against the maxims of statecraft to the point of believing that there was no salvation for those who practised them. But as soon as he was elevated to the court of the empire and became a minister of state he changed his opinion with his circumstances; and so he came to deploy (but with more finesse) those very maxims which he had condemned when they were practised by his predecessors the princes of Aversberg and of Lobkowitz, whose disgrace he had procured, and by Count Augustin de Walstein, his rival for the bishopric of Vienna and as cardinal.[18=**]

We must say something about the work which was written by Innocent Gentillet against that of Machiavelli. In the edition I use,[19=42] its title is *Discours sur les moyens de bien gouverner et maintenir en bon paix, un royaume ou autre principauté* . . . [Treatise on

---

[16=40] M. de Harlai Chanvalon, Préface to his translation of Tacitus.
[17=41] [Amelot de la Houssaie,] in his *Discours critique*, at the beginning of *La Morale de Tacite*, 1686. Since then he [Amelot de la Houssaie] has included it in his French translation of the first six books of the *Annals* of Tacitus.
[18=**] In a manuscript account of the court at Vienna, by a German prince.
[19=42] It is in octavo.

the Means of Governing a State Well and Maintaining a Kingdom
or a Principality in Peaceful Good Order; Divided into Three
Books: Namely, the Council, the Religion, and the Forces of Order
that Should Sustain a Prince. Against the Florentine, Niccolò
Machiavelli]. It is dedicated to the Duc d'Alençon, brother of king
Henry III. It indicates the name of neither author nor publisher,
but merely the date: 1576. This book is usually cited as if it were
entitled *Anti-Machiavelli*: yet this is an abridgement of its true
title though it is from this abridgement that the notion *Anti-
Machiavelli*[20=***] has arisen. Consult M. Baillet.[21=43] I am persuaded
that what I am about to cite from M. de la Popelinière refers to the
treatise of Gentillet. He first condemns the tolerance that is shown
for the works of the Florentine, so full of pernicious maxims; and
then he adds:

> Yet, since Christian magistrates have connived at such
> prejudicial writings: then let a decent thinker emerge among
> the French to confound the errors and the impieties that he
> might judge too open and too commonly favoured; but with
> such poor success at finding authorities, and with so few
> adequate alternative examples, (on which the two parties
> might rely and which the Florentine calls ridiculous); and
> being so short of good arguments, which are the true arms
> under which he exhorts everyone to fight, the poor author
> has been able to draw no reward for taking so much trouble
> to defend state, religion, and the duty of both combined.
> For he receives only threats and insults in place of the hon-
> ours and the stipends that are the proper recompense of
> such detailed and painstaking effort.[22=44]

If one judged a work's merit by the multiplicity of its editions
and translations, that of Gentillet could claim a high degree of glory,
for it has been translated into many languages and reprinted many
times. The edition of Leiden, 1609, mentions that it has been aug-

[20=***] [Note inserted in the edition of 1820–4:] There exists at present under the
same title of *Anti-Machiavelli* a work by the king of Prussia, known as Frederick the Great, and who was then only a royal prince. Voltaire edited it.
[21=43] In vol. II of *Anti-Machiavel* [Gentillet, *Discours sur les moyens de bien gouverner
... un royaume*, 1576], pp. 129 *et seq.*
[22=44] La Popelinière, *Histoire des histoires*, bk 2, pp. 405, 406.

mented by half its length again. The dedicatory epistle has been cut.

If we had the complete work, of which a part was published in 1622, we would perhaps have the best commentary which has been written on Machiavelli's *Prince*. This cut version is entitled: *Fragment de l'examen du Prince de Machiavel* . . . [Excerpt from an Analysis of Machiavelli: Wherein Are Considered Confidential Advisors, Ministers and Counsellors to the Prince, together with the Position of Favourites]. It has 339 pages and is in duodecimo. I have quoted from it in my article on 'Chancellor de l'Hôpital' [above]. A new Latin translation of Machiavelli's *Prince* has been produced in Amsterdam in octavo by Casparao Langenhert, philosopher, who adds his own interpretation. He, who has given us this new translation, 'undertook it only because the one formerly available appeared to him to be defective'.[23=45] . . .

[23=45] *Journal des savans*, 15 March 1700, p. 211, Dutch edition.

Mâcon

[The theme of cruelty perpetrated against a minority in the name of official religion permeates Bayle's work, but in 'Mâcon' Bayle probes the causes and proposes a remedy. The atrocities inflicted in 1562, he contends, were as evil as the barbarities of the most infamous tyrants of antiquity. They were caused, in part, by the abuse of power by officials sent to suppress a disturbance. Yet political theory was equally responsible since it taught, but wrongly, that the republic must maintain a unity of faith, and that the prince who did not could be called 'tyrant'. In Remark (C), Bayle asks whether historians should keep records of atrocities given that some had thought it better for France and for Christianity if their memory were cast into obscurity. They have no alternative, he replies, for if accurate records of abominations are not kept then the imagination will supply them.]

MÂCON, a town of France on the Saône in the Duchy of Burgundy ... This town was afflicted cruelly by the disorders which the Wars of Religion caused in France in the sixteenth century. The Reformers set up a church there in 1560[a=c] and they flourished so considerably that when the massacre of Vassy [1562] obliged them to organise for their own safety, they very easily became masters of the city.[b=d]

It was at the beginning of May 1562 that they established an ascendancy without much violence and without any bloodshed. But

[a=c] Theodore Beza, *Historia ecclesiastica*, bk 3, p. 214.
[b=d] *Ibid.*, bk 15, p. 407.

172

three days later it was learnt that in the city of Lyon, religious images had been smashed, and it then proved impossible for the pastors and the elders to restrain the common people of Mâcon from doing the same, and from that time on, the exercise of the Roman religion was suppressed. Tavanes tried several times to recapture the city, but without success, but finally, having obtained secret intelligence, he took it by surprise on 19 August 1562.^{⊂ᵉ} After violent street fighting against the inhabitants he made himself commander. Every sort of pillage and barbarity (A) was committed and it was then that the atrocities of Mâcon (B) of which I have promised to speak took place. I shall keep that promise and when I do, it will be seen why I discuss these frightful disorders in many places in this work (C). These atrocities have become more infamous than those of the Island of Capri (D).

(A) Every sort of pillage and barbarity was committed.] After the houses of the Protestants had been completely pillaged, and it seemed that there was nothing more to appropriate, Madame de Tavanes managed to unearth hidden supplies so that as her part of the booty she had 480 chests of plunder, as well as yarn, lengths of cloth, all sorts of linen such as bedding, table-cloths and napkins, with which Mâcon was reputed to be better furnished than any other city in France. As for jewels, rings, goblets and other goods, the value was unknown, but those who handled the items reported that Tavanes had enough to turn it into an income of ten thousand livres.[1] After this it is not surprising that the nobles fomented dissension, and fanned the flames of persecution as much as they could; for it was their way of making money and it proved a very lucrative graft.

(B) The atrocities of Mâcon.] I shall use the words of the historian quoted in the preceding remark.[2]

The practice of the Roman religion was also restored without constraint and the priests and monks returned to their

---

⊂ᵉ *Ibid.*, p. 422.

[1] Beza, *Historia ecclesiastica*, bk 15, p. 429.
[2] Beza, *Historia ecclesiastica*, bk 15, p. 429.

former positions together with the brothels.[3] To crown the misery, Saint-Point,[4] a bloodthirsty man and extraordinarily cruel (whose own mother had declared him, in a judgement to discharge her conscience, to be the son of a named priest), had been left by Tavanes as commandant of the city; and who for his sport, after having entertained the ladies, was accustomed to ask if the 'farce' was ready to be enacted (called afterwards the farce of Saint-Point). The word was the signal: his henchmen would bring from the prison one or two captives and sometimes more, whom they led to the bridge of the Saône. There, in the presence of the ladies, and after having asked them some facetious questions, he had them thrown headlong into the river, and drowned. It was also his practice to make malicious provocations and he would drown or shoot a prisoner or any other available person of the Reformed Religion, on the supposed suspicion of their scheming to betray the town.

He was killed by one, Achon, with whom he had fallen out. He was returning from his house near the city where he had hidden away some 20,000 écus of plunder. It happened shortly after the pacification of March 1563. D'Aubigné[5] gruesomely depicts the barbarity of the man through an analogy with a school where, at the end of a day with the fruit and the dessert upon the table, the girls and infants were given lessons in seeing Huguenots pitilessly put to death. He says elsewhere[6] that Saint-Point made merry at the perpetration of his cruelties, and that when his guests departed from his feasts, he entertained the ladies with the spectacle of seeing vast numbers cast down from the bridge. The conduct of this governor was even more barbarous than that of Livius Flaminius[7] who, in order to please the objects of his infamous amours who had never seen an execution, gave orders, while dining, that a criminal should

---

[3] He had said, p. 242, that the ruffians and the debauched priests, who had formerly been thrown out, returned on the day of the seizure and used the houses of the Reformers as schools for teaching brutality, and above all the houses of those who had brought about their eviction.

[4] D'Aubigné refers to him as Saint-Pont.

[5] Théodore Agrippa d'Aubigné, *Histoire universelle*, vol. I, p. 216.

[6] [*Ibid.*,] p. 202.

[7] Plutarch, in the *Life of Flaminius*, p. 379.

be put to death in their presence. But on the other hand, the conduct of these women of Mâcon was much more to be condemned than that of the Roman women who were so strongly censured by a Christian poet for the pleasure they took in seeing the gladiators killed.[8] I do not doubt that, as his excuse, Saint-Point cited the drowning of the soldiers of Montbrison[9] by des Adrets; just as the latter excused himself by the atrocities that were perpetrated at Orange. And thus you see how one example draws endlessly upon another. *Abyssus abyssum invocat* [the abyss calls forth the abyss]. Thus those who provoke first commit the greatest crime and in strict justice it is they who should bear the punishment for all the iniquities which follow. D'Aubigné had not adequately checked his dates when he says[10] that Baron des Adrets, being provoked by the sacking of Orange and the atrocities of Mâcon, then marched to Pierrelate, made himself master of many cities, and came lastly to Montbrison. From Theodore Beza's account,[11] it would appear that by 26 June, Pierrelate and other towns had already been subdued by des Adrets, and that the soldiers of Montbrison were killed on 16 July,[12] and that Mâcon was taken by Tavanes on 19 August.[13]

(C) **It may be seen why I mention those frightful events.**] For the honour of the name of Frenchman and Christian, it should be wished that the memory of these inhumanities had been utterly obliterated and that all the books which mention them had been cast upon the fire. Those who find it wrong that such histories are written – because, say they,[14] history on the subject of the Wars of Religion serves only to teach readers about every sort of crime – are right in certain respects. For they seem highly likely to foster an irreconcilable hatred in the hearts of men, and one of the greatest wonders since the Edicts [of toleration] is that the people of France

---

[8] 'Consurgit ad ictus . . .' ['She rises at each blow. Whenever the vanquisher plunges his sword into his victim's throat, she says that he is her beloved, and the gentle maiden orders the breast of the man lying there to be split open at the turning down of her thumb.'] Prudentius in *Contra Symmachum* [Against Symmachus], 2.1095–8.
[9] See [*Dic,*] article 'Beaumont', Remark (B).
[10] [D'Aubigné,] vol. I, p. 204.
[11] [Beza,] bk 12, pp. 265, 269.
[12] [*Ibid.,*] p. 224.
[13] [*Ibid.,*] p. 422.
[14] See Mascardi, *Discours sur l'histoire.*

of different religions have lived in so much fraternity, notwithstanding that they have continually before them the histories of our civil wars in which they read of nothing but sackings, desecration, massacres, altars overturned, killing, betrayal and acts of violence. Even so, accurate history might be less worthy of admiration than having every individual remain in ignorance of what the histories of each party reproached in the other. Might it not, then, be alleged against me that my purpose when I discuss in my work the most atrocious facts which the history of the sixteenth century records – an abominable century[15] in comparison with which the present generation, though far from true virtue, might pass for a golden age – is to awaken men's anger and to nourish the fires of hatred? It is proper for me to reply to this objection. I say then that even if I wished to arouse storms of anger in the minds of my readers, I should willingly allow that no one should ever be reminded of this sort of event, if it would make anyone learn better, or do his duty better, in the silence of his feelings. But since these matters are dispersed in too many works to hope that the affectation of saying nothing about them would do any good, I have not sought to censor myself, and I have judged that I should discuss freely everything that occurs, letting myself be guided by the chronology and sequence of these events. But since all things have two sides, I must not forget that there are very good positive reasons why it is right for the memory of these frightful disorders to be carefully preserved. There are indeed three sorts of person who ought to reflect on them daily and consider them as a cautionary warning [*un songez-y bien*].

1. Firstly, those who govern states should employ an aide to recite each morning: *persecute no one for his opinions in religion and do not use the right of the sword against conscience. See what Charles IX and his successor achieved by it. It was indeed a miracle that the French monarchy was not destroyed by their Catholicity. Such miracles do not happen every day, so do not count on them. They did not wish to uphold the Edict of January [1562] and it was necessary, following more than thirty years of devastation, after thousand upon thousand torrents of spilt blood, and thousand upon thousand treacheries and conflagrations, to grant them another and more favourable edict* [i.e. the Edict of Nantes of 1598].

2. The second sort of persons who should dwell upon the sixteenth century are those who govern ecclesiastical affairs. When one

---

[15] Cf. [*Dic,*] article 'Lognac', Remark (P).

speaks to them of tolerance they fancy they have heard the most frightful and the most monstrous of all dogmas; and in order to employ the secular arm in their obsessions, they insist that it [tolerance] removes from the government the finest flower of the crown; at least [they say], they must be allowed to imprison and banish heretics. But if they were to consider carefully what is to be feared from a war of religion, they might be more moderate. *You do not wish, you should say to them, that this sect should worship God in its own way nor preach its doctrines; but take care lest the sectarians respond with raised swords and, instead of merely speaking or writing against your doctrines, they overturn your temples and endanger your own persons. What did you gain in France and in Holland by counselling persecution? Nor trust in your superior numbers. Your sovereigns have neighbours, and consequently your sectarians will lack neither protectors nor assistance, even from the Ottomans.*

3. Finally, let these turbulent theologians, who take so much pleasure in innovation, look continuously upon the civil wars of the sixteenth century. The early Reformers pursued their cause innocently; no consideration could stop them since, according to their principles, there was no middle way. Either they had to allow the Papists to be damned eternally, or they had to convert them to Protestantism. But if people fail to respect the possessions of others when they are persuaded that an error does not damn at all; and if such people had rather disturb the public peace than contain their personal ideas, then their conduct cannot be too much deplored. Let them, therefore, consider both the consequences of their innovations and the means they use to bring them about; then, if they can thus embark on their enterprise without an absolute necessity, they must have the soul of a tiger, and a heart more brazen than he who first ventured his life in a ship.[16]

There is no evidence that any party would ever arise among the Protestants to reform their religion in the manner in which they

---

[16] 'Illi robur et . . .' ['That man had a breast of oak and threefold bronze, who was first to entrust a fragile boat to the fierce sea and did not fear the rushing southwest wind as it fought it out with blasts from the north-east wind, nor the gloomy Hyades, nor the rage of Notus. Had he no fear at all of death's approach as he saw, without shedding a tear, monsters swimming in the sea, and swollen waves and the infamous cliffs of Acroceraunia?'] Horace, *Odes*, 1.3.9–20.

reformed the Roman church, that is, on the basis of the principle that they must leave their religion if they did not wish to be damned; and so the disorders that they would have to fear from any future innovating party would be less terrible than those of the previous century. Animosities would be less heated than at that time, especially since no party would find in the other any object of superstition to destroy: no local divinities, no patron saints to be broken or trampled upon, no relics to be scattered, no pyxes or altars to be overturned.[17] There could thus be disagreement between Protestant and Protestant, without need to fear every outrage that had appeared in the quarrels between Protestant and Catholic. Even so, the mischief would still be sufficiently deadly as to deserve our endeavours to warn against it. One would need to remind parties too much addicted to disputes of the horrible commotions they have caused. And one would need to show them, emphatically, that the most fearsome intolerance does not come from sovereigns who use the right of the sword against sectarians, but that it comes from those individual divines who, without a very urgent necessity, rise up against errors protected by custom and the habits of peoples; and who resist them stubbornly even though they see everything around them already in flames.

(D) The atrocities of Mâcon have become more infamous than those of the island of Capri.] And nevertheless a celebrated historian has inserted in his work that in some manner the place is represented as one of the singularities of the island.

> Carnificinae eius (Tiberii) ostenditur . . . ['The place of the executions of Tiberius is known to be on Capri. Here he ordered men who had been condemned to death after long, agonising torture to be thrown headlong into the sea while he watched. A corps of marines fished them out and struck their bodies with poles and oars, so that no life was left in them.']
[18]

But I cannot believe that the Ancients are to be compared to the Moderns in the way in which the same things are transported from

---

[17] There is the appearance that the French and the Spaniards would have spilt Protestant blood less than they did had they not been so angered by the destruction of their images, altars, and relics etc.

[18] Suetonius, *Life of Tiberius*, ch. 62.

book to book. And in consequence the *Sauteries de Mâcon* can be read about in more places, and have more monuments to witness their infamy, than those of the Emperor Tiberius. It was not honourable for those who resorted to these types of torture in the sixteenth century to have retraced the footsteps of such a tyrant. In reading this, one may be reminded perhaps of the comments in the article 'Leucade'.

Mariana

[Historians in the age of Louis XIV were strongly affected by the massacres of the Wars of Religion, and by the memory of the assassinations, by Catholic extremists, of two sovereigns in their recent history: Henry III in 1589, and Henry IV in 1610. After 1598 politiques *and Huguenots insisted, in opposition to Catholic majoritarian doctrine, that the sovereign's first duty was not to impose one religion, but to protect all law-abiding citizens from extremist violence. Mariana, a Spanish Jesuit, had responded to the* politiques *in 1598 with a defence of the people's right to overthrow and replace a tyrant. Bayle's* politique *rejoinder in 1697 provides a clue to his caution in respect of England's Protestant Revolution of 1688. Mariana's defence of tyrannicide, he observed, could support any popular revolution whatsoever – Catholic, Protestant or pagan. The obligation to oppose tyranny could be taken for granted; the issue, however, was about defining it.]*

MARIANA (Jean), born at Talavera in the diocese of Toledo, became a Jesuit on 1 January 1554. He then studied at Complutum until he was twenty-seven years of age. He became one of the most brilliant men of his age. He was a great theologian, a great humanist, profound in his knowledge of both ecclesiastical and profane history, a Greek scholar, and learned in the holy tongue. He went to Rome in 1561 where he taught theology. Four years later he went to Sicily, and taught there for two years. In 1569 he went to Paris, and for five years he interpreted Thomas Aquinas. His health would not permit him to continue and he was obliged to take up less arduous studies. He returned to Spain in 1574 and he spent the rest of his days at Toledo. He died there on 17 February 1624 at the age of eighty-seven [(A)]. The Inquisition made use of him in many affairs of importance, but in other matters his patience was greatly tried [(B)] and he needed great courage not to sink under the trials of adversity.[a] What is observed of his chastity [(C)] is altogether singular. He published several books[b] including, among others, a *History* of Spain which many look upon as his masterpiece [(D)]. It was he who had published a book by Lucas Tudensis about the life to come and against the Albigensians. His treatise on the exchange value of money caused controversy at the court of Spain [(E)] and it exposed him to a penalty which is not well reported by M. Varillas [(F)] ... There would have been more reason to chastise him on account of another book, which was sanctioned in Spain and Italy, but burnt in Paris by decree of the *parlement* because of the pernicious doctrine it contained. Nothing is more seditious than this book by Jean Mariana (G), nor more likely to expose kingdoms to frequent revolutions, and the very lives of princes to the knife of assassins. It exposed the Jesuits, and above all in France, to a thousand bloody reproaches (H), and to very mortifying insults, which are repeated daily and ceaselessly, which impassioned historians copy from one another, and which appear all the more plausible since they are recounted with strong support [(I)]. It has been asserted that Ravaillac derived from it his abominable scheme to assassinate Henry IV and that he declared this when he was interrogated, although this was publicly rebutted [(K)]. Another treatise by this Jesuit has also caused a great controversy. It is the one in which he comments on the faults in the government of his Society [(L)]; though his confrères are not agreed that he is the author of such a book [(M)]. His *scholia* upon the Scriptures have deservedly been praised by Father Simon [(N)]. I ought to have mentioned that his injurious utterances concerning Henry III were, in part, the reason why his book about kings and their foundation was condemned in Paris [(O)].

---

[a] Taken from Natanael Sotuel, *Bibl. script. societ.*, p. 477.
[b] For their titles see Moréri.

I doubt whether he wrote the book *De Republica Christiana* [On the Christian Republic] which is greatly praised by a German writer [(P)].

[Remarks (A)–(F) omitted.]

(G) Nothing is more seditious than this book by Mariana.] Its title is *De rege et regis institutione* [On Kings and the Education of Kings] and it was printed at Toledo in 1598, with the king's privilege and the usual approbations. The author proposing, in the sixth chapter of book 1, to inquire if it is permissible to overthrow a tyrant, approaches this subject with an account of the tragic death of Henry III. He admires the courage of Jacques Clément [Henry III's assassin], and he points out that there were different opinions about the deed of this young monk. Some praised it and thought it worthy of immortality. Others condemned it because they were convinced that it was never lawful for a mere private individual to kill a prince [who had been] declared king by the nation, and consecrated with sacred oil according to custom, although that prince had become a pervert and a tyrant.

> De facto monachi ... ['There is more than one opinion about the monk's deed. Many praise him and believe he has earned immortality. He is censured by others who are highly renowned for their good sense and learning. They argue that it was wrong for a person made king by popular consent to have been overthrown at the bidding of some private individual. They claim it is never justified to kill in this way one who had been anointed and sanctified with sacred oil according to custom, even if he had abandoned morality and had sunk into tyranny.']$^{1=39}$

It is clear that Mariana is one of those who approved the action of Jacques Clément for he rejects the principle by which wise and learned men deplored it. Besides he affects to extol the courage and determination of the assassin without uttering one word that would tend to render him odious to the reader. This observation reveals

---

[1=39] Mariana, *De rege et regis institutione* [On Kings and the Education of Kings], 1.6, p.54.

admirably all the venom in the doctrine of this Jesuit. For it is certain that he used the example of Henry III only to descend from the thesis to the hypothesis, and to demonstrate to peoples a glaring cause of tyranny so that whenever they found themselves in a like situation, they would consider themselves in circumstances where it is permitted to make use of the knife against their monarch. But if it is ever lawful to do this when one finds oneself under a monarch such as Henry III, I do not know where there would be monarchs who would not fear being assassinated or dethroned. For often the good and the evil of two conditions balance one another. It will be said therefore that though the faults of government are not the same as they were under Henry III, they are similar, all things duly considered, and from thence people will conclude that they are in the same condition as the one described by the Jesuit. However, let us continue with our analysis of his system.

Mariana relates the arguments of those who condemned Jacques Clément, that is to say he recounts his understanding of the arguments of those who preached that everyone must patiently submit to the tyrannical yoke of the lawful sovereign. But without further discussion[2=40] of that position, he proceeds to the arguments of the contrary party built upon the following fundamental principle: namely that the authority of the people is superior to that of kings.[3=41] This is his favoured thesis and he devotes two whole chapters[4=42] to its demonstration. Having given an account of the reasoning of each party he declares the following propositions:

1. that, according to the opinions of the theologians and the philosophers, a prince who seizes the sovereign power by force of arms and without the public consent of the nation [*le consentement public de la nation*] is a man whom any private person has a right to kill: 'Perimi a quocunque . . .' ['He can be killed by anyone and stripped of his life and his sovereignty'];[5=43]

[2=40] He refutes them up to the end of ch. 6.
[3=41] 'A republica, unde . . .' ['The state, from which royal power originates, can, should the situation demand it, summon the king to a court of law and if he rejects sound reason, strip him of his sovereignty. It has not transferred the right to power of a sovereign in such a way that it has failed to reserve greater power for itself.'] *De rege et regis institutione*, 1.4.
[4=42] Bk 1, 8, 9.
[5=43] *Ibid.*, p. 56.

2. that if a prince created legitimately, or who is a lawful successor to his ancestors, overturns the [public] religion and the public laws without deferring to the admonishments of the nation, he must be dethroned in the safest and most certain way;

3. that the safest and most certain way of overthrowing him is to summon the Estates, to depose him in this assembly and, if necessary to get rid of tyranny, to order there that arms are taken up against him;

4. that one may put to death such a prince, and that each individual who has the mettle to undertake to assassinate him has the right to do so;[6=44]

5. that if an assembly of the Estates cannot be called, and if it appears nevertheless that the will of the people is to get rid of the tyrant, any individual person in order to satisfy the desire of the people may legitimately kill this prince: *'qui votis publicis . . .'* ['whoever has complied with the wishes of the public by attempting to kill him, I will judge him to have done nothing at all wrong'];[7=45]

6. that the judgement of a private individual or of several is not sufficient; they must act according to the voice of the people and also consult wise and learned men;[8=46]

7. that in truth there is more courage in rising openly against the tyrant; just as there is more prudence in attacking him secretly and destroying him with suitable snares.

> Est quidem majoris . . . ['It is indeed more virtuous and courageous to practise open hostility and to attack in public the enemy of the state. But it is no less judicious to steal an opportunity for deceit and ambush, so that it comes to pass without a rebellion and poses less of a threat to the safety of the public or individuals.'][9=47]

[6=44] 'Principem publicum hostem . . .' ['One should kill by the sword a sovereign declared public enemy. Let any private individual be competent to do this who has cast aside hope of impunity and neglected his own safety in his desire to embark upon an endeavour to assist the state.']

[7=45] *Ibid.*

[8=46] 'Neque enim id . . .' ['For we do not leave this to the decision of some private individual. Nor do we leave it to the decision of the many, unless the public voice of the people is heard and learned and eminent men are consulted.'] *Ibid.*

[9=47] *Ibid.*, 7, p. 65.

He [Mariana] will have it then, that the tyrant should either be confronted in his own palace with armed force, or that a conspiracy should be formed against him. He thus submits that open war, or stratagems, deceptions and treacheries are equally permitted. If the conspirators are not killed in action, he adds, they must be admired as heroes for the rest of their days. Alternatively, if they perish in the attempt they are sacrificial victims, pleasing to God and men, and their endeavours deserve immortal praises.

> Aut in apertam . . . ['Either open violence breaks out, when sedition has arisen and the public takes up arms . . . Or he is killed with greater caution, deceit and craftiness, when one or a few have plotted secretly against his life, and put their own lives in danger in their efforts to protect the state. If they escape death, they are likened to great heroes for their whole lives. If it turns out otherwise, they fall as a sacrifice pleasing to the gods above and to men and are celebrated for all posterity because of their noble deed. Therefore a tyrant can be killed by open force and by arms, either when an attack has been launched against the palace, or when fighting in public has broken out. But an exception has been made also for deceit and ambush.']¹⁰⁼⁴⁸

8. Although there might appear to be no difference between the assassin who kills with the blow of a knife, and the one who poisons, nevertheless, since Christianity has rescinded the laws of the Athenians which appointed criminals to take the poisoned cup, Mariana does not approve of overthrowing a tyrant by means of poison mixed with food. He would have it that it should be applied to the tyrant's clothes or to the saddle of his horse.

> Ergo me auctore . . . ['Therefore, in my view, a poisonous drug should not be given to the enemy nor should lethal poison be mixed into his food and drink to kill him. But it will be permissible to use poison, for argument's sake, in the following way: that the one who is killed is not forced to drink poison, so that he dies by ingesting it, but that it is applied externally without the assistance of him who must

---

¹⁰⁼⁴⁸ *Ibid.*, p. 64.

be killed. Certainly poison has so much strength that it has the power to kill when a chair or a piece of clothing is smeared with it.']$^{11=49}$

Such is the system of this Jesuit. The last article is highly irrelevant. It is a pointless distinction, since a man who drinks poison unknowingly, believing it to be wholesome food, does not in any way contract the guilt of those who take their own life. And yet it is to spare a tyrant from committing such a crime that Mariana would have no one administer poison.$^{12=50}$ Furthermore if it were true that by unknowingly taking poison one would be taking one's life, one would be doing the same by putting on a poisoned shirt. And yet Mariana does not scruple to concede that clothes, saddles, and other items, may be poisoned, or any other things that act from without upon inward parts. I say therefore that Article 8 of this Jesuit is highly unworthy of a man who knows how to reason; and I am surprised that a man who had so much intelligence and so much logic should have resorted to so puerile an argument.

Save on this point, many people are convinced that his system is a fine prescription, that the parts of it are well connected, and that he proceeds logically from one position to its consequence. Suppose, say they, that a monarch has once agreed to the authority of the people as his supreme tribunal, and that he is accountable [*justiciable*] to them for his conduct, all the rest [of his system] logically follows from the principle. Thus we shall see that the author who refuted Mariana had to establish a completely opposite fundamental axiom: namely that sovereign princes answer only to God, and it belongs to him alone to bring about justice.$^{13=51}$ I shall refrain from entering into a discussion of this dogma: it is enough to observe that since the doctrines of Mariana are very harmful to the public good, it might have been better had he argued less consequentially

---

$^{11=49}$ *Ibid.*, p. 67.
$^{12=50}$ 'Crudele existimarunt, atque . . .' ['They have judged it cruel and inconsistent with Christian morality, although there may be overwhelming reasons to drive a man to do violence to himself either through stabbing, or by taking lethal poison mixed with his food and drink. But it is forbidden to do violence to one's own life because that is against both the law of humanity, and the law of nature. We therefore assert that the enemy, whom we have conceded can be killed by deceit, cannot rightly be slain by poison.'] *Ibid.*, p. 66.
$^{13=51}$ Roussel, in ch. 17 of his *Anti-Mariana*.

than pursue, as a good dialectician, the consequences of his principle.

(H) . . . It exposed the Jesuits . . . to a thousand bloody reproaches.] Catholics and Protestants vied with one another to sabotage these doctrines of Mariana, but chiefly after the appalling assassination by Ravaillac. For it was said that reading Mariana had inspired this callous assassin with his infamous scheme to put the knife into Henry IV. Whereupon Father Coton published a letter which he had written to Marie de Médicis, the widow of that prince, wherein he quotes some celebrated Jesuits who taught the contrary to what Mariana had maintained. He went further because at one of their congresses in 1606 he advocated that the book of this Spanish Jesuit should be condemned. . . .

In another work Father Coton returns to his theme. 'The heretics of France', says he,[14=55]

> wanted it to be the case that Mariana had caused Ravaillac to commit his wretched and execrable deed, as if he knew him by heart, to which they replied a hundred and one times, on pain of their honour and life, that Ravaillac had never seen, never read, and never even heard the name of Mariana . . . I add that even if Ravaillac had read it, it remains absolutely false that Mariana recommended the murder and killing perpetrated by that wretch, which is what this scurrilous calumniator attempts to argue in his pamphlet. Thus, in a certain sense he would have wanted Ravaillac to have read Mariana so that it could be understood that Mariana teaches (as Gretsérus shows) that a lawful prince may be killed by an individual on his own private authority.

Father Coton is mistaken: for Mariana's work was highly suitable for inciting the plot to assassinate Henry IV. One can see in it his notion that the action of Jacques Clément was good, and that a private individual may indeed kill a prince if the voice of the people, and the counsel of several learned persons, agree to declare that he oppresses religion. Putting the two things together one could indeed infer from them that the assassination of Henry IV was just. For if

---

[14=55] *Réponse apologétique à l'Anti-Coton*, p. 54.

Henry III, Catholic to the most sovereign degree, was an oppressor of Catholicism because he laboured for the right of a heretical prince who was to be his successor, then one may deduce, in general, that every prince who shows favour to heretics is contriving to oppress religion. Now, if it is permitted to kill an oppressor of religion, it is doubtless permitted to kill that person who has a mind to oppress it as soon as he can. For prudence will not permit us to suffer an evil to increase until it has grown to such an extent that it is difficult to find a remedy. It must be checked while it is still weak. Besides, by 'the voice of the people' one must not understand the judgement of all private individuals. It is sufficient that in every city there are several persons who unite their voices for certain purposes. Now it is indubitably true that the kingdom of France was brimming with people who suspected that Henry IV had a mind to make the Reformed religion triumphant as soon as he could, and that he engaged in war against the House of Austria precisely upon this prospect. Thus Ravaillac, in reasoning according to the principles of Mariana, and joining to them a sense of *accommodation* in the usual way, might very well have believed that he had no less right than Jacques Clément to attempt assassination. He found only too many learned persons, and in his sense very prudent, who confirmed him in his pernicious design, and all for the good of religion. See in Remark [(K)] his answer to those who asked him why he had committed this assassination, and recall that he declared before his judges that 'his wish to kill the king' came to him because that prince 'had not endeavoured (though he had the power) to restore those of the supposed Reformed religion to the Catholic, apostolic and Roman Church',[15=56] and because 'he had heard' that the king 'wanted to make war against the Pope, and translate the Holy See to Paris'.[16=57] For 'making war against the Pope', said he,[17=58] 'was to make it against God, inasmuch as the Pope was God and God was the Pope'. A Catholic writer, who refuted the declaration of Father Coton in a book entitled *L'Anti-Coton*,[18=59] reveals certain matters which deserve a place here. 'This book of Mariana', declares he,[19=60]

[15=56] *Mercure Français*, vol. i, fol. 440. See also fol. 442, verso.
[16=57] *Ibid.*
[17=58] *Ibid.*, fol. 443.
[18=59] This book has been wrongly attributed to Pierre du Moulin.
[19=60] *Anti-Coton*, 1610, pp. 12, 13.

having been first printed at Toledo, was brought into France and presented to the king. When the seditious clauses of this book were brought to the attention of His Majesty [Henry IV], he sent for Father Coton and asked him whether he approved of this doctrine. But the said Jesuit, who accommodated himself to circumstances and trimmed to the times, declared that he did not approve of it. Following which His Majesty, on the advice of M. Servin, his Advocate-General, ordered Coton to write against it, but the latter excused himself, knowing very well that he could not write against it without contradicting the General of his order, the Provincial of Toledo and a body of Jesuits who had approved the book. But when he saw that through the assassination of the king [Henry IV] the Jesuits had became the objects of universal hatred, and that he was under pressure from the *parlement* and from the Sorbonne, he wrote a preliminary declaration wherein he formally condemned Mariana, but in terms so weak and so doubtful that it plainly appeared that he was afraid of causing offence. For he says merely that it showed the rashness of a bold pen, whereas he ought to have accused the author of heresy, perfidious and barbarous treason, and the doctrine of impiety and hostility against God and men . . . When he [Coton] did reprove Mariana as he deserved, it was too late; he should have written when the king commanded him and not allowed an opinion to take root in the minds of the people which would cost the king his life a few years later.

Father Coton identified eight falsehoods in this account. See his apology in response to the *Anti-Coton*.[20=61] Moreover, the Jesuits in France were not the only ones to be harassed on account of their confrère, Mariana; those in Germany also had a share of the storm, as is shown by the apology which Jacques Gretsérus was obliged to publish.[21=62] Let us add a passage from Conringius:

Prodiit et alius . . . ['Another small book by Mariana appeared, *De institutione regis*, which contains many notorious ideas. In this book, he draws very frank conclusions

---

[20=61] Page 37. See also Eudaemon, Johannes, *Réponse à l'Anti-Coton*, p. 54.
[21=62] See his *Vespertilio Haeretico-Politicus*. Father Coton refers to it in his Declaratory Epistle, p. 7 and in his *Réponse apologétique*, p. 33.

about how kings should be educated. But he has had no hesitation in openly teaching also that if a king is declared heretical or excommunicated, and has become somewhat separated from the Roman church, it is permissible to punish him with the sword, certainly with burning at the stake. He wished, however, to be seen to have scruples, when he said that it was not permissible to kill a king with poison, as if in all sincerity. This book has in fact been burned in Paris on account of such a terrible doctrine, and the Jesuits were forced to repudiate it publicly. Mariana even had no hesitation in saying that the assassin of Henry IV, king of France, was among the saints.']²²⁼⁶³

I think Conringius is twice mistaken: Mariana did not assert that it is lawful to kill a prince who departs ever so slightly from the communion of Rome, or who is simply excommunicated; and since his book pre-dated the assassination of Henry IV by more than ten years, he could not have been referring to Ravaillac. If, in other works, he had spoken of that monster, Ravaillac, as a saint no one would have failed to reproach the Jesuits on whatever occasion, after such works, they had advanced an account of the seditious maxims of Mariana. But I do not think that anyone ever did. A great distinction has always been made between Ravaillac and Jacques Clément. The latter received public approval, and some even sang his praises; but Ravaillac never had any that I know of. The reason for this is patently obvious: Henry III had already been excommunicated when he was assassinated, but Henry IV had for a long time been reconciled with the Pope.

Let us take the opportunity of pointing out that M. Seckendorf can be criticised. He alleges that the doctrine of Mariana consists in this: that a mere private person, motivated either by his own zeal, or on orders from the Pope, may make an attempt upon the life of heretical kings.

Dudum quoque male ... ['The Society of Jesus, said he, has also a little while ago acquired a bad reputation on account of the doctrine of J. Mariana, himself a Spanish

---

²²⁼⁶³ Hermanus Conringius, *De regno Hispaniae, apud* Pope Blount, *Censura Auctorum* [On the Kingdom of Spain, in Pope Blount, Critique of Famous Authors], p. 614.

Jesuit, and of those others who have declared it to be lawful, indeed praiseworthy, if anyone, even a mere subject or private individual, kills an heretical king or sovereign, or removes him from the state by whatever means, when the Pope commands it.']23=64

But it is certain that Mariana laid down his position in general terms, and that he said nothing in particular about either heretical princes or about the permissions and dispensations of the court of Rome. His maxims relate to all nations and to all tyrants. He does not exclude Protestants from his principles should they live under a tyrannical government; and he excludes neither Mahometans nor pagans. He treats the question altogether as Aristotle would have done. Nor do I see anything that Milton and his sort, of whom there is such a great number, could reply against the hypothesis of this Spaniard, unless they were to condemn the preamble which he uses to support Jacques Clément. But this preamble is not his precise doctrine. It merely indicates through inference the application which the author sought to make of his maxims.24=65

23=64 Seckendorf, *Historia lutherana*, 3, p. 332.
24=65 See what is said in Remark (G) above, and note that Jacques Gretsérus has shown that there are many books more pernicious than that of Mariana. See also the work entitled *Recueil des pièces concernant la doctrine et pratique romaine* ... [Collection of Pieces Concerning Roman Doctrine and Practice on the Dethronement of Kings and the Disposal, which it Entails, of their Lives and Estates], printed in Geneva, p. 251.

Navarre

[In an article which pays homage to an obscure princess of the Renaissance and the Reformation, a reader can observe in microcosm the range of Bayle's public concerns. For, in his Life of Marguerite de Valois, he identifies religious diversity, enlightened government, philosophic scepticism, conquest of prejudice, historical accuracy, interest in imaginative literature, and their connection to the ideas of tolerance and freedom. He succeeds, additionally, in portraying the exceptional person as one who can be active in a public calling, prudent in administration, a scholar of distinction, and an individual of moral sensibility. The article reflects, too, Bayle's recognition that the attainment in Stoical virtue of an educated woman can match that of an educated man.]

NAVARRE (Marguerite de Valois, queen of), the sister of Francis I, was born in the city of Angoulême on 11 April, 1492.[a] She was a princess of extraordinary merit who attracted admiration for her piety, intelligence, and the creations of her pen. She was educated with very particular care at the court of king Louis XII and she married the Duc d'Alençon in December 1509.[b] She became a widow in April 1525.[c] Her affection for her brother, king Francis I, was to be admired. She moved to Spain when he was a prisoner there and served him in all the ways open to a good and ingenious sister [(A)]. She was very useful to him in the affairs of [(B)]

---

[a] Anselm, *Histoire généalogique*, p. 83.
[b] Hilarion de Coste, *Eloges des dames illustres*, vol. II, p. 269.
[c] *Ibid.*

government. He in turn felt for her an extreme consideration and friendship of which he gave proof even before the recovery of his liberty [(C)]. He arranged for her marriage in 1527 to Henri d'Albret II, king of Navarre, and secured for her important advantages in the marriage contract [(D)]. She diligently applied herself with her husband to every appropriate activity likely to raise their states to a more flourishing condition [(E)], and for a time she desired to foster the ecclesiastical Reformation there. She had strong leanings towards what were called the New Opinions and she protected those who were persecuted for them [(F)]. She wrote a book that was censured by the Sorbonne and she found herself exposed to the indignation of the theologians [(G)]; and therefore the king her brother was forced to employ his authority to restrain their insolence. She took steps which might have induced him to favour the Reformation,[d] had the excesses of certain turbulent parties who posted placards in 1534 not exasperated him to such a degree as to make him afterwards a violent persecutor of Lutheranism.[e] She was obliged after this to be cautious and to rule her conduct by a method that the Calvinists have greatly condemned, but which gave the Papists reason to say that she had completely renounced her errors [(H)]. There is evidence that she took very great pleasure in reading the Bible [(I)]. She had some afflictions to bear from her husband, and she did not like to converse about death [(K)]. Her curiosity in observing a dying person attentively reveals clearly that on the nature of the soul she did not affirm the views which a true philosopher ought to maintain (L); but there are some very great minds and some very great philosophers who have thought no better than she upon that important article. Her *Heptaméron*, a book in the style of the novels of Boccaccio, has some wonderful qualities quite remarkable for the *genre*. She died in December 1549 [(M)] and was honoured with numerous eulogies.[f] Of the four children whom she had by her second marriage, a son and three daughters, only one daughter was spared.[g] . . .

---

[d] *Ibid.*, bk 1, p. 15.
[e] They at that time named as 'Lutheranism' in France what afterwards was called 'Calvinism'.
[f] Hilarion de Coste, *Eloges des dames illustres*, vol. ii, pp. 275, 276; De Thou, bk 6, p. 117.
[g] *Ibid.*

It would be superfluous to warn my reader here that *L'Histoire de Marguerite de Valois, reine de Navarre, sœur de François I*, printed in Amsterdam in 1696,[h=i] is, from beginning to end, a tissue of fiction and romantic chimeras based upon little historical fact. It would have been better if the person who abused his leisure concocting such fables had spent it giving us the true and complete history of this illustrious princess . . . There is infinitely less heroism in the supposed passion which is invented by the writer[i=l] than there is in the generosity with which our Marguerite de Valois effectively protected many worthwhile persons persecuted for the sake of religion (P).

[Remarks (A)–(K) omitted.]

(L) Her curiosity . . . in observing a dying person attentively, reveals clearly that on the nature of the soul she did not affirm the views which a true philosopher ought to maintain.] Here is something singular:

I have heard it said of her – these are Brantôme's words . . . that, having heard many learned men disputing whether the soul and spirit [*l'âme et l'esprit*] depart from the body as soon as it is deceased, she wished to see whether there proceeded from it, at the point of separation, any wind or noise or the least sound, but that she perceived nothing at all . . . and added that had she not been well settled in her faith, she would have been able to think of nothing else but this progression and departure of the soul . . .[l=54]

This passage would bear many reflections but we shall observe here only two things; one is that this princess may be excused for

---

[h=i] After the Paris edition.

[i=l] Note that, according to ordinary notions of human conduct, honourable behaviour is compatible with a girl's love for a man even though she does not know if she will ever be able to marry him; but according to perfectionist notions, such love is quite contrary to honour. One ought as a rule, therefore, never to use as a model of perfection the notion of a girl intending to be pleasing. It is to this that writers of romantic novels are unable to conform because they yield to the idea that love is at the centre of their work.

[l=54] Brantôme, *Mémoirs des dames illustres*, pp. 319, 320. [Brantôme was author of *Vies des dames galantes*, and *Vies des hommes illustres*. Bayle probably intended to indicate the former.]

having conceived man's mind [*l'esprit*] as a being which separates locally from the body at the moment when man expires; for in that century this was universally the opinion of the theologians and the philosophers, and it continues to be the opinion of all doctors today who are not Cartesians. They supposed that the soul [*l'âme*] is locally present in the human body and that it is co-extended with the matter that it animates; but that at the moment of death, it ceases to occupy that space and passes actually and physically into another place. I confess that this does not prove that we ought to believe that this transmigration is accompanied with any noise or sibilation as the queen of Navarre envisaged; but it is not at all strange that a woman, who carried her views further than the ordinary, should suspect that a subtle, invisible, and yet actually extended substance must escape from the body with some sort of noise, as when an arrow is in flight, or some spirituous liquors find their way out of some chink in a vessel that contains them. The other thing I have to say is that, in her doubts, the queen of Navarre conducted herself in the wisest manner possible. She imposed silence on her reason and her curiosity, and submitted herself to Revelation. . . .

[Remarks (M)–(O) omitted.]

(P) The generosity with which our Marguerite . . . protected . . . many persons persecuted for the sake of religion.] I refrain from examining whether Florimond de Rémond took it from reliable sources that she protested to her death that her protection of the followers of the New Opinions proceeded rather from compassion than from any ill will to the ancient religion of her fathers.[2=92] Let us assume that her insistence was sincere: I maintain in that case that there was something more heroic in her compassion and generosity than there would have been had she been persuaded that the fugitives she protected were orthodox. For a princess, or for any other woman, to do good to those whom she takes to be of the conventional faith is not out of the ordinary, it is the natural consequence of a moderate piety; but for a queen to grant her

[2=92] Florimond de Rémond, *L'Histoire de l'hérésie*, bk 7, ch. 3, p. 856.

protection to a people persecuted for the opinions she believes to be false, to open a sanctuary to them, to preserve them from the flames in which their enemies would have burnt them to death, to provide them with a subsistence, liberally to relieve the toils and inconveniences of their exile, is a heroic magnanimity which has hardly any precedent. It is an effect of a superiority of reason and soul to which very few can ascend. It is to be able to pity the misfortune of those that err, and to admire at the same time their constancy to the dictates of their conscience. It is to know how to do justice to their good intentions and to the zeal they express for the truth in general. It is to grasp that they are mistaken in the application of a principle but that in the principle itself they conform to the immutable and eternal laws of the natural order which requires us to love the truth and to sacrifice to it the temporal conveniences and comforts of life. It is, in a word, to know how to distinguish in one and the same person his opposition to particular truths and his love for the truth in general; a love that he evidences by his great attachment to the doctrine he thinks to be true. All this characterised the judgement of the queen of Navarre. It is difficult for any person to attain this level of knowledge; but it is especially difficult for a princess such as she, who had been educated in the communion of Rome, in which nothing was talked of for many ages but the burning and hanging of those that err. Furthermore, family prejudices powerfully reinforced all the obstacles that education had put in the path of this princess. For she entirely loved her brother, the king: an implacable persecutor of those they called heretics – a people whom he caused to be burnt without mercy wherever the indefatigable vigilance of informers unearthed them. I cannot conceive by what method this queen of Navarre raised herself to so high a point of equity, reason and good sense. It was not through indifference to religion, for it is certain she had a great piety and that she studied the Scriptures with a singular application. It must therefore have been the fineness of her intelligence and the greatness of her soul that perceived a path which hardly anyone had trodden. It might be said to me perhaps that she needed to consult only the fundamental and general ideas of the natural order which show most clearly that involuntary errors do not hinder a man who entirely loves God, as he has been able to discover him after all possible enquiries, from being reckoned the servant of the true God, and that we ought to respect in him the rights of the true God. But I would immediately have replied that in the matter of being clear and self-evident, this maxim is itself the subject of mighty disputes. Besides, these basic ideas seldom appear to our understanding without limitations and modifications, which obscure them a hundred ways according to the different prejudices produced by education. For party loyalty, attachment to a sect, and even zeal for orthodoxy, produce a kind of ferment in the humours of our body and thereby the medium through which our reason ought to consider those basic ideas is muddied and darkened. These are the infirmities that will cloud our reason for as long as it is dependent on the ministry of the bodily organs. It is like the lower and middle regions of the air suffused with vapours and meteors. Few can lift themselves above these clouds, and attain for themselves a true serenity.[3=93] Could anyone do that, it would have to be said of him as Virgil said of Daphnis:

> Candidus insuetum miratur lumen[4=94] Olympi,
> sub pedibusque videt nubes et sidera Daphnis.[5=95]

['Radiant Daphnis marvels at the unusual light of Olympus and sees clouds and stars beneath his feet.']

And he would resemble less a man than those immortal beings who are placed upon a mountain[6=96] higher than the region of the winds and the clouds etc. To fully understand a certain sort of truth, it is hardly less important to transcend the passions than it is to do virtuous deeds. Now we know that this mountain is the symbol of the person of good intent whom no passion can turn from the path of justice.

> . . . Sed ut altus Olympi . . . ['The lofty summit of Olympus, which leaves wind and storm far behind, is, in its perpetual serenity, never desecrated by any cloud, rising higher than the rain, listening to the torrents cascading beneath its feet

---

[3=93] '. . . Munita tenere / edita doctrina sapientum templa serena.' ['To inhabit lofty, serene sanctuaries which are fortified by the teachings of the wise'.] Lucretius, *De rerum natura* [On the Nature of Things], 2.7.

[4=94] Most editions say 'limen'.

[5=95] Virgil, *Eclogues*, 5.56.

[6=96] That of Olympus. See Apuleius, in his book *De mundo* [On the World], and the lines he cites from Homer.

and trampling under foot the loud rumbling of thunder. In such a way, amidst so much turbulence, the serene spirit soars free and true to itself. Hatred does not compel it, nor friendship urge it, to be diverted from the right path.']⁷⁼⁹⁷

Through this fine passage I maintain that I have indeed conveyed the heroism of the queen of Navarre.

[7=97] Claudian, *De Mallii Theodosii consulatu* [On the Consulship of Mallius Theodosius], p. 6, col. 2.

Nicole

*[The Jansenist Pierre Nicole died in 1695 giving Bayle the oppor-
tunity to include in the Dictionary's first edition an appreciation of
his work. The article is, I believe, a landmark in political theory
insofar as it shows, a century before Kant, that Bayle foresaw an
evolving role for the* philosophe théologien. *For ecclesiastics were
apt to believe that their judgements concerning heresy should, as
under a once-united church, remain binding on every Christian. Bayle's
view, hardly grasped by those whom he challenges, was that a
theologian had no more claim than any lay thinker to escape assess-
ment by peers in the republic of letters. When Bayle refers to a
'death of controversy' he is mocking the prediction of 'certain persons'
for whom the outcome of such respect for religious 'error' would
supposedly be religious apathy.]*

NICOLE (Pierre), one of the finest pens in Europe, was born at
Chartres in 1625 ... He was a member of the party of the Jansenists, and collaborated on many books with M. Arnauld,[a] whose 'loyal
companion he was during the last ten or twelve years of his exile'.[b]
It was he who put into Latin M. Pascal's *Provincial Letters* and
added a commentary to them [(B)]. He did not follow M. Arnauld
when the latter left the kingdom in 1679, and he even consented, it
is said, to an accommodation with the Jesuits, which consisted of
agreeing to write nothing against them while not breaking with his

---

[a] See the book entitled *Question curieuse: si M. Arnauld est hérétique*, pp. 150 *et seq.*,
1695.
[b] *Ibid.*

old friends. One of his finest works is that entitled *Essais de morale.* What he wrote against those of the Reformed religion is very subtle. No one has so forcefully put the objections to schism; but certain prudent persons are of opinion that he would have done better to suppress it than to publish it. For apart from the fact that the Roman church gains nothing from it, since all the arguments of M. Nicole can be turned against her, all his works, together with the answers made to them, can unfortunately encourage in their perverse dispositions all who have a leaning towards Pyrrhonism (C), and all who do not consider with sufficient attentiveness the spirit and the character of the Christian religion. His treatise concerning the unity of the church shows the hand of a master, and yet he has not attacked his adversary [(D)] in his weakest parts, which is a manifest proof that with all his penetration he did not discover them. He died in Paris on 16 November 1695 a few days after his treatise on the Quietists was published. He was well versed in letters. The *Delectus epigrammatum* [Selection of Epigrams] – which has seen several reprintings – and the learned preface that accompanies it are attributed to him [(E)]. In the rest of this piece I shall write more extensively about the implications of one of his books, since men of judgement have persuaded me that facts of this sort, accompanied by comments, are of the province of this Dictionary, and provide the variety that should stimulate the reader. This is the true reason why here, and in many other places, I use this method. . . .

[Remarks (A)–(B) omitted.]

(C) His works . . . may give encouragement . . . to those who have a leaning towards Pyrrhonism.] I have in mind here only two works by M. Nicole. One is entitled *Préjugés légitimes contre les Calvinistes*[1=10] and the other *Les Prétendus Réformés convaincus de schisme.*[2=11] In the first case I consider only chapter 14, where the author claims to show 'that the method proposed by Calvinists to

[1=10] [Well-grounded Prejudices against the Calvinists,] Paris, 1671, Holland, 1683.
[2=11] [The So-called Reformed Church Convicted of Schism,] Paris, 1684, Holland, the same year.

teach men the way to the truth is ridiculous and impossible'. He says there is no man who can reasonably be instructed in this method without first being assured of the following: 1. whether the passages of the Scripture put to him are taken from a canonical book; 2. whether they agree with the original; 3. whether there are not several ways of reading them that weaken their evidence. After this, M. Nicole deploys all the subtleties of his rhetoric to show in particular the difficulties that are encountered in the discussion of these three points. He presses this much further in another book in which he claims that those who left the Roman communion in the sixteenth century could not have done so without being extremely foolhardy: unless they had an exact knowledge of the reasons for supporting it and the reasons against it and, in general, of all the objections that might be formed upon the passages of the Scripture offered on both sides. He shows what they were required to do in order to be certain that it was their duty to leave the Roman church and to join the communion of the Protestants; and he introduces so many details into the investigation that necessarily led to a similar certainty that there is not a reader who will not perceive that, of ten thousand persons, he might, with difficulty, find four who could fulfil this duty. What benefit has he reaped from so many meditations? An advantage which ends in himself; for he has consolidated his reputation as a subtle disputant and as a philosophical theologian [*philosophe théologien*] who is inordinately capable of carrying any cause whatsoever, and of pursuing difficulties as far as they will go. But he has done nothing for his party: for M. Claude has answered his first book, and M. Jurieu has answered his second, and both have demonstrated that a person in the Roman communion is exposed to all the same difficulties. The more one embarks on the ocean of tradition, the more it is necessary to run through all the ages of the church, all the history of the Councils, and all the disputes concerning the Pope's authority – inferior to Councils according to some, superior to Councils according to others – so that the way of authority by which the Catholics profess to guide themselves is the high road to Pyrrhonism. A man who wants to assure himself legitimately that he ought to submit to the authority of the church is obliged to know whether the Scriptures will have it so. Thus you see him exposed to all the difficulties raised by M. Nicole;[3=12] and he must know, furthermore, whether the doctrine of the Fathers and of all the ages of Christianity is in conformity to his submission. He must be exceedingly indefatigable if he does not prefer to doubt everything than engage in so many inquiries; and he would be very subtle if, taking all the trouble that it requires, he finally discovers the light. It is thus a path to Pyrrhonism.[4=13]

The response by M. Claude [a Huguenot pastor] to M. Nicole entitled: *Défense de la réformation*[5=14] is a masterpiece. He has not only turned his adversary's objections against him, but he has also directly clarified them in a way that edifies pious souls without teaching to libertines a method of insulting religion. Many would be glad if as much might be said for M. Nicole's other adversary [Jurieu] but this could not be done without flattering him blatantly. For he has not been content to teach the Jews how they could convict of an unworthy temerity those of their ancestors who embraced the Gospel – and to declare ultimately that the Synagogue had become a false religion[6=15] – but he has created for us I know not what grotesque distinction between an 'examination through discussion', and an 'examination through attention',[7=16] as absurd, at least, as the distinction between formal quantity in respect of itself [*à soi*], and actual quantity in respect of place [*au lieu*] – 'quantitas formalis in ordine ad se, et quantitas actualis in ordine ad locum' – which Roman Catholic faculties retain; and he agrees that the faithful are led to orthodoxy not by evident proofs but by proofs of feeling, and that they discern the truth through taste and not through distinct ideas. This dispute has had some repercussions:

[3=12] See *Nouvelles de la république des lettres*, November 1684, art. 1, p. 888.
[4=13] M. Turretin … defended an excellent thesis at Leiden … in 1692, entitled *Pyrrhonismus pontificius, sive Theses theologico-historicae de variationibus pontificiorum circa ecclesiae infallibilitatem* [Pontifical Pyrrhonism, or Theologico-historical Theses on the Differences between Pontiffs Concerning the Church's Infallibility]. See also the book by M. de la Placette: *De insanibili romanae ecclesiae scepticismo* [On the Absurd Scepticism of the Roman Church], Amsterdam, 1696. The journalists of Leipzig have printed an extract, June 1697, pp. 264 *et seq.* It has been printed in English, London, 1688.
[5=14] Rouen, 1673, Holland, 1682.
[6=15] See M. Jurieu's book entitled *Le Vrai Système de l'église*, Dordrecht, 1686, bk 2, ch. 13, pp. 333 *et seq.*
[7=16] *Ibid.*, ch. 22, p. 402.

since, on the one hand, M. Pellisson[8=17] and the author of the *Commentaire philosophique sur les mots Contrains-les d'entrer* [Bayle, 1686] and M. Papin[9=18] have written books in which they have shown more and more cumulatively the insurmountable difficulties concerning the way of conversion through examination; and, on the other hand, some ministers have complained very energetically about the response which has been made to M. Nicole in respect of the basis of belief. The author of this reply, far from retracting or taking any steps backward, has explained himself afresh more precisely. He has just brought out a thick book to maintain not only that proofs of the divinity of the Scripture are not proposed to us by the evidence of the spirit of God who converts us, and that it is not evident that God reveals his word to us in such and such a mystery, but also that those who put the foundation of belief on the evidence of witness teach a pernicious and highly dangerous doctrine.[10=19] There are those who say that this is to lead religion to the edge of a precipice, and that if the Celsuses and the Porphyrys had found it in such a position, and if they had been required to combat Christian doctrines that had made so many advances and so many converts, they could not have stood their ground for a quarter of an hour. I do not think they are right, or that they have meditated sufficiently on the nature of Christianity. I do not know, furthermore, the outcome of the dispute between the minister of Rotterdam [Jurieu] and the minister of Utrecht [Saurin]: but it seems that if we lived in a time of crisis and in a ferment of controversy which produced so catastrophic an impact in previous ages, we should be liable to see vast changes. *Deus omen avertat* [May God avert the bad omen].[11=20]

[8=17] In his *Réflexions sur les différens de la religion*. See *Nouvelles de la république des lettres*, July 1686, art. 1.

[9=18] A minister who has become a Papist. See his book entitled *La Tolérance des protestans, et l'autorité de l'église* ... M. de Beauval refers to it in *L'Histoire des ouvrages des savans*, January 1693, art. 7.

[10=19] See the work of M. Jurieu entitled *Défense de la doctrine universelle de l'église ... contre les imputations et les objections de M. Saurin*, Rotterdam, 1695. M. Saurin is minister at the Walloon church at Utrecht.

[11=20] This was how I spoke of it in the first edition of this work, when this dispute had not yet come to an end; but at the time of the second edition, that is in December 1700, I can say that it is spoken of no more than Flaccianism, forgotten for a hundred years.

There are, perhaps, people who would like the doctrines of the minister of Rotterdam [Jurieu] to be embraced by every divine. They imagine that, afterwards, people would dispute no more, and that it would be the veritable death of controversy: for, given that one does not dispute about taste, as soon as every theologian had reduced the analysis of faith to taste, one would no longer dispute about religion.

I believe, says the one, *that I am in possession of truth because I have the taste and the feeling of it; and I also,* would say the other. *I do not claim,* would say the one, *to convince you by self-evident reasons, I know that you are able to elude all my proofs; nor I neither,* the other would say. *My conscience is convinced,* the former would say, *it tastes a thousand consolations, although my understanding has yet to see clearly in these matters; and mine also,* would say the latter. *I am persuaded,* the first would continue, *that the interior working of the mind of God has led me to orthodoxy; and me too,* says the second. *Let us dispute no more, let us persecute one another no more,* they would say in unison. *For if I propose objections to which you cannot reply, I cannot fail to hope to convert you; for since you do not claim that evidence is the mark of theological truth, the obscurity of your reason and the weakness of your arguments will never seem to you a mark of falsehood. It would thus be in vain for me to reduce you to silence. Your taste would, for you, take the place of a demonstration; just as, in respect of meats, we trust more to our palates and to the good effects they produce upon our health than to the speculative reasoning of a cook or a physician, though we are unable to give a reason why these meats either please us or fortify us. Let us agree together therefore not to cause one another trouble and let us be content to pray to God for each other's welfare.*

Thus you see the fruit that could be born of this doctrine for which certain people yearn, and who remember a maxim of Saint Augustine: namely that the discernment of the true and the false being a very difficult matter we should not get too angered with those who err.

Illi in vos saeviant ... (says he [Augustine] to the Manicheans): ['let them rage against you, who do not know with what toil the truth is found, and how hard it is to avoid error. Let them rage against you who do not know how extraordinary and how difficult it is for the religious mind to overcome by means of serenity the phantoms of the body. Let them rage against you who do not know how difficult is the task of healing one's inner eye so that one can see one's own sun. Let them rage against you who do not know what sighs and what lamentations are poured forth so that God can be grasped in even the smallest measure.']¹²⁼²¹

Observe, I say, what fruit this doctrine might produce if we were to believe certain persons; but I myself doubt it – *sed non ego credulus illis* – when I consider that the minister of Utrecht¹³⁼²² – though persuaded that the Scriptures do contain an evident proof of our mysteries – does not approve of the persecution of heretics; while by contrast his adversary [Jurieu] – though convinced that we can put forward no good proofs¹⁴⁼²³ either of the divinity of the Scriptures *vis-à-vis* infidels, or of the testimony of our mysteries *vis-à-vis* the Socinians – strongly advocates that magistrates should persecute heretics.¹⁵⁼²⁴ What contradictions are here! We must count on nothing, even when we suppose that men will act according to their principles, and that they construct their systems logically. It is not that I claim that the minister of Utrecht [Saurin] reasons badly when he joins two such assertions together: the one that there is in the Scriptures the sound evidence for those matters that God illuminates; and the other that one should not institute civil penalties for those who do not believe in the mysteries of the Trinity and the Incarnation, etc. I attribute inconsistency only to his adversary. This is patent: for if, on the one hand, it suits him to say that he cannot give good proof¹⁶⁼²⁵ that God clearly reveals his mysteries in his word, one is very much in the wrong to claim that a man, who does not believe in them, deserves to lose his goods, his liberty and

---

¹²⁼²¹ Augustine, *Contra epistulam Manichaei quam vocant 'fundamenti'* [Against the Letter of the Manichean which is called 'Fundamental Principles'], 2.

¹³⁼²² M. Saurin.

¹⁴⁼²³ We understand by good proofs those which offer evidence.

¹⁵⁼²⁴ See his [Jurieu's] treatise *Des Droits des deux souverains* [On the Rights of the Two Sovereigns], and his *Tableau du socinianisme* [Portrait of Socinianism], letter 8.

¹⁶⁼²⁵ See note 14=23 above.

his country: because, in his understanding, he has the light of reason on his side, and you cannot deny that he acts reasonably in refusing to renounce his light unless it appears that it is evidently contradicted by the testimony of God. He is ready to sacrifice his most distinct ideas as soon as it appears clearly that the authority of God requires it. You recognise that you are incapable of making this appear so to him; and you say that grace may indeed persuade him of it, though not reveal it to him evidently. Thus all that reason and charity require of you is to pray to God for him,[17=26] and to act through the path of moderate instruction so that he finds less probability in his opinions than in yours. If you cannot succeed, then let him enjoy his estate and his country, and do not attempt to arm the power of his sovereign against him. These are matters that follow naturally and consequentially, and yet the minister of whom I speak here [Jurieu] separates them from one another, so matchless is the contrary turn of his mind. To remark in passing: was anything more preposterous than to condemn, as he did, the author of the *Commentaire philosophique* [i.e. Bayle], and then adopt the fundamental principle of his system? It might easily be shown that his hypotheses are most admirably fitted to confirm those of the commentator;[18=27] but this would carry me rather too far from M. Nicole. So, let us return to him.

Let no one say to me that this author has succeeded only too well since his books have provoked disputes such as these among the ministers of Holland [the Huguenots in exile]. This is a chimerical advantage to his communion [Catholicism], and it has caused real harm within Christianity by raising controversies that demonstrate that neither by the way of authority nor by the way of examination[19=28] can one choose a party with the satisfaction of telling oneself that one has made good use of one's reason. For this good use consists in suspending one's judgement until the evidence of proof becomes available. Philosophic minds would rebuke, as a great fail-

---

[17=26] See [Bayle,] the preface to *Le Supplément du commentaire philosophique*, where it is shown that the obscurity of a controversy is an invincible reason for tolerance.

[18=27] The commentator [Bayle] has shown in his preface to part 4 that with regard to the rights of the erring conscience, M. Jurieu, by seeking to refute it, refutes himself. One may extend that to other articles.

[19=28] His adversary has renounced the examination of discussion and the claims of self-evident arguments.

ing, the spontaneity with which they had accepted truths which had been put to them only obscurely. They [philosophic minds] would not exonerate themselves at all for having given a judgement in a cause, had they decided it prior to a rigorous examination of all the depositions of the contending parties. They give the contemptuous term 'opinionated' to those who commit themselves to one side without being, as it were, forced to it by incontestable arguments. They maintain that one can acquire thereby only a false science; and they say that ignorance is worth far more than that false science which makes one imagine that one knows what one does not know at all. For as Saint Augustine has most judiciously observed in his book *De l'utilité de la créance* [On the Utility of Belief], this attitude of mind is to be condemned for the following two reasons: firstly, because he who persuades himself falsely that he knows the truth thereby renders himself incapable of instruction; secondly, because this presumption and impulsiveness is a sign of a mind that is immature. 'Opinari, duas ob res . . .' ['It is highly improper to be opinionated, and for two reasons: because the person who is convinced that he already has knowledge can learn nothing, and the very lack of considered thought is, in its own right, a sign of an ill-developed intellect.'] For the word 'opinari' in the pure Latin original signifies the disposition of a mind which assents too lightly to propositions that are uncertain, and without being aware of what it does not know. This is why every philosopher should maintain: 'sapientem nihil opinari' [the wise man has no opinions] and why Cicero, castigating himself for that vice, said he was 'magnus opinator' [dreadfully opinionated].[20=29]

Not only philosophers but everyone in general should acknowledge this maxim: 'in order not to be rash it is not enough to tell the truth, one must also be aware that it is the truth. He who affirms that the grains of sand upon the seashore are of an even number might be telling the truth, but he certainly could not fail to be guilty of temerity.'[21=30] Thus M. Nicole's book has been effective only for fostering the irresolution of vacillating minds, and for giving new pretexts to sceptics in religion. One might perhaps say of the first of these works what the ancients said of the first ship: would to

[20=29] [Arnauld and Nicole,] *L'Art de penser*, part 1, ch. 3, pp. 54, 55.
[21=30] Nicole, *Les Prétendus Réformés convaincus de schisme*, bk 1, ch. 2, p. 15.

God that the tree felled to build it were still standing! Cicero applies this thought to reason:

> 'O utinam igitur, ut illa anus optat . . .' [' "Oh", as the old woman exclaimed, "that the fir tree had not been axed in the Pelian grove", and likewise that the gods had not given men their inventiveness! For very few put it to good use, and they are outweighed by those who use it badly; moreover the multitude uses it wickedly.']22=31

But since every argument has two sides there is some reason to hope that honest minds will gain something from such a rancorous dispute. They will learn to apply to their own domain Descartes's maxim concerning the suspension of our judgement.23=32 They will learn, since our reason is so imperfect, to be mistrustful of natural light [*des lumières naturelles*], and to have resort to the way of the spirit of God. They will learn to what extent it is necessary to rely on the doctrine of grace, and how much our humility is pleasing to God since he has sought to shame us even in the possession of his truths. For he has precluded us from discerning them by means of that sort of philosophical investigation by which we arrive at a scientific knowledge of some things.

22=31 Cicero, *De natura deorum* [On the Nature of the Gods], 3.30.
23=32 On the disastrous effects of this maxim if transposed into religion, see *Nouvelles de la république des lettres*, by the author [Bayle] of *La Critique générale*, pp. 799 *et seq.*; M. Jurieu, *Le Vrai Système de l'église*, pp. 373 *et seq.*, *Nouvelles de la république des lettres*, November 1684, art. 1, p. 889; July 1686, art. 1, p. 745. See also [*Dic*,] Remarks to the article 'Pellisson'.

Ovid

[Bayle uses his article on Ovid to show that theories of creation remained speculative. For life's origins, whether attributed to God or Nature, posed problems for natural philosophy. Contemporaries – he mentions Descartes, Newton, and the atomist, Lami – were engaged in showing the falsity of many commonly held notions, but their improved alternative theories were not necessarily the last word. Through his discussion of Epicurus, who had posed a theory of creation through chance, Bayle recovers a pre-Christian theory of natural selection. In Remark (H), he relates the debate to moral psychology, asking if the contest between reason and passion in the human being might parallel the clash of the elements in the natural world.]

OVID NASO (Publius) ... was one of the greatest poets of the age of Augustus ... Nature endowed him with so strong a gift of poetry that out of love of the muses he laid aside those projects and strategies that are necessary for attaining positions of dignity. Yet while the inclination to poetry extinguished in him all fire of ambition, it warmed in him, on the other hand, the fervour of love. He was ardently devoted to the pleasures of Venus [(A)], and that was almost his only vice. Not content with loving and making conquests in the way of gallantry, he also taught the public art of love and making oneself loved; that is to say he reduced to the consistency of a system that pernicious science in which Nature gives us only too many lessons ...

Ovid's finest work is his *Metamorphoses*. This judgement was that of the author himself, and he hoped that it would be principally though this work that his name would be immortalised . . . [(F)] This prediction has not so far been contradicted. Among its finest parts is the *exordium* or beginning of the poem. It is a description of chaos, and of the manner in which the universe was formed out of it. Nothing could be more elegant or more lucid than his magnificent description if we consider it only as poetry; but if we examine its doctrines we find them inconsistent and self-contradictory and amounting to a rather greater chaos than the one which he describes. This gives me the opportunity of fulfilling a promise which I made earlier.[a=c] I shall examine whether the ideas of the Ancients who speak of the chaos were right, and whether they could have said that the state of confusion no longer exists (G). I shall demonstrate that the struggle of the four elements did not, as they suppose, cease at the production of the world. Furthermore, I shall show that, in any case, they ought to have excepted the human race from their general law since it is subject to disorders and contradictions quite as fearsome as those that must have existed during the chaos (H).

[Remarks (A)–(F) omitted.]

(G) I shall examine whether the ideas of the Ancients who speak of the chaos were right, and whether they could have said that such a state no longer exists.] To proceed methodically in this task, it is necessary first to give an account of the description of the chaos left to us by Ovid. His rendering is none other than a statement, or rather a paraphrase, of what he had met with in the writings of the ancient Greek philosophers.

> Ante mare et terras . . . ['Before there was sea and earth and the sky which covers everything, throughout the whole world nature had one appearance, which men have called chaos, an unformed, confused mass. Nothing existed except inactive weight and the conflicting elements of ill-fitting matter heaped in one body. No sun yet provided the world

---

[a=c] In [*Dic*,] 'Anaxagoras', Remark (H).

with light. No waxing moon renewed its horns. The universe was not suspended in the surrounding air, balanced
there by its own weight. Nor had the ocean stretched out
its arms round the shores of lands. But wherever there was
earth, there was also sea and air. Thus earth gave no foot-
hold, water could not be swum in, sky had no light. Nothing
maintained any fixed shape, but everything got in the way
of everything else, because within that one body, cold was
fighting against hot, wet against dry, soft against hard, lightness against weight . . .']$^{1=42}$

You thus see that, by chaos, they understood a shapeless mass of
matter, in which the particles of all individual bodies were jumbled
together to the ultimate degree of confusion. Air, water and earth
were everywhere combined; every part was opposed to every part;
cold and heat, wetness and dryness, lightness and weight opposed
each another in one and the same body over the whole of the vast
extent of matter. Now here is how Ovid supposes this state of confusion was unravelled:

Hanc DEUS, et melior . . . ['This dispute was settled by God or
superior Nature. For he divided the earth from the sky and
the water from the earth, and separated the clear sky from the
thick atmosphere. After he had untied these elements and
removed them from the chaotic heap, he united them in
peaceful harmony, each in a different place. The fiery, weight-
less ether shot up to form the vault of heaven and took up its
place at the top of the sky. The air, closest to it in lightness,
came next in place. The earth, heavier than these, drew with
it large particles and sank down, pulled by its own weight.
Water flowing round took possession of the last remaining
place and encompassed the firm earth. When that god, whichever god he was, had divided the mass so as to arrange it thus,
he confined it to its separate parts.']$^{2=43}$

You see that he says that this war among the confused and
entangled elements was brought to an end by the authority of a god
who separated them, and who allocated to each its proper place;

$^{1=42}$ Ovid, *Metamorphoses*, 1.5–20.
$^{2=43}$ *Ibid.*, 1.21–33.

assigning fire to the uppermost region, earth to the lowermost, air immediately below fire, and water immediately below air; and then forging a bond of amity and harmony among the four elements now spatially separated. It follows that the analysis of our poet's discourse can be reduced to the following six propositions.

I. Before there was a sky, an earth and a sea, nature was a homogeneous whole.[3=44]

II. This whole was merely a heavy mass[4=45] in which the principles of things were contained confusedly and without any symmetry, and in a discordant fashion.

III. Heat struggled with cold in the same body; moisture and dryness did likewise; and lightness and weight were the same.

IV. God put an end to this war by separating the combatants.

V. He assured them of distinct dwelling places according to the lightness or weight which belonged to them.

VI. He formed between them an appropriate relationship.

Here, in general, are the inherent defects which can be found within Ovid's doctrine. I do not know whether his work has ever been criticised from a philosophic perspective or whether commentators have examined this part of the *Metamorphoses*: but had they done so, I think they might easily have perceived the following points:

1. In the first place, that the first proposition is hardly consistent with the second; for if the parts of a whole are composed of contrary seeds or principles then that whole cannot pass for homogeneous.

2. In the second place, that the second proposition does not accord with the third; for one cannot say that a whole in which there is as much lightness as weight is just a heavy mass.

3. In the third place, that this heavy mass cannot be looked upon as inactive weight, *pondus iners*, since contrary principles are mixed in it without symmetry, from which it follows that their actual struggle must end in the victory of one or the other.

4. In the fourth place, that the first three propositions being once true, the fourth and fifth are superfluous; for the elementary qualities are a principle of sufficient force to disentangle the chaos without

---

[3=44] 'Unus erat toto naturae vultus in orbe.' ['Throughout the whole world, Nature had one appearance.']

[4=45] 'Nec quicquam nisi pondus iners.' ['Nothing existed except inactive weight.']

the intervention of another cause, and to set the parts at a greater or a lesser distance from the centre proportionately to their heaviness or lightness.

5. In the fifth place, that the fourth proposition is false upon another score; for since the production of sky, air, water and earth, the struggles between cold and heat, wetness and dryness, heaviness and lightness would remain as great in the same body as ever they could have been before.

6. In the sixth place that, for the reason last mentioned, the sixth proposition is false.

From which it appears that this description of the chaos and its development is composed of propositions more opposite to one another than were the elements during the chaos.

It is unnecessary to enlarge upon all of these errors of Ovid, but some of them merit a detailed clarification.

1. I say therefore that there is nothing more absurd than to suppose a chaos that has been homogeneous during all eternity, notwithstanding that it had elementary particles: i.e. those that are termed changing, which are heat and cold, wetness and dryness, and those which are called moving, which are lightness and weight, and which cause upward movement and downward movement. Such matter cannot be called homogeneous, and must necessarily contain all sorts of heterogeneities. Heat and cold, wetness and dryness cannot mingle without their action and reaction modifying them and converting them into other qualities which make the form of mixed bodies; and since this modification can according to its diversities make countless combinations, it was necessary for the chaos to have contained in it an unbelievable multitude of composite species. The only way to imagine it as homogeneous would be to say that the . . . qualities modified themselves to the same degree in each of the molecules, so that they had everywhere the same warmth, the same softness, the same odour, the same taste etc., but that would be to undermine on the one hand what one had built up on the other; that is through a contradiction in terms, to call chaos a most orderly work, the most wonderful in symmetry, and most admirable in matter of proportion that one can conceive. I agree that man's taste feels more comfortable with a diversified work than with a uniform work; but our ideas should not prevent us from apprehending that the harmony of contrary qualities, uniformly

conserved throughout the universe, would be a perfection as marvellous as the unequal division which succeeded the chaos. What
science, what power, would not ask for this uniform harmony,
spread throughout nature? It would not be enough to put into each
mixed thing the same quantity of each of the four ingredients; one
would need to put more in some, and in others less, as the strength
of one is greater or smaller for acting than for resisting,[5=46] since
one knows that the philosophers allocate in different degrees the
action and the reaction of elementary qualities. All considered it
will be found that the cause which metamorphosed the chaos would
thus have wrested it not from a state of confusion and of warfare,
as is supposed, but from a state of wholeness the most complete
possible, and which, through a reduction to an equilibrium of
opposing forces, would have held it in a condition of repose equivalent to peace. It is thus patent that if poets wish to save the homo-
geneity of the chaos, they must efface all that they add concerning
this bizarre confusion of contrary elements, this undigested mixture,
and this perpetual warfare of antagonistic principles.

II. Let us pass over this contradiction since there are others . . .
Let us recommence our attack with eternity. Nothing is more
absurd than to postulate, during an infinite period of time, the
admixture of insensible parts of four elements; because as soon as
you suppose in these parts the activity of heat, the action and the
reaction of the four primary elements and, in addition, the movement towards the centre of the elements of earth and water, and
the movement towards the circumference of those of fire and air,
you establish a principle which will necessarily separate one from
another these four types of body, and which will require only a
finite period of time . . .

One can use another comparison which is to suppose that the
chaos was similar to new wine in the process of fermentation. It is
a condition of flux. The spirituous parts and the solid parts brew
together. One can perceive in them neither the appearance nor the
taste of what is properly wine and what is only sediment or lees.

[5=46] 'Calor qui maxime . . .' ['Heat which is especially active has the least resistance.
But on the contrary dryness, which is less active, has greater resistance. Cold,
which comes second in being active, comes third in resistance. Finally wetness
comes last in being active, but second in resistance.'] Arriaga, *Disputatio de
generatione* [Treatise on Generation], sect. 11, no. 178.

This confusion excites a furious warfare between these diverse parts of matter. The energy is so great that the vessel is sometimes incapable of containing it. But two or three days, more or less, sees an end to this internecine war. The crude parts separate and descend through their own weight. The more subtle parts separate also and evaporate[6=47] through their lightness, and in this way the wine finds itself in its natural state. This is what would happen in the chaos of the poets. The opposition of principles confusedly mixed together produces a turbulent fermentation, but which, at the end of a certain time, would have been the cause of the descent of earthly bodies, and the evaporation of the spirituous parts, and, in a word, of the appropriate ordering of each body with regard to its lightness and weight. There is, then, nothing more contrary to experience and to reason than to postulate a chaos of an infinite duration, notwithstanding that it contains all the energy that has appeared in nature from the formation of the world. For we should take care to note that what we call general laws of nature, laws of movement or principles of mechanics, are the same thing which were called by Ovid and the Peripatetics heat, cold, wetness, dryness, heaviness and lightness. They claimed that all the energy and all the activity of nature, all the principles of generation and alteration of bodies, were comprehended within the sphere of these six qualities. Since, therefore, they have acknowledged them in the chaos, they have necessarily recognised them as the very same qualities which bring about generation and alteration in the world, including the winds and the rains, etc.

III. From this emerges another objection which is hardly less strong than the foregoing. Ovid and those whose opinions he paraphrased had recourse without any pressing need for the ministry of God for unravelling the chaos. For they acknowledged all the energy that was inherently capable of separating the parts and assigning to each element its proper situation; why then was there a need to call upon any external cause? Would it not be to imitate those theatrical and inadequate poets who brought in God to remove a very small perplexity? To reason rightly upon the production of the world we must consider God as the author of matter,

---

[6=47] One always finds a space in the barrel once fermentation has stopped, evident proof that some parts have escaped through the sides of the barrel.

and as the first and sole principle of motion. If we cannot raise our minds to the idea of a creation properly so called, we shall never get ourselves off the rocks; and whichever side we take, we shall utter things that our reason can never accommodate: for if matter exists of itself we cannot easily conceive that God could or should have given it motion. It [matter] would be independent of any other thing as to the reality of existing: why then should it not have the power to exist forever in the same place with regard to each one of its parts? Why should it be forced to give way to the desires of another substance with respect to a change of position? Add to this the objection that if matter had been moved by an external principle, that would be an indication that its necessary and independent existence were separate and distinct from motion; the conclusion of which is that matter's natural state is that of repose, and consequently that God could not move it without introducing disorder into the nature of things, there being nothing more conducive to order than following the eternal and necessary institution of nature. Of this I speak more considerably in other places.[7=48] But of all the errors into which one falls when one strays so far as to reject creation, there is none so piteous, it seems to me, as to suppose that though God is not the cause of the existence of matter, then he is at least the first mover of bodies, and in this capacity is the author of elementary properties and the author of the order and the form that we see in nature. The supposition of his being the first mover of matter is a principle that yields naturally the following consequence: that he formed the heavens and the earth, the air and the sea, and that he is the architect of this great and marvellous edifice which we call the world. But if you remove from him this quality of first mover, if you affirm that matter moved itself independently of him and that it had of itself its diversity of forms; that with respect to some of its parts its motion tended towards the centre, and that with respect to others it tended towards the circumference; that it contained corpuscles of fire, corpuscles of water, corpuscles of air, and corpuscles of earth: if, I say, you profess all these things with Ovid, you employ God needlessly and inappropriately in the construction of the world. Nature might well be considered as the ministry of God, since she had sufficient energy to separate the

---

[7=48] See [*Dic,*] article 'Epicurus'; see also [*Dic,*] 'Hiéraclès, philosophe', Remark (A).

different particles from the elements, and to put together those of the same sort.[8=49] Aristotle has fully grasped this truth and in this respect he holds a much sounder opinion than Plato who postulated a disorderly motion in elementary matter before the production of the world. Aristotle shows that this supposition demolished itself since, to avoid falling into an infinite regression, one would have to say that there was indeed natural motion in the elements. If it were natural then some would veer to the centre, and others to the circumference: they were thus organising themselves in the way that they have to do to form the world that we have today; therefore there was a world at the time of this motion that was allegedly disorderly and antecedent to the world – which is a contradiction. . . .

Aristotle observes,[9=50] and very reasonably, that Anaxagoras, who postulated that no motion preceded the first formation of the world, had in this respect seen more clearly than the rest.[10=51]

The Peripatetics of today, who are most zealous for evangelical orthodoxy, can find nothing to condemn in these words of Aristotle. For they admit that the altering and moving qualities of the four elements are, in themselves, sufficient for the production of all the effects of nature. They would have God intervene only as the conserver of these elementary faculties of which he is the first cause, or rather they would have him intervene only through a general concurrence; and they are agreed that they [these elementary faculties] do nearly everything and that they are, as a secondary cause, the complete principle of all generation.[11=52] Thus a Scholastic theologian would admit without difficulty that if the four elements had existed independently of God, with all the faculties they have today, they would of themselves have formed the machine of the world and have maintained it in the state in which we see it. It follows that he would recognise in the doctrine of the chaos two major faults. The first, and indeed the principal one, is that it removes from God the creation of matter and the construction of the qualities belonging to fire, air, earth, and sea. The other is that having

[8=49] Cf. [*Dic*,] article 'Anaxagoras', Remark (G), no 8.
[9=50] Aristotle, *De caelo* [On the Heavens], 3.2, p. 370.
[10=51] I have cited Aristotle's words, in [*Dic*,] 'Epicurus', citation 161.
[11=52] One must except the soul of man.

removed that role from God, it then introduces him quite unnecessarily into the theatre of the world to allocate the places of the four elements. Our new philosophers would find the same faults in Ovid's description of the chaos, though they have rejected the elements and the faculties of Peripatetic physics. For what they call the general laws of motion, principles of mechanics, modifications of matter, figure, situation, and order of the corpuscles, signify nothing other than those active and passive qualities of nature which the Peripatetics understand as the altering qualities [*qualités altératrices*] and the moving qualities [*qualités motrices*] of the four elements. According to the doctrine of the Peripatetics, those four bodies – positioned according to their lightness and weight – constitute sufficient principle for all generation; therefore the Cartesians, the Gassendists, and all the other modern philosophers should maintain that the motion, the situation, and the shape of the parts of matter are sufficient for the production of all natural effects, including even the general arrangement which has positioned the Earth, Air, Water and the Stars where we see them today. Thus the true cause of the universe and of the phenomena produced in it is not different from the principle that gave motion to the parts of matter; whether it assigned to each atom a pre-determinate shape as the Gassendists will have it; or whether, as in the hypothesis of the Cartesians, it just gave a push to cube-shaped parts which in the course of movement under certain laws subsequently assumed all manner of shapes. Both the one and the other should agree, in consequence, that if matter had so existed before the generation of the world, as Ovid claims, it would have been capable of extricating itself from the chaos by its own efforts, and giving itself the shape of the world without the assistance of God. They must therefore charge Ovid with committing two mistakes; one is in supposing that matter without the assistance of the deity contained the seeds of all the mixed bodies, heat, motion etc.; and the other is in saying that without the intervention of the divine hand matter could not have extracted itself from its state of confusion. This is conceding too much and too little; it is refusing aid when it is most wanted, and asking for it when it is not necessary.

I know there are some who do not support the speculation advanced by M. Descartes concerning the manner in which the world might have been formed.[12=53] Some ridicule it and believe it injurious to God; others find in it either falsities or impossibilities. To the former it may be answered that they do not understand the subject, and that if they did they would admit that nothing is more fitting for giving a gracious idea of the infinite wisdom of God than to affirm that out of a shapeless matter he could have made our world in a certain time, by the bare conservation of a motion initiated once, and reduced to a small number of simple general laws. As for those who reject Descartes's system as containing some things contrary to the laws of mechanics and the actual state that astronomers have discovered in the vortices of the heavens, I shall reply to them that this only argues that the bulk of his hypothesis may be right and reasonable; and I am fully persuaded that M. Newton, the most formidable of all M. Descartes's critics, has no doubt that the effective system of the world could be the production of a small number of mechanical laws established by the author of all things: because as soon as you postulate bodies disposed to move in straight lines and to veer either towards the centre or towards the circumference every time they are obliged to move in a circular motion because of the resistance of other bodies, you establish a system that will necessarily produce great varieties in matter; and if it does not form this particular system, it will form another.

It is not just the foolish and extravagant hypothesis of the Epicureans that possesses what is required to construct a particular world. Allow them different figures of atoms with the inalienable energy to move themselves according to the laws of gravity and mutual repulsion, and to encounter one another, and to deflect in this or that manner according to whether they collide diametrically or obliquely, and you will no longer be able to deny that the fortuitous meeting of these corpuscles can form masses where there will be hard bodies, and fluid bodies, heat and cold, opacity and transparency, vortices etc. All that could be denied them is that chance could produce an assemblage of bodies as our world is, in which there are so many things that persevere so long in their regularity,

---

[12=53] See Descartes, *Principes* [Principles], part 3, nos. 46 *et seq.*

so many natural organisms [*machines d'animaux*] a thousand times more industrious than those of human art which require necessarily an intelligent direction.

Let us take the opportunity of examining a notion of M. Lami, doctor of medicine in the faculty of Paris, who is as great a partisan for atoms [chance creation] as he is adversary of the Peripatetics and Descartes. This appears in his work *De principiis rerum* [On the Principles of Things].[13=54] Here is what he replies to an objection which is commonly advanced against the hypothesis of Epicurus. The argument proceeds by the following comparison: by joining together a random conjunction of characters one would never compose Homer's *Iliad*; therefore the casual meeting of atoms could never produce a world. He replies that there is a great difference between these two cases. The *Iliad* can be constructed only through the precise and pre-determined bringing together of a certain number of characters. The method of composing it is thus unique among an infinity of ways of arranging characters: therefore it should not be thought strange that chance could never hit upon this one way among an infinity of others. But for making a world, generally speaking, this one or others, there is no need for atoms to meet and combine in a certain and precise manner, unique and determined; for in whatever way they cluster together they will necessarily form accumulations of bodies, and consequently a world. He does not stop there, he gives the comparison another turn: however random they are, he says, the casual conjunction of letters and syllables will make words, therefore the chance meeting of atoms will necessarily form bodies. If you put it to him that these words formed by chance have no meaning, his answer will be that it is because words signify only what man makes them mean; and that to have meaning they must be arranged in conformity with human institutions; but the virtue of atoms, being independent of man, is to produce considerable effects, which can evoke his admiration whatever their arrangement may be.[14=55] There is no great necessity to discuss all this. For we may grant him a part of his claim and at the same time deny that our world, in which there are so many

[13=54] The *Journal de Leipsic*, 1682, p. 155, gives an abstract from it, and note that it was printed in Paris in 1680; but that was a revised date. I read it in 1678 and even then it was not new.
[14=55] Taken from bk 3, ch. 39 of Guillaume Lami, *De principiis rerum*.

regular things tending to certain ends, can be the complete effect of chance. . . .[15=56]

IV. The last observation that remains to be illustrated relates to Ovid's assertion that the war of the four elements, having been continuous during the chaos, was brought to an end by the authority of the god who formed the world. Is that not to say that since that time the elements have lived at peace with one another? And is the claim not very ill founded, and does experience not contradict it? Does war ever cease between heat and cold, moisture and drought, lightness and weight, fire and water, etc.? Since Ovid supported the hypothesis of the four elements he ought to have been aware that the antipathy of their qualities always exists and that they never agree to either peace or truce; no, not even when they constitute a temperament of mixed bodies. They enter that state only after a war in which they have reciprocally struggled with one another; and if there were periods when their fight happened to be interrupted for some moments, it was because the resistance of the one party is precisely equal to the activity of other. When they can do no more they breathe again, being always ready to harass and destroy one another as their strength permits. The equilibrium cannot last long, for each minute it comes to the assistance of either the one or the other; and of necessity the one must lose what the other gains. Thus Ovid saw that, as in the time of the chaos, their war continued to reign everywhere, and in the smallest recesses of the same mixed bodies: 'within that one body, cold was fighting against hot, wet against dry, soft against hard, lightness against weight'.[16=57]

The laws of this engagement are that the weakest must be entirely ruined according to the full extent of the power of the strongest. Clemency or pity have no place there; no proposals for accommodation are heard. This internecine war makes way for the dissolution of the compound and sooner or later it accomplishes that end. Living bodies are more exposed than others, and would soon perish if nature did not furnish them with resources; but finally the contrast between natural heat and radical moisture becomes fatal to them. The power of time which consumes all and

---

[15=56] Cicero, *De natura deorum* [On the Nature of the Gods], 1.32.
[16=57] ' . . . corpore in uno / frigida pugnabant calidis, humentia siccis, / mollia cum duris, sine pondere habentia pondus.' Ovid, *Metamorphoses*, 1.18.

which Ovid describes so brilliantly in the fifteenth book of his *Metamorphoses*[17=58] has no other foundation but the conflict of bodies. In fashioning that description, our poet no longer remembers what he had stated in the chapter on the chaos. Thus to convict him of contradiction we need only compare the beginning of his work with the end. In the first chapter he affirms that a stop was put to the discord of the elements, and in the fifteenth he tells us they take turns to destroy one another and that nothing continues in the same state.

> Haec quoque non perstant . . . ['Even those things which we call elements do not persist . . . All the elements are derived from each other and sink back into each other. Earth is broken up and liquefied into running water. Water is rarefied into breezes and becomes air. Air also loses its weight and when it has been greatly thinned, shoots up to the fiery ether above. Then they revert to their former state and the same arrangement is restored. For the fiery ether condenses and turns back into the thicker atmosphere, air into water and water under pressure solidifies into earth. Nor does anything maintain its form. But Nature, renewer of creation, repeatedly produces one shape from another.'][18=60]

He then recounts several instances of conquests made by water upon the earth and by earth upon the water. Where, then, is this pacification to which he was so partial in the first book? See note.[19=61]

Even if our poet did not contradict himself, we might still rightly censure him; for since the world must become a theatre of vicissitudes nothing could be more improper than to depict the four elements in a state of peace; and given that during the initial chaos they had had an accommodation, the cessation of the chaos, far

---

[17=58] 'Tempus edax rerum, tuque invidiosa vetustas . . .' ['Time, devourer of the world, and you, envious Old Age, you both destroy all things and, gnawing away at them, you gradually consume everything in a lingering death . . .'] *Metamorphoses*, 15.234–6.

[18=60] *Ibid.*, 244–53.

[19=61] Let no one say here, to excuse him from contradiction, that he was making Pythagoras speak here. For the greater part of the things that he makes him say are either histories, or ideas in conformity with those who explained growth and decay by the quality of the elements.

from putting an end to their quarrels, would on the contrary have set them against one another. It is through their friction that nature becomes fertile; their harmony would keep her barren, so that, without the implacable war which they unleash wherever they connect, we should see no generation. The production of one thing is always the ruin of another.[20=62] *Generatio unius est corruptio alterius.* ['The generation of one thing is the disintegration of another.'] That is an axiom of natural philosophy. It was thus necessary for Ovid to have pre-supposed that the god who allotted distinct places to the four elements enjoined them to fight without quarter, and to act the part of highly ambitious conquerors who leave no stone unturned to invade the possessions of their neighbours. The orders given them would have been like Dido's curse: 'I pray that now, hereafter or whenever you are granted enough strength, your shores oppose their shores, your waves their waves. I pray that you force them and their descendants after them into war.'[21=63]

And, in effect, they act just as if they had received such orders, and as if they were inspired with the fiercest passion to put them into full execution. Cold enlarges its sphere as much as ever it can, and there destroys its enemy: heat does likewise and these two qualities are by turns mistresses of the campaign, the one in winter, the other in summer. They imitate those victorious armies which, after the triumph of a decisive battle, constrain the enemy to fly to his citadels and, pursuing him, then lay siege to him and reduce him to extremity. In the summer cold escapes to caverns and subterranean cavities; and to prevent its being entirely sunk redoubles the effort of its resistance, and fortifies itself in the best manner that it can, by the virtue called 'antiperistasis': as in winter heat takes the same course. Philosophers of the elements who offer this explanation of nature tell us that each quality strains itself so much to vanquish its enemies that, not satisfied with making them its vassals and ordering them to wear its livery, it endeavours to transmute them into its state: 'omne agens', say they, 'intendit sibi assimilare pas-

---

[20=62] 'Nam quodcumque . . .' ['For whenever something undergoes change, passing outside its boundaries, death at once befalls what was there before.'] Lucretius, *De rerum natura* [On the Nature of Things], 1.670–1.

[21=63] Nunc, olim, quocunque dabunt se tempore vires, / littora littoribus contraria, fluctibus undas / imprecor, arma armis, pugnent ipsique nepotes. Virgil, *Aeneid*, 4.627–9.

sum' ['every active quality strives to assimilate whatever is subject to it']. Can one meet with a more hostile and a more ambitious animosity than this? Empedocles was mistaken when he associated Amity and Enmity with the four elements, one to unite them and the other to disunite.[22=64] One can agree with him that the union and the separation of parts are very necessary for the productions of nature, but it is certain that amity has no hand in it; for only discord and antipathy among the elements connect bodies in one place, and disperse them in another. These two qualities of Empedocles can be attributed at most only to living bodies; but air and fire, water and earth have no connection other than enmity.

Living bodies execute very effectively the command to engage in mutual destruction, supposed by Ovid to have been ordered by him who disentangled the chaos. For it is true to the very letter that they feed only upon destruction: whatever serves as a support for life loses its shape and changes its state and its species. Vegetables destroy the constitution and qualities of all the liquids they can absorb. Animals commit the same ravages upon all that serves them for food. They eat one another and there are several species of beast that fight only to devour the enemies they kill. In some countries men follow the same course, and everywhere they are great exterminators. I do not speak of the slaughter arising from ambition, avarice or cruelty, or from the other passions that give rise to war. I speak only of the consequences of the efforts we make to nourish our bodies. Upon this score man is a principle so injurious and so destructive that if all other animals did as much in proportion, the earth would not be able to furnish them with sufficient sustenance. When we see in the streets and in the market places of the great cities that prodigious bulk of vegetables, fruits and the infinite number of other things destined for the feeding of its inhabitants, is one not apt to exclaim: here is enough for the week? Is it imaginable that the display has to be replenished each day? Would we believe that a slit as small as the human mouth were a gulf, an abyss, which would devour all and in so short a time? Experience alone can persuade us. In the recently published *Saint Evremoniana* I came across the following words:[23=65] it is said that in Paris there

[22=64] See Aristotle, *Physics*, 8.1; Diogenes Laertius [Lives of the Philosophers], 8.76, and therein Aldobrandius and Menagius [Gilles Ménage].
[23=65] Dutch edition, 1701, p. 293.

are 4,000 oyster sellers; that each day are consumed 1,500 large oxen, and more than 16,000 sheep, calves and hogs, in addition to a prodigious quantity of poultry and game. Judge what happens in those countries where people eat more meat, and eat better.

Given therefore that this is the condition of nature – that beings are produced and preserved by the destruction of one another – it cannot be asserted that the war of the elements was pacified when the world began and when the chaos ended.[24=66] It would be enough to say that the situation and the energy of the combatants were so regulated and so balanced that their continual hostilities did not bring about the destruction of the enterprise but only the vicissitudes that are its ornaments, *per questo variar natura è bella* ['nature is beautiful because of her variety'], as the Italians say. Some perhaps will imagine that, since war did not cease on the ordering of the elements, it was not so much a cessation of the chaos as a rough draft for the disentanglement; and that after this preparation, that is to say our World, has continued for a certain number of ages it will be succeeded by a much finer world from which discord will be eliminated. And they will claim perhaps that Saint Paul[25=67] confirms their sentiments by saying that all creatures sigh for their deliverance from the state of vanity and corruption in which they find themselves. They may say what they please but I shall not engage in examining their thoughts.

Observe that through the principles of mechanics, which the new philosophers use to explain the effects of nature, it is more easy to understand the perpetual war of bodies than through the physics of the four elements. Since all the actions of the six elementary qualities are nothing other, according to the new philosophy, than local motion, it is clear that each body assails everything it encounters, and that the parts of matter tend only to knock, break, and impact upon one another according to the full rigour of the law of the strongest.

(H) They ought to have exempted the human race from their general law since it is subject to disorders and contradictions

---

[24=66] See *Bibliothèque universelle*, vol. XVIII, p. 23, a remark in opposition to what Gregory Nazianzus said in his twelfth speech: 'that it is peace that makes the world go round'.

[25=67] Romans, 8:19. The passage gives commentators great trouble.

quite as fearsome as those that must have existed during the chaos.] But if, putting aside the arguments set out in the previous remark, we grant that Ovid could have maintained that creatures, generally speaking, had been extricated from the chaos, that does not allow us to claim that he could rightly have said that man in particular was included in this favour. I consider here only the views one might hold when one is destitute of the light of Revelation. In that state how could one prevent oneself from believing that, with regard to mankind, the horrors of the chaos are still in being? For apart from the perpetual conflict among the elements which reigns a little more in his machine than in most other material beings, is there not a war between his soul and his body, between his reason and his feelings, between his feeling soul and his reasoning soul? Reason should calm this disorder and pacify those internal conflicts, since reason is not only judge, but a party to the dispute; its verdicts are not executed and they only increase the harm.[26=68] . . .[27=69]

[Bayle dissects at length the ideas of several authors of his age who had considered the differing psychologies of reason and passion as they were treated in classical and Christian texts. His last textual critique, which follows, is of a work of 1678 by a Catholic contemporary, Esprit, entitled: De la fausseté des vertus humaines *(On the Deceptiveness of Human Virtue).]*

Here I shall copy for you a long passage in which there are some fine things but certain errors as well:

The philosophers were unacquainted with the nature of the motivation of men's hearts, and they had no enlightenment nor any suspicion of the strange change whereby reason becomes slave to the passions . . . True, they may be excused for not knowing the origin of this change, but they are not at all excusable for not perceiving the change itself . . . For how can it be conceived that enlightened people did not discover through their own insight, and through their own experiences, that reason, with all its power and all its indus-

---

[26=68] Concerning the objections that are made against reason, see [Bayle,] *Nouvelles Lettres contre M. Maimbourg*, pp. 755 *et seq.*; and in [*Dic*,] Remark (E) of the article 'Paulicians', certain passages from Cicero.

[27=69] Mme Deshoulières, *Idylles des moutons* [Idylls of the Sheep], Amsterdam, 1694, pp. 32, 33.

try, is incapable of destroying a passion which has taken root in the heart of man ... and that they did not see and that they did not feel what is seen and felt by more ordinary people? A small measure of attention to what they experienced themselves would thus have enabled them to familiarise themselves with the state of reason, and convince them of their fragility, and cause them to grasp that the man who inhabits that serene and luminous realm in the most elevated part of his soul, from which he observes and regulates his own exterior and interior actions, is suddenly plunged into the senses, whose pleasures he devours as if he were born for them. By the same means he might have perceived also that though reason might have lost the power it had within man, it has not nevertheless entirely lost its illumination: since sufficient is left to point out to him his duties.[28=75]

M. Esprit is the author who speaks thus in a work which he published in 1678. Everything he asserts about the weakness and the slavery of reason is certainly true, but he is wrong to accuse philosophers in general of failing to recognise such servitude, and of having no notion of its cause. For it is undeniable that several pagans possessed enlightenment in that very respect which he supposes they did not. I know well enough that the Stoics spoke too extravagantly of the empire of reason, and that their idea of the sage was lofty to such a degree that certain things escaped them. But their weakness was not in supposing that, in being freed from the passions, man would constantly observe the laws of order and decency but in supposing that it was wholly possible for men to extirpate their vices. That was their great mistake; it was there that they betrayed their ignorance of the human condition [*la condition humaine*]. The other part of their doctrine makes good sense; namely that man, having once taken charge of his passions, would find no difficulty in practising virtue and arriving at perfection.[29=76] In any case M. Esprit should have concentrated on the Stoics and not given so large a sweep to his censures. Who told him that the ancient philosophers did not know that the soul of man is inseparable from the senses? Was Cicero so ignorant of it in his words from

---

[28=75] Esprit, preface to the book *De la fausseté des vertues humaines*.
[29=76] See [Bayle,] *Nouvelles Lettres* against Maimbourg, p. 758.

the third book of the *Republic* which Saint Augustine has preserved for us, and which contains so vivid a description of the soul's slavery under the empire of the passions?

> Homo non ut a matre . . . ['Man was brought into being not by a mother, but by a step-mother, Nature. He had a body which was naked, frail and infirm. Moreover, he had a mind which grew anxious when troubles arose, abject when fears struck, weak when there was any toil, inclined to lusts, a mind in which a certain divine spark of inner intellect and spirit was, as it were, eclipsed . . .']30=77

Did he have no insight, nor any suspicion of the astonishing change which takes place within man when reason becomes enslaved to the passions? What did the words mean that the same Saint Augustine has preserved for us, where Cicero appears to support the ancient prophets of paganism, who had thought that the birth of man was the penalty for a sin committed in an earlier life?31=78 . . .

In short, I do not understand how M. Esprit can assert that the ancient philosophers were unaware that the power of reason may be lost, while its insight [*sa lumière*] nevertheless can remain. Did not Euripides, the dramatic philosopher, after meditating at length upon the depravity of men, say that he found that they sin not in the corruption of their understanding but rather because, knowing the good, they turn away from it: some through sloth, others through the love of voluptuousness. He puts these fine maxims into the mouth of Phedra.

> Iam saepe mecum . . . ['I have often needed to reflect during the long night hours upon how men's lives are ruined. This is not, to my mind, the fault of their inborn nature, but rather that they behave badly despite it. For many men do have a right understanding of life. We need rather to consider the problem in the following manner: that we know and hold on to what is good, but we do not put it into

---

30=77 See *Fragmens de Cicero* [Fragments from Cicero], collected by André Patricius. He cites it as taken from Saint Augustine, bk 4, *Contra Pelagium* [Against Pelagius].

31=78 See [*Dic,*] article 'Tullie', Remark (R).

practice; some fail to do so through indolence, while others prefer pleasure to honest pursuits.']³²⁼⁸¹

Could one improve on the following words of Ovid for describing the incapacity of reason to oblige us to do those things of which she makes us approve?

> Concipit interea validos ... ['Meanwhile, Medea, daughter of Aeetes, became inflamed with overwhelming passion. For a long time she struggled against it, but her reason could not overcome her madness. She told herself, "you resist this in vain, Medea, for some god or other is standing in your way" ...']³³⁼⁸² Excute virgineo conceptas ...³⁴⁼⁸³ [' "Cast from your maiden heart, if you can, the flames that have been kindled there, unhappy creature! If I could, I would be more rational. But a strange force overcomes me against my will. Desire urges one thing, intellect another. I see which is the better course and approve of it, but I follow the worse path." ']³⁵⁼⁸⁴

Take care to note, if you please, that she imputes to some god this compulsion which she finds impossible to resist. That was the usual refuge of the pagans with respect to passions which destroyed a man in spite of his mental insight and his knowledge of his true interests.³⁶⁼⁸⁵ They found in it something of the divine, and nearly always a punishment of some antecedent sin: which shows that they were not so ignorant as M. Esprit supposes, and that they sensed, in some measure, what the theologians teach about the loss of free will through sin, and the forsaking of those who abuse the favours of God.

Instead of Ovid I could have cited various other authors who were philosophers by profession. But I thought the quotation from Ovid to be more suitable for showing the error by M. Esprit; since

---

³²⁼⁸¹ Euripides, *Hippolytus*, vss. 375–82.
³³⁼⁸² Ovid, *Metamorphoses*, 7.9–12.
³⁴⁼⁸³ *Ibid.*, 17.
³⁵⁼⁸⁴ She admits in Euripides that she knows very well the nature of the crime that she is about to commit, but that her anger has more strength than her discernment. 'Et intellego quidem ...' ['I fully grasp the terrible nature of the evil I plan to do. But anger is more powerful than good sense.'] Euripides, *Medea*, 1078–9.
³⁶⁼⁸⁵ See [*Dic*,] article 'Helena', Remark (Y).

it is less pardonable to be ignorant of what is to be found in a poet such as he, than to be ignorant of what is said by the Greek authors. I could equally have collected many other testimonies highly capable of convincing us that it was very well known [in pagan antiquity] that mankind continued to flounder in chaos. But the very finest descriptions of the pagans by the orators, the poets, or the philosophers cannot give us so vivid an idea of the matter as that which Saint Paul has left us. We need only cast our eyes upon the picture painted by this great apostle, directed by eternal truth, in his epistle to the Romans. 'That which I do',[37=86] says he, 'I allow not; for what I would, that I do not; but what I hate, that I do . . . That when I would do good, evil is present with me: for I delight in the law of God after the inward man . . . I find then a law that when I would do good, evil is present within me . . . Oh wretched man that I am, who shall deliver me from the body of this death?'

Observe that I have considered the chaos within man only with regard to the interior war that everyone feels within himself. Had I considered the discord which reigns among peoples, and even between one neighbour and another, and all the hypocrisies, frauds, and acts of violence that attend them, I would have had a very vast and fertile field for proving what I set out to establish.

[37=86] Epistle to the Romans, 7:15.

Sainctes

[When Bayle uses the word 'intolerance' he is sometimes referring to the theory of government which upheld a single public religion and criminalised other sects. Yet sometimes he uses the adjective 'intolerant' to mean a bigoted temperament of the sort that incited others to violence. He associated Claude de Sainctes with intolerance in both senses of the word. In Remark (F), Bayle praises Henry IV's politique *use of the civil power to quell such incitement to religious hatred and violence, and he urges contemporaries to read the most modern writing on the idea of toleration, including that of Van Paets, de Beauval, Locke, Jurieu, and himself. Posterity, he hopes, of whatever religion, will rise above the hypocrisy of asking if the unorthodox should be executed or 'merely' banished.]*

SAINCTES (Claude de), in Latin Sanctesius,[a] one of the chief polemicists of the sixteenth century, was from Perche [(A)]. He took the habit of canon regular in the year 1540[b] at the monastery of Saint-Chéron near Chartres[c] and was sent to Paris some time later, where he studied the humanities, philosophy and theology at the college of Navarre.[d] He became doctor of theology in 1555,[e*] after which he applied himself to controversy and was admitted into the

---

[a] M. de Thou calls him Sanctius.
[b] Moréri, under the word 'Claude de Sainctes' and the letter 'C'.
[c] 'In Coenobio sancti Carauni ad Carnutum.' ['In the monastery of Saint Chéron at Chartres.'] Johannes Launoïus, *Historia gymnasii Navarrae* [Jean de Launoi, History of the College of Navarre], p.769.
[d] *Ibid.*
[e*] [Note by Beuchot:] It would be in the year 1556, according to Leclerc.

household of the Cardinal de Lorraine.[f=e] In the year 1561, he was one of the disputants for the Roman party at the Colloque de Poissy and was afterwards one of the twelve theologians whom Charles IX sent to the Council of Trent. In 1566, he and Simon Vigor debated with two [Calvinist] ministers at the house of the Duc de Nevers.... He was so bigoted against those of the Reformed religion that he maintained that those whom they had baptised were to be baptised again [(B)]. He left no stone unturned to have them excluded from his diocese and to have every canon of the Council of Trent recognised in the kingdom without restriction [(C)]. He did not scruple to assert that Calvin and Beza taught atheistical notions.[g=h]

He supported the party of the League with such anger that he maintained that Henry III had been rightly assassinated and that Henry IV deserved the same punishment (D). The manuscript in which he asserted this doctrine was found in his office. It was discovered, I believe, when Biron made himself master of Louviers and imprisoned this wretched prelate. He was thus not treated according to martial law but was sent to Caen[h=i] to be tried. Since he obstinately persisted in his support of this treasonable assertion, he might have been put to death had Cardinal de Bourbon and certain other ecclesiastics in the king's circle not prevailed upon him to commute the death penalty to perpetual imprisonment. He died soon after in the year 1591.[i=k] It should be recalled that in a previous work, and out of hostility to those of the Reformed religion, he had argued that subjects ought never to oppose the ordinances of their sovereigns (E). In 1561, he published a short work to show that princes should not tolerate heretics (F). This opinion is very ancient and is still very generally held today, even though no dogma whatsoever has been refuted with more substantial arguments.[k=l] You will find the titles of his other works in the history of the college of Navarre....

[f=e] *Ibid.*
[g=h] See the work which he entitled *Déclaration d'aucuns athéismes de la doctrine de Bèze et de Calvin* [Statement Concerning Atheistic Notions in the Teaching of Calvin and Beza].
[h=i] The *parlement* of Normandy had been transferred there.
[i=k] De Thou. See his words in Remark (D) below.
[k=l] See Remark (F), below.

[Remarks (A)–(C) omitted.]

(D) He held that Henry III had been rightly assassinated, and that Henry IV deserved the same punishment.] Let us give M. de Thou's account.

> Captus in oppido . . . ['Claude Sainctes, bishop of Evreux, famous theologian, who was extremely hostile to the royal party [of Henry IV], was captured in the town,[1=4] along with his books and papers. Writings were discovered among them in which he upheld the position that the assassination of a king was a just act, and he defended the view that the same deed could lawfully be committed against the king of his own day. Action was taken against him, therefore, but not according to martial law; he was sent under guard to Cadomus [Caen] so that the senate could indict him and sentence him to a punishment as if he were a public enemy. For, in a case of high treason, the privilege of holy orders is no longer recognised by us but the severity of the law is exercised against whomsoever is convicted under it, be he priest or bishop, just as if he were released from his orders and had become an ordinary citizen. Moreover, the sentence for this crime was execution. Sainctes was condemned, since he was by nature headstrong and he resolutely defended his misdeed. But afterwards Cardinal Bourbon and other churchmen, who were in the king's circle, interceded on his behalf. They argued that instead of receiving the death penalty, which he deserved according to our laws as they themselves admitted, he should be sent to prison for life. He died there shortly afterwards.][2=5]

On that occasion Henry IV was undoubtedly motivated by the principles of clemency and generosity that came naturally to him. But he mixed with them a little of that apprehensive prudence which so often tempered his great courage after he had perceived that the monstrous League which he had to defeat – now more cruel and more dangerous than the hydra of Hercules – would become even more ferocious and even more unmanageable through

---

[1=4] That is to say Lupariae, in Louviers in Normandy.
[2=5] De Thou, bk 101, p. 418.

the shedding of blood. Clemency, on the one hand, and prudence
[*la politique*], on the other, saved Claude de Sainctes from the shame
he deserved of losing his life on the scaffold.[3=*]

**(E) He had said in a written work that subjects should never
oppose the laws of their sovereign.[4=6]**] The book in which he
advanced this opinion was printed at Paris in 1561. It is entitled:
*Confession de foi catholique, contenant, en bref, la réformation de celle
que les ministres de Calvin presentèrent au roi en l'assemblée de Poissy*
[Confession of the Catholic Faith, Containing, in Brief, a Reformu-
lated Version of the one that Calvin's Ministers Presented to the
King at the Assembly of Poissy]. Article 57 of this confession contains these words:

> We hold, therefore, that we should obey their laws and ordi-
> nances, pay tributes, taxes and other duties, and bear the
> yoke of allegiance with a good and free will, *even when princes
> are natural infidels and the empire of GOD does not everywhere
> reign in its entirety*. We thereby abhor those who seek to
> reject superior authorities, put cantons and communities
> under their own command, introduce confusion in the own-
> ership of wealth, and reverse the procedures of justice. *We
> reject also* all murderers, gunmen, assassins and mercenaries,
> hired and sworn to accompany and support sects, *and those
> who declare death sentences at their pleasure* and without trial,
> on all who displease or resist them, *and who have kings*,
> gentry, churches, and towns, molested *under pretext of the
> word of GOD*.

[3=*] [Note added by the editors of the edition of 1820–4:] Joly, who sought to weaken
the testimony of de Thou, observes that Sainctes was buried in the cathedral of
Evreux, and he thinks that this refuted the account of his imprisonment. He
adds however that the body of the prelate had been transferred to the cathedral
from the place where he had died.

[4=6] This was the position of the Roman Catholics before the League; but they
changed their vocabulary shortly afterwards, since one of their number condemned it among the Leaguers in a work entitled Déploration . . . [Condem-
nation of the Assassination of Henry III, and of the Scandal Caused by it in the
Church], Caen, 1590. They themselves, says he, p. 54, had at the beginning of
the troubles used this argument against the Huguenots: they are heretics since
they take up arms against the magistrate. They do not wish to obey him, and
they wish to implant their religion through the sword which is given only to the
magistrate.

Its author [Sainctes] claimed to show that Catholics were more loyal in their allegiance than the Calvinists, since the latter had appended a clause to the article whereby they had indicated their position on the obedience of subjects: *provided*, according to the Calvinists, *that the sovereign empire of God do remain in its entirety.*[5=7]

Despite those who have on many occasions glossed over this clause as full of specious generalisation, it is, if properly interpreted, very sound and completely correct, even though one can abuse the intentions of its authors. But it is certain that Claude de Sainctes banished it from his confession only out of mischief and through animosity towards Geneva. For no man ever contradicted himself more flagrantly than he: that is commonly the fate of those who reason without integrity, and who seize upon a principle only to distance themselves from the opinion of their enemies, or to find grounds for insulting them and rendering them suspect. As soon as this obsession ceases, or the interest and the needs of their party demand another topic, they abandon their first opinion, and espouse a completely contrary one. We have seen some very recent examples of it.

(F) He published a short work . . . to show that princes should not tolerate heretics.] His book was entitled: *Ad edicta veterum* . . . [On the Edicts of Past Princes concerning the Authorisation of Sects within the Christian Religion. And on the Methods Used by the First Catholic Sovereigns to Combat Sectarianism]. In it, he advocates the death penalty for heretics, and he declares that if they [the government] had not extinguished the fires lit to destroy Calvinism in France, their sect would not have survived.

> Audivi Severum Sulpitium . . . ['Severus Sulpitius . . . circulated what might be called a decree of amnesty among the homes of certain judges when capital punishment for religious matters was still exercised in Gaul in accordance with the edicts of the most Christian of kings . . . I understand that more damage was inflicted upon our faith by that historic act than by Calvin's books and followers. For had the fires not been hastily extinguished, and their doctrine made public by saboteurs of religion and the state, they

---

[5=7] *Confession de Genève*, art. 11.

would have expanded neither so far, nor so quickly, nor attracted so many to their sect . . .']⁶⁼⁸

The whole thrust of his book follows only from custom and usage, since he offers hardly any arguments and few that are sound. Anyone who would compare, without prejudice, the arguments for intolerance with those for tolerance must acknowledge that he could never have provided such arguments even had he been more able. The present-day arguments for tolerance have been very recently propounded by certain modern authors. See the prefaces of [Benoist,] the historian of . . . *l'Edit de Nantes* [Delft, 1693–5]; and the book [by Jurieu] whose title is: *Traité de la liberté de conscience ou de l'autorité des souverains sur la religion des peuples, opposé aux maximes de Hobbes et de Spinoza, adoptées par le sieur Jurieu dans son Historie du papisme, et dans son Système de l'église;*⁷⁼⁹ and the *Commentaire philosophique sur ces paroles de l'Evangile Contrains-les d'entrer* [by Bayle]; as well as the *Epistle* in Latin printed at Tergou in the year 1689. M. de Beauval⁸⁼¹⁰ has attributed the latter to M. Bernard, a French minister very well known by his works and wholly capable of writing a book that requires such close reasoning; but it is known for certain that he is not its author, and it is believed that it should be ascribed to an Englishman,⁹⁼¹¹ whose books on metaphysics and morals appear in the journals. But should anyone wish to avoid a long work, they would need only to read a concise piece that an illustrious magistrate from a town in Holland composed in London in 1685.¹⁰⁼¹² It is entitled *H.V.P. ad B**** de nuperis Angliae motibus epistola in qua de diversorum a publica religione*

---

⁶⁼⁸ Claudius de Sainctes, in *Methodus quam secuti sunt principes* [The Methods which were Followed by Rulers], ch. 13, fol. 112 verso.

⁷⁼⁹ [I.e. Treatise on Liberty of Conscience. Or, Concerning the Authority of Sovereigns over the Religion of Peoples, Opposed to the Maxims of Hobbes and Spinoza, Adopted by M. Jurieu in his *History of Papism*, and in his *System of the Church*] Amsterdam, 1687.

⁸⁼¹⁰ *Histoire des ouvrages des savans*, September 1689, article 2.

⁹⁼¹¹ M. Locke.

¹⁰⁼¹² M. Paets. See his obituary in *Nouvelles de la république des lettres*, October 1685, art. 2. This distinguished man died on 8 October 1685. [Adriaan Van Paets, lawyer of Rotterdam and a politician of the de Witt tendency, had been Bayle's patron, and was ambassador to London when he wrote the pamphlet which Bayle translated into French.]

circa divina sententium disseritur tolerantia.[11=*] This letter was printed in Rotterdam in 1685 in Latin, French and Dutch.

It is imperative that the arguments put by supporters of toleration should be cogent. For those who have employed the subtleties of the mind and the artifices of the pen to reply to them have been obliged to resort to dishonesty, and to say merely that the penal laws against heretics should not include the death penalty.[12=13] Their bad faith is revealed, however, in their attempt to demonstrate that all who support toleration must be crypto-Socinians; in that they seek to undermine government by depriving the sovereign authority of one of its most important and God-given rights. This is a base and prejudiced sophistry: for according to that logic we would not be allowed to condemn the harsh laws which have sent so many Protestants to the stake – whether in France, or the Low Countries, or Spain or Italy – simply because they are cruelties which the Socianians likewise devote all their energy to denouncing. Neither would we be allowed to protest against the Papists, who executed the Protestant martyrs, any more than we should be allowed to remonstrate with the Protestants who put to death Servetus and Gentilis, etc. In short we should not be allowed to write anything further against the Pope, or the Jews, or the Turks etc., simply because it is patent that they are people whom Socinus and his followers do not spare, and do their utmost to refute. So that if the act of insisting that no sovereign should institute penal sanctions against those that err in matters of faith is to show lack of respect; and if it is to repudiate one of the sovereign's God-given rights [i.e. to punish heretics], then our first [Protestant] critics of intolerance must also have been accomplices in that crime, since they too believed that one should not go so far as to shed blood. Yet, would not that also be to deprive sovereigns of the finest plume in their crown? For does not the right of the sword make them master over the life and death of the criminal? And is it not to mock the magistrates of Holland, and to expose them to the contempt of their subjects etc., to argue that God has given them the power of the

---

[11=*] [A Letter from H.V.P. to B**** (Van Paets to Bayle), Relating to Recent Disturbances in England, in which is Discussed the Toleration of Dissenting Opinion Concerning God, Differing from that of the Public Religion], 1685.

[12=13] See [Jurieu,] *Tableau du socinianisme*, letter 8.

sword not so much to punish those who violate the first table of the Decalogue [idolatry and blasphemy], as to punish those who offend against the second [murder, theft, adultery] etc.? And if that were true, would the tolerance that they had for idolatry [i.e. Popery] not be as criminal as the tolerance that they had for murderers and highwaymen? And besides could anything be more absurd than to be satisfied with the penalty of mere banishment for those who made a profession of indiscriminate assassination or mass poisoning?[13=14] Consider the dispute of Messieurs des Wallemburch[14=15] on the question as to whether magistrates, given that they have a right to eliminate heretics with penal sanctions, have a concomitant right to punish them with death. It is to this level that they reduce the dispute against the Lutherans; for they take the side of the famous Gherhard, who did undoubtedly want to use penal sanctions against sectarians but not the ultimate sanction of the death penalty. They make him see invincibly that this is an irrelevant distinction. But in order to see the inconsistency of those who support intolerance, it is sufficient to be alert when they make that slip of saying that sovereigns who oppose the introduction of the true doctrine are highly commendable. 'I am unable to condemn the Swiss', says one, 'who cannot abide the growth of any new sect amongst them. Holland overflows with many different religions; yet it could be wished that they had smothered these disorders at birth.' . . .[15=16]

[13=14] Note that one can turn against him the maxims of the author [Jurieu] of the eighth letter of the *Tableau du socinianisme*. See [*Dic*,] article 'Loyola' [above], n. 10=106. [Bayle aimed to show that though Jurieu advocated toleration for sects where Calvinism was in the minority, he simultaneously advanced objections to such freedom in countries where Calvinism had become the public religion. Such inconsistency was common but far from Bayle's own understanding of toleration.]

[14=15] See their book *De unitate ecclesiae* [On the Unity of the Church], bk 6, part 1, ch. 2, pp. 2 *et seq.*, Cologne, 1656.

[15=16] [Jurieu,] *Esprit de M. Arnauld*, vol. II, p. 355.

Sainte-Aldegonde

[In 1581 the Netherlands declared their independence from Catholic Spain and became the United Provinces, embracing Calvinism as the religion of the people. In his article on the patriot Philippe de Marnix, Bayle seized the chance to show support for a republican uprising that had turned out well. De Marnix who, in the cause of liberty, had taken up pen, diplomacy, song writing, and even the defence of dancing, deserved fulsome praise. Yet Bayle had some advice for successful revolutionaries. Having overthrown the oppressor, they had invariably to learn that it was unjust to punish minorities who held opinions different from the new orthodoxy. For that would be to imitate the tyrant they had replaced, and they would be reduced to the absurdity of asserting that the dissenters' doctrines were heretical and that their own were true.]

SAINTE-ALDEGONDE (Philippe de Marnix Seigneur du Mont). Born in Brussels [(A)] in the year 1538, he became famous through his deeds and his writings. He took refuge in Germany when liberty of conscience was oppressed in the Low Countries by the Spaniards, and he was honoured in Heidelberg with the office of advisor to the ecclesiastical counsel. He returned to his country in 1572 so that he might offer his talents to the cause of liberty and to the good of the Reformed religion [(B)]. He was highly esteemed by the Prince of Orange to whom he rendered many important services, not so much by his sword as by his pen [(C)]. He was one of the deputies whom the Estates sent into England in 1575 to solicit the protection of Queen Elizabeth. Three years later he was sent by the Archduke

Matthias to the Diet of Worms, where he made a fine speech and courageously denounced the Spanish tyranny [(D)]. He was one of the plenipotentiaries whom the Estates sent to France in 1580 to make representations to the Duc d'Alençon [(E)]. He was Consul at Antwerp in 1584 when the town was besieged by the Duke of Parma. In the year 1593, he escorted to the Palatinate Princess Louise Julienne[a] who had been betrothed to the Elector Frederick IV.[b]

The books he published [(F)] were not the least of his achievements. Some were about politics and others about controversy; some were serious and others light-hearted, but the latter proved more useful [(G)]; moreover it was not only from his songs that the new republic derived many advantages (H). He translated the Psalms of David from the Hebrew into Flemish verse, though the translation was not made use of in churches [(I)]. When he died in Leiden on 15 December 1589, he was working on a Flemish translation of the Scriptures.[c] Shortly before, he had made a journey into France on business for the prince.[d] He was not immune from slander [(K)], and it was said that his retirement was a sort of disgrace. He was strangely perplexed when complaints were made that he had exhorted the Estates to persecute the sects (L). I have seen a book in which it is observed that he had a passion for dancing which may serve to overcome the scruples of the *précisistes* (M). It would be unfair to refuse him a place among the illustrious men of the sixteenth century. For he demonstrated great zeal for his religion, a fine intelligence and great learning; and he was well versed in the civil law, politics, diplomacy, theology, as well as Hebrew, Greek, and Latin and many modern languages.[e]

[Remarks (A)–(G) omitted.]

(H) He brought many advantages to the new republic, and not only by his songs.] I could have cited above Verheiden rather

---

[a] Daughter of William of Orange, the first of the name.
[b] In Melchior Adam, in *Vitae jurisconsultorum* [Lives of Jurists], pp. 333 *et seq.*
[c] *Ibid.*, p. 334.
[d] See his *Réponse apologétique au gentilhomme allemand* [Rejoinder to a German Gentleman], at the beginning.
[e] Verheiden, *Elogia aliquot theologorum* [Sayings of Various Theologians].

than Melchior Adam who merely copied him. But I think that is an indifferent matter provided that one cites the original initially. I do it another way here. I report the words of Verheiden. 'Ab hoc viro', he says,

> etiam profecta dicitur . . . ['This man is said to have been the author of that much sung ballad, composed in praise of Prince William of Orange, and circulated among the Belgians who had been oppressed by the tyranny of the Duke of Alba. This song, in fact, was so finely arranged, so appropriate in its harmonious rhythms and melody, that it aroused in emotions of ordinary people an intense love for the prince and for the liberty of their homeland. In this, Sainte-Aldegonde thus showed himself to be, as it were, another Tyrtaeus (the poet), so often praised by Plato . . .'][1=30]

There is good reason to say that nothing could have better suited the needs of the times than a clever song, full of invective against the Duke of Alba, and praise for the Prince of Orange. The plan to create a republic out of certain provinces of the king of Spain required many feats of daring; and in particular ceaseless activity to forestall the suggestions of those who might have argued that it was almost impossible to hold out against so powerful a monarch; or that the cost of waging a war against him would hugely exceed what he exacted; therefore that it was a great folly to give all that one possessed rather than put up with a tax.[2=31] There were a hundred good reasons for refuting this, but it was important to impress them upon the people either from the pulpit or through books. But nothing could assist such a purpose as effectively as a song; for that is a something that stays in the heart, and everyone, even the peasants and serving girls, daily repeat it with joy and exaltation. This, therefore, was one of the more important services performed by Philip de Marnix. It reminds me of the hymn *De l'Escalade* which they sing in Geneva on the day of their founding anniversary, an act almost indispensable to the ceremony. I am convinced that this has always left the most vivid impression on people's minds.

[1=30] Verheiden, in *Elogia aliquot theologorum*, p. 145.
[2=31] 'Omnia dabunt ne decimam darent.' ['They will give away everything to avoid parting with a tithe.']

[Remarks (I)–(K) omitted.]

(L) **It was complained that he exhorted the Estates to persecute the sects.**] I have said more than once when there was occasion for it that there was no issue more embarrassing for the writers of the Protestant communion in the sixteenth century than the necessity, to which they thought themselves reduced, of urging the magistrates to punish heresy; whilst thinking it strange, at the same time, that Catholic princes should persecute the Protestants. Naturally their own arguments were used against them and they could extricate themselves from their disarray only by supposing, as all parties do, that their own doctrine was true. Sainte-Aldegonde must have been more embarrassed than many others, since he had taken so many journeys, made so many speeches, and written so many books for a state which had taken up arms against the Spaniards, precisely to free itself from the yoke of the Inquisition. What might not have been said when he was seen to urge the sovereigns of that same state to wipe out certain sects? You will see here the evidence of his embarrassment. He supposes 1. that these words only were complained of.[3=59] 'It is high time, my noble and venerable lords, that you should seek to defend the honour of God in this world, if you desire him to protect the safety of our country.' 2. That the *Antidote* that they opposed to such a counsel consisted in this: 'We ought to live with our neighbours, allow each person to believe in his own fashion without concerning ourselves in it, and without interference. "Permitte divis cœtera." ["Leave the rest to the gods."]' He cites page 9 and page 41 of the *Antidote*, but there is on page 9 a clause omitted by him. These authors reproached him for using these words: 'to suppress and entirely annihilate that fatal poison'. It was further said[4=60] that he thought it very strange 'that there should still be around men so faint-hearted as to question whether the magistrate ought to inflict corporal punishment and fines on insolence perpetrated in the service of God and the faith'. What he suppresses, what he would seemingly have us believe, was in fact not objected to; and this alters the state of the question by removing the awkward part of it. Can good faith be consistent with

---

[3=59] Sainte-Aldegonde, *Réponse apologétique*, fol. A4.
[4=60] *Antidote*, p. 10.

such a procedure? Can it permit him to reduce the *Antidote* to a single proposition on page 41, without considering the many other good arguments that preceded it? Let us concede that in another place in his work[5=61] he examines what he had left out at the beginning, but that it reveals a man who was thoroughly embarrassed. Note that it is many a year since anyone found enthusiasts vexing. See the letter he wrote to Theodore Beza on 10 January 1566.[6=62]

(M) It was observed that he loved dancing, a fact that might refute the scruples of the *précisistes*.]

[In the middle of Remark (M) Bayle quotes at length from various authors, classical, Catholic, and Calvinist, who had condemned sexually provocative dancing. He uses citations to show how common it was for moralists to describe lewd dancing in explicit detail, especially that of their religious or political enemies, while defending the dancing which, to them, seemed agreeably innocent.]

See Schoockius[7=63] who has inserted in one of his books a letter written by Sainte-Aldegonde in 1577 to Caspar Verheiden, the celebrated Dutch minister.[8=64] That letter seems to me very judicious. I shall take from it two or three curious things. The author affirms that many people were troubled because dancing was disapproved of in the Reformed churches and that this made them reluctant to join; but that many were cured of their irritation against the Protestants when they came to learn of his opinions and practice in the matter. From that he infers that too rigid a morality about this bodily exercise was unworthy and far from edifying.[9=65] He says that the prince[10=66] himself was very much irritated when he heard it said that one could not even dance at a wedding without incurring the censure of the ecclesiastical discipline. He thinks that dancing

---

[5=61] Aldegonde, *Réponse apologétique*, fol. G5 *et seq.*
[6=62] *Lettres de Béza*, letter 6.
[7=63] Schoockius [Martinus Schoock], *Exercitatio academica* [Academic Exercise], 23, p. 317.
[8=64] *Epistolae illustriae Belgarum* [Letters of Famous Belgians], letter 1, vol. II.
[9=65] 'Plane censeo . . .' ['I certainly believe not only that is there no edification in this churlish moroseness and in censorship renewed at the whim of someone's opinion, but I even think it an incredible scandal.'] Schoockius, p. 318.
[10=66] I suppose he speaks of the Prince of Orange.

is a good and commendable thing in the Netherlands because it keeps people from gambling or getting drunk after supper.[11=67] He consoles himself for having lost his esteem among the zealots: on the grounds, says he, that it was for superficial rather than substantial things. 'Existimationis certe . . .' ['As the sure basis of esteem (since all the zealots, you say, think I have, for that reason, lost it), I have resolved never to trust in external appearances, but in the things themselves.'][12=68] However, he approves of the conduct of the Church of Geneva which by forbidding dancing suppressed certain indecent things that habitually took place there: it having been the custom in those parts to take young girls to a dance in the evening and then torment them with lewd posturing. He does not think one could be present, let alone participate, at such a spectacle without becoming depraved. His expressions, being stronger and more extensive than my own, are cited here for the benefit of those who understand Latin more readily than French.

> Ut ego Genevates . . . ['I think that the people of Geneva deserve to be praised, since they have curbed with appropriate severity, and by means of a single prohibition, the most scandalous indecencies, which were committed daily without shame. For it was very common [for the local men] . . . to lure innocent girls to dances at an untimely hour of the evening, without any chaperone. They would take them off to dances wherever they wished, for as long as they wished, and at any time of the year, and would wear them out *ad nauseam* with shameful and obscene gesticulations, almost without respite under the pretext of dancing. I think it wrong just to watch these practices, let alone to condone them by taking part.'][13=69]

One cannot sufficiently praise the discipline of the Reformed churches when they forbade that sort of dancing; and it would be foolish to imagine that the ministers condemned it merely in the sense that it was a skill in the art of stepping or skipping to rhythm.

[11=67] 'Immo vero his locis . . .' ['In fact, I believe dancing in these places to be wholesome, for it can be put to good use after banquets to keep drunks from drink and gamblers from gaming.'] *Ibid.*

[12=68] *Ibid.*, p. 139.

[13=69] *Ibid.*, 23, p. 320.

Under such a notion it is a very lawful exercise. It is neither good nor bad morally speaking. But the manner of it then occasioned a thousand disorders, and, in the very rooms where the ball was held, it made dangerous inroads upon a woman's chastity. The proverb concerning cloisters, 'as dangerous as returning from matins', might with a small alteration have produced another: 'as dangerous as returning from the ball.' . . .

It is clear that if dancing is accompanied with that many irregularities it deserves the castigation of all who are concerned with morals. Sainte-Aldegonde would not have approved of it. Count de Bussi Rabutin condemned the event of the ball as a very dangerous occasion: reason and his own experience obliged him to speak of it.[14=81] All casuists have, in this respect, to be either *précisiste* or *rigoriste*. The philosopher who attacked the *précisistes* declared[15=82] that he condemned dancing of that sort, but he said that he did not believe its nature to be the same among the Protestants of Germany; and that the *précisistes*, who are scandalised by the custom in that country whereby both sexes dance together, should bear in mind that they do not disapprove of certain customs which are highly likely to offend the Germans . . . He draws a parallel between the custom of kissing and that of dancing; and he maintains that the former can more easily shock foreigners than the latter shocks the *précisistes* . . . He concludes that nations ought to excuse one another and consider, above all else, that an ancient and long-standing custom may make the same thing innocent in one country that is indecent in another. He gives the example of English women being escorted by men other than their husbands.[16=85]

What has been said of kissing can also be applied to the English custom of wives being escorted by men other than their own husbands.[17=86] Belgians of the highest rank have now begun to practise this custom too. Such women have

---

[14=81] See [de Bussi Rabutin,] *Retour des pièces choisies*, his letter to the bishop of Autun, concerning the ball and the dance, part 2.

[15=82] 'Nulla ratione tamen . . .' ['In no way do I wish to defend modern dances, which are not different from the rhythms of Bathyllus, and which are more suited to the lecher and the sodomite than to the Christian.'] Martinus Schoockius, *Exercitatio* . . . 23, p. 327.

[16=85] *Ibid.*, p. 329.

[17=86] Henri Etienne has spoken of this custom in his Latin 'Apology for Herodotus'.

indeed offended wives in [more] northern countries who are quite astounded that these and similar practices are tolerated without criticism by those theologians whose zeal is every day directed at dancing and drinking. But I can extricate myself with constancy from all these difficulties without casting aspersions, by teaching that the customs and practices of peoples in such matters should above all be examined, and that one should allow English wives their practice of being escorted by husbands other than their own, just as the stricter *précisistes* grant Holland her pleasures. So they should not begrudge other peoples their dancing, provided that this involves neither wantonness nor that 'art' of arousing *libido* devised by idle profligates.

You may observe if you wish that this philosopher [Schoockius] had in no way the same motives as Sainte-Aldegonde for working on his treatise on dancing. He protested that he had never in his life dreamt of dancing, and that he would not himself have been troubled if the laws of the magistrate had abolished dancing forever.[18=87] Sainte-Aldegonde could hardly have spoken with any sincerity in those terms.

[18=87] 'Protestationi hoc unum . . .' ['I add a further point to my protestation . . . I have not even dreamt of taking part in such dances in my whole life. This life of mine . . . led according to God's will, to which I freely give my consent, is bound by the chains of troubles and cares. I could, for that reason, equally well put up with those edicts of the magistrate which command dancing to be abolished in perpetuity.'] Schoockius, *Exercitatio* . . . 23, p. 321.

Socinus (Marianus)

[The Socinian sect was considered throughout western Christendom – by Lutherans and Calvinists as well as Catholics – as a heresy that should not be tolerated. Bayle traces the movement's history from its origins in Renaissance Italy to its quest for refuge in Transylvania and Poland. He infers from the mixed fortunes of the Socinian sect in Poland that a government must not only have the desire to protect a law-abiding minority, it must have the power to carry out its commitments.]

SOCINUS (Marianus) celebrated jurist, was born in Sienna, on 4 September, 1412 ... [and died on] 30 September, 1467. ...

SOCINUS (Marianus), grandson of the foregoing,[a] was not less celebrated in the profession of the law than his forebear. He was born in Sienna on 25 March 1582 [*sic; recte* 1482]. ...

Were we to believe Ponciroli,[b=d] he had thirteen children, of whom only two survived him, Celsus and Philippe ... Ponciroli should have known that there was a third named Laelius Socinus, the first author of the Socinian Sect (B). Alexander Socinus, son of Marianus and father of Faustus Socinus, of whom I shall speak below, died very young but with a reputation as an erudite jurist.

[Remark (A) omitted.]

(B) Marianus left a third son named Laelius Socinus, the first author of the Socinian Sect.] He was born in Sienna in

---

[a] He was the son of Alexander Socinus, son of Marianus. They surnamed the first *Senior*, and the second *Junior* to distinguish between them.

[b=d] Panzirolus [Ponciroli], *De claris legum interpretibus* [Famous Legal Commentators], p. 341.

1525.[1=2] Having been destined for the law by his father, he soon began to seek the basis of that science in the word of God, and through this study he discovered that the communion of Rome taught many things that were contrary to Revelation. Seeking to probe more deeply into the meaning of the Scriptures, he studied Greek, Hebrew, and even Arabic, and soon left Italy for Protestant countries. Fear also contributed to his withdrawal since he knew that his particular views on matters of religion would not be permitted. In the year 1546 he began his travels, and in four years he saw France, England, the Low Countries, Germany and Poland, and finally Zurich. He made the acquaintance of the most learned men of the age, who witnessed their esteem for him in their letters, but since he revealed through his doubts that he was tainted with the Arian or the Photinian heresy [denying Christ's divinity], he attracted a certain suspicion. In the year 1552 Calvin gave him some sound advice on the matter: 'Quod pridem testatus sum ...' ['Having seen this going on for some time, I again earnestly warn you that unless you soon check this obsession for asking questions, you will bring down upon yourself worse persecution.'][2=3]

Laelius Socinus, benefiting from this advice, and even more from the torture and death of Servetus [in Geneva in 1553], did not reveal his thoughts until the time and place were right, and he conducted himself with so much circumspection that he lived among the most extreme enemies of his convictions without coming to harm: an example which is proposed by his nephew, in the *Life*, to those who give themselves precipitately to martyrdom, sometimes more out of ardour for a great reputation than for zeal for the truth. 'Sciant, quos nimia ...' ['They ought to know that excessive liberty to express the truth has often thrown men into untimely danger, and that the ideas which they defend may be more securely protected by prudent circumspection than by unbounded zeal. Men who wantonly put themselves at risk seem bent more on private glory than on benefiting the public cause.'][3=4] He found certain disciples who listened with respect to his teaching: they were Italians

[1=2] *Bibliotheca Antitrinitaria* [Anti-Trinitarian Library], p. 18.
[2=3] See *Vie de Faustus Socin* at the beginning of vol. 1 of *Bibliotheca Fratrum Polonorum* [Library of the Polish Brethren].
[3=4] *Ibid.*

who travelled in Germany and in Poland. He also communicated his errors to his relatives through writings which he had kept in Sienna. He made a visit to Poland after the death of his father ...[4=5] The journey from Poland occurred in about the year 1558 ...[5=6] His family was dispersed at that time, since they were suspected of heresy: some ... had been imprisoned and certain others, his nephew Faustus among them, had followed him in flight. Laelius returned to Switzerland and died in Zurich in May 1562. Faustus was then in Lyon and left immediately he heard of the death of his uncle. He arrived in Zurich before they could remove any of Laelius's papers of which he took possession and made use in due course.[6=7]

You may find further details in the *Bibliothèque des Anti-Trinitaires*. Laelius Socinus, born in 1525, began to discuss matters of religion in the year 1546 with some forty others. They met secretly on Venetian territory,[7=8] calling principally into question the mystery of the Trinity and Jesus Christ's absolving power. Attending these meetings were Ochin, Valentin, Gentilis and Paul Alciat but they were exposed. Some of these innovators [*novateurs*] were seized and condemned to torture and death, while the others dispersed. The chronology of this author [Zanchius] is unsatisfactory, since Ochin left Italy in about 1542. Zanchius testified that Laelius Socinus had attempted to harm him with his heresies, not through supporting them formally but by proposing them as doubts and by way of debate. He added that he was a very learned man, well schooled in Greek and Hebrew and very correct in his behaviour.

> Fuit is Laelius ... ['Laelius was such a man: descended from a noble and honourable family, learned in Greek and Hebrew; he appeared blameless in his way of life. On account of these qualities I had become involved in no ordinary friendship with him. But the man harboured a variety

[4=5] Who had died ... in Bologna, in 1556.
[5=6] *Vita Fausti Socini* [Life of Faustus Socinus], p. 2.
[6=7] Taken from the *Life*.
[7=8] 'Circa annum 1546 ...' ['Around the year 1546, in the dominion of Venice, he had established with over forty of his friends who were also Italian a society for the discussion of religion.'] *Bibliotheca Antitrinitaria*, p. 18.

of heretical ideas, which, however, he would never lay before
me, except for argument's sake, and he would always pose
questions as if he wished to be instructed.']⁸⁼⁹

When Zanchius spoke in that way, he was certain that Laelius
had written a paraphrase of the first chapter of Saint John,
suffused with Photinianism.⁹⁼¹⁰ The same Laelius composed a
dialogue in the year 1554 against the work which Calvin had
published concerning the right to put heretics to death. *Calvinus*
and *Vaticannus* are the adversaries in this dialogue.¹⁰⁼¹¹ Some
attribute this work to Castalion, but others, such as Clopen-
bourg¹¹⁼¹² and Hoornbeek,¹²⁼¹³ attribute it to Laelius Socinus . . .

[8=9] Zanchius, in the preface to the book *De tribus Elohim* [The Three Gods], in *ibid.*,
p. 19.
[9=10] He wrote it in 1561. *Ibid.*, p. 21.
[10=11] It was reprinted in Holland in the year 1612, with some other pieces of the
same sort. In the following year it was reprinted in Flemish in the same country.
Ibid., p. 29.
[11=12] In the preface to the *Compendium Socinianum confutationum* [The Compendium
of Socinian Rebuttals].
[12=13] In *Summa Controversiarum* [Comprehensive Study of Controversies].

Socinus (Faustus)

[In the article on Faustus Socinus Bayle continues the story of the sect's persecution but he also makes original observations about the epistemology and the psychology of religion, and about human behaviour. The Socinians questioned the Scriptures' divine inspiration, and rejected, inter alia, the doctrines of the Trinity and Hell. Orthodox Christians responded with the argument that carried weight with civic educators, that to deny divine retribution was to weaken the fear of God and so undermine public morals. In Remarks (I) and (L), Bayle restates his proposition of empirical politics (made earlier in his Pensées diverses sur la comète*) that the presumption of a causal connection between absence of such beliefs and unsociable conduct was refuted by the evidence.]*

SOCINUS (Faustus) was grandson of the foregoing [Marianus Socinus: 1482–1556], and main founder of a highly erroneous sect that goes by his name and which, notwithstanding persecution, flourished for a considerably long time in Poland (A). He was born in Sienna, on 5 November 1539. He studied indifferently in his youth. He knew only the classics and the basic elements of logic. The letters his uncle wrote to the family whereby they and their wives imbibed the seeds of heresy[a] made a strong impression on him. So, not confident of his innocence, he fled with the rest when the Inquisition began to

---

[a] 'Hos inter quoque . . .' ['Laelius, that remarkable master of speculation about the truth, had sown the seed of his ideas throughout his family. Despite distance, he retained influence over them with such persistence that . . . he involved in his sect the wives of some of his relatives.'] *Vita Fausti Socini* [Life of Faustus Socinus].

persecute the family. He was in Lyon when he heard of his uncle's death and he immediately set about gathering all the writings of the deceased. He returned to Italy and became so acceptable to the Grand Duke that the charms of the court, and the honourable employments in which he engaged, made him forget that he had been thought of as the man who would complete the system of Samosatenian theology which his uncle Laelius had begun. Finally, the search for the truths of the Evangelist appeared preferable to the enjoyments of the court. He withdrew voluntarily and went to Germany in the year 1574, and ignored the Grand Duke's exhortations to return. He spent three years in Basel where he studied theology with great application. Having embraced principles very different from those of the Protestants, he set about maintaining them and propagating them. To this end he composed a work *De Jesu Christo servatore* [On Jesus Christ the Saviour] [(B)]. At the beginning of the year 1578, he debated in Zurich against François Puccius. It happened that the disputes concerning the honours and the powers of the son of God arising from the dogmas of François David caused much disorder in the churches of Transylvania. Blandrata, a man of strong authority in those churches and at court, sent for Socinus, perceiving him as an instrument well qualified to pacify those troubles. He lodged him in the house of François David but the latter did not allow himself to be disabused, and maintained his opinion so openly and so boldly that he was imprisoned. His death, shortly afterwards, caused Socinus to be ill spoken of on that account, though it is affirmed that he had no hand in the counsels that were given to the prince of Transylvania to oppress François David. He withdrew into Poland in the year 1579 and sought to join up with the communion of the Unitarians. But since he differed from them on some points and had no desire to be silent about them, he met with a rejection. Nevertheless he wrote in favour of their churches and against their enemies. The book he wrote against Jacques Paléologue provided his enemies with a pretext to provoke the king of Poland and yet no book could have been less seditious (C). Though a perfunctory reading of his work would have been sufficient to refute detractors, Socinus judged it appropriate to leave Cracow, though he had lived there for four years, and to take sanctuary in the house of a Polish nobleman.[b] He lived more than

---

[b] Christophorus Morstinius Pawlicovii dominus [Christopher Morsztyn, master of Pawlikow].

three years under the protection of several noblemen and even married the daughter of such a family. She died in the year 1587 which afflicted him extremely [(D)] and to complete his distress he was deprived through the death of Francesco de Médicis, grand-duke of Florence [(E)], of the revenues from his patrimony. The consolation he had of seeing his doctrine finally approved in 1598 was very small compensation given that he received countless insults in Cracow, and it was only with difficulty that he was rescued from the hands of the mob. He lost his household goods and some of his manuscripts which upset him greatly (F). Among other works, he lost the piece which he had written against atheists. To avoid the recurrence of similar perils, he withdrew to a village some nine miles from Cracow where he spent his remaining years in the house of Abraham Blonski, a Polish gentleman.[c] He died on 3 March 1604.[d] His sect did not die with him but survived. It has declined since 1658 when it was expelled from Poland, and is very much diminished in respect of its visible condition. I express myself so because many people are persuaded that it has multiplied invisibly, and that it becomes daily more numerous. It is even thought, given present conditions, that all Europe might suddenly find itself Socinian should powerful princes publicly embrace this heresy, or if they were merely to decree that the civil disadvantages against those who profess it might be lifted. This is the feeling of many persons, and this feeling causes their anxiety and panic. But others assert that one should dismiss such fears, and that princes will never embrace a sect which does not approve of war and the holding of public office (G). This fact, say they, will always turn individuals from Socinianism. For there are very few people capable of renouncing ambition and the bearing of arms (H). One has only to consult experience and to consider what is daily practised. They advance yet other reasons (I) which show that this sect is hardly on the verge of a popular explosion. Those who say that the Socinians have a full liberty of conscience in the United Provinces are little acquainted with history (K) and can be soundly refuted by reading

[c] 'Cum ad tam . . .' ['Since threats were getting close to being acts of physical violence, he left Cracow for Lustawice in the countryside some nine miles from Cracow, which became famous for being his last home and the place of his death. Here he lived for some years, a neighbour to Stoinius, enjoying the hospitality of the nobleman Abraham Blonski.'] *Vita Fausti Socini*, fol. **3.

[d] Taken from the *Life*, written by Przipcovius, Polish gentleman. It is at the beginning of vol. I of the *Bibliotheca fratrum polonorum* [Library of the Polish Brethren].

the replies made to the letters of M. Stoupp.[e] They will see there a
great number of decrees passed against the sects. I shall say something
of those that relate to the Socinians, and expand a little further on
those of the year 1653 (L). . . .

A German historian[f=i] has condensed the doctrine of the Socinians into 229 propositions.

The most general objection that one may propose against them [the
Socinians] is that by refusing to believe what appears to them to be
contrary to philosophic reason [*lumières philosophiques*] and by refusing to submit their faith to the incomprehensible mysteries of the
Christian religion, they pave the way to Pyrrhonism, deism, and atheism. One might perhaps object that they open the same door, at least
indirectly, through the manner in which they interpret the passages
of Scripture which concern the consubstantiality of the Word. For it
would seem that it follows from their analysis that the Apostles,
motivated by an ardent zeal for the glory of Jesus Christ, employed,
when speaking of his perfections, the most exaggerated ideas and
expressions that devotion could express. It is thus that the devotees of
the Holy Virgin have taken things as far as they have, and as near as
they could to a veritable deification. But if one had to ascribe all the
utterances of the Apostles to zealous enthusiasm, and not to the direct
intervention of the Holy Spirit, everyone would see that Scripture has
hardly more authority than the panegyrics upon the saints. Furthermore, by demolishing the divinity of Scripture, one would overturn
Revelation completely, so that it would become, in consequence, no
more than a dispute among philosophers. . . .

**(A) A sect . . . which, notwithstanding persecution, flourished
for a considerably long time in Poland.]**

*[Bayle compares the betrayal and persecution of the Socinian
sect in Poland with that of the Huguenots of his own day, and
he discusses the mixture of theological and pragmatic justification
for it. He takes most seriously the received diplomatic wisdom of
the day, supposed empirically demonstrable but which he judged*

---

[e] Jean Brun, *Apologie pour la religion des hollandais*, 1675.
[f=i] Daniel Hartnaccius, in the continuation of Johann Micraelius's *Syntagma historiae
ecclesiasticae* [Treatise on Church History].

*fallacious, that unity of religion was a practical condition of
every nation's stability.]*

Sigismund Augustus granted liberty of conscience to the sects that
forsook the church of Rome. They formed no separate bodies at
first, but when the evangelicals came to know the opinions of the
Unitarians [i.e. Anti-Trinitarians] they would have nothing further
to do with them, which occasioned two different communions. That
rupture began in Cracow in consequence of Gregorius Pauli. The
Unitarians had several churches in Poland and Lithuania, some in
the large towns[1] and others in the country on the estates of the
gentry. They established their base in Racovia ... and they held
their annual synod there. They erected a college and set up a printing house. Some Catholics sent their children to that college, and
there were also those who joined the communion of the heretics.
Certain Protestants did the same and a vast quantity of books came
out of the printing house at Racovia, and were dispersed in foreign
countries. This state of prosperity was interrupted in 1638 when
certain scholars of the college of Racovia stoned a wooden cross set
up in a main street. It was ordered by the Diet of Warsaw that the
college be demolished, that the church of Racovia should be shut
down, that the printing house of the Unitarians should be demolished, and that the ministers and the regents be banished.[2] Some
time after, the judges of Lublin destroyed the church of Kesalin
and that of Beresac in the Volhinie under the pretext that the ministers of Racovia and the teachers of the college had fled there. The
Diet of the year 1647 banished Jonas Slichtingius for having published a book entitled *Confessio christiana* [Confession of Christian
Belief] and that book was burnt at the hand of the public hangman.
But notwithstanding those humiliations, the Unitarians performed
their religious exercises in many places of that kingdom until the
year 1658. They were then expelled. Advantage was taken of the
fact that some of them had put themselves under the protection of
the king of Sweden who had conquered the greatest part of Poland.
However they did not give that reason in the Edict of Banishment
lest it should anger the Swedes who had procured a general amnesty

---

[1] As Cracow, Lublin and Novogorod.
[2] I shall cite in Remark (L) an author who denies that the Diet's decree did entail
all that.

for all subjects of the king of Poland who had supported them during the invasion. The penalty of exile was based upon their doctrine alone, it being alleged that in order to draw God's blessing upon the kingdom, it was necessary to exclude those who denied the eternal divinity of the Son of God. They were therefore ordered to leave, and the death penalty was instituted against those who would not submit to the order. All their possessions were confiscated; and it was forbidden under the same penalty for anyone to show any assistance or any mark of good will or kindness towards them in their exile.[3] . . .

Usually those who complain of their sufferings suppress whatever makes their persecution look less painful. And therefore, in order to represent the state of the matter accurately, I shall give a further account of it which is contained in the passage which follows:

During the last campaign of the Swedes in Poland, it was discovered that the Arians and the Socinians, intending to raise themselves on the ruins of the state, kept in contact with Ragozki, prince of Transylvania, who attacked the kingdom at the same time. The Catholic nobility in the General Diet of Warsaw in the year 1658 used the opportunity therefore to exterminate in Poland that abominable heresy which might still bring down God's wrath upon the state. The Lutheran and Calvinist deputies who were in that Diet, being apprehensive that a law exacted against those heretics might be a precedent for a law against themselves, and that, in time, they too would be so treated, came together in order to oppose it. But as there were very few of them in comparison with the Catholics and because there was some interest in letting them retain their liberty, and as, in addition, they did not love the Arians [i.e. Trinitarians] – having more than once demanded that they should not be tolerated in Poland – a law was finally enacted by common consent under which Arianism was proscribed; and the Arians and the Socinians, understood under the same term, were then obliged either to abjure their heresy or to leave the kingdom within the two years allowed them to sell

[3] Taken from the Preface to the *Bibliotheca Fratrum Polonorum*.

their goods. That law which was subsequently confirmed in other General Diets was not like those which are diminished by time or, being born in the heat of a zeal conceived in the face of public disorder, gradually lose their impact. It was executed and remains in force to this day.[4=6]

Should anyone think that the Jesuit, Maimbourg, has falsified this part of his history to have the king and the Estates of Poland praised for having observed a certain degree of moderation, I must inform the reader that Socinian writers[5=7] report that the Edict of the year 1658 allowed them a three-year period in which to sell their possessions, and that, subsequently, one of those three years was revoked, so that the day appointed for their departure was set for 10 July 1660.[6=8] One can find hardly anything more lamentable than the description they give of the miseries to which they were subjected from the year 1648 until they left Poland. They suffered every sort of harassment, they could not sell their belongings except at very low prices, and their wretchedness was aggravated by all sorts of duplicities. They omit neither the infringement of supposedly perpetual and irrevocable edicts, nor the royal oaths under whose protection they had lived unmolested for nearly one hundred years. Nor do they forget either that it was ecclesiastics who forced the Estates of the kingdom into this infraction, and King John Casimir into violating the oath he had taken ten years before . . .[7=9] . . .

He [Maimbourg] gives an account of the oath made by the king in the year 1648. And then he says,

> Decimo post anno . . . ['Ten years later, many men became bewitched by the Pope's sorcery. The kingdom's Estates, formerly bound by the most sacred of obligations, shamefully forgot their pledge, honour, and conscience. Those who had decent attitudes were overwhelmed by a violent, howling, and threatening mob. The majority overturned the most hallowed and most beneficial law of peace, formerly

---

[4=6] Maimbourg, *Histoire de l'arianisme* [History of Arianism], bk 12, pp. 375–6 of vol. IV, Dutch edition.
[5=7] See the two letters printed at the end of *Historia Reformationis Polonicae* [History of the Polish Reformation], pp. 278 *et seq.*
[6=8] *Ibid.*, p. 294.
[7=9] *Ibid.*, p. 290.

established by the guarantees, agreements, covenants, and stipulations of countless assemblies, and of the many kings who succeeded Sigismund Augustus in a continuous line and who ratified it with public oaths. This law had only recently been reaffirmed for us with great care and formality. But they annulled it, striking us with this terrible decree, which banished us from the land of our birth.'][8=10]

To understand the persecution to which they were subjected prior to the revocation of the Edicts, you need only read the Latin passage I am about to cite, and note two points. The first is that the king and the republic of Poland had struck a gradual succession of blows before inflicting the final extremity. It was thus that France behaved towards its Reformed communities.[9=11] The second is that the Unitarians attributed every misfortune in Poland to the persecution perpetrated in the kingdom contrary to the spirit of the edicts, on the sects not belonging to the church of Rome.

Poloniam deinde infausto omine . . . ['Then they speak of our homeland, Poland, with ominous foreboding. This country broke the pledge of her oaths and her covenants, taking away places of worship, not just from us but also from evangelicals and others. She destroyed our freedom to practise our religion, and proved herself an enemy by inflicting various penalties upon us on account of our differing religious beliefs. She called herself the avenging hand of God, and she became involved in devastation and disaster to which, at present, we see no end. Yet just as long as she maintained and protected each citizen's freedom of conscience and religion, the country flourished with the greatest of peace and prosperous good fortune. But when that obligation began to weaken, those who could disagree about religious matters under a just law began to investigate every thought.'][10=12]

It was thus that they spoke in an address which they presented before the Estates of the Province of Holland in the year 1654.

[8=10] *Ibid.*, p. 293.
[9=11] That is to say before the Revocation of the Edict of Nantes, in 1685.
[10=12] *Apologia pro veritate accusata, adversus edictum ordinum Hollandiae* ['Defence of Truth Accused, against the Edict of the Estates of Holland'], p. 40.

[Remark (B) omitted.]

(C) That they preached nothing that was less like sedition.]
He [Faustus Socinus] condemns subjects taking up arms against
their prince and those Protestant theologians who say that it is permissible to resist oppressors of liberty of conscience; and with such
ardour that perhaps never did partisan of the despotic and arbitrary
power of sovereigns seem to speak more vehemently. He writes
more as a monk who had sold his pen to arouse hatred for the
Reformation than as a fugitive from Italy.... .[11=16]

Hoornbeek ... having cited [Faustus Socinus] ... observes,
among other things,[12=17] that such a malign criticism of the conduct
of the Dutch against Philip [of Spain] could well have been used
by the Estates General when, in 1598, they expelled the Socinians.
The words of Cocceius deserve a place here. We learn from him
that in 1654 the Socinians praised inordinately the very conduct
[taking up arms against Spain] which [Faustus] Socinus had condemned in 1581. Socinus in *Contra Paleologum* ... says

> 'Ex quo intelligi ...' ['From this it can be grasped how
> preposterously men behave when they take up arms against
> those who govern, supposedly with a view to defending the
> worship and religion of God.' The foregoing is what Socinus
> said in 1581. But no one, I think, believes that he meant the
> princes of these Provinces. These ... [Socinian] gentlemen
> ... now claim that the war was indeed waged on behalf of
> that presumed freedom of conscience and that God indeed
> chose this noble republic.][13=18]

But let us remark in passing that there is nothing of which a
hostile polemicist is not capable. For to the king of Poland they
depicted Socinus as the author of an insurrectionary pamphlet;[14=19]

[11=16] Socinus, in the book *De magistratu adversus Paleologum* [On the Magistracy
against Paleologus], part 1, in J. Hoornbeek, *Apparatus ad controversias socinianas* [Remarks on the Socinian Controversy].

[12=17] *Ibid.*, p. 59.

[13=18] J. Cocceius, in his *Examen apologiae equitis poloni* [Examination of the Apology
of a Polish Knight], p. 141.

[14=19] 'Stephanus tunc regnum ...' ['At that time Stephen was king of Poland. An
informer poisoned his mind with an accusation which charged Socinus with
having written seditious ideas. It was argued that it was intolerable for such
insolence to go unpunished because the author was a wandering exile from

notwithstanding that he forthrightly condemned every author who had defended both the insurrection of subjects, and their self-elevation as the judge as to whether their prince reigned tyrannically.

I do not believe that it has yet been maintained among the Socinians that it is right and proper to take up arms against one's prince. But that is because the sect has not so far needed to justify its position. In that particular, it retains its virginity and does not resemble certain others who might, like the courtesan of Petronius, say: *nunquam memini me virginem fuisse etc.* [I cannot recall that I was ever a virgin etc.]. It seems that the opportunity for imitating others in that respect has been lacking.

[Remarks (D)–(E) omitted.]

(F) He lost ... some ... manuscripts which upset him greatly.] Though he was sick, certain scholars of Cracow, having stirred up the mob, entered his house and snatched him half-naked from his room. They paraded him through the streets; they clamoured for his hanging; they beat him up; and it was with extreme difficulty that he was rescued by a professor from the hands of those ruffians. His house was plundered, he lost his furniture; but none of this upset him so greatly as the loss of his manuscripts, which he would have redeemed with his blood . . .[15=22]

(G) Princes will never embrace a sect which does not approve of war and the holding of public office.]

[Though the Gospel clearly taught the renunciation of killing, violence and revenge, even the Christian ruler was suspicious of a Christian sect which refused to bear arms. Bayle, in a vain attempt to explain this paradox, resorts to humour.]

How many sovereigns do we see who make a traffic of their own subjects as a private individual deals in horses or sheep? Some raise

Italy. The pamphlet *De magistratu adversus Paleologum* was cited. Though no other evidence would have been required than for him to have read the pamphlet himself, it would be convenient for him to avoid taking the risk.'] *Vita Fausti Socini*, fol. **2, verso.
[15=22] *Vita Fausti Socini*, fol. **3.

troops not to defend their frontiers or to attack their enemies, but in order to make money from them in the service of other princes.[16=23] They are delighted to have subjects always ready to enlist at the first beat of a drum. They profit from it greatly; and they are therefore irritated by Socinians since their treasury gains nothing from them. Additionally most sovereign princes enjoy making incursions into neighbouring states and aligning themselves with those who are at war; and it is of importance to them to make it known that they cannot be attacked with impunity. For all these reasons nothing could be more pointless than to command men who, out of a principle of religion, are engaged not to bear arms. A story is told, which is perhaps a jest, that the king of Poland, under attack from rebellious Cossacks and the Tartars, and having need of all his subjects to repulse the enemy, sent word to the Socinians to take up arms. They answered that their conscience did not allow them either to shed human blood or to do any harm to reasonable creatures. Whereupon it was proposed to them to go to war but without putting any shot in their muskets. You will make up the numbers, they were told, and that will count for something since the enemy will fear us more. But they had some trouble in selling that expedient. See the end of the next remark.

I have it on good authority that some Polish gentlemen of the Socinian persuasion would go to war when the laws of the kingdom required it, and that some of them even make a profession of the military life, though not obliged to do so from the necessity of obeying the laws of the kingdom. In the latter case their sect did not approve their conduct.

(H) There are very few people capable of renouncing ambition and the bearing of arms.]

[Completing the discussion of the rarity of the refusal to bear arms, Bayle floats the speculative opinion that the Socinian sect might have been founded to instigate a specifically Italian Reformation and so deflect support from the innovations of Luther and Calvin.]

Those who enjoy war are innumerable and they act from highly compelling motives. Gentlemen and nobility are prompted either

---

[16=23] See [*Dic*,] article 'Anabaptists', Remark (E).

by the sole ambition to advance themselves and gain reputation or, in addition to these desires, by the need to deliver themselves from poverty. Soldiers are prompted by both idleness and gratification. They hope for the greater part of the time to be free from labour; they hope also for some pillage and plunder and for good wine and easy women. In every town in the world those of a rank with a claim to office aspire to great positions with eagerness, and engage in a thousand activities to acquire them. As soon as there is a vacancy, many candidates emerge who have long before paved the way by their intrigues and liberalities: an evident sign that the desire for honours and dignities is very intense and very general – from which one should conclude that the Socinian religion is made neither for a whole people, nor for the greatest number. It is appropriate only for certain choice temperaments. And if it is true that a pope, having heard it said that Protestants tolerated neither adultery nor fornication, exclaimed that their religion would be of no long duration,[17=24] then it may be inferred that his prognosis would have been more apt had he applied it to a sect which renounces both arms and honours. Let me communicate to my readers at this point an observation I have heard, which refutes those who say that all those Italian intellectuals who forsook Calvinism to set up a new Arianism had a plan to form a party greater than that of the reformers in Germany and Geneva. It is supposed that though believing that there were incomprehensible mysteries, they pretended to oppose them in order to attract many followers. For to convert the human understanding to a belief in three persons in the divine nature, and in a God made man,[18=25] is a very heavy burden for reason. One comforts Christians immensely therefore if one relieves them of such a burden; and consequently it might be argued that if one removes such a yoke, one will be supported by a great multitude. Thus it was that those emigrants from Italy, who were transplanted into Poland, came to deny the Trinity, the Hypostatic Union, original sin, and absolute predestination, etc. They thought that if Calvin had won so many followers by avoiding the need to believe all the incomprehensible doctrine associated with transubstantiation, they would make greater progress still if they rejected

---

[17=24] See [*Dic*,] article 'Abelians', note 3.
[18=25] See *L'Esprit de M. Arnauld*, vol. 1, ch. 7, p. 231.

all the other inconceivable matters which that reformer had retained. To this one can, however, reply that if they attempted to deceive others through this artifice, then they were very foolish and very unworthy of their Italian education. For the speculative mysteries of religion trouble hardly anyone, though they may indeed exhaust a professor of theology who contemplates them with intensity, whether to explain them or to respond to the objections of heretics. Certain other studious persons who examine them with great earnestness may likewise be fatigued by the resistance of their reason; but all other men remain in a perfect tranquillity in respect of such matters. That is to say, they believe – or believe they believe – what is said of these things and remain at peace in their persuasion. One would therefore be something of a visionary dreamer [*visionnaire*] should one believe that the citizen [*le bourgeois*], the peasant [*le paysan*], the soldier [*l'homme de guerre*], and the gentleman [*le gentilhomme*] would be relieved of a heavy burden if he were dispensed from belief in the Trinity or the Hypostatic Union. They feel far more at ease with [it is thought] a doctrine that is mysterious, incomprehensible, and above reason. They suppose that one is more apt to admire what one does not understand; since one thereby creates for oneself an idea more sublime and more consoling. In consequence all the ends of religion are better sought in objects that one does not understand: they inspire more admiration, more respect, more awe, and more confidence. If false religions have had their mysteries it is because they have been forged in imitation of the true one. Thus God, through an infinite wisdom, has accommodated himself to the human condition [*l'état de l'homme*][19=26] by mixing darkness with light in his revelation. In a word, we must admit that incomprehensibility in certain matters is agreeable to us.[20=27]

If one were to invent a hypothesis only for philosophers, worthy of being called the religion of the physician, one would, seemingly,

---

[19=26] According to Caesar, *De bello civili* [The Civil Wars], 2.4, this condition would be cruel. 'Communi fit vitio . . .' ['Our universal natural failing is to have more faith in unseen, hidden and unknown things, and thus to be the more violently struck with terror.']

[20=27] Mme de Sablé says in one of her maxims (the thirty-ninth), 'One makes more impression on others by going beyond their understanding, for one always presumes more when something is only half-visible.'

consider oneself obliged to separate from it doctrines that are too hard to grasp. But, at the same time, one would have to renounce the vanity of being followed by the multitude. . . .

But suppose we agree that those Italians were foolish enough to think that people would be freed from an intolerable yoke if they were dispensed from believing in the Trinity etc., must we also agree that they did not think the prohibition on civil and military employment to be a burden infinitely harder to bear? Will anyone be so unreasonable as to require that we should entertain such a notion of those people, a people who lacked neither wit nor address, as nobody denies? What I am going to say is doubtless the *dénouement* of the problem. When men of ability, planning to set up a new sect, decide upon a smooth path and propose to substitute an easy doctrine in place of a difficult one, one may well assert that they do not alight upon the most effective means of success; but one would not expect that they would be content to modify the speculative mysteries and retain the full weight of the practice, or that they would even increase the burden of the practical precepts. And yet this is precisely what must be supposed concerning the founders of the Socinian heresy; and therefore what is said of their intentions must be a mistake. They are more rigid than other Christians both in respect of their prohibition against vengeance, and in respect of their renunciation of worldly honours; for they seek no mitigation whatsoever, nor figurative explanations of those texts in the Scriptures which relate to morals. They have revived the severity of the primitive church which approved neither of the faithful being involved with the magistrature, nor of their putting a neighbour to death,[21=29] to the point of not even permitting them to bring charges against a malefactor. The prohibition against bringing charges, and against making war, is a heavier burden even than the prohibition

---

[21=29] 'Non enim cum occidere . . .' ['For when God forbids us to kill, he not only prohibits us from being mercenary soldiers, which is not allowed even under public laws, but he also warns us against participating in activities which men think lawful. Thus it is right that the occupation of soldier is forbidden him whose campaign is for justice itself; it will not be allowed either to prosecute anyone on a capital charge, since there is no difference between killing by argument and killing by the sword, given that killing itself is prohibited. It is essential, therefore, that to this precept of God no exception at all be made, for it will always be wrong to kill a man, whom God has willed to be a holy, living being.'] Lactantius, *Divinae institutiones* [Divine Institutions], 6.20.

against vengeance. For it excludes the expedients of either deceiving oneself, or of deceiving others. Those who preach the renunciation of revenge with the greatest fervour manage to find a thousand distinctions to elude that precept. Some say that they do not hate their neighbour in the sense that he is a man, but in the sense that he is an enemy of God, while others protest that they do no harm in avenging a private quarrel in the interest of God. This is to return by detours to the very path of vengeance that one had professed to renounce. Some deceive themselves, others are mere hypocrites who deceive the world: but on the renunciation of war and honours there can be no subterfuge. One is absolutely obliged to practise what one preaches. The practice cannot be separated from the theory; there are neither distinctions nor equivocations. It is therefore a very effective constraint. It is no passing abstinence, like that of those who discipline themselves once a year: it is a perpetual and continuous condition. Let us conclude, then, that those Italian refugees were no charlatans. They were mistaken in their subtleties, and in deferring too much to natural reason [*la lumière naturelle*]; and if they retained one part of Christianity rather than another it is because they were led to this proposition or to that, through their first principle, whereby they would admit nothing that was directly contrary to the light of their reason. This, seemingly, is the origin of their choice. Had they been greedy or manipulative sectarians, they would have gone about things in quite another way. Let us therefore oppose their principle as an erroneous route, but let us not usurp the place of those [philosophers] who listen to beating hearts. Their principle undervalues religion and changes it into philosophy; for the magnificence, the authority and the sovereignty of God require that along this path we travel by faith and not by vision. . . .

The pagans said that the secrets within mysteries make God appear more exalted and that they are a semblance of his nature, given that it is hidden from the senses . . . 'Mystica sacrorum occultatio . . .' ['The mystical cloak of rites gives majesty to a deity, because it is a way of concealing these mysteries from the observation of the senses.'] It is Strabo who speaks thus in book 10, p. 322.

But what I am about to say may disabuse those who flatter themselves that the aversion of the Socinians to arms and honours will always be a powerful obstacle to the progress of that sect. It is no article of the Socinian faith that one ought to renounce civil and military office. The Socinians, in that respect, are more indulgent of the passions than the Mennonites. They do not scruple to hold public employment in Transylvania and, seemingly, they would bear arms like other men were they to have a sovereign of their religion.

(I) They advance yet other reasons.]

[Bayle's advocacy of suspension of judgement on questions of scientific uncertainty or metaphysical obscurity was often misrepresented. His true position was to assert, as a fact of psychology, that suspension of judgement is rare, since the ordinary human reaction to uncertainty is to jump to a conclusion. He shows with what arguments a clever polemicist can convince a magistrate of the truth of the fallacious proposition that persons or communities who are uninstructed in the metaphysical doctrine of divine retribution are a necessary threat to public order.]

For most people are inclined to yield to the evidence of inward feeling than to follow the thread of numerous connected consequences which proceed from clear and distinct ideas. Since one may be confused quickly and easily by the paradoxes which reason exposes, it will appear somewhat likely that the Socinian system is hardly suitable for converting the people. It is more appropriate for leading studious persons, and those who are engaged only in analysis and speculative thought, into scepticism (*pyrrhonisme*). Adversaries will always encounter reason's weak points, which will provide them with the means of disheartening people: thus, the infinity of matter, God's physical extension and its limitations; the notions of divine knowledge, the punishments of Hell, are among Socinian doctrines which, being represented to sovereigns and to peoples with but a touch of rhetoric, can fill them with horror. For if it is agreeable for each individual to have no fear of the punishments of the next world, it is rather disconcerting for them to imagine that they might daily have to encounter other such people. It is not in the interest of individuals, therefore, that any dogma tending to lessen the fear of Hell should establish itself in their country. And it is likely enough that preachers of this sort of permissive temperament will always be found more offensive than acceptable to the public. An author has said recently that the very people who reject the Gospel because of the austerity of its precepts would reject a religion with an even greater horror if it enjoined them to steep themselves in infamous disorders; I mean, if such were presented to them when they were in a state of reason, and before they had been immersed in the prejudices of their education'.[22=30] He has given reasons for that; but he has omitted one of the better considerations; for he has not touched on the matter of self-love [*l'amour propre*] or personal interest [*l'intérêt personnel*]. It is true that a degenerate person would find his preference respecting his conscience in a doctrine which allowed murder, adultery, perjury etc., but in many other respects he would not see it that way at all. He has a mother, wife, sister and nieces who would vex him mortally should they grow infamous through their impropriety. There are more people who can murder, rob and defraud him etc. than there are people against whom he can commit these same crimes. Everybody is more capable of being offended than of offending. For among twenty equal persons it is evident that each one of them is less strong against nineteen than are nineteen against one.[23=31] It is supposedly in the interest of each private individual, therefore, however dissolute he may be, that a code of morality is taught which is suitable for sensitising the conscience.

(K) Those who say that the Socinians have a full liberty of conscience in the United Provinces are poorly acquainted with history.] The Unitarians made several attempts to establish themselves in Holland . . . The third attempt was that of Ostorode and Vaidove who came from Poland to Amsterdam in 1598 with many Socinian books, both in print and in manuscript, which they began to get translated into Flemish.[24=32] The magistrates, having had all the books seized, sent them to the academy of Leiden and then to the Estates General. Having learnt of the judgement of the academy of Leiden concerning those works, they ordered that they be burnt in the presence of Ostorode and Vaidove, and that these

---

[22=30] [Bayle,] *Pensées diverses sur les comètes*, n. 189, p. 592.
[23=31] And that supposes that the nineteen do not act in concert against the twentieth.
[24=32] Taken from Gibertus Voëtius, *Disputationes*, vol. III, p. 811.

two Socinians had ten days to leave the country.[25=33] The judgement of these theologians of Leiden was that these writings differed very little from Mahometanism, and that they contained blasphemies that could not be permitted among Christians without extreme impiety.[26=34] . . .

(L) I shall expand a little further on the decree of the year 1653.]

[Bayle condemns the vehemence and violence with which ortho-dox Calvinism in the United Provinces had responded to the Socinians' rejection of the Trinity, eternal punishment, and the bearing of arms. He observes that other advanced thinkers, lay and ecclesiastic, without necessarily subscribing to Socinianism, preferred likewise to emphasise God's magnanimity rather than his supposed severity.]

I do not know what the Estates of Holland answered in 1628 to the remonstrances of their synods, but I have read the proceedings of what was done in a similar case in 1653. The deputies of the same synods protested that the Socinian sectarians – whose doctrines concerning the resurrection of the dead, the hope of life eternal, etc., undermined everything in Christianity – had dared to come into United Provinces, and principally into Holland, to pervert the faithful, and to tear the church apart; that the zeal of the Ragorskis against those heretics was well known in Transylvania, and that certain decrees had been passed against them in Poland in the years 1638 and 1647; that they had been expelled from Poland, that their temple, their library, and their printing house had been destroyed because they had in press a very shocking book against the mystery of the Trinity . . .[27=46] . . .

The Socinians did not remain silent; they employed one of their finest pens to compose an apology; it appeared in the year 1654 with the following title: *Apologia pro veritate accusata etc* . . . This piece is well written, since all the expertise of the art is observed. It diffuses an air of moderation combined with a brave tenacity

---

[25=33] J. Hoornbeek, *Apparatus ad controversias Socinianas*, p. 98.
[26=34] *Ibid.*
[27=46] See the reply by Cocceius to the *Apologiae equitis Poloni* [cf. n. 13=18 above], fol. ****2, verso.

in denying every accusation. The author deploys the same general arguments[28=54] made use of by Tertullian in his *Apologetic*, and by Calvin in the Epistle Dedicatory to his *Institutes*, and by many other reformers in their writings against the accusations of the Sorbonne. It is an unavoidable inconvenience that when a false church pleads for toleration and complains of the penal laws, it advances the same commonplaces as the true church in a similar position. When the true church requires of sovereigns the extirpation of the false church, it uses the same arguments and the same proofs advanced by the false church when it requires the extirpation of the true church. It were indeed to be wished that communions as different in their tenets should not be so alike in their use of the same mode and the same theme; but that is a blessing which cannot be promised in this world. The abuse, in that respect, is without remedy: for among other skills, man would need to possess the art of finding the real truth from among a hundred other claimants to it, who, in respect of general reasons, would express themselves in the same way. But let us pass to another matter. . . .

A synod should never rely on vague rumour without a source when it makes legal representations to a sovereign, and when the purpose is to obtain the suppression of a sect. In accusations which concern doctrine, it is easier to defend oneself against a charge that is not exact. For example, they stated as fact in the Remonstrance that the Socinians destroyed the resurrection of the dead and the hope of eternal life. The faculty of theology at Leiden insisted likewise that, like the Sadducees, Socinians denied the life of the soul separated from the body, and the resurrection of the wicked. The Polish gentleman says that in that respect they were calumniated.[29=62] . . .

I shall observe in passing that nothing has proved more prejudicial to the Socinians than a certain doctrine that they thought highly useful for removing the greatest stumbling block in our theology as it appeared to philosophic minds. Every great thinker who consults only natural reason and the euphoric notion of an infinite goodness which, morally speaking, constitutes the principal quality

---

[28=54] I use this adjective [i.e. 'general'] since the circumstances relating to the severity of the penal laws are not the same as the circumstances that occasioned the apologies of Tertullian and Calvin, etc.

[29=62] *Apologiae equitis Poloni*, pp. 73, 74.

of the celestial nature will be offended by what the Scriptures tell us of the infinite duration of the pains of Hell. This is especially so if one adds to it the many detailed accounts that are to be found in many books.[30=66]

According to the pagans of antiquity 'Deus optimus maximus' [a God who is finest and greatest] indicated the common and ordinary qualities of the divine nature. It was their set expression when they spoke of God, and they never said 'Deus severissimus, implacabilissimus' [a God who is sternest and most implacable]. This manner of address contained two epithets, 'optimus' [fine] and 'maximus' [great], which, to speak correctly, were but the image and the expression of a single quality: I mean a sovereign goodness [*une bonté souveraine*]; for if the notion of God's goodness is to be properly used, it must be accompanied by the notion of greatness. And what is it, I pray you, if it is not magnanimity, generosity, munificence, or the effusion of good? This natural concept, which caused the Gentiles to speak in this way, finds a confirmation in the Scriptures, since there reigns in them, if I dare express myself so, a perpetual attempt to raise the goodness of God above his other attributes. Doing good work and showing mercy is, according to the Scriptures, the daily and preferred work of God; but chastising, punishing and showing severity is his unusual and disagreeable work. Thus, insofar as one stops there, and does not humbly submit to the authority of certain texts of the Gospel, one will regard with horror the dogma of infinite penalties and punishments for all or almost all men.

The Socinians, deferring too much to reason, have put limits on these sufferings, but with rather more care than when they considered whether men were made to suffer for suffering's sake; and whether to take into account either the benefit to the sufferer or the benefit to spectators: for who has never profited from the example of a well-regulated tribunal? They supposed that they would win for Christianity those who were alarmed by an idea which seemed so little compatible with the sovereign good. But those heretics did not realise they would be thought more odious on this account and more unworthy of tolerance, than on account of all their other

---

[30=66] See the work entitled *Les Merveilles de l'autre monde* [The Wonders of the Other World], by a Canon de Reis, surnamed Arnoux.

dogmas. Basically, there are very few people who are outraged by the doctrine of eternal punishment; and few share the perverse thinking of Theodore Camphusius.[31=67] He was a minister of religion and a native of Gorcum in Holland who turned Socinian. He declared publicly that he would have lived without religion had he not come across books in which it was taught that the punishments of Hell will not last for ever. 'Memini, meminerunt et . . .' ['I recall, as do others, that it was a certain Didericus Camphusius (Dirk Raphaels Comphuysen)], who in a published letter, which accompanied his songs, professed that he had been inclined to abandon all religion, until he chanced upon those books which teach that perpetual fires and eternal tortures are without existence.']]$^{32=68}$

[31=67] In the vernacular, Dirk Raphaels Comphuysen. He was born in 1536, and died in Dockum, Frisia, in 1627. See *Bibliothèque Anti-Trinitaire*, p. 112 . . . He was author of many works in Flemish and one, among others, was reprinted more than twenty times in various forms, and consisted of songs and spiritual poems, of which much was made by connoisseurs of Flemish poetry. The author has cleverly inserted his opinions about many dogmas of Christianity, and principally on matters of morals.

[32=68] Cocceius, *Examen apologiae equitis Poloni*, p. 305.

Synergists

[Alongside the theology of free will and predestination lay the juridical question of an individual's responsibility for his harmful acts, and whether other factors, such as grace or destiny, played a part. Bayle uses this piece to show that there were better and worse ways of handling the problem. This irreconcilable debate was familiar because of the dispute between Jansenists and Jesuits, satirised in Pascal's Lettres provinciales *(1656–9). Bayle proposes (in Remark (C), and n. 10=23) that if progress were to be made, it would be by employing the cosmologists' method of exploring rival propositions as hypotheses. By applying to dogmatic theology the method of critical science Bayle can avoid saying that certain truth is never attainable in some matters. At the same time, he can show that honest support for a mistaken theory should never, in justice, be a civil offence.]*

SYNERGISTS. The name given in the sixteenth century to certain theologians in Germany. Finding Luther's hypothesis on free will too severe, they taught that men are converted not through the grace of God alone but with the aid of the human will. This was the fifth schism that arose in the communion of the Lutherans.[a] Melanchthon laid its foundations, while Victorin Strigelius and certain other ministers, who respected his authority, drew attention to certain passages that they found in his writings which strongly emphasised man's will. This is why they maintained that the natural power of free will [*franc arbitre*] concurred with the grace of God

---

[a] Johann Micraelius, *Syntagma historiae ecclesiasticae* [Treatise on Church History], p. 865.

in the conversion of a sinner. George Major, Paul Eber, Paul Crellius and Piperin were the other principal apologists for this opinion,[b] and they were persecuted by the faction of Illyricus. It is certain that Melanchthon could not agree with the rigid approach of Luther and Calvin on the subject of grace (A), and it would be useless to assert, as apparent proof of his sharing their opinion on this article, the fulsome praise he bestowed upon their piety. For he was unusually skilled at deflecting the unsavoury consequences of prejudice. He believed that men may err from honest motives (B). My remarks on the subject will give me an opportunity to link to the present discussion a rejoinder (C) which was made to a passage in the *Commentaire philosophique sur contrains-les d'entrer.*

(A) Melanchthon could not agree with the rigid approach of Luther and Calvin on the subject of grace.] Baudouin provided good proof of this when he published the extract from a letter which Melanchthon had written to Calvin, 11 May 1543 . . .

Let us see what Theodore Beza replied to that part of Baudouin's work. Firstly he denies that Melanchthon had written such a letter . . . In the second place, he put forward a fragment of the letter to show that in the matter of dogma there was complete agreement between Calvin and the doctor of Geneva . . . The second part of Beza's reply had no force because the praises which Melanchthon bestowed upon Calvin do not prove that he agreed with his opinion. He was so imbued with fairness, moderation and decency that he treated justly even those who maintained opinions which were not to his taste. His own preference for free will [*libre arbitre*] did not prevent him from discerning the strength of mind, the piety and the eloquence displayed by Calvin when the latter postulated the fragility of the human will. He was inhibited neither from praising him for his perspective, nor from complimenting him on being the protagonist of such a work. We shall say more about this idea below.[1=10] . . .

[b] Balduinus [Baudouin], *Responsio altera ad Johannem Calvinum* [Second Response to John Calvin], p. 139.

[1=10] In Remark (B).

(B) Melanchthon believed that one may err from honest motives.] A domineering divine with a choleric temperament will be so excessively fond of his opinions that he thinks none can oppose them without acting against the light of conscience or common sense. To the extent that he is pursued and contested, he protects and entrenches himself more and more within his prejudices. But a modest, humble and moderate divine of a phlegmatic temperament, such as Melanchthon, takes a different course. For though he rejects an opinion as false and dangerous, that does not prevent him from being fair to those who support it. He points out that very specious arguments lead them to maintain their opinion, but he acknowledges that they have other excellent qualities for which he commends them. He thereby guards against breaking with them or loosening the bonds of fraternity so long as the dissension is kept within certain bounds. From whence it appears that neither Melanchthon's Letters to Calvin, nor the praises he bestowed upon him in printed books, can prove that he agreed with him on the dogma of free will. All that can be inferred is that he was sufficiently fair to make a distinction between the two following things: Calvin's doctrine as it appeared to him, and that same doctrine as it seemed to Calvin. It seemed to him that according to the doctrine, God was the author of sin, but he was also well aware that Calvin did not teach it from that point of view, and that he would have looked upon such a notion as abominable. He was fully aware of how Calvin understood it; that is as a system apparently grounded upon several passages of the Scriptures, which served to support both the sovereignty of God's Providence and that of the dispensation of the New Law. He was aware that in Calvin's eyes the system of free will appeared only under a monstrous form, that to him it seemed to be destructive of Providence, directly contrary to St Paul's Epistles and to the glory that accrues to God for his redemption of man. Therefore Melanchthon, though not approving of Calvin's opinions, believed nevertheless that they were grounded upon a motive worthy of a good man, zealous in the service of God. Nor was he prevented from being of one mind with the doctor of Geneva in the following maxim: that of two opinions one should always choose the one which conforms more with the Scriptures and with the interests of the Creator. Their perfect agreement in respect of this thesis was the cause of their disagreement. For in pursuing this maxim, Calvin embraced the hypothesis of necessity, and Melanchthon that of free will. One of them believed that the sovereign empire of God over all things and the rights of a providence worthy of an infinite Being required an absolute predestination. The other believed that the goodness, the holiness and the justice of the Supreme Being required a contingency in our actions. Such were their respective principles. Each aimed at the same goal, namely at the greatest glory of God, but they pursued their aim through different paths. Was this then a sufficient reason for them not to own one another as brethren, and as fellow labourers in the Lord's vineyard?[2=15]

I foresee that it will be put to me that the difference between those different paths ought to have obliged those two doctors to anathematise one another, given that Melanchthon would have believed that Calvin, under the supposition of maintaining the rights of divine authority, had annihilated the goodness, the holiness and the justice of God by making him the author of sin and hell; while Calvin, on the other hand, would have believed that Melanchthon, under the supposition of emphasising those three attributes, had overturned providence and the empire of God by giving man a free will. But here is a solution. Suppose Calvin had contended in the following way: not being able to preserve all the attributes of God I renounce some in order to preserve the others, and I would prefer to sacrifice the moral virtues to the physical virtues, rather than the other way round – in short, I would prefer a powerful master to a good one – if this had been his argument it follows that he would indeed have deserved to be anathematised by all men. But in fact, he maintained in all debates that in asserting the supreme authority of God, he made no inroads on his goodness, his holiness or his justice. Melanchthon therefore would have been very unfair had he resorted to personal wrangling; I mean had he drawn the consequences which, in the last analysis, would have proceeded from his doctrine, since Calvin disowned them. Let us recount the words of his [Melanchthon's] denial:

> Ubique in scriptis suis . . . ['Wherever sin is treated in his
> writings, Calvin proclaims that God's name must not

[2=15] Note that we do not claim to extend this notion to every sect which finds itself in agreement on the general maxim to accord honour to God.

become embroiled in the discussion. For only perfect righteousness and justice befits God's nature. How outrageous, then, is the false accusation which implicates a man, who deserves well from God's church, in that crime of making God the author of sin. He does indeed teach consistently that nothing can happen without God's will. However, he maintained that wickedness committed by men is controlled by a hidden judgement of God, in such a way that He has nothing resembling the faults of men. The main point of his doctrine is that God, in a wondrous way and in a manner unknown to us, directs everything towards whatever end He wishes, so that his eternal will remains the primary cause of all things. But Calvin argues that God's reason for willing what does not seem to suit us at all is incomprehensible. He states that it should not be questioned too closely or too presumptuously, for the following reasons: since God's judgements and mysteries, which rule over our superficial condition, are infinitely deep, it is appropriate to worship Him with reverence rather than to examine Him. Nevertheless, he maintains this principle, that although the reasons for God's purpose are hidden from us, praise for God's justice must always be accorded to Him, because the rule of justice is his highest will.']³⁼¹⁶

Fervent and passionate men will not be placated with such a wise reply. Melanchthon loved accord, however, and from his store of equity and modesty, he was able to develop a mental clarity with which he penetrated the strengths and weaknesses both of the opinions he approved of and those he rejected. Melanchthon, I say, having such a disposition, was always ready to do justice to Calvin. This is conduct which everyone should imitate! Though you prove invincibly to an apologist of predestination that his system is necessarily and inevitably linked with the following consequence, 'God, therefore, is the author of sin', you should be content with the following answer as to his integrity: I see as well as you do the

<hr>

³⁼¹⁶ Calvinus [Calvin], *Brevis responsio ad diluendas nebulonis cuiusdam calumnias, Tractatus theologicorum* [Brief Response to the Calumnies of a Certain Miscreant, Theological Tracts], p. 730. See [*Dic*,] vol. xv, citation 49, 'Clarification on the Manicheans'.

connection between my principle and that consequence, but though I observe that my reason which perceives it does not provide me with sufficient insight to make me understand how I am mistaken, I remain strongly persuaded that God, in the treasury of his infinite wisdom, finds a certain way of breaking that connection; a certain way, I say, completely infallible, though it is unknown to me, and though it exceeds the limits of my understanding [*mes lumières*]. A Christian ought to pride himself mainly in his submission to God's authority. To disbelieve what one sees must often be one's motto, as well as to believe what one does not see. Here, in its essence, is the sense of the passage from Calvin which we have just cited. Melanchthon, and the other theologians who propound man's free will, would do better to be satisfied with this answer, because they too might be obliged to resort to such a *dénouement*. For, from the moment they show a modicum of good faith, they acknowledge that what is incomprehensible to them is the link between the free will of the creature, and the providence and foreknowledge of God.[4=17] Thus they are driven towards the very same precipice to which they have driven others; and they, in their turn, take refuge in the incomprehensibility of God's nature and in the weakness of our limited reason.

This is why one cannot be sufficiently distressed when one sees disputes about grace producing such venomous disputes. Every sect carries animosity to its ultimate limits and accuses the others of teaching frightful impieties and blasphemies. Yet it is precisely in respect of such doctrines that one should practise forthwith a mutual toleration. One might pardon intolerance in a party which could clearly prove its opinions, and answer all objections precisely, categorically, and in a convincing manner; but intolerance is inexcusable among people who are obliged to say that they have no better solution to offer than secrets impenetrable to the human mind, and hidden in the infinite treasury of God's incomprehensible immensity; and – I say – especially people who are proud, who unleash the thunder of anathema, who banish and hang those who dissent from them. Melanchthon was more humane. He did not

---

[4=17] Theodore Beza objects that they have no other answer when they are hard pressed. I have quoted his words in Remark (H) of the article [in *Dic*] 'Castalion', n. 93.

believe that those who deny free will are unworthy of being called God's servants. He excused them on account of the obscurity of the subject matter and the goodness of their motives.

Nothing could be more useful than to make profound reflections upon what has been said about this controversy in a work by M. Burnet, bishop of Salisbury.[5=18]

(C) The rejoinder that was made to a passage in the *Commentaire Philosophique sur contrains-les d'entrer*.] It seems to me that one of the things which inspired in Melanchthon the spirit of conciliation and decency [*honnêteté*] displayed in his conduct was that he considered that the manner in which God willed to act had been chosen from an infinite number of other ways, all equally worthy of a sovereignly perfect Being. Now here is the consequence of that notion: namely, that a person may be mistaken in explaining theological matters without necessarily ascribing to God anything which is prejudicial to his perfections. For, notwithstanding that those who advance a hypothesis which fails to correspond with what God has actually done may be mistaken if their theory conforms to one of these other ways which God might have chosen, he ascribes to him a conduct completely worthy of him. Let us elucidate this with an example. Let us suppose that Solomon, familiar with exchanging diplomatic correspondence with the king of Tyre,[6=19] one day wrote him an encoded letter in which he discussed a matter of state. Let us suppose that Titius and Mevius, being ordered to decipher the letter, did not make use of the same key. One took for an 'A' what the other took for an 'O', and so on with the other characters. In consequence Titius uncovered Solomon's true intention but Mevius did not. Nevertheless Mevius constructed a message so reasonable and so coherent that it did as much honour to Solomon's wisdom as that of Titius. One could have objected to Mevius that he ascribed some things to Solomon inconsistent with the ordinary course of prudence. But he could have replied that an intelligence as vast as Solomon's exposed depths in political affairs that surpassed the capacity of other minds. Let us assume, he might

---

[5=18] M. de Beauval has given an extract from it in his *Histoire des ouvrages des savans*, October 1699, pp. 435 *et seq.*, and also M. Bernard in the *Nouvelles de la république des lettres*, August 1700, pp. 155 *et seq.*

[6=19] Josephus, *Antiquitates judaicae* [Jewish Antiquities], 8, 2.

have said, because of his extraordinary wisdom, what surprises us here. One could have made a similar objection against Titius, and he would not have failed to extricate himself in a similar way. The superiority of mind of the great king of Jerusalem could have served as a new key in the particular difficulties of deciphering the characters. Solomon alone could have determined whether Titius was more able or more fortunate than Mevius. But perceiving, on the one hand, that Mevius ascribed to him a sublime reasoning, and on the other that if there remained any awkwardness in it, it was removed by a supposition exceedingly glorious to his wisdom, he might have been as pleased with Mevius as with Titius. He might have addressed them in the following terms: one of you makes me say what I really thought, and the other what I might have thought, but each with an equal glory.

It will readily be granted to me that in this, we have a portrayal of the destiny of astronomers who explain celestial phenomena with opposite systems. Such phenomena resemble an encoded letter which God presents to astronomers to be deciphered. As their key, some take the motion of the earth and the others its repose. For some the spinning of the earth upon its axis serves as the cause of the precession of the equinoxes,[7=20] while the others prefer spiral trajectories[8=21] and so on. Thus, the three systems, of Ptolemy, Copernicus and Tycho Brahe, different as they are, each explain the apparent facts. However, only one of them conforms to the truth. This was what M. Marion[9=22] meant when he insisted that 'the system of Copernicus was an opinion true in art but false in nature'. But since all the proponents of these various systems concur in admiring the infinite power and wisdom of the craftsman who produced the construction, they are in no way afraid of offending God should they be mistaken. They judge that if he does not do things in the way they imagine he does, he *could* do them thus without the least prejudice to his perfections. They judge that a knowledge as infinite as his has an infinity of designs for the world – all perfectly beautiful and all worthy of a Being who is infinitely wise and infinitely powerful. I am convinced that a Copernican,

---

[7=20] See Rohault, *La Physique*, vol. II, ch. 19, p. 77; Regius, *La Philosophie*, vol. III, bk 3, part 2, ch. 6, p. 128, edition in duodecimo.

[8=21] See the work entitled *Uranie ou Tableau des philosophes*, vol. III, p. 44.

[9=22] Arnauld, in one of his *Plaidoyers*, *difficultés à Steyaert*, part 9, p. 101.

having strongly disparaged the system of Ptolemy, its superfluity of cycles and epicycles, and the wastefulness of the prodigious speed of the firmament, etc., will admit, if he thinks carefully about it, that all the faults he observes in that hypothesis can be compensated for by certain of its advantages which are not to be found in the more simple mechanism of the spinning of the earth. As soon as one contemplates the notion of an infinite science [*une science infinie*] one sees the possibility of such a compensation; one grasps that man may not be the only being at whom such great marvels are directed. He will grasp that the inconceivable rapidity of the celestial spheres could have wondrous uses in relation to parts of the universe which are beyond the range of our vision. In a word, if Ptolemy's system is false, that does not prevent it from being possible, and consequently worthy of the wisdom of the Creator. For if it were unworthy it would not be possible. I think that no astronomer strongly convinced that he preferred this system to all others only because, all things duly weighed and considered, he believed it more consonant with God's choice would be afraid of appearing before the judge of the world with such an opinion, even though it should be found false. I believe that he would hope that both a Copernican and himself would receive an answer rather similar to that which one assumes that Solomon would have made to Titius and Mevius. Few people would deny that; except if it concerned a matter of theology, and then an abundance of divines would do so.[10=23] I make the conjecture that Melanchthon would not be among the latter on the matter of the two systems relating to predestination: that of liberty and that of necessity. He would suppose that the false theory is plausible, possible, and not contrary to God's perfection.

I do not, in this context, touch at all on questions of right [*du droit*]; but here is a matter which it will be highly appropriate for me to mention. For the rules of history fully authorise it and, more-

---

[10=23] If it were only a question of predicting eclipses and other phenomena to satisfy our curiosity, or for practical results, one might have a choice of systems: one might reconcile different hypotheses with the same phenomena; moreover, if one had poor results one would be acquitted of having made a mistake, or of having measured inaccurately, or calculated wrongly. Whether we follow Ptolemy's system or Tycho Brahe's, or Kepler's, or that of Copernicus, it would matter very little, provided one did not positively affirm matters of which one did not have mathematical certainty. But it is not the same thing with systems of religion. Saurin, *Réflexions sur les droits de la conscience*, p. 335.

over, were I to mix a little criticism with my summary, I should do nothing that exceeds the remit of this Dictionary. A minister from Utrecht [Saurin] reflecting recently upon the *Commentaire philosophique* has confuted very strenuously the following passage:

Here is a project to dispel the phantoms and attacks of panic [*terreurs paniques*] which have so long assailed theologians in the chapter of errors. Namely, that the reason why the human mind finds so many arguments, all equally sound in appearance, to maintain true and false propositions, is that most of the false propositions [*les faussetés*] which they discuss are as possible as the true propositions [*les vérités*]. In effect we all suppose that Revelation [Creation as taught in the book of Genesis] follows from a free decree of God, for he is not required by his nature to make men or any other beings. In consequence, he might, had he wished, either have produced nothing, or have produced a world different from the present world; and in the case where he wanted to make men, he could have directed them to his purposes by methods quite contrary to those he has chosen, and which would have been equally worthy of the sovereignly perfect Being. For an infinite wisdom has infinite ways of manifesting itself, all equally worthy of it. That being so, one should in no way be astonished that theologians find as many good arguments to support man's free will as to impugn it. For we have ideas and principles to conceive and to prove both that God could have made man with free will, and that he could have made him without it, through the liberty, as it is called, of *indifference*; and thus of a hundred other contradictory propositions. Vol. II, *Supplément à la Com. phil.*, ch. 24, pp. 308, 310.[11=24]

His [Saurin's] reflections upon the preceding passage, to the extent that they concern the subject under discussion, can be reduced first to this interrogative: *Who told him* [Bayle] *that we have ideas and principles to conceive and to prove that God was able to make man free; but not able to make him free for the liberty of indifference?*[12=25] I believe that M. Saurin would not have posed such a question

[11=24] *Ibid.*, p. 323.
[12=25] *Ibid.*, 324.

had he recalled that for a period of 150 years vast quantities of
books for and against free will have been published unceasingly all
over Europe, and in which each party has made triumphant objections. He would have been the first to concede then that we do have
'ideas and principles to conceive and to prove etc.' Let him peruse any
of the books written by the Arminians, the Calvinists, the Molinists
or the Jansenists, and he will see that those ideas and principles are
to be found in abundance in the human mind. He adds[13=26] *'that
there are contradictory things opposed to the essence of God and in
consequence impossible ... that God could not create bodies without
extension and without three dimensions; nor minds which were not beings
that think'*. But all this is to no point, since the commentator [Bayle]
had said nothing whereby he insinuated that there are no things
absolutely impossible. Of what use is it, then, to remark that the
attributes which make up the essence of a creature cannot be separated from it? Would he doubt this truth? *'If God'*, he [Saurin] continues,[14=27] *'did not make man with his liberty of indifference, our philosopher [Bayle] could not have known whether he could have created
him with this liberty; or whether this liberty is not as contradictory as
a square circle, or as an independent creature'*. I do not grasp this
sufficiently well to be able to confute it, but I think that Melanchthon, were he to reply in a similar case, would have restricted himself to saying: I do not like cavilling on such a matter. I will conform
to ordinary notions: I believe that God has freely made all the works
of creation, and I find it very odd that a minister calls this fact into
question.[15=28] I find it even stranger that he [Saurin] suggests that
liberty of indifference is as contradictory as a square circle given
that shortly afterwards he asserts *'that it is impossible for God to
create an intelligent creature without giving him laws'*.[16=29] The laws
God gave to Adam were accompanied with threats and promises.
This supposes clearly that Adam could either obey or disobey.
Those most rigid theologians, Saint Augustine and Calvin, teach
expressly that men have lost free will only because of the poor use
made of it by Adam in the earthly paradise. I ask no more than that

[13=26] *Ibid.*
[14=27] *Ibid.*, p. 325.
[15=28] These [very] words, 'if God did not make man with his liberty of indifference',
contain this doubt.
[16=29] Saurin, *Réflexions sur les droits de la conscience*, p. 330.

to be confident that it is possible for God to give to man liberty of indifference. For had he not bestowed it upon Adam all our systems of religion would founder. From which I conclude that God did give him such a liberty. Furthermore, everyone knows that one may infer from action the power to act;[17=30] but I conceive that he might have created him resolved towards good actions, and held him there in so secure a manner as to prevent him from wavering between doing good things and doing harmful things. This is why I find possible both the hypothesis of liberty and the hypothesis of necessity. This, it seems to me, is what Melanchthon might have answered. I think also that he would have found it highly unacceptable for the author of the *Reflections upon the Commentaire philosophique* [Saurin] not to declare his own position, but to be content with an '*if God etc.*', a vacillating phrase and from which one may infer that the deprivation of free will is contradictory. For assuming that God created Adam without a liberty of indifference, it could follow that it was a liberty that implies contradiction. Others will maintain, assuming that he created him with a liberty of indifference, that the result would be that his determination to one or the other of these contrary sides would be as impossible as a square circle. I pass over what the author of the *Reflections* [Saurin] says against the assertion by the author of the *Commentaire* [Bayle] that the proofs of false things are sometimes as good as the proofs of true things. What M. Saurin answers to that is full of irrelevance. For it is pointless in a dispute to prove to an adversary what he does not contest. The one thing that does not seem superfluous is his saying that '*the arguments which determine us to our choice of a religion should be moral demonstrations*';[18=31] but even that counts for nothing in the controversy about free will as it has been discussed by the commentator; for since each party prides himself on having for himself this sort of demonstration, it is to resort to equivocal positions.

Here is another passage from the *Commentaire philosophique*:[19=32]

> What happens, then, when Revelation is doubtful on some point? Some explain it by one system and others by another.

[17=30] 'Ab actu ad potentiam valet consequentia' ['from the act we can infer the capacity to act'].
[18=31] Saurin, *Réflexions*, p. 326.
[19=32] *Ibid.*, p. 327.

I mean that the system of some is consonant with the method that God has actually chosen, which does not prevent the other system from being consonant with what he might have done, entailing as much worth and glory for him as anything else; since we conceive that God could have done things otherwise than he did and in a hundred different ways, all worthy of his infinite perfection. For without that possibility he would have no liberty, and would not differ from the God of the stoics locked into an inevitable destiny: a dogma hardly better than spinozism. Consequently there can be no crime in false systems except where a theologian constructs one upon a notion which he himself believes to be contrary to what God himself has said, and therefore disparaging to his greatness. But I do not believe such theologians are to be found anywhere. [Bayle], *Supplément à la Com. phil.*, vol. II, ch. 24.

M. Saurin, comparing those words with another passage in which the commentator [Bayle] says that '*he will not take advantage of the comparison of a prince whose vast empire may contain many nations that have different laws, customs and languages*', finds[20=33] that the commentator, in making that assertion, justifies not only every sect of Christianity but also every sect of paganism. I am surprised that he did not perceive that his adversary limits himself to the systems that are based on the various interpretations that are advanced in Scripture.[21=34] I am going to show you another passage which will surprise you. '*God could have done things otherwise than as he did, and in a hundred different ways all worthy of his infinite perfection.*' M. Saurin,[22=35] having quoted once again those words from the *Commentaire philosophique*, confutes them with a distinction between the essential parts and the non-essential parts of a religion; after which he [Saurin] says:

the author [Bayle] does not make this distinction; his proposition is universal: '*God could have done things otherwise than he did, and in a hundred different ways.*' And what is remark-

---

[20=33] *Ibid.*, p. 329.
[21=34] 'What happens, then, when Revelation is doubtful on some point?' *Commentaire philosophique* cited by M. Saurin, *ibid.*, p. 327.
[22=35] *Ibid.*, p. 329.

able is that among those different ways he includes those which are envisaged by the poets of paganism and by the Chinese philosophers; for he seeks to justify every system of religion that has been invented by doctors, and received by peoples. To demonstrate his thesis, he postulates God's liberty. *'For without that'*, says he, *'he would have no liberty, and would not differ from the God of the stoics locked into an inevitable destiny: a dogma hardly better than spinozism'*. Were this consequence valid, God would have the most dreadful liberty of *'indifference'* imaginable. He might lie and perjure himself when he swears in his own name: he might command us to hate him and forbid us to love him; he might command treason and perjury, and, in a word, all sorts of crimes. In short, he might make a vice of every virtue, and a virtue of every vice.[23=36]

To refute those reflections, one needs to be mindful only of the following few words: EACH WORTHY OF HIS INFINITE PERFECTIONS. They entail, with the ultimate degree of evidence, that God's liberty does not consist in the ability to behave well or badly, wisely or imprudently; but in being able to follow among an infinity of plans, all equally fine and good, this one or that one, as he chooses. Can this mean that he could have been author of the false cults whose praises were sung by the heathen poets? Are they the way of his infinite perfections?

[23=36] *Ibid.*, p. 330.

Xenophanes

*[In 'Xenophanes', Bayle explores two notions that were subjects of controversy in classical, Christian, and heretical writings: 'acatalepsy' (or 'scepticism'), and 'evil'. The first, examined in Remark (L), is raised in the context of the postulate: 'Xenophanes believed in the incomprehensibility of all things.' The second concerned harm (*le mal*) – meaning both 'the crimes of humankind' and 'the unhappiness of humankind'. In Remark (E), Bayle explores gross moral evil, including war, mass slaughter, extortion, great superstitions, and the abuse of the innocent. He asks if the belief that there are two warring empires in the universe, namely, the evil empire and God's empire, can be sustained either theologically or philosophically. In Remarks (F), (H) and (K), Bayle turns to 'happiness', asking if 'the sweet things of life' equal its 'bitter draughts'. He infers that if philosophers were to deepen their knowledge of empirical psychology they could well improve their moral insight.]*

XENOPHANES, a Greek philosopher, native of Colophon who was, some tell us, a disciple of Archelaus.[a] On this account he should have been a contemporary of Socrates.[b] Others will have it that he taught himself all that he knew[c] and that he lived at the same time as Anaximander.[d] In that case he would have flourished before Socrates, and at about the sixtieth Olympiad as

---

[a] Diogenes Laertius[, Lives of the Philosophers], 9.18.
[b] He was a disciple of Archelaus.
[c] Diogenes Laertius[, Lives of the Philosophers], 9.18.
[d] *Ibid.*

Diogenes Laertius asserts.[e] He lived a long time, since verses are cited in which he declares 1. that his works were applauded in Greece for sixty-seven years; and 2. that he began to be famous at the age of twenty-five [(A)].[f] He wrote several poems on philosophical subjects, as well as 2,000 on the foundation of Colophon,[g] and on the colony of Elea.[h] He maintained an opinion on the nature of God that was very little different from Spinozism [(B)]. He composed some verses against Homer and Hesiod[i] on the follies that were sung of the gods. He held a maxim which completely undermined the pagan religion: namely that it is not less impious to assert that the gods are born than to assert that they die, since in either of the two cases it will be equally true that they do not exist eternally.[k] This doctrine is very true, and it is not at all contrary to the doctrine of the incarnation. He believed the moon to be an inhabited country [(C)]; and that it was impossible to predict future events;[l] and he claimed that, if the supposition of a learned critic is well founded, the good surpasses the bad in nature [(D)]. He would not have been the only one to have had this notion, but it seems that he held a completely different opinion. And if it had been only about harm morally considered (E), I do not believe he would have found an opponent. For everybody admits that good and decent people are rare; and that nothing is more common than a person who strays from the rules of virtue. But Xenophanes, without any doubt, intended to speak of physical harm; and his sense was that the sweet things of life do not equal the bitter draughts that she obliges us to swallow (F). Many people are persuaded that this is true, and they do not lack plausible arguments, as we shall see below. Even those who recognise that nature has provided the human race with an infinity of good things, and

---

[e] *Ibid.*, 20. See Remark [(A)].
[f] Diogenes Laertius [, *Lives of the Philosophers*], 9.19.
[g] *Ibid.*, 20. Note that Moréri reduces all the verses of Xenophanes to this number. Athenaeus often cites many of this philosopher's verses.
[h] A town in Italy.
[i] Diogenes Laertius [, *Lives of the Philosophers*], 9.18. . . .
[k] 'Ut Xenophanes dicebat . . .' ['Xenophanes said that those who claim that the gods are born and also say that they die are impious. For in both instances it is the case that they are not gods at any time.'] Aristotle, *Rhetoric*, 2.23, p. 446.
[l] Cicero, *De divinatione* [On Divination], 1, at the beginning.

that she has destined for humankind the use of all other things, consider man from another aspect as an unhappy being [(G)]. No small part of the harshness of his condition is the terrible need to which so many people are reduced, of seeking the remedy for their anxieties among forbidden pleasures (H). Whichever is the case, we may cite here the authority of Aristotle. For this great intellect, who philosophised with so much application and penetration, recognised that in nature there was more harm than good. Aristotle supposed that it was for this reason that Empedocles disliked the hypothesis of a single principle and so began to propose two principles: one for good, and the other for evil [(I)]. Holy Scripture has so emphatically depicted the wretchedness of this life[m] that it offers a conclusive argument on this controversy. I am surprised that Rabbi Maimonides, who had great knowledge and much judgement, and who was a very sound philosopher, could believe that he had adequately refuted the doctrine of which I speak (K). There is some intimation that Xenophanes believed in the incomprehensibility of all things (L). He gave good guidance to the Egyptians when he saw them engaging in lamentations at their festivals. 'If the objects of your cult are gods', said he,[n] 'do not weep for them; if they are men, offer them no sacrifices at all'.

Others claim[o] that he uttered this thought when the Eleatics desired to know if they should make sacrifices to Leucothia and whether or not to shed tears for her. It must not be forgotten that he was banished from his country, that he retired to Sicily[p] and lived at Zancle[q] and Catana, that he founded the Eleatic sect,[r] that Parmenides was his pupil, and that he complained of his poverty (M). His retort to a man with whom he refused to play dice was very worthy of a philosopher. He called him a coward: yes, replied he, I am extremely so with respect to disreputable activities.[s]

[m] See particularly the Book of Job, and Psalms in various places.
[n] Plutarch, *De superstitione*, at the end, p. 171.
[o] Aristotle, *Rhetoric*, 2.23, p. 447.
[p] Diogenes Laertius[, Lives of the Philosophers], 9.18.
[q] It is the same town as Messena, today Messina.
[r] Cicero, *Academica*, 4. Clement of Alexandria, *Stromata*, 1, p. 301.
[s] 'Fassus est ad res inhonestas . . .' ['He admitted that in base activities he was very cowardly.'] Plutarch, *De vitioso pudore* [On Compliancy], p. 530.

[Remarks (A)–(D) omitted.]

(E) If it were only about harm morally considered.] There
would be a hundred things to observe upon the question as to
whether Pliny is more believable than Euripides and so many other
great men who have supposed that the bad things in human life
surpass the good. Let us pause here a little; and say first that if it
were only about moral or criminal harm [*du mal de coulpe*], the
contest would soon be over in favour of Pliny. For where is the
man who would dare maintain that acts of virtue are as one in a
thousand compared with the crimes of human kind? Let us say in
the second place that if it is a question of natural harm or accidental
suffering [*du mal de peine*] then Euripides will find his supporters.
I shall refer the second point to the following remark [see Remark
(F)], and offer here something on the first.

Though the dogma of the 'two principles' has always seemed
detestable to all Christian communions,[1=56] it has not prevented the
recognition in Christianity of a subordinate principle of moral or
criminal harm [*du mal morale*]. For the theologians teach us that
when a great number of angels sinned, they formed a party against
God in the universe. For brevity's sake, this party goes under the
name of the devil or demon, and it is recognised as the cause of the
fall of the first man, and as the perpetual tempter and seducer of
human kind. This party, having declared war on God from the
moment of its fall, has always continued in its rebellion without
there ever being peace or truce. It continually applies itself to
usurping the rights of its creator and to corrupting his subjects so
as to make rebels of those who serve under its banner against their
common master. Once the first hostilities with regard to man had
succeeded, this party attacked the mother of all living creatures in
the garden of Eden and vanquished her; then immediately afterwards it fell upon the first man and overthrew him. Thus you see
it as the master of the human race. Yet God did not allow it to keep
this prey; but he delivered human kind from its slavery, rescuing it
from its state of corruption by virtue of the satisfaction that the
second person of the Trinity was able to exact for his justice. This
second person undertakes to become man, and to take on the task

[1=56] For the Marconites, Manicheans, etc., do not deserve the name of Christian.

of mediator between God and the human species, and redeemer of Adam and his posterity. He undertakes to fight the party of the devil so that he might be leader of God's party against the party of the devil who was leader of the rebel creatures. It was a question not of conquering all the descendants of Adam, since they were all under the power of the demon, because of the circumstances of their birth; it was about conserving or recovering the conquered territory. The purpose of the mediator, Jesus Christ the Son of God, was to retrieve; that of the devil was to hold firm. The victory of the mediator would consist in making men walk in the path of truth and virtue; that of the devil would consist in leading them through the ways of error and vice. So that to know if moral good [*le bien morale*] equals moral evil [*le mal moral*] among men, one has only to compare the victories of the devil with those of Jesus Christ. Furthermore, in combing history we find only a few triumphs for Jesus Christ,

Apparent rari nantes in gurgite vasto,[2=57]

and we encounter everywhere the ravages of the devil. The war between these two parties is a continuous, or nearly continuous, process of conquests for the devil's side, and if the rebel party were to keep chronicles of its exploits, there would never be a day that was not marked with abundant occasion for celebratory bonfires, triumphal anthems, and other rituals of mighty success. There would be no need for the gazetteers to use hyperbole or flattery to have the superiority of this faction recognised. Sacred history[3=58] speaks of only one virtuous man in all Adam's family, and reduces the family of that good man to a single virtuous man and so on, through subsequent generations until Noah, in whose family are found three sons whom God saved from the deluge together with their father, mother and wives. . . .

Error and vice soon raised their heads in Noah's family after the flood. His descendants sank into idolatry and all manner of depravities . . . That is to say, the devil kept his usurped power over them. As to orthodoxy, there was no more than a handful of people, confined to Judaea, that escaped the devil, and further-

---

[2=57] ['Men are seen swimming here and there in a vast open sea,'] Virgil, *Aeneid*, I.118.
[3=58] Compare this with Remark (G) of [*Dic*,] article 'Orosius'.

more the arms of the true party were somewhat unreliable with respect to that also, since every so often the people lapsed into idolatry so that their conduct was an alternation between true worship and false worship. And with regard to vice there was never a real interregnum among the Jews, any more than among other peoples, and consequently the devil kept one foot in the small domain which the true party recovered. There came a happy revolution at the birth of Jesus Christ; his miracles, his Gospels, and his apostles made splendid gains. The empire of the devil received a very great reverse, and a considerable part of his territory was wrested from him. But it did not retreat so far, or without leaving behind an intelligence network and a great many officials. It maintained itself by planting abominable heresies. Vice was never entirely uprooted, and soon after it re-entered as if in triumph. Error, schism, contention, and conspiracy were introduced, together with that deadly train of shameful passions which generally accompany them. The heresies, superstitions, massacres, frauds, extortions and debaucheries which have appeared throughout the Christian world for many ages are matters which I could only imperfectly describe though I had the eloquence of Cicero. What was said by Virgil is true to the very letter.[4=59] Thus while the devil reigned supreme outside the frontiers of Christendom, he continued to dispute territory within it in such a way that the progress of his arms was incomparably superior to that of truth and virtue. In the sixteenth century he was checked and perhaps forced to retreat a little, but what he lost on one side he regained on the other. And what he did not achieve by lies he gained by the corruption of manners. There is no asylum, no fortress in this particular depravity where the devil does not make men feel the effects of his power. Leave the world, incarcerate yourself in a monastery and he will follow you. He will introduce intrigues, envy, faction, or if he can do no worse, lewdness. This last resource is almost infallible: 'Diaboli virtus in lumbis est' ['The devil's power is in the loins'], says Saint Jerome.[5=60] ...

[4=59] 'Non mihi si linguae . . .' ['Had I a hundred tongues and a hundred mouths, or an iron voice, I could not cover every type of crime.'] Virgil, *Aeneid*, 6.625.
[5=60] Montaigne, *Essais*, bk 3, ch. 5, p. 134.

Let us take note of two things: that war lasts at least as long as peace among Christians. I limit myself to Christianity because it is unnecessary for me to speak of infidel nations; for they are continually in the service of the devil, and subject to his empire; and there, the usurper is not in the least disturbed. It cannot be denied that warfare is the devil's time or, if I may so express it, his turn to reign. For without mentioning the violence and the debaucheries, everyone in wartime is necessarily obliged to declare that he will suffer no injuries. Either he must renounce his profession completely, or take revenge for an affront. Now this, manifestly, is to withdraw allegiance from the empire of Jesus Christ and to desert to the other camp. Peacetime may not seem so favourable to the empire of the devil, and yet it is very much so, insofar as people enrich themselves,[6=65] they become more voluptuous, and they wallow even more in debauchery and idleness. My next remark is more decisive. Catholics and Protestants agree that very few escape damnation. They allow none to be saved except the orthodox who lead good lives and repent their sins in detail at the point of death. They do not deny that habitual sinners may be saved by a sincere death-bed repentance, but they maintain that nothing is more rare. Accordingly, it is plain that for one man saved there are perhaps a million damned.[7=*] Moreover, in the war which the devil wages against God, the issue is about winning souls; it is therefore certain that victory is on the devil's side; he wins all the damned and he loses only the small number of souls predestined for paradise . . .[8=66] Death puts an end to the war; Jesus Christ does not fight to save the dead: so we must say that this war ends with the advantage on the devil's side. . . .

Observe that everything that I have been saying is preached daily, and without anyone pretending to award victory to the Word Incar-

[6=65] 'Nunc patimur longae . . .' ['We now suffer the evils of a long peace. Luxury more dire than warfare has taken hold of us, and punishes the world it has conquered.'] Juvenal, *Satires*, 6.292.

[7=*] [The comment which follows was inserted by the editors of the edition of 1820–4.] David Durand, author of *La Vie de Vanini*, 1717, reproaches Bayle for having reproduced powerfully and eloquently the arguments of Vanini without reporting the reply given to them by Vanini himself, and for advancing certain arguments repeated later by Joly. Joly gives certain facts about Vanini, this victim of fanaticism, which, as might be expected, are not to his advantage.

[8=66] That is to say, all those whom he has gained in making the first man fall since, from that moment, the whole of posterity becomes slave to the devil.

nate. No one wishes to say otherwise (which is also my opinion), namely, that man is, by his nature, so naturally prone to do harm that, except for the small number of the elect, all other men live and die in the service of the evil spirit [*l'esprit malin*], and they render the paternal love of God ineffectual either to remedy that malignity [*la malice*], or to bring them to repentance.

(F) His meaning was that the sweet things of life do not equal its bitter draughts.] Those who hold the contrary opinion chiefly rely upon a parallel between sickness and health. There are very few persons, they say, of whatever age who cannot reckon on incomparably more days when they feel well than when they feel ill, and there are many who in the space of twenty years do not have as many as fifteen days' illness together. But this comparison is deceptive[9=68] since health considered alone is rather an indolence than a sense of pleasure. It is more of an exemption from misery than a good, while sickness is worse than a privation of pleasure. It is a positive state which plunges the mind [*l'âme*] into a sense of suffering and which weighs it down with pain. It has been judiciously said[10=69] that health on its own is a good which is not much appreciated, and that sometimes it serves only to make us desire more ardently all the other pleasures which we cannot have. Let us make use of a comparison taken from the Scholastics. They say that rare or porous bodies contain but very little matter under a great extent, and that dense bodies contain a great quantity of matter enclosed in a small volume [*étendue*].[11=70] According to this principle one has to say that there is more matter in three feet of water than in 2,500 feet of air. This is an apt image of sickness and health. Sickness resembles the dense bodies, and health the rare. Health lasts many years and yet contains only a small portion of happiness. Sickness lasts only a few days and yet comprehends vast misery. If we had scales to weigh an illness of fifteen days against health of fifteen years, we should observe what is proved when we weigh on a balance a bag of feathers and a piece of lead. On one side we see a mass that fills a great space, and on the other a body

---

[9=68] See [*Dic*,] article 'Pericles', Remark (K).
[10=69] I believe it was by Mlle de Scudéri.
[11=70] 'Rarum est quod . . .' ['A porous object contains little material within a large compass, but a dense object contains much matter within a small compass.']

that is tiny. However there is no more weight enclosed in the great space than there is in the small. Let us be on our guard therefore against the illusion to which we might succumb in the parallel between sickness and health, and their extent. You are going to say to me that health is important not only because it exempts us from a very great misery but also because of the liberty which it affords us to taste a thousand active and intense pleasures. I grant all this but it must also be considered – there being two sorts of hurt to which we are subject – that it secures us from only one of them and leaves us wholly exposed to the other. We are subject both to pain [*la douleur*] and to sadness [*la tristesse*], two scourges so frightful that it cannot be decided which is the greater. The most vigorous health does not secure us from grief. For grief flows in upon us through thousand upon thousand of channels, and it is of the nature of dense bodies. It encloses very much matter in a very small volume. Distress is enclosed, compressed, heavy. There is more hurt in one hour of grief [*chagrin*] than there is good in six or seven pleasant days. I was told the other day of a man who killed himself after being in a state of melancholy for three or four weeks. Each night he laid his sword under his pillow in the hope that he would have enough courage to end his life when darkness increased his melancholy. But his resolution failed for several nights successively. Finally, he had no further strength to resist his distress, and he cut the veins of his arms. I maintain that all the pleasure that this man had enjoyed for thirty years would not equal the evil [*le mal*] which tormented him during the last month of his life if one weighed both on accurate scales. Return to my parallel of dense and rare bodies and remember that the good things of this life are less good than the bad things are evil. Hurtful things are generally more pure and unmixed than good things; the active sense of pleasure does not last. It soon evaporates and is followed by distaste.[12=71] What appears to us as a great good when we do not possess it, scarcely touches us while we are enjoying it. So we acquire what we have with a thousand pains and a thousand anxieties, but we possess it with no more than a moderate enjoyment. And most often, our fear of losing

---

[12=71] 'Omnium quidem satietas . . .' ['One can have a surfeit of everything: of sleep and of love, of sweet song and of excellent dancing.'] Homer, *Iliad*, 13, p. 636. See a similar sentence of Pindar, quoted in [*Dic*,] article 'Bérénice', citation 4.

the good we possess surpasses all the sweetness of its enjoyment. . . .

Many people say that most individuals who have reached a certain age think like La Mothe le Vayer, who had no wish to pass again through the bad times or the good that he had known in his life.[13=80] If that is so, it might be believed that everyone, all things considered, finds that the pleasures which he enjoys do not equal the pain and suffering with which he is afflicted. I do not allege that no one is content with his lot[14=81] for there is no proof that every man considers himself less happy than unhappy. Four burdens [*incommodités*] combined with twenty benefits [*commodités*] would be sufficient to oblige a man to wish for another state, I mean one where there are no burdens and where there are only one or two out of forty benefits. On the other hand, no one ought to allege against me with Lactantius[15=82] that men are so delicate that they complain of the least hurt, as if they had forgotten all the good things they have enjoyed; for it is irrelevance here to consider what might be the absolute quality of good and harm dispensed to man; we must consider only their relative quality; or, to express myself more clearly, we ought to consider nothing but the feeling of the mind [*l'âme*]. A good, very great in itself, but which arouses only a weak pleasure, ought to pass for only a mediocre good; but a small hurt, though very little in itself, which arouses an anxiety, a sorrow, or an unbearable pain, ought to pass for a very great evil: so that for a man to be considered less happy than unhappy it is enough for him to be afflicted with three hurtful things for thirty good things, if those three hurtful things, though as little in themselves as you please, give him more anxiety than the thirty good things afford him pleasure, though as great in themselves as you please. The position of a governor of a province is, in itself, a much greater good than a decoration; yet if a duke and peer feels more joy on receiving a sash from his mistress than in obtaining the government of a province from his king, then a decoration, I say, is a greater good to him than the office of governor. By the same token, it would

---

[13=80] See [*Dic*,] article 'Vayer', Remark (F).

[14=81] These lines of Horace, *Satires* I.1, at the beginning, encapsulate a very certain fact. 'Qui fit, Maecenas . . .' ['Why is it, Maecenas, that no one lives content with the lot which his judgement has chosen for him or which fortune has cast in his way but praises those who follow different paths?']

[15=82] I have cited these words in [*Dic*,] article 'Tullie', n. 85.

be, for him, a greater evil to be deprived of that decorative thing than to be deprived of his post if he feels more grief over the loss of the decoration than over the loss of his office. This is why no one is able to judge rightly either the unhappiness or the happiness of his neighbour.[16=83] We do not know what another feels, we know only the outward causes of good and harm; and these causes are not always in proportion to their effects; those which seem small to us often produce an intense feeling; and those which appear severe to us often produce a slight feeling. The following words of Tacitus are revealing: 'Neque mala vel bona ...' ['Good and evil are not what they are commonly asserted to be. Many who appear to be afflicted by adversity are happy. On the other hand, a lot of people are utterly miserable although they have great riches. The former endure great misfortune with tranquillity, while the latter experience their favourable circumstances with no consideration.']][17=84] We need only extend the meaning of the word 'consideration' in order for it to embrace that disposition of temperament which causes us to possess the favours of fortune with anxiety rather than joy.

All this indicates that no one can judge with certainty how the destiny of his neighbour has been squeezed from Homer's two barrels[18=85] so that the portion of good is as strong as, or stronger than, the portion of harm. All that can be said with complete certainty is that no man's fate was ever drawn uniquely from the good barrel ... It is certain that those who would like to find people who have felt more happiness than unhappiness would be more likely to meet them among peasants or small artisans than among kings and princes.[19=90] Consider the following words of a distinguished man:

> Do you believe then that uneasiness and the most mortifying sorrow are not concealed beneath the purple, or that a kingdom is a universal remedy against all miseries, a balm that assuages them, or an enchantment that annuls them? Whereas, by the course of divine providence which knows

---

[16=83] 'Felicitas cui praecipua ...' ['The question as to which man has experienced the greatest happiness is not one for human judgement. For each man defines prosperity itself in a different way and according to his own character.'] Pliny, [*Natural History*,] 7.40.

[17=84] Tacitus, *Annals*, 6.22.

[18=85] See [*Dic*,] article 'Manicheans', Remark (C).

[19=90] See Horace, *Epodes*, 2.

how to counterbalance the most exalted conditions, this *grandeur* which we admire at a distance as something more than human is less impressive among those who are born to it, or confounds itself in its own plenty; while among the newly elevated it is accompanied by a new sensitivity to grief whose impact is the harder, because they are less ready for it.[20=91]

Thus you see two sources of unhappiness among the great: their habituation to the pleasant side of their condition makes them unappreciative of pleasure but greatly sensitive to pain. When three pieces of good news, and one of bad, are brought to them, they feel hardly any happiness at the former, but they are caused great distress by the latter. Can there be any advantage not threatened by some disgrace? Consider what Gustavus Adolphus [of Sweden] achieved in Germany, and you will find a surplus of good fortune which has few parallels; yet, nevertheless, you will find mingled with it such a great diversity of disastrous events that you will easily realise that he was beset by countless troubles.[21=92] For when you suppose that the victories obtained in some provinces do not equal the losses that one suffers in others, you have reason to believe that your joy is not at all pure. A hundred unwanted reflections come to disturb it. One imagines that the attack was made too soon or too late; or that one lost too many men, or that one did not follow up the disarray of the vanquished, but permitted them to recover from their confusion; or that by a different strategy one might have had a more substantial victory. How many generals are there who pass the night very uneasily after a complete victory? They are aware that they are in debt to a lucky chance, to a mistake of the enemy, and sometimes even to their own faults. They suppose that they have not done what they might have done. They are apprehensive of the comments of the experienced, and of the malicious reflections of their enemies. In a word, they cannot bear a good testimony of themselves nor internally support the eulogies

[20=91] Jacques Bénigne Bossuet, bishop of Meaux, *Oraison funèbre* [Funeral Oration] *de Marie Thérèse d'Autriche, reine de France*, pp. 78, 79, Dutch edition.
[21=92] For he was obliged to publish manifestos against those who condemned him for not having prevented the taking of Magdeburg [in 1631, during the Thirty Years War].

bestowed on them. This disturbs and torments them. Whilst their consciences are dull with regard to the law of God, they are still moved to the very quick with respect to the transgression of some martial law, and the non-observation of certain rules which a very able general would have followed. Observe that the most successful princes, whether at winning battles or at conquering towns, are those who are afflicted mercilessly by the defeat of an army, or the loss of a city . . .

What has just been said about rulers may be said, proportion-ately, about any person whom providence raises to an eminent post, and who participates in any sort of distinction. Their lot is a package in which anxiety finds it easier to predominate. Great learning and great intellect do not exempt men from this fatality. No, look for happiness rather amongst the most ignorant multitude than amongst illustrious and learned men. The glory that surrounds authors and celebrated orators does not secure them from a thou-sand cares. It exposes them to envy in two unfortunate ways: they have rivals who persecute them, and they are jealous, in their turn, of the praise which is received by others. One typographical error can make them more wretched than four letters of recommendation can cause them pleasure. The glory which they have acquired acquaints them with flattery, and increases their sensitivity to being deprived of it, as well as to censure, and to the sharing of fame. Furthermore, the more learned they are, the more they know that their works are imperfect. If they guard against the weaknesses of prejudice, and against the irregularities of a hundred mean passions, and seek to rule their utterances and their conduct by this state of mind, they are detested, and so are obliged to renounce the pleas-ures of sociability. For not participating in the quest does not put them outside the sphere of its activity. On the contrary, by not entering in, they expose themselves all the more to its ravages. If they conform outwardly to the depraved taste of the world, they reproach themselves a hundred times a day for their ignominious hypocrisy, and thereby they disturb their repose. There are very few who, like Democritus, can appreciate the extravagance of the passions and use it to divert themselves. How enlightened in this respect was that philosopher! Read the 'Letter from Hippocrates to Damagetes', as well as the summary published by an author of the sixteenth century.[22=105] He elegantly and accurately unfolds what the Greek author said in general. He plays with this censure, and one may perceive that he was touched by pain himself, and that had he been asked:

> What dark humour
> Makes you see so contrarily?

He could have replied:

> It is because I am not among that number
> Of authors who are happy.[23=106] . . .

It is time to bring these general ideas to a conclusion. Let me summarise with four small points. I. The first is that if we considered mankind in general, it seems that Xenophanes could indeed have said that grief and pain prevail over pleasure. II. The second is that we can presume that there are a few individuals who taste, in this life, much more good than harm. III. Thirdly, that there are others who, it may be believed, have a far larger share of harm than good. IV. Fourthly, that my second proposition is, above all, probable with respect to those who die before old age; and that my third appears especially certain among those who reach a declining old age. When Racan insisted

> Que pour eux seulement les dieux on fait la gloire
> Et pour nous les plaisirs.[24=108]

he was thinking only about the prime of life. It is then that enjoyment predominates and pleasure tips the scale. That is the time when the pagan Nemesis offers advances and credit, allowing accounts to be rendered without payment; but she obtains her reimbursement in old age. . . .

[22=105] Alardus Amstelredamus. This summary of the 'Letter from Hippocrates' was composed in the Abbey of Egmont in Holland in 1526. The edition used is Salingiaci in [the collection of] Johannes Soter, 1539.

[23=106] These words are from an opera by Quinant . . .

[24=108] ['That the Gods invented glory for themselves alone / And pleasures for us'.] See his letter to Balzac in vol. II of *Recueil des lettres nouvelles*, Paris, 1684, p. 300.

[Remark (G) omitted.]

(H) Of seeking among forbidden pleasures the remedies for their anxieties.] Is this not to deliver oneself from a physical harm through a moral harm? And is the remedy not worse than the disease? And is one not very wretched if one has no better refuge than this? It is very certain that a vast number of people can find no other respite. Domestic brawls and the display of ill management in the home force men out of doors to gaming, or to drinking at the tavern. Without it they cannot drive away their melancholy; and this is the sole distraction with which they assail their anxiety [*chagrin*]. There are even those who deliberately intoxicate themselves to avoid the sorrows of the night, the time when they are most distressed. They find that they are denied their slumber since their thoughts dwell too cruelly upon their misery. Which is why they use wine to procure a profound sleep. It is time snatched from ill fortune, and it secures the most formidable part of the day's twenty-four hours. Generally speaking, women cannot make use of this buttress against anxiety, and therefore their condition is more to be pitied than that of men – which is why Medea in Euripides declares that a woman ill married is in so wretched a condition that it is better for her to die than to live with her husband. For she cannot, like men, go beyond her house to seek out the necessary consolations.

> Et si nobis haec ... ['If we behave well and our husband does not resist the yoke of marriage but stays at home with us, our lives are blessed indeed. If not, it would be better to die. For a husband, when he is upset by problems at home, can go out and calm his anger by turning to a friend or peer. But we can only rely on one person for comfort.']²⁵⁼¹¹⁷

[Remark (I) omitted.]

(K) I am surprised that Rabbi Maimonides ... could have thought that he had adequately refuted the doctrine of which I speak.] He admits that the pagans and even some rabbis have

---

²⁵⁼¹¹⁷ Euripides, *Medea*, 241.

made assertions about the preponderance of harm, which he calls mad and absurd . . .[26=121]

He says that the cause of their extravagant error[27=122] is that they imagine that nature was made only for them, and that what has no relevance to their persons counts for nothing; from whence they infer that when something goes badly for them, all is amiss in the universe. He adds that were we to consider the smallness of man in relation to the universe, we should soon be convinced that the predominance of unhappiness has no meaning among the angels, or the celestial bodies, or among the elements and the mixed inanimate substances, or among many sorts of animal. Yet this observation of Maimonides does not address the point; because those whom he refutes mean only that among men the wretched things surpass the good things . . . Subsequently, Maimonides says that the afflictions of mankind may be reduced to three categories: the first proceeds from man's having a body; the second proceeds from men's machinations one against another; the third is those which a man brings on himself by his own avarice. He makes fine remarks on all this, but they are irrelevant to the question. For the dispute is not about the cause of man's unhappiness, but about whether it is a matter of fact that the afflictions which he suffers surpass the good things which he enjoys. It means nothing to tell us that we, ourselves, are the cause of our misfortune; that we often trouble ourselves without good cause; and that the pleasures of life are countless, and sometimes long lasting. For none of this is capable of solving the difficulty. A grain of evil, so to speak, spoils a hundred measures of good;[28=123] a tiny fragment of iron heated to the seventh degree annihilates more than a hundred feet heated to the fourth degree. No evil is small when it is looked upon as great, and nothing troubles an uneasy man more than to know that he has no reason to be troubled. 'There is', says M. de Saint-Evrémond,

> a sort of pain whose cause I cannot fathom, and since one is not able to find its true nature, I think it very difficult to

---

[26=121] Moses Maimonides, in *More Nebuchim* [Guide to the Perplexed], part 3, ch. 12, p. 355.

[27=122] 'Causa erroris fatui . . .' ['That is the cause of the foolish error of that man and of all his associates.'] *Ibid.*, p. 355.

[28=123] Sea water whose taste is not bearable in fact contains forty or forty-two times more fresh water than salt.

allay, or to preserve oneself against . . . This sort of distress is common to all men. It is the anxiety that makes us fall out with ourselves and which shows us that we have no reason to be troubled, and forces us, in spite of self-love, to confess within ourselves that we are unjust and unreasonable.[29=124]

(L) Xenophanes believed in the incomprehensibility of all things.] Let us begin this remark with a passage from Diogenes Laertius . . . that is: 'Sotion, who says that Xenophanes was the first who maintained that all things were incomprehensible, was mistaken.'[30=125]

One does not learn from these words whether Diogenes Laertius is contesting what Xenophanes had understood by incomprehensibility; for he cannot contest it and at the same time accuse Sotion of error. The accusation would be accurate if, before Xenophanes, others had taught that all objects of our mind are beyond our understanding. There are countless similar such passages in Diogenes Laertius; it hardly does him credit: for an exact mind would have avoided these ambiguities and obscurities. I make the conjecture that he intended to say that Xenophanes did not teach incomprehensibility;[31=126] but at the same time I think that he was wrong to assert it about this philosopher. All the appearances lead us to judge that Xenophanes taught that one could not understand anything in the nature of things. Plutarch attributes to him the view that our senses and our reason are deceptive faculties.[32=127] Others claim that he rejected the evidence of the senses in order to conclude that we must append faith to reason only, and they say that he was the first author to have held this doctrine. 'Sensus visaque omnia . . .' ['They believe that we must utterly reject the senses and all visible things, and that we must trust in reason alone. They claim that Xenophanes

---

[29=124] Saint-Evrémond, *Discours des ennuis et des desplaisirs* [Discourse on Troubles and Anxieties], . . . p. 137. My edition (vol. IV, p. 45), the Dutch one, 1693, contains only part of what that critic [i.e. Saint-Evrémond] mentions.

[30=125] Diogenes Laertius [, Lives of the Philosophers], 9.20.

[31=126] See below citation n. 47=142, the passage from Sextus Empiricus.

[32=127] 'Sensus fallaces esse . . .' ['He argues that the senses are deceptive, and he also criticises reason along with them, as being defective in every matter.'] Plutarch, *Stromata*, in Eusebius, *Praeparationes evangelicae*, 1.8.

and Parmenides were the first thinkers to hold this doctrine.']³³⁼¹²⁸
I believe that Plutarch represents the system of Xenophanes more
faithfully than did Aristocles. I believe that Xenophanes had hardly
any more confidence in reason than he had in the senses: this is
what persuades me. He was the first who taught that everything
which has been made is corruptible.³⁴⁼¹²⁹ He taught also that all
things were only one being; that there was no generation and no
corruption; and that this sole being remained always the same and
could not be subject to any change.³⁵⁼¹³⁰ 'Hi quicquid esset . . .'
['These men were convinced that whatever existed was only one
being, that nothing existed which differed from it, that nothing was
born, or corrupted, or changed in any way.']³⁶⁼¹³¹ But here, more
succinctly, are the principles of Xenophanes connected sequentially.
Firstly, he asserts³⁷⁼¹³² that nothing is made of nothing; that, to
remove all ambiguity, is to say that a thing that has not always
existed can never exist. He concluded from this that everything
which is, has always existed; therefore, he adds, what has always
existed is eternal; what is eternal is infinite, what is infinite is
unique; for if it contains several beings, one of them would put an
end to the other, therefore it would not be infinite. Furthermore,
he says, what is unique is, above all, like itself; because if it contained any difference, it would not be one being but several beings.
Finally, this unique being, eternal and infinite, must be immobile
and unchangeable; since if it could change its position, there would
be something beyond itself; thus it would not be infinite: and if
without changing its place it could be altered, something which had
not existed from all time would begin to be produced, and something which had existed from all time would cease to be. Therefore,
that is impossible; because anything which, not having existed eternally, begins to exist would be produced from nothing, and anything
which has had no beginning has a necessary existence; it cannot

---

³³⁼¹²⁸ Aristocles, *De philosophia* [On Philosophy], 8, in Eusebius, bk 14, 17, p. 23B.
³⁴⁼¹²⁹ 'Primus definivit omne . . .' ['He was the first to define everything which is
made as being liable to corruption.'] Diogenes Laertius[, Lives of the Philos-
ophers], 9.19.
³⁵⁼¹³⁰ See Plato, *Sophists*, p. 170C.
³⁶⁼¹³¹ Aristocles, in Eusebius, [note 33=128] above.
³⁷⁼¹³² See the treatise by Aristotle on *Xenophanes, Zeno* and *Gorgias*, in his *Works*,
vol. I, Geneva edition, 1605.

therefore ever cease to exist. Thus you can see, if we are to accept Aristotle, what his principles were.[38=133] I do not doubt at all that they seemed evident to him and that he believed that, in them, there was a train of consequences necessarily drawn from an incontestable principle. Orthodox theologians deny his principle that nothing can have a beginning. But they concede that the being that has never had a beginning is unique, infinite, immobile, and unchangeable; and that everything whose existence is necessary is indestructible. They teach, and reasonably, that God is subject to no change; since if any change occurred he would either acquire something or lose something. What he acquired would either be distinct from his substance, or a mode identical with his substance. If it were a distinct being, God would not be a simple being; and, which is worse, he would be composed of a nature both created and uncreated.[39=134] If it were a mode identical with his substance God would be able to produce from it only by producing himself: therefore, since he exists independently of his will and since he did not give himself his existence in the beginning, it follows that he can never give it to himself. Furthermore, nothing that exists necessarily can cease to exist, therefore it must necessarily be the case that God can never lose what he once had. Further, everything that one calls a modification or *ens inhaerens in alio* [one being clinging to another] is of such a nature that it cannot be produced except through the destruction of another entity [*modalité*], just as when a new figure is necessarily the destruction of the old. This is why, were God to acquire something new, he would necessarily lose some other thing; because this new acquisition would not be a substance but an accident or an *ens inhaerens in alio*. Therefore, since nothing which exists necessarily can cease to exist, it follows that God can never acquire anything new. Here you see the immutability of God based on evident ideas. Xenophanes added to these maxims the following: that nothing is made from nothing, or that each accident produced anew and distinct from divine substance would be drawn from the nothing. It must be denied therefore that the eternal being could acquire any new mode distinct from its own substance. But he

---

[38=133] *Ibid.*

[39=134] When a being is distinct from another it is not composite; thus every being distinct from every other being is made out of nothing; it is thus created.

found himself very embarrassed when they drew his attention to the continuous generation that occurs in nature, and that they are not false appearances. They prove both that the universe is not a single being, and that it contains something that is changeable, since it actually changes. To extricate himself from this objection he denied the evidence of the senses. He said that they deceive us; that it is not true that there is generation in nature, and that they are only false appearances. But, it was doubtless said to him, the appearances of the senses would not change if our mind remained always the same, and if the beings that are outside us do not change in any way; it is therefore necessary at least that what in us is the passive subject of the perceptions (what you call the deception of the senses) comes from a moveable and alterable being; it is thus not true (as you claim) that no change occurs in the universe. I do not see that he could have replied in any other way than as follows. Our reason is as fallible as our sense perceptions; everything is incomprehensible to it. For if our reason, even when it is based on evidence which is *non plus ultra* [incapable of improvement], does not encapsulate the truth, then this is a sign that the truth is an incomprehensible and impenetrable thing. Furthermore, relying on notions of evidence, I had insisted that nothing can be made out of nothing: from which it follows necessarily that nothing can begin, and everything that has once existed always exists, which proves evidently the immobility and the immutability of everything; I had, I say, understood that clearly, and nevertheless the experience of my senses and my feelings convinces me that I am changeable; thus I have understood nothing with certainty; and thus I have no faculty proportioned to the truth. It was in this way, we can suppose, that he reasoned, and from this we can conclude that the sects of the Acataleptics[40=135] and the Pyrrhonians had as their cradle nothing other than the principle of the immutable unity of all things maintained by Xenophanes.

I do not claim that he was right in the consequences that we have just seen; I assert all this only so that one may see that I refute this philosopher[41=136] out of the proper motives of the

---

[40=135] It was they who taught incomprehensibility.
[41=136] See my citation from Diogenes Laertius at the beginning of this remark [30= 125].

historian. I have on my side firstly the testimony of Sotion,[42=137] that of Cicero,[43=138] that of Plutarch,[44=139] and certain lines of Xenophanes,[45=140] which were not unknown to Diogenes Laertius.[46=141] In the second place, I can say that Xenophanes had principles which necessarily required him, as I have just given proof, to support incomprehensibility. Let us state the lines in which he asserts his position.

> Nullus aperte vir scit, sed neque vir sciet unquam
> De diis et cunctis a me quae dicta fuerunt.
> Namque licet sit perfectum quod dixerit ille,
> Ille tamen nescit, cunctis et opinio in his est.

['No one clearly knows, or will ever know, about the gods and all the claims I make about them. For although someone might say something excellent, he does not know for certain that it is so, since, in every one of these matters, it is simply his opinion.'][47=142]

In these words one sees manifestly that Xenophanes says that no one can arrive at a clear and certain knowledge of the truth; and that although a man may encounter the truth, he could not know that he had encountered it. In all matters, he continues, there are only opinions to grasp. Sextus Empiricus[48=143] places him firmly among those who denied that there is a *criterium veritatis*, or a rule, or a measure, of the truth. I admit that he does not adopt the view[49=144] of those who number him among the Acataleptics, but he attributes to him, however, the belief that one could never understand anything with the degree of certitude which amounts to knowledge [*la science*]; and that one never attains anything other than judgements of apparent truth [*vraisemblance*], or probability [*probabilité*]. Is that not, at base, to support acatalepsy, or the incomprehensible nature of things? . . .[50=147]

[42=137] See above, n. 30=125.
[43=138] See below, n. 50=147.
[44=139] See above, n. 32=127.
[45=140] See citation n. 47=142, relating to Sextus Empiricus.
[46=141] He cites them at the beginning of *Vita Pyrrhonis* [Life of Pyrrho], 9.72.
[47=142] Xenophanes, in Sextus Empiricus, *Adversus mathematicos* [Against the Mathematicians], pp. 146, 157, 280. See also Plutarch, *De audiendis poetis* [On Heeding the Poets], p. 17E.
[48=143] *Ibid.*, p. 146.
[49=144] *Ibid.*, and pp. 156, 157.
[50=147] Menagius, in Diogenes Laertius [, Lives of the Philosophers], 9.20.

In respect of the particular question as to whether this philosopher is the first to have opted for incomprehensibility, as Sotion
asserts, it is no longer a subject on which to suspend judgement,
since Plato says that before Xenophanes others believed in the unity
of all things,[51=148] a dogma which seems to me to be the high road
to incomprehensibility. Nothing is more curious than the lines of
Timon reported by Sextus Empiricus . . .[52=149] . . .
I observe in passing that the Jesuit who commented on Cicero's
De natura deorum [On the Nature of the Gods] took the side of
Xenophanes against Aristotle somewhat inconsiderately.

> Dubio procul exciderit . . . ['Without doubt the said Velleius
> failed to notice the judgement which Aristotle cast upon
> Xenophanes in the *Metaphysics*, 1.5, where he remarks on
> the obscurity of that person, both in his manner of thinking
> and in the expression of his thought. Moreover he has con-
> tempt for Xenophanes as being uncultivated and a man of
> considerable negligence, and he thinks that he should be
> excluded from the whole confraternity of philosophers.
> However, he attributes to Xenophanes that view about God
> which suggests a mode of thinking which is far from unculti-
> vated . . .']53=155

That priest was greatly in the wrong to attribute to Xenophanes
a reasonable position on the nature of God; for the opinion of this
philosopher on that subject is an abominable impiety. It is a Spinozism more dangerous than the one I refute in the article on Spinoza,
because Spinoza's hypothesis carries within it its own antidote
through the mutability, or the continual corruptibility which,
having regard to its entities [*modalités*], it attributes to the divine
nature. This corruptibility overturns common sense, and shocks
both ordinary and distinguished minds; but the immutability of all
matter, which Xenophanes attributes to the infinite and eternal
being, is a dogma of the purest theology; it can thus be very persuasive in favour of the rest of the hypothesis. . . .
But the Jesuit, whom I refute, was not wrong in everything; for
he is able with justice to condemn Aristotle for scorning the intelli-

[51=148] Plato in *Sophist*, p. 170.
[52=149] Sextus Empiricus, *Pyrrhoneioi Hypotuposeis* [Outlines of Pyrrhonism], 1.33, p. 46, edition of Geneva, 1621.
[53=155] Lescalopier, in his comments on Cicero, *De natura deorum*, 1.28, p. 44.

gence of Xenophanes; although a true greatness of mind and a strong capacity for reasoning do not allow one to fall in this manner, it is however true that a moderate intelligence would never fly so high as Xenophanes, nor fall so low. He reasoned more consequentially than Aristotle, who, admitting no creation, recognised an eternal matter susceptible successively to an infinity of shapes. For, if elephants have not to fear such spiders' webs, flies should fear them even less. It is not mediocrity of spirit which makes one doubt[54=156] one's capacity to arrive at a legitimate certainty[55=157] – mediocrity is more suitable for inflating one's confidence than for raising one's doubts[56=158] – and one can say of the Acataleptics, 'faciunt intelligendo ut nihil intelligant' ['they convey by understanding that they understand nothing'].[57=159] They arrive at the dogma of incomprehensibility not through knowing nothing about it, but through apprehending such things far better than the greatest part of the world apprehends them; although they do not know them in the right way. . . .

The Socinians themselves are, in certain respects, Acataleptics; they cannot say sincerely that it is not incomprehensible that a nature which exists of itself is changeable. It seems, therefore, that in certain respects their boldness surpasses that of Xenophanes. He, finally, takes the position of saying that he understands neither whether an eternal nature is changeable, nor whether it is unchangeable; but as for them [the Socinians], they conclude that it is changeable: from which it follows that a being which exists from all eternity is indeed destructible,[58=164] and that is the one thing in the world which is most contrary to the evidence of our ideas.

I cannot conclude without making the following two obser-

[54=156] Socrates, Zeno of Elis, Arcesilaus, and similar adversaries of certitude were the most sublime minds of antiquity.

[55=157] 'Qui plura novit . . .' ['He who knows much has all the more doubts.'] Gabriel Naudé, *Addition à la vie de Louis XI* [Addition to the Life of Louis XI], p. 38, cites this as from Aristotle, *Rhetoric*; but others cite it as from Aeneas Silvius.

[56=158] 'Imperitia audaciam, ratiocinatio vero metum affert.' ['Ignorance makes one bold, whereas reasoning makes one fearful.'] Thucydides, 2, p. 26A.

[57=159] Terence said the same concerning another matter, in the prologue to *Andria*.

[58=164] They say that in making the world God gave to matter the form that he wanted to give to it. He thus destroyed the eternal form of matter. Whether this form made a mode or a distinct accident is of little importance. It was a real thing which perished, although it had never begun, and had no efficient cause.

vations: firstly, that the evidence from the principles of Xenophanes on the immutability of what is eternal accords, in every degree, with what one sees in the clearest notions of one's mind; so that besides it being incontestable that change takes place, evidenced by things that take place outside ourselves, the best position that our reason can adopt is to say that everything, apart from God, has a beginning. You see here the dogma of creation; because to claim to explain nature's generation (through postulating several eternal principles, whose diverse actions and reactions diversify what would otherwise remain uniform, should nothing external intervene) is to flee from one inconvenience by leaping into a greater one. My second observation is that the evidence of these principles of Xenophanes provides us with an excellent demonstration against Spinoza, for if everything which has no point of beginning is unchangeable, the God of Spinoza is incapable of any change; for he is thus not the immanent cause of the changes which take place in the universe.[59=165] Every immanent cause produces something in itself; for this thing is either a mode that is *identical* with the substance that it modifies, or it is a quality, absolutely and really distinct from its subject of *inhesion*. If it is an identical mode, God cannot produce it; for, since that divine substance exists necessarily, it cannot follow from any efficient cause. If it is a distinct quality, God can, therefore, create beings distinct from himself, and from that moment the hypothesis of Spinoza has no further place. Add to this that the production of one mode or accident[60=166] is the destruction of another; from which it follows that if God were the immanent cause of change in nature, there would be eternal modes which would have perished; for Spinoza would not have been able to say, without contradicting himself, that what he calls God did not always have modes. Examine his distinction between *natura naturans* [a nature that creates nature] and *natura naturata* [a nature created by nature], and you will see that it is, at base, a receptacle of contradictions.

[59=165] Note that if the Church Fathers had believed what the minister [Pierre Jurieu], author of the *Pastorales*, imputes to them concerning the generation of the Word, they would have had, on the mutability of God, a notion almost as impious as that of Spinoza. See [Bayle,] *Janua coelorum reserat* [Heaven's Gate is Closed, *OD* II, pp. 817–902], pp. 128 *et seq.*

[60=166] I refer to the accidents which are *ens inhaerens in alio*.

(M) He complained of his poverty.] I am so poor, said he one day to Hiero, king of Syracuse, that I can afford to keep only two servants. Fancy that, replied Hiero:[61=167] Homer, whom you never cease to decry and dead though he is, was able to support ten thousand!

[61=167] Plutarch, *In Apophthegm.* Amyot's version, p. 157.

Clarifications: On Atheists *and* On Obscenities

[Shortly after publication in 1697 formal charges were laid against the Dictionary at the instigation of Pierre Jurieu. Its references to Epicureans and atheists, and its obscenities, the theologian alleged, were offensive to religion. After deliberating for a year, the Consistory of the Calvinist Church in Rotterdam cleared Bayle but on condition that he made changes. (See Dic, vol. XVI, pp. 287–300.) In the second edition of 1702 Bayle accordingly amended the articles 'David' and 'Xenophanes', and included four vindicatory essays. The latter were entitled: I. On the praises bestowed on certain persons who have denied either the providence of God, or the existence of God. II. On the objections to the Manicheans. III. On the objections to the Pyrrhonians. IV. On obscenities. *Of these Clarifications the First and the Fourth are included here.*

Bayle denied the charge that he had defended atheism, explaining that he had sought to examine a more testable proposition that had a bearing on the persecution of the religiously unorthodox: namely, whether human conduct was motivated solely by the individual's love or fear of God, or whether by a combination of natural factors such as love of praise and fear of disgrace. A political reading of the defence indicates that Bayle's target was not religion's truth, but religion's supposed utility, and the fallacy of the age, believed by politiques *to be true, that a public religion was an indispensable instrument of government. The persecution of sects, in Bayle's view, had been reinforced by this fallacy and the error continued to block the way to true toleration and freedom.*

Bayle's First and Fourth Clarifications insisted therefore that a 'utilitarian' case, not just a 'humane', or 'charitable' case, should be made for religious and intellectual diversity. The well-governed republic had everything to gain from examining all ideas, and by ensuring the freedom of the printed word.]

First Clarification: On Atheists

The comments that have been made in respect of the good morals of certain persons who had no religion at all cannot in any way prejudice the true faith, and are no affront to it.

Those who have been offended at my saying that there have been atheists and Epicureans whose propriety in moral matters has surpassed that of most idolaters are entreated to reflect carefully upon all the considerations which I am going to propose. If they do, their indignation will evaporate and entirely disappear.

I. The fear and love of God are not the sole basis of human action. There are other principles that motivate a man: the love of praise, the fear of disgrace, qualities of the temperament, the punishments and rewards available to the magistrates, all have immense influence upon the human heart. Were anyone to doubt it, he would have to be unaware of what takes place within himself and what the common occurrences of daily living regularly reveal to him. But does it appear that anyone is so artless as to be unaware of such things? What I have established concerning these other springs of human action may, therefore, be placed among the number of common notions.

II. Fear and love of the Divinity are not always a more active principle than all the others. Love of glory, fear of disgrace or death or suffering, or the hope of preferment, all act with greater effect upon some men than the desire of pleasing God and the fear of breaking his commandments. Were anyone to doubt it they would be unconscious of a part of their own motives and they would know nothing of what takes place daily among humankind. The world abounds with people who would rather sin than offend a prince who can promote or ruin their prospects. Men daily subscribe to confessions of faith against their conscience either to save their possessions, or to avoid imprisonment, exile, death and so on. A soldier who has given up everything for his religion, but finding himself obliged either to offend God if he avenges himself for a trifle, or to be thought a coward if he does not, gives himself no rest until he has received satisfaction for the affront, notwithstanding that he is in peril of killing or being killed, and thereby of being in a state that must be followed with eternal damnation. It is not likely that anyone is so ingenuous as to be ignorant of such facts. Therefore, let us place among agreed ideas about morals the following aphorism: *that the fear and the love of the Divinity are not always the most active principles motivating the actions of men.*

III. That being so, it ought not to be reckoned as a scandalous paradox, but rather as a very likely possibility, that some men without religion are more motivated to lead a decent, moral life by their constitution, in conjunction with the love of praise and the fear of disgrace, than are some others by the instincts of conscience.

IV. There ought to be a greater outrage that so many people are seen to be convinced of the truth of religion while at the same time being steeped in crime.

V. Indeed, it is stranger that pagan idolaters should have performed good actions than it is strange that atheistical philosophers should have lived like virtuous men, since those idolaters must have been encouraged to commit crimes by their very religion. For if they were to emulate their gods, which is the essence of religion, they must have believed that they were required to be envious and deceitful and to engage in fornication, adultery and pederasty, etc.

VI. From which it may be concluded that the idolaters who lived virtuously were guided simply by ideas of reason and decency, or by the desire for praise, or by their natural constitution, or by such other principles as may be found in the absence of religion. Why then should we expect to find more true virtue under a regime of pagan idolatry than under a regime of irreligion?

VII. Observe, I entreat you, that in speaking of the decent morals of certain atheists, I have not ascribed to them any true virtues. Their sobriety, chastity, probity, contempt of wealth, zeal for the public well-being, their desire to be of service to their neighbour, did not proceed from their love of God, and did not tend to honour and glorify him. They themselves were the origin and the object of their behaviour: *l'amour-propre* [love of self] was its foundation and the term is self-explanatory. Their actions were merely *splendida peccata*, glorious sins, as St. Augustine says of all the magnificent actions of the pagans. To say what I have said is thus in no manner to disparage the prerogatives of true religion. It is still the case that truly good works are produced only from spiritual motives. And what is it to the true religion if the worshippers of Jupiter and Saturn are no better in their actions than those who have no religion?

VIII. If those who are offended claim that, with respect to a virtuous life, one cannot praise the decent morals of Epicurus without supposing that it is the same thing to have *no* religion whatsoever as to profess *any* religion, they are defective in the art of consequential reasoning, and they have completely misunderstood the nature of the question. I have compared atheism only with paganism. Therefore true religion is not under comparison, and is excluded from our discussion. The issue is only about cults introduced and inspired by the devil; and about whether those who have professed such forms of worship, infamous in origin and content, have been more regular than atheists in the practice of decent behaviour. I presume, as a point indubitable and fully agreed, that in the true religion there is not only more true virtue than anywhere else, but that outside this religion there is no true virtue at all, nor any *fruits of righteousness*. What purpose does it serve then to claim that I injure true religion? Does it lessen the harm that may be alleged of the false religion? And should it not rather be feared that the display of such zeal will be offensive to moderate people, and over-nice to a cult supposed, by every doctor of theology, to be created by the devil and detested by God?

IX. I could not rightly have taken exception to these complaints had I written a romantic novel in which my characters were depicted as both atheistical and truly virtuous; for since I would have been master of their words and deeds, I would have had the option of describing them in a manner suited to the taste of the most scrupulous reader. But since my Dictionary is a historical work, I have no right whatsoever to represent people as others would like them to have been. I must represent them as they actually were; I can suppress neither their faults nor their virtues. Seeing then that I advance nothing concerning the conduct of certain atheists other than what the authors I cite relate of them, no one has cause to take offence. To encourage my critics to reflect further upon the truth of what I say, I need only ask them whether they believe the suppression of true facts to be the duty of a historian. I am sure that they would never subscribe to such a proposition.

x. Not that I doubt that there are people artful enough to admit that a factual truth [*une vérité de fait*] ought to be suppressed by a historian if it is likely to lessen the abhorrence of atheism, or the veneration of religion in general. But I most humbly entreat them not to take it amiss if I continue to believe that God has no need of the artifices of polemic, and though it might have a place in a poem or in a work of oratory, it does not follow that I ought to allow it in a historical dictionary. They must permit me to inform them that it is sufficient to work for the *right* religion, since all that would be done for religion in general would be as useful equally for paganism as for Christianity.

xi. I should have been much more deserving of censure had I suppressed the facts objected to; for besides contravening the fundamental rules of historical scholarship, I should have omitted matters which, in their essence, are highly advantageous to the true system of grace. I have shown in another place[1] that nothing can be more suitable for demonstrating the corruption of the human heart, a corruption naturally invincible and surmountable only by the Holy Spirit, than to show that those who have no spiritual assistance are as wicked under the practice of a religion as those who live under atheism. I add here that one could give no greater joy to the Pelagians than to say that the fear of false Gods was able to induce the pagans to renounce some vices. For if, out of fear of incurring the wrath of heaven, they had abstained from doing evil, then they could also have been led to virtue through the desire for spiritual rewards, and so procure for themselves the love of God. That is, they might have been able not only to fear but also to love the Divinity, and so act upon this proper principle. The two handles by which one motivates man are the fear of punishment and the desire of reward. If he can be moved by the former he may also by the latter; for one cannot rightly admit the one and reject the other.

xii. If certain persons more than ordinarily fair and enlightened cite, as their sole reason for being offended, the artifice which has been used, in their opinion, of raising the virtuous lives of atheists

---

[1] See *Pensées diverses sur les comètes*, pp. 437, 490, 599; and *Additions aux pensées diverses*, pp. 58, 110. [For these same works in Bayle's *Œuvres diverses*, see *PD*, *OD* III, pp. 1–160; and 'Additions aux *Pensées diverses sur les comètes* ou réponse à un libelle intitulé, "Courte Revue des maximes de morale et des principes de religion de l'auteur des *Pensées diverses sur les comètes*, etc." ', *OD* III, pp. 161–86.]

with my readers, I would beg them to consider that, in the present case, subterfuge could be highly excusable and might even be looked upon as a subject of edification. To perceive this, one need only call to mind an episode of my treatise on *Comets*. The true purpose of that book was to confute with an argument from theology what is commonly said about comets as ill omens.[2]

The need to strengthen this argument led me to draw a comparison between atheism and paganism. For without that, my demonstration would have been exposed to an objection which would have rendered it unfit to evince what I needed to prove. Therefore, it was necessary for me either to leave that objection unanswered, or to refute the arguments of those who say that pagan idolatry was not so great an evil as atheism. The complete success of the encounter depended largely upon the success of this line of argument, and therefore, according to the rules of debate and by virtue of the rights belonging to an author, I was obliged to avail myself of whatever logic and history could afford to answer the objection. It was not, therefore, out of frivolity or perversity that I related certain matters of fact tending to reveal that atheists are not necessarily more disorderly in their behaviour than idolaters. The rules of debate and the right everyone has to rebut the objections to which he sees his thesis exposed thus laid upon me the indispensable need to take such a course. Loud protests were made about this part of my work and some even tried to make it appear pernicious. I was therefore obliged to defend it as far as reason and fact would permit and, consequently, nobody ought to be surprised if, when occasion offers, I tell my readers that history informs us that this or that person, who denied either the existence or the providence of God, or the immortality of the soul, did nevertheless live like a virtuous man. This assertion, which would perhaps be a just cause of offence in another book, is none at all in mine. On the contrary it might edify my readers since it shows that I have not advanced a paradox out of a principle of vanity, but that I have made an observation which is fundamentally certain and which seems false only to those who have failed to examine it. Nothing is more offensive than a

---

[2] See *Préface* to the third edition. [For the full reference in the *Œuvres diverses*, see *PD*, *OD* III, pp. 161–8, 'Préface de la troisième et quatrième édition ... 1699, 1704', pp. 7–8.]

man who, to give himself some distinction, brazenly affects to depart from the common path: but if there are authors who have opened themselves to the suspicion of having such an inclination, not through their own fault but because readers were not thoroughly acquainted with the matter, nothing can be more edifying than to see them justify themselves.

XIII. In order to remove any suspicions of a perverse affectation completely, I have taken care to remark as often as possible on the improper conduct of atheists.[3] If I have not done so more often it was only because the material was lacking. The public was aware that I called for examples to be pointed out to me.[4] Nobody has taken the trouble and I have not as yet been able to discover them by my own inquiries. I do not pretend to deny that in all countries in all ages there have existed persons who, through their debaucheries and their long-standing criminal habits, have smothered explicit faith in the existence of God. However, since history has not conserved their names it is not possible to speak of them. It is conceivable that amongst those criminals, ruffians and celebrated assassins who commit crimes of that sort there are some who have no religion, but the contrary is still more probable given that among the many malefactors who pass through the hangman's hands, there are none that are found to be atheists.[5]

The ministers who prepare them for death always find them ready enough to desire the joys of paradise. As for those profane hearts steeped in excess who, in the judgement of Father Garasse and many other writers, are avowed atheists, I have not brought them into the discussion; the question here being not about people who are called practical atheists – people who live without fear of God though not without belief in his existence – but about those understood as theoretical atheists – as for example Diagoras, Vanini, Spinoza, etc. I mean people whose atheism is attested either by historians or by their own writings. The question turns uniquely upon the moral conduct [*les mœurs*] of this category of atheist. It is

---

[3] As in [*Dic*,] articles 'Bion Borysthénite', vol. III, pp. 445, 448 and 'Critias', vol. V, p. 331.

[4] See *Additions aux Pensées diverses sur les comètes*, p. 86; see also p. 75. [See n. 1 above.]

[5] I speak thus because I do not recall having read any account of the final atheism of this sort of people, nor heard of any.

with regard to them that I wished to be given examples of a dis-ordered life. If I had found any I would have made full use of them. There is nothing more ordinary in history than to encounter reprobates whose repulsive acts elicit disgust but whose very impiet-ies and blasphemies indicate that they believed in the Divinity. Observe that as a natural consequence of the constant teaching of theologians, the devil, who is the most evil of all creatures but incapable of atheism, is the instigator of all the sins of humankind; further, that it follows that the most outrageous malignity of man must have the same character as the malignity of the devil; that is to say that it must be accompanied by the belief in the existence of God. A maxim of the ancient philosophers confirms this reasoning.[6]

XIV. If what I have previously said is capable of edifying sensitive consciences by making them see that the principle which alarms them agrees with the most orthodox principles, they will find no less edification in what I am about to propose. That the greatest reprobates are not atheists, and that since most of the atheists whose names have come down to us have been persons of virtue as the world goes, it is a mark of the infinite wisdom of God, and a reason for admiring his providence. For it has sought to set limits to the corruption of man so that there might be societies upon earth; and if it has favoured only a few with sanctifying grace, it has everywhere dispersed a *restraining* grace,[7] which, like a strong floodgate, holds back the waters of sin to prevent a general inundation which would destroy every state, whether monarchical, aristocratic or democratic, and so on. It is commonly said that the means used by God to achieve this end have been to preserve in the mind of man the idea of virtue, vice and a sense of a Providence which takes care of creation, and which punishes the bad and rewards the good. You will find this idea in the common notions of divinity and in an abundance of other orthodox works. Now what is the logical out-come of this proposition? Is it not to conclude that if there are people whom God does not permit to fall into the systems of Epic-

---

[6] 'Propter quod unumquodque . . .' ['What causes an attribute to apply to a subject always possesses that attribute in an even greater degree.'] Aristotle, *Analyt. Poster.* [Posterior Analytics], 1.2. See also his *Metaphys.* [Metaphysics], 2.1.

[7] I have been informed by a theologian that it is by virtue of this idea that one can speak of God's Providence in the sense that it never permits crime to get so out of hand that it reaches the point of destroying societies.

urus or the atheists, they are principally those brutish beings whose cruelty, presumptuousness, avarice, rage and ambition can swiftly bring about the ruin of a great country? Is it not to say that if he forsakes certain people to the point of permitting them to deny either his existence or his providence, they are principally persons whose temper, education, positive ideas of virtue, love of noble glory, and sensitivity to dishonour serve as sufficient restraint to enable them to do their duty? You see thereby two consequences that follow naturally from the principles of theology which I have mentioned above. Therefore by pointing out to my readers in various parts of this Dictionary that the greatest profligates have had some religion, and that other persons, who have had no religion at all, have lived according to the rules of decency, I have said nothing whatsoever that does not accord with these two consequences; and that it follows that no one can reasonably continue to take offence.

xv. It would be far more legitimate to see the hand of God in all these matters, as well as the admirable way of his providence which attains the same ends through different paths. Thus the *restraining principle* [*le principe réprimant*], so necessary, according to theologians, for preserving societies, exerts its effect by the brake of idolatry in some countries and persons, and by the constitution or strength of ideas and a taste for moral virtue in certain others. The Greeks, inventive and hedonistic, and thereby susceptible to a terrible succession of crimes, had need of a religion that would encumber them with an infinity of rituals. Had the diversity of ceremonies, sacrifices, and oracles not offered them many distractions and if superstitious terrors had not caused them fear, they would have had too great an opportunity to fall into harm. The Scythians, a rough people with neither currency, nor apparel, nor good food, merely despised sensual pleasures or knew nothing of them.[8] This was enough to maintain their republic and to prevent them from injuring one another. They were so fashioned that each was content with

---

[8] 'Aurum et argentum . . .' ['Gold and silver they reject just as the rest of the human race pursue them. This plain living has also produced in them an uprightness of character, since they covet nothing which belongs to others. For wherever riches have a use, people are greedy for them. I most certainly wish that the rest of the human race had the same self-restraint and absence of covetousness . . . In short, it seems strange that what gives them their nature is what the Greeks cannot attain for all their philosophers' precepts and their sages' extensive teachings.'] Justinian, *Institutiones*, 2.2.

what he had. There is no need at all for codes or digests among such people.[9]

Thus you see fifteen considerations which seem to me sufficient to remove the problems which according to some can be found in certain parts of my Dictionary. They might provide the basis for a substantial book, but here I have been content to present them briefly, given that I have discussed them elsewhere[10] in somewhat greater detail, and that I intend to consider them more fully in a future work.[11]

Fourth Clarification: On Obscenities

That if there are obscenities in this work, they are not of the sort that can reasonably be censured.

I. When it is said that there are obscenities in my work one needs to be aware that the following distinct meanings may be under consideration.

1. *Either* that the author, making use of vulgar words, gives a description of his own debaucheries, that he applauds himself, that he congratulates himself, that he exhorts his readers to abandon themselves to impurity, and that he commends it to them as the surest way of enjoying life, and that he asserts that ordinary conventions should be ridiculed and the maxims of the virtuous should be treated as old wives' tales.

2. *Or* that the author relates in a free and jovial style certain passionate adventures, fabricated as to the substance, or at least as to the detail and circumstance; and that he introduces into his narrative many amorous incidents, which he embellishes with every possible relish in order to make them entertaining, and thus more suitable for nurturing the yearning for romantic intrigue than for any other purpose.

3. *Or* that the author, contemplating revenge upon an unfaithful mistress, or to excuse the transports of his passion, or to cast invective upon a courtesan, or to celebrate the marriage of a friend, or

---

[9] 'Justitia gentis ingeniis culta non legibus.' ['This people's sense of justice was cultivated through their natural disposition, not by law.'] *Ibid.*

[10] In *Pensées diverses sur les comètes.*

[11] See the *Préface* to the third edition of these *Pensées* [see n. 2 above].

to divert himself by revealing his thoughts, gives free scope to his muses, and writes epigrams, epithalamiums and so on, in a style which is characterised by a number of lewd expressions.

4. *Or* that the author, inveighing against wantonness, describes it too nakedly, too vividly and too coarsely.

5. *Or* that the author, in a tract of physics, or of medicine, or of jurisprudence, expresses himself directly either upon the subject of generation, or upon the causes and remedies of infertility, or upon grounds for divorce etc.

6. *Or* that the author, commenting upon the Latin texts of Catullus, Petronius, or Martial, has inserted a profusion of foul and vulgar expressions.

7. *Or* that the author, recounting the history of a sect or a person whose actions were infamous, has included very ingenuously a great many things which are wounding to chaste ears.

8. *Or* that the author, considering cases of conscience and particularly of the different species of carnal sin, has said many things that modesty cannot easily accommodate.

9. *Or*, lastly, that the author relates historical facts, which have been taken from other authors, which he has accurately quoted: the said facts being vile or immoral; that to contribute a commentary upon his historical narrations and to illustrate them with testimonies, reflections, and evidence, etc. he sometimes reproduces the words of certain writers who have spoken very freely: some in the capacity of physician or jurist, others as soldier or poet; but that he says nothing that constitutes, either implicitly or explicitly, an endorsement of immorality; but that, on the contrary, he undertakes in his many narrations to create an abhorrence for it and to refute moral indifference.

These are, it seems to me, the chief circumstances in which one may encounter writers who can be accused of discussing obscenities. In the first instance cited, these writers deserve not merely castigation of the severest sort under canon law, but they should also be prosecuted by the civil magistrate as disturbers of public morals and as professed enemies of decency.

As to the second, third, fourth, fifth, sixth, seventh and eighth class, let each individual judge them as he sees fit; for they do not concern me, as I consider myself to be in only the ninth category, and it is sufficient for me to consider obscenities of the last type.

Nevertheless I shall make two or three general reflections upon the others.

II. I say in the first case that there are various gradations within the seven classes of writing which I surrender to the reader's judgement.[12=1] One may stay within certain bounds, or one may exceed them, since the distinctions and the degree vary prodigiously. And it would be exceedingly unfair were one to pronounce the same sentence against every writer who falls into the second category. For example, the recent *Cent Nouvelles*,[13=2] or the tales of the Queen of Navarre, or Boccaccio's *Decameron*, do not deserve the same severity as Aretino's *Raggionamenti*, or the *Aloisia Sigoea Toletana*. The authors of these last two works deserve to be banished with Ovid to the first category of obscene authors.

I observe, in the second place, that in all ages an abundance of people have agreed in condemning obscenities; and yet their decisions have not elicited the respect of the authors judged; nor were they such that poets or commentators and so on ever felt obliged to conform to them upon pain of being excluded from the status of moral person. Censors of obscenities seem to be far more capable of closing the question with an arbitrary sentence upon the whole of the republic of letters than of forming a broad senate of opinion encompassing many sorts of person. For within it one should see not only people venerated for the austerity of their lives or their sacred profession, but also swordsmen, professed gallants and, in a word, the sort of person whose hedonistic living was an occasion of scandal. This could be a factor of great weight; for the right to compose wanton verses would, undoubtedly, be a bad thing if it were denounced by the very persons who live in a worldly manner. But though people habitually pontificate against obscene writing, this has never ensured that, henceforward, their judgements could be used to distinguish between decent and indecent authors. In the republic of letters a right, or a liberty, to publish works of this nature has always been upheld. Authors have never allowed such a right to be circumscribed; for many people of merit have prevented its limitation by virtue of the freedom which they

---

[12=1] Note that I am not prevented from confirming as sound the comments I have made in certain places, as for example [in *Dic*] in the article on the poet Lucretius, vol. IX, p. 507, and the article 'Quillet', vol. XII, p. 393.

[13=2] Recently reprinted, Amsterdam, 1701 in 2 vols., in duodecimo.

themselves have appropriated to produce that sort of work; and
without attracting any adverse comment, and without rendering
themselves any less eligible for every honour and every privilege
belonging to their estate, or for acceding to the preferments that
fortune has promised.[14=3] . . .

III. Let us see if the Protestants have been more severe. . . .

The exhortations of Theodore Beza did not prevent Theodore
de Juges from bringing out an edition of Petronius with prolegomena in which he sought to justify those who commented on the
salacious conduct of the Romans. We find that Theodore de Juges
suffered no damage either to his reputation or his fortune . . . Let
us not, then, be at all surprised if the faction which opposes those
who condemn obscenities has always protected itself in the republic
of letters. For, as well as advancing many reasons for their opinion,
its members shelter under the authority of many examples. You
may see those two lines of argument in the prolegomena of Petrone
de Goldast. All those who have defended authors who, in the
capacity of physician or casuist, discuss obscene[15=13] material, are
able to pit argument against argument, and authority against authority. They lack neither great names nor serious testimony.

> . . . magnos se judice quisque tuetur.

['Everyone maintains that great men support their view.'][16=14]

But do not, I entreat you, suppose that I wish to place the arguments of protagonists and their adversaries on an equal footing. For
I have declared often enough and in several places that I wholly
condemn the lewdness of Catullus and that of his imitators; and I
add here that the arguments of those who plead for the freedom to
insert obscenities in an epigram seem to me to be very weak in
comparison with the arguments which oppose it.[17=15] I add also that
an obscenity, slightly coarse, intended only to amuse, seems to me
more deserving of condemnation than an invective which is exceed-

---

[14=3] I do not claim to apply this to particular cases exceeding certain limits, or to
those persons who in addition deserve infamy in consequence of their actions.

[15=13] See [*Dic,*] article 'Albert the Great', Remark (D); 'Sanchez (Thomas)', Remark
(C).

[16=14] Lucan, *Pharsalia*, 1.127.

[17=15] One may compare the reasons for and against if one reads Father Vavasseur in
the book *De epigrammate* [On the Epigram], ch. 2, entitled 'De obscenitate in
epigrammate vitanda' [On the Avoidance of Obscenity in Epigrams].

ingly coarse, but intended to inspire a horror of lubricity. And as for the obscenities of the theatre I am strongly of the opinion that magistrates should treat them severely. They can only be a school for corruption, and belong more to the first category than to the seven categories which follow it, and which are here the subject of my preliminary remarks. I have one more argument to propose.

IV. For I say, in the third place, that should anyone allege that it were better for the writers, who fall into these seven categories, to apply themselves only to serious matters and to treat their work with the degree of modesty required by the Gospel, he would indeed miss the point of the discussion. Such advice, though very good in itself, would not be pertinent since these authors might reply that the question is not about deciding whether they have chosen the better part, and whether they have alighted upon the best possible use they might have made of their leisure and their pen, but that it is solely about determining whether they have taken a liberty punishable under the statutes of the republic of letters, or by the rules of civil order, or by the law of the state. They will have no difficulty at all in agreeing that they could not avoid condemnation if they were to be judged according to the rules of the Evangelist. But they would argue that all authors find themselves more or less in the same position, given that there is not one among them of whom it might not be said that he could have chosen an occupation more Christian than that which he has at present. For example, even a theologian who has dedicated himself to commenting upon Scripture could have put his life to a more Christian use. For would it not be of more value were he to divide his time between devotion to prayer and works of charity? Could he not devote one part of his day to meditating on the greatness of God and the four last things? And could he not use the other part to run from hospital to hospital assisting the poor, or from house to house consoling the afflicted and instructing small children? Since all men without exception, such authors will say, are incapable of giving a good account of their time before the severe tribunal of divine justice, and since all have need of divine mercy, in respect of their surfeit of useless activities and their failure to choose what was the most essential, we request then another jurisdiction. That is, we will ask if we have done things which, either in the judgement of the public, or before the tribunal of the civil magistrate, debase the

standing of a decent man [*honnête homme*], and make him ineligible
for the status, and the privileges, which are enjoyed by men of
honour. We request what cannot be denied to countless honest
women, who go to the theatre or to the ballet, who enjoy gaming
and fine clothes, who look after their appearance and who studiously
assess how to present themselves with the most effect. For they are
not so blind as to be unaware that they fall short of the precepts of
the Gospel; but so long as they do only that, they may properly
claim the name, the quality, the rank, and the privileges of a
respectable woman. They deserve, perhaps, the censure of Christian
moralists, agreed; but until the judgement of the public, or the
magistrate, has attached a mark of infamy to their way of life, one
cannot designate them as dishonest women, and whoever attempted
to do so would be required to make suitable reparation. They can
invoke the custom and practice of centuries, since there have always
been women of virtue who have played cards, who were fond of the
cabaret, the theatre, or jewellery; and who contravened neither the
civil law, nor codes of human honour, nor abandoned themselves
to the disorderly living of courtesans of a certain sort. Thus poets
who too explicitly describe a wedding night can invoke the same
defence. They can acknowledge that their muse might not only have
employed them in a more laudable task, or that a Christian sonnet
would have been preferable, but that even that sort of composition
could have been bettered. It would have been more worthy still to
have prostrated themselves in a life of prayer, emerging only to
serve the sick in hospitals, etc. Thus there is no occupation whatsoever that is not vulnerable to the argument that a better one might
have been chosen – or, that of all the occupations in life, there is
almost none more deserving of censure, if one judges it according
to the rules of religion, than that which is the most ordinary; I mean
the occupation of people who earn a living whether in commerce or
in other legitimate ways. For the most lawful means, humanly
speaking, of enriching oneself are contrary not only to the spirit of
the Gospel but also to the literal prohibitions of Jesus Christ and
his Apostles. It is therefore in the interests of everyone in general
that God should be merciful about the ways in which they employ
their time. The poets of whom I speak, having established the principle, add that they have done no more than follow in the footsteps
of certain persons who were illustrious for their virtue and their

wisdom; that the liberty which they have seized has never died among honest people; that if it had been abused for many centuries to serve only debauchery it would be inexcusable, and that one might properly proceed against the miscreants for their misuse of it; but it would be found that the right of possession was on their side, and that a thing which so many persons of honour have practised is honestly defended.[18=16] Here is a maxim from Pliny on the subject. He was among the finest minds and the most honest men of his age, but he composed verses that were found too wanton.[19=17] He was accused, but he defended himself with an abundance of good examples. Yet he would not cite the Emperor Nero, for I know – added he – that things in no manner become worse because wicked people do them occasionally, but that they are honest because good people do them often.[20=18] That will suffice with regard to poets. Let us now examine whether writers who belong to the other categories under consideration can use the same arguments. There are even those who say something more controversial – that a physician, for example, and a doctor can maintain that it is their duty to explain what concerns generation, anaemia, sterility, childbirth, uterine flux, exactly as one explains fermentation, indigestion, or gout, etc. A casuist will argue that it is no less necessary to instruct confessors and their penitents in the various ways in which one may sin against chastity, or commit every sort of commercial fraud.

In the last resort one must do these authors the justice of not judging their lives by their writings.[21=19] For there is no necessary relationship between the first of these two matters and the second. There are poets who are chaste in their verses and in their conduct; just as there are poets who are neither chaste in their verses nor in

[18=16] I say nothing of the licence which M. de Voiture uses in his poetry. Nor is it only today that poets make vicious use of this liberty. They have for a long time prostituted the chastity of the muses; and they defend themselves by their numbers. Yet one can no longer dispute a possession that they have acquired by common consent over many centuries, and in all nations. Girac, *Réponse à la défense de Voiture*, p. 74.

[19=17] See Pliny, *Letters*, 4.14 and 5.3.

[20=18] 'Neronem transeo, quamvis . . .' ['I pass over the case of Nero, although I know that things are not made worse because wicked men do them from time to time, but that they remain honest because good men do them quite often.'] *Ibid.*, 5.3, p. 289.

[21=19] See above, [*Dic*,] article 'Vayer', Remark (D), vol. XIV, p. 289.

their conduct. Likewise, there are those who are chaste in their verses but not in their lives; just as there are those whose passion is all in the head,[22=20] who are unchaste in their verses but not so in their lives. In the latter case their wanton epigrams are exploits of the mind alone, and their Candidas and their Lesbias are merely fictional mistresses. The Protestants of the Reformed religion will not deny that it was so in the case of Theodore Beza who asserted that when he wrote his *Juvenilia*, which he came to regret so much, he lived a very regular life.[23=21]

v. Following these general remarks, let us now apply them to the particular case of my Dictionary. Let us begin by saying that if one refuses to accept them as good arguments, then that in no way prejudices my position, but if one does accept them then they will serve me very well. I argue that I am situated in an infinitely more favourable position than the other authors I have mentioned;[24=22] for though one may condemn Catullus, Lucretius, Juvenal, or Suetonius, one can hardly condemn a writer who cites them. These authors are on sale in all the bookshops. They can do no more harm through the passages which cite from them than they can in the original. . . .

This will seem clearer if I add that, in addition to the definition I have given above[25=23] of the nature of my task, I have avoided three things from which anyone who wishes to avoid well-founded objections should always abstain.

In the first place, wherever I speak on my own behalf I have avoided words and expressions that might scandalise civility and the common well-being [*la bienséance commune*]. That is sufficient in a work such as this, which combines history and discussion of every sort. For to claim that a compilation – in which one introduces matters of physics, letters and jurisprudence according to the various topics under consideration – must be written in conformity with the seemliness of a sermon or a work of piety, or a romantic novel, would be to confuse the boundaries of things, and lead to a tyranny

---

[22=20] Compare with this what Count de Bussi Rabutin related concerning Mme de . . . 'The warmth of lively conversation carried her away and in such a situation she listened happily to all that was freely expressed, provided it was veiled: she even replied in kind believing he would leave if she did not say more than he said to her . . .' *Histoires amoureuses des Gaules*, p. 174, etc.

[23=21] See [*Dic*,] article 'Beza', Remarks (V) and (X).

[24=22] That is, the eight categories of author referred to above.

[25=23] Above, § 9 [p. 321].

over minds. A particular word which would seem too gross in the mouth of a preacher, or in an ordinary novel, is not too gross in the brief of an advocate or in the testimony of a physician, or in a work of science, or even in a work of literature, or in a true rendering of a Latin work, as for example in the account of the unfortunate Abelard. . . .

In the second place, I have avoided expressing in our language the sense of a quotation which contains something too coarse, and I report it only in Latin. . . .

In the third place, I have avoided making any mention, in any language whatsoever, of anything which might have a character of extravagance or affront, and is not common knowledge . . . I cite only authors known everywhere and who are reprinted nearly every year . . .

[In short, Bayle insists, criticisms of his Dictionary can be reduced to two questions, namely:]

1. Whether I have not sufficiently disguised with euphemisms some of the lascivious facts which are found in history, and 2. whether, given that I have not suppressed entirely this sort of fact, I deserve some sort of censure.

vi. The first of these two questions is, strictly speaking, the province only of grammarians, since morals have no relevance to it; and thus these matters are within the remit of neither the intendant of police . . . nor the 'command of the *praetor*'. Moralists or casuists have nothing to do with it either: the sole action they could bring against me being a question of inelegance of style, at which point I would ask to be referred to the *Académie française*, the natural and proper judge of this sort of dispute; and I am sure that it would not convict me, since all the expressions which I have used may be found without any mark of dishonour in its own dictionary.

[Bayle gives examples, including some from the play Les Précieuses ridicules, *pointing out that some moralists had failed to see the irony of Molière's famous satire on the supposed impropriety of certain words and utterances.]*

vii . . .

VIII . . . Thus we see to what the delicate taste of our purists is usually reduced. They condemn one expression and approve another, although it evokes in the mind of the listener or reader the very same idea of impurity. The remarks against M. Mézerai, printed in Paris in 1700, will be highly gratifying to these critics. See note [26=44]. He is condemned[27=45] for making frequent use of the expressions 'concubine', 'bastard' and 'adultery' which 'offend the delicacy of our age'. No one would condemn, I am sure, the expressions 'favourite', 'natural offspring', or 'conjugal infidelity', which have exactly the same meaning. What an irrelevance!

IX. One may find less unreasonable the caprice of fashion which, so I have heard, includes among obscene expressions the words '*lavement*'[28=46] and 'medicine' and substitutes the general word 'remedy'. They had banned the word 'enema' as soon as they realised that it evoked the activity too specifically. Initially they had substituted [for 'enema'] the word '*lavement*' [washing out] whose meaning was more general. But when the idea of '*lavement*' became specific and invoked too much of the activity, they had to abandon that in order not to sully or stimulate the imagination, and they could no longer use the more general 'I am undergoing treatment', 'a remedy was prescribed for him', etc. . . .

To recapitulate this part of my clarification, I observe:

1. That the matter relates not to morality but to grammar, and it is to be decided by those who judge style.

2. That I acknowledge humbly that I do not seek the glory that such a degree of politeness might procure.

3. That it does not seem to me that every author is obliged to submit themselves to such a style for, if they did, one would need a further dictionary for *précieuses* and pedants.

4. That the rules of this new politeness are not so well established that they have acquired the force of law in the republic of letters,

---

[26=44] In which Mézerai reported that a priest was dismissed on being surprised with a woman, and mutilated in those parts which are of no use to a good ecclesiastic. The author of the *Observations*, p. 64, criticises him in the following manner: 'Would it not have been more felicitous if he had written only that "he was mutilated"? Would not the rest have been fully comprehensible? And, in any case, could he not have found a less scandalous mode of expression?'

[27=45] On pp. 18 and 19.

[28=46] See *L'Apologie de Garasse*, p. 107.

since the former right[29=47] still exists and one may use it until it is repealed.

5. That, in a work such as this, it suffices not to offend universally received usage; but while respecting this principle with all the care[30=48] I have taken to respect it, it is wholly permissible for me to make use of expressions that would not be fitting in a sermon or a text book. It is allowable if they are appropriate in books of anatomy, or briefs of advocates, or in the conversation of educated people.[31=49]

x. But to show more clearly that the matter in question does not affect morals, I must cite an example given by my critics. Let us see if they can sustain the argument that every expression which offends modesty is an attack on morals since it undermines chastity. I first make the following observation: that all who assert that certain things offend modesty must mean either that they weaken chastity or that they evoke anger in persons already chaste. One may argue that in the first case their proposition ought to be rejected, and that if women were appointed judges of the question, the proposers would undoubtedly lose their case. Furthermore women, without doubt, are the most competent judges in such matters since they are endowed with incomparably more refinement and modesty than men. Let them tell us, if it pleases them to do so, what passes in their minds when they hear or when they read a crude passage which wounds or which offends against modesty. What they will not say, I am convinced, is that it imprints foul ideas on their imagination, or that it excites lascivious desires in their heart which they have great difficulty in controlling and, in a word, that they

---

[29=47] The friends of M. Ménage were charged with obscenity in 1695 for a book printed with the official privilege.

[30=48] I have even observed the precept of Quintilian regarding those words which the corruption of readers has made obscene. 'Vel hoc vitium . . .' ['There is the fault (of the vulgar innuendo) which is called *kakophaton*. This term applies when perverse usage distorts an expression so that it takes on an obscene meaning: thus '*ductare exercitus*', and '*patrare bellum*' and such expressions used by Sallust in their old and pure sense make us laugh, I am sorry to say. I do not think it is the writer who is to blame, but his readers. We ought to avoid the fault, for we have corrupted decent words by our immorality, and are forced to surrender to vice. Also, the fault known as *kakophaton* applies when the combination of sounds produced by a word resembles something foul.'] Quintilian, *Institutio oratoria* [The Education of an Orator], 8.3, p. 307.

[31=49] As with those of the *Mercuriale* by M. Ménage.

are exposed to temptations which undermine their virtue, and which lead them to the very edge of the precipice. Let us be persuaded that, in place of that, they will rather reply that an idea which excites them in their imagination in spite of themselves causes them at the same time to feel a most unbearable shame, disgust, and indignation. Furthermore, it is certain that nothing is more appropriate for strengthening chastity and for erasing the toxic influence of the obscene object which is imprinted in the imagination. So that instead of saying, as in the first sense, that what wounds modesty puts chastity at risk, one is obliged to argue to the contrary that it is a reinforcement, a protection, and a fortification for this virtue. And in consequence if we understand the phrase 'such a thing wounds modesty' in the second sense, we are obliged to conclude that this object, far from weakening chastity, strengthens it and restores it.

Thus it remains true that a prosecution made against an author who has failed to deploy a refined and polite style is effectively a prosecution of grammar in which morals play no part.

XI. If it is replied that the prosecution response is indeed moral, given that the author has expressed himself in a manner which gives pain to the reader, I will respond that they [the prosecution] base their observations on a false hypothesis, since there is no writer who can spare his reader from resentment, grief and outrage in a thousand and one ways. Every writer on controversy who defends his cause with subtlety continuously enrages his readers who are zealots of the opposing party. Anyone who, when recounting his travels or the history of a people, reports things glorious to his own country or religion, and derogatory to the country or the religion of strangers, cruelly distresses readers whose prejudices are not the same as his own. The very perfection of a good history is to be disagreeable to all sects and to all nations, given that it proves that the author flatters neither one party nor the other, but that he gives his frank opinion of each. There are many readers who become so incensed when they read such matter that when they come across them they tear out the page, or write in the margin: 'Wretch, you lie', and 'You deserve to be thrashed!' There is nothing in this that provides a good reason for saying that the authors are indictable before a tribunal for morals. They need answer only before a tribunal of critics.

It remains to argue only that a representation of lewd objects is relevant to morals since it evokes harmful desires and impure thoughts. But this objection is infinitely less valid against me than against those who use the wrappings, detours and delicate manners that it is complained that I have *not* used; for they do not prevent the impure object from being painted upon the imagination, and are indeed the reason why they can be depicted there without evoking feelings of shame or anger. Those who make use of these disguises in no way pretend to be unintelligible. They know very well that everyone will grasp what is involved and that everyone will understand perfectly what they wish to convey. The delicacy of their portrayal produces only this: that people approach their work with less caution than they would were they expecting to confront nudity. One's presence of mind is disturbed only if one casts one's eyes upon naked impurity; but if impurity is wrapped in transparent material, one does not scruple to examine it from head to toe without shame and without feelings of outrage towards the painter. And thus the object may insinuate itself into the imagination more easily, and so touch the heart, and extend its malign influence more easily than if the mind had been overcome with shame or anger; since these are the two emotions which bruise nearly every activity of the mind, and which put it in a state of distress little compatible with other feelings. At the very least it is certain that impurity cannot act so easily upon minds overwhelmed with shame and shock as it can upon minds which experience no confusion and no distress.

Pluribus intentus minor est ad singula sensus.

['When the faculties are considering several things, they can give less attention to each individually.']

What the mind gives to one passion weakens thereby what it can give to another. Add to this that when one depicts an obscenity in part, but in such a way that supplying the rest is not difficult, those whom one addresses arrive by their own efforts at the portrait which sullies the imagination. They thus play a more active part in the production of this image than if it had been explained to them in full. In the latter case they would have been only a passive subject, and in consequence the reception of the obscene image might have been very innocent. But in the former case they become an active subject, and thus they are less innocent, and have more to fear from the contagious consequences of the object, since it is in part their own creation. Thus these supposed ameliorations for the sake of modesty are in fact a dangerous snare. They begin to dwell upon the foul material in order to find the remainder of what has not been expressed in precise words. Is that the sort of meditation that one should encourage? Might it not be better done by the means that prevent people from lingering there too long?

XII. This point is even stronger against those who seek detours. Were they to alight upon the first word they find in the Dictionary, they would easily make their point. But the cloaks which they so artfully seek ... mean that they can spend hours on the problem. They snake around the topic as if they had a certain regret at leaving such an agreeable place ... It is certain that if one excepts those who are truly devout, the greater part of our other purists, through carefully avoiding the expressions of our ancestors, think nothing of the interests of decency. They were the Don Juans by profession who took up with one woman after another, blonde after brunette, and who often enough had two mistresses, one whom they paid and the other who paid them. How easily they sit beside those who quibble over words that offend modesty and who perform such delicate operations with words that leave nothing to the imagination! ...

The Jansenists are considered the most able in the doctrine of morals. Moreover, it is upon their notions that I base my comments when I say that a coarse obscenity is less dangerous than an obscenity expressed elegantly. 'I well know', says one of them,[32=53] 'that one calls "filth" only words that are extremely coarse, and that one calls "banter" [*galanteries*] those words which are uttered in a manner that is refined, delicate, or ingenious: but smut, when under the cover of inventive equivocation as under a transparent veil, is not less unclean, and it is not less wounding to Christian ears ...'
. . .

This Jansenist, having reported certain notions that Father Bouhours had uttered through a character in a dialogue, continues thus: 'There are no parents, I say, not even among those who are the

---

[32=53] *Réponse à l'Apologie du Père Bouhours*, pp. lxiii *et seq.*, 1700 edition. See also *Lettres curieuses de l'Abbé de Bellegarde*, p. 253, The Hague, 1702; and [*Dic*,] Remark (C) of the article 'Accords'.

most worldly, who do not believe that to expose the young to such nonsense is to spoil the mind, to corrupt the heart, and to instil within them the worst sort of character, and that it is more dangerous than gross filth.'[33=55] We have seen above[34=56] a passage from M. Nicole, where it is asserted that criminal passion is more dangerous when it is covered with a veil of propriety . . .

There are people of intelligence who approve of Saturnalia. They will insist that the satires of Juvenal are a hundred times more likely to evoke a disgust of debauchery than the most modest and most chaste diatribes against vice. They will insist that Petronius in his coarse parts is incomparably less salacious than is the Comte de Rabutin, who dresses them up delicately, so that when one reads his *Amours des Gaules* one finds its '*galanteries*' far more likeable than Petronius.

Despite this, one would be wrong to conclude that the lesser harm would be to use the expressions of the street. For that does not follow. I am aware, of course, that the Stoics mocked those who made distinctions between words, and held that each thing must be called by its name, and that given there was nothing indecent in conjugal duty, the act could not be represented by a word that was indecent: meaning that the word used by peasants to indicate it was as good as any other. You will find their sophisms in one of Cicero's letters.[35=58] Perhaps it would be hard to reduce the Stoics to silence through debate; but they do not deserve to be allowed to dispute the issue. For since time immemorial it has proved necessary in all societies and with the unanimous consent of the public for there to be a code of seemliness and decency as an incontrovertible first principle against which one cannot speak. Thus once a people agrees together to treat as improper certain words which even the most uncouth people, who use them habitually, consider improper, and abstain from using in decent company, and would be shocked should they hear them pronounced in a public place, then it should no longer be permitted for individuals to oppose that judgement. Everyone who is part of a society is obliged to respect it. The courts of justice give us a good example; for they do not permit advocates

---

[33=55] See *Journal de Trévoux*, February 1703, p. 312, French edition, on the novel *La Princesse de Porcien*.

[34=56] See citation 11 of the article [in *Dic*] 'Marets (Jean des)', vol. x, p. 239.

[35=58] Cicero, *Ad familiares* [Letters to his Friends], 9.22.

to use the same words when they demand the punishment of those who have used such words to injure their neighbours. Their desire is that public decency is respected in the auditorium: but when they pronounce judgement on the other hand they permit it. For not only do they allow the prosecutor to utter the expressions of the accused, however foul they may have been, but they also insist on it. A counsellor of the *parlement* of Paris informed me some years ago that having attempted to use a substitute for the word on the first occasion he was prosecutor, he was cautioned by the judge that it was not a matter of assuaging chaste ears, it was a matter of assessing the extent of the offence, and that therefore he must utter the exact expression which was at issue. I believe that the Inquisition did likewise. . . .

I perceive a further objection. It will be said that it is an incivility to put in a book what cannot be said in the presence of an honest woman. Therefore, since incivility is an indictable offence morally speaking, the case that might be made against a transgressor is no trial of grammar, but a true trial of morals.

I reply firstly that incivility, morally speaking, is an offence only when it arises out of arrogance, and from a precise intention of showing contempt for one's neighbour; but if one lacks civility either because one is innocently ignorant of good manners, or because one judges reasonably that it is not necessary to follow them, one does not offend . . .

I reply secondly that it is not true that one must exclude from a book every word that one dare not utter in the presence of an honest woman. I cite as my witness a man who is acquainted with the etiquette at court. I mean M. de Saint-Olen. He did not wish to repeat in a serious discourse before ladies what he had written on the matter of marriage among African tribes.[36=64]

The freedom that one may take to say more extensively in a book what one may not say before a live audience is founded on many sound reasons. An obscenity uttered before honest women in respectable company can considerably embarrass them . . . The shame that an obscene idea can evoke is much greater when surrounded by witnesses who can observe our countenance. The confusion and the embarrassment in which an honest woman may find

---

[36=64] In his *Relation de Maroc*, Paris, 1695.

herself is an inconvenient state; nature has made it so. Such an idea arouses in her mind a feeling of indignation, since people do not usually speak in an obscene way before a woman who is believed virtuous, but only before a woman of whom one has a poor opinion. Nothing of that sort is involved with a book. You are required only to read, or not read, what is not very chaste, in your opinion. You can be warned for example about what you will find in my Dictionary in the article on the courtesan Lais, and that it will be illustrated with citations which contain indecent facts: so do not read them. Have the places marked by a *confidant* before embarking on your reading. Tell them to indicate what should be avoided. But over and above that, a woman who is alone when she reads a book is not exposed to the looks of others which is what embarrasses her and which discountenances her more;[37=65] and since the author addresses only an individual, she need not suppose herself to be either despised or offended. . . .

But how does it happen, I will be asked, that an honest woman takes no offence at a veiled word and yet feels insulted by a coarse word? I reply that it is because of the accessory ideas which accompany a coarse word, but which do not accompany a veiled one. The impudence and the lack of respect that she observes in people who express themselves grossly constitute the true cause of her indignation. One may see three ideas underlying this mode of expression: the first is direct and predominant, and the two others are contributory. The direct idea represents the impurity of the object, though it does not represent it more distinctly than any other word that might be used. But the indirect and subsidiary ideas represent the disposition of the person who speaks: his insensitivity, his contempt for the person who listens, and the intention which he has of insulting an honourable woman.[38=71] These are what cause offence. It is not because she is modest that she is offended, for under this notion nothing can offend her except the object which stimulates her imagination: that is, it is not to this thing that she objects, since if it had been imprinted by other phrases as evocative

---

[37=65] The most modest people have no shame when they are alone about the state they are in when they get out of bed, but they are self-conscious if others see them.

[38=71] Compare with [*Dic*,] article 'Beza', in which I cite *L'Art de penser* [by Arnauld and Nicole].

of the obscenity as the coarse word she would not have been indig-
nant. Therefore she is irritated for other reasons, by which I mean
on account of the incivility that is shown to her. For that reason it
happens very often that a women who is a free spirit shows more
outrage than a chaste woman against those who utter obscenities in
her presence. For they take it as an insult, and as a serious affront.
It is thus not love of chastity that animates them but pride and the
desire for self-protection. And, insofar as all women of honour are
angered by a coarse obscenity, they become so out of a very reasonable self-interest. For interest [*la raison*] requires that they are sensitive to an injury which attacks them in their possession of the
respect which is accorded to their sex. Interest [*la raison*] likewise
requires that they maintain a good reputation, which they would
not do were they to be seen enduring patiently the low sort of
raillery that must be suffered by women of a dissolute life.

This is how I prove that it has been impossible to exclude from
this Dictionary everything that might sully the imagination. For
however delicate the language, one necessarily sullies the imagination whenever one mentions that Henry IV had natural children.

Thus it is certain that it is sufficient for me to have kept within
the limits of common decency [*civilité ordinaire*]. For a person who
has a great love of purity, or who seeks to incite no improper desire
in their heart, or who attempts to avoid all thought of obscenity,
could only attain such an end by losing his eyes, his ears, and the
very memory of the many things which he has been unable to avoid
hearing and seeing. One cannot aspire to such perfection as long as
one is able to see people and animals; and as long as one knows the
meaning of certain words which necessarily find their way into the
language of any country. It does not depend upon our receiving
certain ideas at the moment when such and such an object makes
an impact upon our senses, for such notions in any case imprint
themselves upon our imagination. To possess them has nothing to
do with chastity, provided the heart detaches itself from them and
disapproves of them. Were chastity about avoiding any stimulation
of the imagination, one would need to avoid going to temples where
impurity is censured, or where one may read about forthcoming
marriages. One would have to avoid hearing the liturgy read at the
marriage ceremony, or reading the holy Bible – the most excellent
of all books; and one would have to flee all occasions where there is

talk of pregnancy, childbirth or baptism. For the imagination is so agile that it runs from effect to cause with intense rapidity. It finds the path so smooth that it goes from one end to the other before reason has had a chance to restrain it.

There is another argument which teaches those who compile literature that it is enough to stay within the bounds of ordinary common sense. That is that they should not expect that they will be read by people whose ears and imagination are so tender that the smallest obscene particular can cause dangerous surprises. I do not know if they supposed correctly in ancient Rome that the rude words that little pages recited in the nuptial suite came as a shock to the ears of young brides,[39=72] but I am persuaded that today, whatever one's sex, one has only to be in the world for four or five years to know by hearsay countless rude things. This is true mainly in countries where jealousy is not tyrannical. For in such places one sees real freedom: games, conversations, amusing parties, festivals, and country outings are almost daily fare. The aim is only to amuse one another and to raise the spirits. The presence of the opposite sex is very much the reason why obscenities do not enter except in a veiled way, but that does not mean that they are not present under a mask. They emerge in disguise which, as I have proved above, allows the crude object to paint itself upon the imagination just as if one had made use of the rough expressions of a peasant. It is out of fear of being mocked as prudes and *précieuses* that women dare not show their indignation except on those occasions when one overstates these expressions. It is purely a question of terminology, a true dispute about words: the thing intended is communicated, though not every word which signifies it. Thus an author can suppose that he will not take his readers by surprise since they will already be habituated and prepared by common usage. . . .

Let us examine here three objections commonly used. It is said, 1: that doctors or moral thinkers are obliged by the nature of their profession to attend to the detail of such matters but that my work is not; 2: that those who write in Latin can take liberties not permissible in the vernacular; 3: that what was permitted in previous centuries should be forbidden in ours because of today's prodigious corruption. . . .

[Having disposed of the first two objections, Bayle turns to the third.]

[39=72] See [*Dic,*] article 'Lycurgus', Remark (G).

I have some difficulty in believing that the corruption of our times is at all equal to that of the reign of Charles IX and Henry III. But let us not disagree over that; let us employ the *dato non concesso* [granted but not conceded] of the logicians and accept their supposition. I shall deduce from it precisely the opposite of what they deduce. For it is never more necessary to depict the ugliness of crime strongly and vividly than when it does most harm. And it is a poor way of stopping the course of impurity to decry it with smooth words, or to fear giving an odious name to women who prostitute themselves. Furthermore if today's corruption is so great, what purpose has been served by this chastity of words incorporated into the French language – according to the calculation of M. Chevreaux – for at least sixty years? Is it not a sign that the prohibition of these supposedly coarse words has remedied nothing? And who has told you that they must proscribe them for fear of corrupting modesty? Have you consulted those women for whose benefit you refrain from using these expressions? Have they informed you that they are terms which they find a great threat to their honour? Will they not tell you rather that it is to calumniate them to suppose that they are not able to withstand an idea and a word? Will they not rather tell you that if they do want a language which portrays lubricity less outrageously, it is in order to create a notion more faithful to the reality of their nature, and more sensitive to their modesty, than was the idea of their forebears? Therefore they do not fear coarse objects as a temptation, since they only give new vigour to their modesty. They insist on formality rather because of the discourtesy and the incivility that they find in certain words. It follows that those who claim that one must abstain from all utterance of words supposed coarse, given the infinite corruption of our times, are like a traveller who to prevent his muddy coat from becoming fouler refuses to hang it in a smoke-filled room. If the corruption of the heart is so great that a base fact of history can push a young person into promiscuity, be assured that he is already a corrupt young knave whose corrupt condition you fear to worsen by putting him in bad company. A polished style and delicate wrappings will not cure such a person, nor pull him back from the brink.

Assuredly one may discern in this an example of the sophism *non causa pro causa* [not the cause of the issue]. The origin of chastity is not to be found here: you do not get to the root of the problem. It requires other remedies. Such youth are already steeped in obscenity, in words at least, and they will have received their tuition in smut and dirt well before they have read Suetonius. Carnal conversation, inevitable among young boys who are unattended, does a thousand times more damage than the histories of corruption. Yet, a very able man has said that Amyot's translation of Plutarch 'is dangerous to morals because it depicts images too freely and too frankly, and because it uses expressions which today have a foul meaning'.[40=106] I beg him to let me disagree. Amyot's rendition and expression are nothing by comparison with what one hears and sees in the course of everyday life. Add to this that if his translation of Plutarch were dangerous to morals then it would be so with all other versions, at least those which do not expurgate what is depicted 'too freely and too frankly'.

Here there is no middle ground: it is necessary either that a book make no mention of anything impure, or that our censors admit that an obscenity will always be dangerous however delicately it is expressed. One translation may be more elegant than another, but if they are faithful one will find in them the images of impurity that are recounted in the original. . . .

[Bayle asks if he could be accused of having contravened a maxim of Isocrates but he defends himself.]

'. . . Quae factu sunt turpia . . .' ['You should believe that if a thing is indecent to do, it is also indecent to say.'][41=119] . . . One would need to be demented to suppose that the precept of Isocrates meant that a young person could not give a rendering to a teacher or a parent of their reading of the *Iliad*, or of the exploits and adulteries of the gods.

If one sought to oppose every excess one would assert that it is indecent to steal, to betray, to lie and to kill, and that it is not at all indecent to talk about these crimes; but as it is evident that the precept of Isocrates concerns only sins against chastity, one would be a pedant were one to put that objection to him. The Cynics and the Stoics in justification of their dogma asserted that there was no

---

[40=106] A. Dacier, preface to his translation of some of Plutarch's *Lives.*
[41=119] Isocrates to Demonicus.

harm in any word. Cicero refuted the view but only by relying on the supposition that there is such a thing as natural shame.[42=121]

It is time to bring this dissertation to a close. It has proved more difficult to compose than I supposed. I hope that my defence will seem evident, if not by those who have too much presumption to be able to understand that they are being disabused, then by those who acquired their beliefs either on the testimony of others, or on the basis of arguments insufficiently examined. If they are to be pardoned for having been deceived by specious argument before I gave these ... clarifications, they cannot expect to be pardoned if they continue in their delusion. They would have done well to follow the precept of Jesus Christ who said: 'Judge not according to appearance, but according to a right judgement.'[43=122]

They put their trust in first impressions instead of waiting until they had heard the arguments for each side. Yet to do so is always essential, above all when the matter is about judging a writer who does not follow the most common path. They should first suspect that he had his reasons, and that he would not have undertaken his time-consuming task had he not considered its various aspects more carefully than those who merely read it. This well-founded presumption should inspire patience and diligence as well as suspension of judgement. But what is done is done. One can only hope that second thoughts will prove better than first.

I shall warn my readers that immediately after many passages in this Dictionary, they will find my justification for topics[44=123] that may shock tender minds. . . .

[42=121] 'Nec vero audiendi . . .' ['We should pay no attention to the Cynics, or to the Stoics who are practically Cynics, who criticise and make fun of us for maintaining that it is shameful to name in words deeds which are not base, while certain other deeds, which are base, we call by their actual names. Robbery, fraud and adultery are wrongful acts, but it is not obscene to mention them. To beget children is a worthy act, but it is obscene to mention it. These philosophers attack modesty with many other arguments of the same type. But let us conform to Nature and avoid any reference to what eye or ear cannot approve.'] Cicero, *De officiis* [On Duties], 1.35.
[43=122] John, 8:2.
[44=123] Principally with regard to obscenities.

Index

Entries in SMALL CAPITALS and page numbers in **bold type** denote Dictionary articles; letters in **bold type** refer to Bayle's 'Remarks'.

the real world, 86; analogous to theorems of geometry, 87; that the ship of state should be steered from a sidewind, 98–9; and the aims of republics, 97–9; must resist injustice, 107–9; must pursue goals with determination, 106–10; by peoples, turbulent, 113; must use suitable and flexible means, 116–117; by women, 140; those who govern states, duties of, 176–7; *see also* BODIN; HÔPITAL, de l'; MÂCON

governments and *parlements*: their need for mediators, 110–13; republic's vulnerability to their reciprocal abuse and neglect, 104–6; and the example of de l'Hôpital, 110–13; *see also* BODIN; government; *parlements*

Greece and Rome, de l'Hôpital resembled the most eminent men of, 96

Greek and Latin languages, 6

Greek philosophers, 210

Greeks, compared with Scythians, 319–20 and n

GREGORY I, Pope, 47, 48; **64–78**; biography, 64–7; and conversion of the English, (D) 67–9; want of principle in making conversions, (E) 69–74; credulity when reporting miracles, (R) 74–8; his *Dialogues* cited, 67; converted the French, 69; saw little difference between infidels and heretics, 70; his lack of critical judgement, 76

Gregory of Tours, his *Historia francorum* [History of the Franks] cited as evidence of a priest who expected no resurrection, 77 and n

Gretsérus, Jacques: defended Mariana, 189, 191 n; his *Vespertilio Haeretico-politicus*, cited 189 n

grief, in the human condition, 294

Grotius, Hugo, xxvi, 30, 57; his *De jure belli et pacis* cited, 124 n, 154; *Historia* cited, 154 n

Guicciadini, Francesco, xxvi; his cynicism disapproved by Montaigne, 86 and n

Guise, duc de, 23, 100, 114

Guise, House of, xxviii, 19, 22, 23, 98, 112, 118

Guise, Madame de, 101

Gustavus Adolphus of Sweden, 197

Hamon, children of, 49

Hannibal, 14

happiness: whether the natural state of humankind, 293; and health, 293–4; and temperament, 296; among peasants and small artisans, 296

harm: morally considered, 289; whether humankind intends it, 293; *see also* chaos; war; XENOPHANES

Hartnaccius, Daniel, 254 n

hearsay, 74

Hebron, 45

Hegel, G. W. F., xix

hell, doctrine of, 266, 270, 271

Henri d'Albret of Navarre, 193

Henry III of France, 18, 21, 22, 28, 122, 188, 233, 339; France wretched during reign of, 111; murder of 159, 180, 182, 183; excommunication of, 190

Henry IV of France, xxvii, xxx, xxxiii, 57, 61; 113, 118, 122, 159; assassination of, 180, 181, 187, 189; suspected of seeking to impose Reformation, 188; his response to the book *De rege*, 190; and his prudence, 233, 234

Henry VIII of England, 55, 58

Hercules, 27, 31, 139

hereditary kingdoms: right of eldest in, 53–4; on exclusion from the succession, 53

hereditary monarchies, 58

heresies, xxii and n, 105, 199; rulers no duty to extirpate, xxxv, 158; de l'Hôpital on civil jurisdiction over, 97 n; whether reason for dethronement of a prince, 151; capital vs non-capital penalties for, 238; and the Socinian sect, 247, 251, 264; some teach abominable doctrines, 291; *see also* heretics

heretics, 70, 187; many to convert in the age of Pope Gregory I, 77; de l'Hôpital's policy on, 109; Hotman's defence of, 125; if sovereigns should punish them, 157, 158; Jurieu's

Mennonites, sect of the, 266
Mephiboseth, 47, 48
Mercure français, 188 n
Mersenne, Marin, philosophised with
  Hobbes, 80
Mézérai, François Eudes de, his *Abrégé
  chronologique* cited, 22, 58, 59, 95,
  106, 125 n, 127 and n, 329 and n
Mézeriac, 8
Mical, concubine of king David, 44, 48
Michelangelo, 8
Micraelius, Johann, his *Syntagma* cited,
  272 n
Mill, J. S., xix, 1
Milton, John, his views on tyrannicide
  similar to Mariana's, 191
mind, 12, 13, 15, 228, 241, 293, 327; and
  impenetrable secrets, 277; tyranny
  over minds, 327–8
Minerva, daughter of Juno, 8 n, 139,
  140 n
minorities, protection of, xxxix
miracles, 64; Pope Gregory's credulity
  concerning, 74–8
miraculous causes, 148; *see also*
  superstition
missionaries, in Japan, 128; and Francis
  Xavier, 130; their reports, 131
Moabites, David's torture and murder
  of, 49
mob, Faustus Socinus attacked by, 260
moderation, that of Melancthon to be
  emulated, 272
Moderns, vs Ancients, 2, 47
molecules, their modificaction, 213
Molière (pseud. for Jean-Baptiste
  Poquelin): his *Comédie du cocu
  imaginaire* cited, 10 and n; his
  Précieuses ridicules, 328
Molinists, and the doctrine of free will,
  282
monarchs: authority of, 19, 20; doctrine
  that it is unlimited, 23–7; doctrine
  that it is restrained, 28–9; as
  officials of peoples, 157; impossible
  to dethrone them without force,
  158; that from God vs that from
  peoples, 159; *see also* BODIN;
  HÔPITAL, de l'
monarchy, hereditary, 58; in Japan, 128
Monconys, Balthasar, wrongly accused of

libertinage, his *Voyages de Monconys*
  cited, 90 and n
Monluc, Jean de, 119
Montaigne, Michel de, xxiii, 122, 291;
  refused to attribute ill motives to
  every deed in history, 86; on
  political doctrines as 'migratory
  birds', 125; his *Essais* cited, 125 n
Montmorenci, Connétable de, 97 n, 108
moral theorists, 48, 49, 243
morality, 45, 53, 61, 162, 243; and moral
  evil, 290; *see also* natural morality
morals, confused with logic by some
  Jesuits, 160
More, Thomas, his *Utopia* cited, 86
Moréri, Louis, 14, 57, 96, 128, 181 n,
  231 n, 287 n
Moses, 27
motion, laws of, 218
Moulin, Pierre du, 67, 188 n
mutual toleration, vs venomous disputes,
  277
mysteries, their enduring attraction, 263;
  views of the pagans concerning, 265

Nabal, 41, 42, 52 n
Nathan, the prophet, 53
natural law, xxxiii, 24; *see also* law
natural morality, 52; *see also* morality
natural passions, xxv n; *see also*
  happiness; unhappiness; war
natural philosophy, xxiv, 209, and the
  new philosophy, 225; its notions of
  generation and destruction, 233
natural reason, thinkers who consult
  only, 269
nature: confused state of, 42; her many
  examples of love, 209; laws of, 215;
  if nature is minister of God, 216; or
  becomes fertile through friction, 223
Naudé, Gabriel, 19, 61; his praise of de
  l'Hôpital; 97; his *Coups d'état* cited,
  97 n, 167 n; on Machiavelli's
  indebtedness to Tacitus; 168; his
  scepticism, 308; his *Addition à la vie
  de Louis XI* cited, 308 n
NAVARRE, Marguerite de Valois, Queen
  of, 192–8; heroic magnanimity of,
  xxxiii; biography 192–4; her stoical
  virtue, 192; her *Heptameron*, 193;
  her reading of the Bible, 193;
  questions of concerning philosophy

Index

Sicily, 180, 288; methods of converting
Jews in, 71
sickness, and health, 293, 294
Sienna, 247, 248
Sigismund Augustus of Poland, 255, 258
Silius Italicus, 83, 139; his *Punic Wars*
cited, 84
Simler, Josias, and Hotman's
Franco-Gallia, 127 n
Simon, Richard, his *Dictionnaire du Bible*
cited, 40
sin, 321; whether God author of, 274–6;
pagan doctrine of antecedent sin,
229
Sisyphys, misery of, Juno's compared
with, 146
Sixtus, Pope, 57
Skinner, Quentin, xi, xxvii, xxi n,
xxxiii n
Slichtingius, Jonas, his *Confessio
Christiana* cited, 255
societies, 318 n, how preserved, 319
Socinian sect, history of, 247–8; Laelius
their first author, 247–8; its
Bibliotheca Antitrinitaria cited, 249
and n; its founders' torture and
death in Italy, 249, 251; its
theological doctrines: on
Photinianism, 249, on Revelation,
254, on denial of Trinity, 262, on
life of the soul, 269; decrees passed
against in Poland, 254–6; its
practical doctrines: on arms bearing,
253, on non-resistance to
persecution, 259–60, on public
office-holding, 260–1, 265–7;
reason, its first principle, 254, 265;
psychological critique of its
teachings, 266–7, 269–70, 268;
judged unworthy of tolerance in
Holland, 268–70; its doctrines
compared with those of the
Acataleptics (sceptics), 308 and n;
see also SOCINUS (Marianus);
SOCINUS (Faustus);
XENOPHANES
SOCINUS (Faustus), 251–71; biography
251–4; Socinian sect and Poland (A)
254–8; his *De Jesu Christo servitore*,
252; his writing against atheism,
253; his repudiation of seditious
preaching (C) 259–60; his

commitment to non-violence, 259–
60 and nn; his distress over loss of
manuscripts (F) 260; assaulted by
mob, 260; why princes view pacifist
doctrines unfavourably (G) 260–1;
sects that renounce arms bearing
(H) 261–6; reason's weak points
discussed (I) 266–7; Socinian sect
excluded from United Provinces (K)
267–8; hostile decree of 1653 (L)
268–71
Socinus, Laelius, uncle of Faustus, 247–
50 and nn; 251 n, 252; his *De tribus
Elohim* [The three Gods] cited,
250 n
SOCINUS (Marianus), 247–50; biography
of Marianus (b.1412); biography of
Marianus (b.1482); biography of
Laelius, son of Marianus, (B) 247–
50; *see also* Socinus, Laelius
Socrates, 286
sodomy, 133
Solier, François, 131; his *Histoire
ecclésiastique du Japon* cited, 131,
amended 135 n
Solomon, king, 47, 49, 50, 53, 54; and
king of Tyre, 278 and n
Sorbière, his translation of Hobbes's *De
Cive*, 84
Sorbonne, 189, 193, and accusations
against Reformers, 269
Sotion, 302, 306, 307
Sotuel, Natanael, 153 n, 181 n
soul, immortality of, 77 and n, 77–8,
128, 193, 193–4, 195, 226, 227, 227–
8, 269, 316
sovereigns, xxix, 46, 72 n, 158, 183 and
n; 269; how to judge them, 61;
rebellion considered the worst
crime, 133; if they can rule without
sin 165; *see also* duties of sovereigns;
monarchs
sovereignty, can be removed violently, 28
Spain, 151, 152, 192, 239; and the
Japanese, 132; and the Jews, 69; *see
also* Spaniards
Spanheim, Ezechiel de, his erudition, 7 n
Spaniards, cruel maxims of, 132; *see also*
Spain
Spinoza, Baruch, 129, 307, 309; the
Japanese religion taught similar
ideas, 129; example of a theoretical

Cambridge Texts in the History of Political Thought

Titles published in the series thus far

Aristotle *The Politics* and *The Constitution of Athens* (edited by Stephen
Everson)
0 521 48400 6 paperback

Arnold *Culture and Anarchy and Other Writings* (edited by Stefan
Collini)
0 521 37796 x paperback

Astell *Political Writings* (edited by Patricia Springborg)
0 521 42845 9 paperback

Augustine *The City of God against the Pagans* (edited by R. W. Dyson)
0 521 46843 4 paperback

Austin *The Province of Jurisprudence Determined* (edited by Wilfrid E.
Rumble)
0 521 44756 9 paperback

Bacon *The History of the Reign of King Henry VII* (edited by Brian
Vickers)
0 521 58663 1 paperback

Bakunin *Statism and Anarchy* (edited by Marshall Shatz)
0 521 36973 8 paperback

Baxter *A Holy Commonwealth* (edited by William Lamont)
0 521 40580 7 paperback

Bayle *Political Writings* (edited by Sally L. Jenkinson)
0 521 47677 1 paperback

Beccaria *On Crimes and Punishments and Other Writings* (edited by
Richard Bellamy)
0 521 47982 7 paperback

Bentham *A Fragment on Government* (introduction by Ross Harrison)
0 521 35929 5 paperback

Bernstein *The Preconditions of Socialism* (edited by Henry Tudor)
0 521 39808 8 paperback

Bodin *On Sovereignty* (edited by Julian H. Franklin)
0 521 34992 3 paperback

Bolingbroke *Political Writings* (edited by David Armitage)
0 521 58697 6 paperback

Bossuet *Politics Drawn from the Very Words of Holy Scripture* (edited by
Patrick Riley)
0 521 36807 3 paperback

The British Idealists (edited by David Boucher)
    0 521 45951 6 paperback
Burke *Pre-Revolutionary Writings* (edited by Ian Harris)
    0 521 36800 6 paperback
Christine de Pizan *The Book of the Body Politic* (edited by Kate
    Langdon Forhan)
    0 521 42259 0 paperback
Cicero *On Duties* (edited by M. T. Griffin and E. M. Atkins)
    0 521 34835 8 paperback
Comte *Early Political Writings* (edited by H. S. Jones)
    0 521 46923 6 paperback
Conciliarism and Papalism (edited by J. H. Burns and Thomas M.
    Izbicki)
    0 521 47674 7 paperback
Constant *Political Writings* (edited by Biancamaria Fontana)
    0 521 31632 4 paperback
Dante *Monarchy* (edited by Prue Shaw)
    0 521 56781 5 paperback
Diderot *Political Writings* (edited by John Hope Mason and Robert
    Wokler)
    0 521 36911 8 paperback
The Dutch Revolt (edited by Martin van Gelderen)
    0 521 39809 6 paperback
Early Greek Political Thought from Homer to the Sophists (edited by
    Michael Gagarin and Paul Woodruff)
    0 521 43768 7 paperback
The Early Political Writings of the German Romantics (edited by Frederick
    C. Beiser)
    0 521 44951 0 paperback
The English Levellers (edited by Andrew Sharp)
    0 521 62511 4 paperback
Erasmus *The Education of a Christian Prince* (edited by Lisa Jardine)
    0 521 58811 1 paperback
Fénelon *Telemachus* (edited by Patrick Riley)
    0 521 45662 2 paperback
Ferguson *An Essay on the History of Civil Society* (edited by Fania
    Oz-Salzberger)
    0 521 44736 4 paperback

Filmer *Patriarcha and Other Writings* (edited by Johann P. Sommerville)
0 521 39903 3 paperback
Fletcher *Political Works* (edited by John Robertson)
0 521 43994 9 paperback
Sir John Fortescue *On the Laws and Governance of England* (edited by Shelley Lockwood)
0 521 58996 7 paperback
Fourier *The Theory of the Four Movements* (edited by Gareth Stedman Jones and Ian Patterson)
0 521 35693 8 paperback
Gramsci *Pre-Prison Writings* (edited by Richard Bellamy)
0 521 42307 4 paperback
Guicciardini *Dialogue on the Government of Florence* (edited by Alison Brown)
0 521 45623 1 paperback
Harrington *A Commonwealth of Oceana* and *A System of Politics* (edited by J. G. A. Pocock)
0 521 42329 5 paperback
Hegel *Elements of the Philosophy of Right* (edited by Allen W. Wood and H. B. Nisbet)
0 521 34888 9 paperback
Hegel *Political Writings* (edited by Laurence Dickey and H. B. Nisbet)
0 521 34898 9 paperback
Hobbes *On the Citizen* (edited by Michael Silverhorn and Richard Tuck)
0 521 56797 1 paperback
Hobbes *Leviathan* (edited by Richard Tuck)
0 521 56797 1 paperback
Hobhouse *Liberalism and Other Writings* (edited by James Meadowcroft)
0 521 43726 1 paperback
Hooker *Of the Laws of Ecclesiastical Polity* (edited by A. S. McGrade)
0 521 37908 3 paperback
Hume *Political Essays* (edited by Knud Haakonssen)
0 521 46639 3 paperback
King James VI and I *Political Writings* (edited by Johann P. Sommerville)
0 521 44729 1 paperback
Jefferson *Political Writings* (edited by Joyce Appleby and Terence Ball)
0 521 64841 6 paperback

John of Salisbury *Policraticus* (edited by Cary Nederman)
  o 521 36701 8 paperback
Kant *Political Writings* (edited by H. S. Reiss and H. B. Nisbet)
  o 521 39837 1 paperback
Knox *On Rebellion* (edited by Roger A. Mason)
  o 521 39988 2 paperback
Kropotkin *The Conquest of Bread and Other Writings* (edited by Marshall
  Shatz)
  o 521 45990 7 paperback
Lawson *Politica sacra et civilis* (edited by Conal Condren)
  o 521 39248 9 paperback
Leibniz *Political Writings* (edited by Patrick Riley)
  o 521 35899 x paperback
Locke *Political Essays* (edited by Mark Goldie)
  o 521 47861 8 paperback
Locke *Two Treatises of Government* (edited by Peter Laslett)
  o 521 35730 6 paperback
Loyseau *A Treatise of Orders and Plain Dignities* (edited by Howell A.
  Lloyd)
  o 521 45624 x paperback
Luther and Calvin on Secular Authority (edited by Harro Höpfl)
  o 521 34986 9 paperback
Machiavelli *The Prince* (edited by Quentin Skinner and Russell Price)
  o 521 34993 1 paperback
de Maistre *Considerations on France* (edited by Isaiah Berlin and Richard
  Lebrun)
  o 521 46628 8 paperback
Malthus *An Essay on the Principle of Population* (edited by Donald
  Winch)
  o 521 42972 2 paperback
Marsiglio of Padua *Defensor minor* and *De translatione imperii* (edited by
  Cary Nederman)
  o 521 40846 6 paperback
Marx *Early Political Writings* (edited by Joseph O'Malley)
  o 521 34994 x paperback
Marx *Later Political Writings* (edited by Terrell Carver)
  o 521 36739 5 paperback
James Mill *Political Writings* (edited by Terence Ball)
  o 521 38748 5 paperback

J. S. Mill *On Liberty*, with *The Subjection of Women* and *Chapters on Socialism* (edited by Stefan Collini)
o 521 37917 2 paperback
Milton *Political Writings* (edited by Martin Dzelzainis)
o 521 34866 8 paperback
Montesquieu *The Spirit of the Laws* (edited by Anne M. Cohler, Basia Carolyn Miller and Harold Samuel Stone)
o 521 36974 6 paperback
More *Utopia* (edited by George M. Logan and Robert M. Adams)
o 521 40318 9 paperback
Morris *News from Nowhere* (edited by Krishan Kumar)
o 521 42233 7 paperback
Nicholas of Cusa *The Catholic Concordance* (edited by Paul E. Sigmund)
o 521 56773 4 paperback
Nietzsche *On the Genealogy of Morality* (edited by Keith Ansell-Pearson)
o 521 40610 2 paperback
Paine *Political Writings* (edited by Bruce Kuklick)
o 521 36678 x paperback
Plato *Statesman* (edited by Julia Annas and Robin Waterfield)
o 521 44778 x paperback
Price *Political Writings* (edited by D. O. Thomas)
o 521 40969 1 paperback
Priestley *Political Writings* (edited by Peter Miller)
o 521 42561 1 paperback
Proudhon *What Is Property?* (edited by Donald R. Kelley and Bonnie G. Smith)
o 521 40556 4 paperback
Pufendorf *On the Duty of Man and Citizen according to Natural Law* (edited by James Tully)
o 521 35980 5 paperback
The Radical Reformation (edited by Michael G. Baylor)
o 521 37948 2 paperback
Rousseau *The Discourses and Other Early Political Writings* (edited by Victor Gourevitch)
o 521 42445 3 paperback
Rousseau *The Social Contract and Other Later Political Writings* (edited by Victor Gourevitch)
o 521 42446 1 paperback
Seneca *Moral and Political Essays* (edited by John Cooper and John Procope)
o 521 34818 8 paperback

Sidney *Court Maxims* (edited by Hans W. Blom, Eco Haitsma Mulier and Ronald Janse)
o 521 46736 5 paperback

Spencer *The Man versus the State* and *The Proper Sphere of Government* (edited by John Offer)
o 521 43740 7 paperback

Stirner *The Ego and Its Own* (edited by David Leopold)
o 521 45647 9 paperback

Thoreau *Political Writings* (edited by Nancy Rosenblum)
o 521 47675 5 paperback

Utopias of the British Enlightenment (edited by Gregory Claeys)
o 521 45590 1 paperback

Vitoria *Political Writings* (edited by Anthony Pagden and Jeremy Lawrance)
o 521 36714 X paperback

Voltaire *Political Writings* (edited by David Williams)
o 521 43727 X paperback

Weber *Political Writings* (edited by Peter Lassman and Ronald Speirs)
o 521 39719 7 paperback

William of Ockham *A Short Discourse on Tyrannical Government* (edited by A. S. McGrade and John Kilcullen)
o 521 35803 5 paperback

William of Ockham *A Letter to the Friars Minor and Other Writings* (edited by A. S. McGrade and John Kilcullen)
o 521 35804 3 paperback

Wollstonecraft *A Vindication of the Rights of Man* and *A Vindication of the Rights of Woman* and *Hints* (edited by Sylvana Tomaselli)
o 521 43633 8 paperback